THE HEIDEGGER READER

T·H·E
HEIDEGGER
READER

Edited with an introduction by

GÜNTER FIGAL

Translated by Jerome Veith

Indiana University Press
Bloomington & Indianapolis

This book is a publication of

Indiana University Press
601 North Morton Street
Bloomington, IN 47404-3797 USA

http://iupress.indiana.edu
Telephone orders 800-842-6796
Fax orders 812-855-7931
Orders by e-mail iuporder@indiana.edu

⊕ The paper used in this publication meets
the minimum requirements of the American
National Standard for Information
Sciences—Permanence of Paper for Printed
Library Materials, ANSI Z39.48-1992.

Manufactured in the United States of
America

Library of Congress Cataloging-in-
Publication Data

Heidegger Lesebuch. English.
   The Heidegger reader / edited with an
introduction by Günter Figal ; translated by
Jerome Veith.
   p. cm. — (Studies in continental thought)
   Includes bibliographical references.
   ISBN 978-0-253-35371-9 (cloth : alk. paper)
—ISBN 978-0-253-22127-8 (pbk. : alk. paper) 1.
Philosophy, German—20th century. I. Figal,
Günter, date II. Veith, Jerome, date III. Title.
   B3279.H47E5 2009
   193—dc22   2009015549

         1 2 3 4 5   14 13 12 11 10 09

CONTENTS

TRANSLATOR'S FOREWORD

───────────── ❧ ─────────────

Despite having its beginnings over ninety years ago, and despite our biblio-graphic overview of completed and projected publications of his works in supplement 4, Heidegger's oeuvre remains a dense landscape, impossible to survey at a glance, in which much territory is still uncharted. In the English-speaking world the difficulty and deferral of translation continually com-pounds this exploration.

The importance of this Heidegger reader, then, is twofold. Firstly, in drawing on works from the entire course of Heidegger's thought, Dr. Figal's selection encourages a synthetic approach to the various "thought-paths" that weave throughout Heidegger's *Gesamtausgabe*—the 102 volumes of his collected works. This enables one to trace thematic developments and contributes to an understanding of Heidegger's work as a whole. Dr. Figal's thorough introduction, as well as the chronology and *Gesamtausgabe* list at the back of the volume (supplements 2 and 4), further contextualize the works selected here. The present volume is thus suited to all levels of Heidegger scholarship, and nicely complements existing collections of his essays.

Secondly, the volume provides, for the first time, translations of texts which might otherwise have remained obscured or delayed by the immen-sity of Heidegger's collected works. In addition to these new translations (chapters 9, 12, 13, 15, 16, 17, 19, and 22), I have polished and occasionally retranslated previous English versions of the selections, emending minor errors and editing for overall consistency. Thus, for example, by using the edition of the *Spiegel*-interview that Heidegger himself sanctioned, the translation published here (supplement 1) fills in important omissions of several previous versions, and can be viewed as definitive. For ease of reference—and perhaps as a reminder that many of these selections are not self-enclosed essays—each chapter includes the standard pagination of the collected works (indicated by GA), or else that of the original source of publication. To this end as well, a concise list of the sources for all selections in the volume appears in supplement 3.

I have tried wherever possible to provide English citations of the texts Heidegger cites, and have taken care to distinguish his notes from mine or the editor's. Notes are distinguished as follows: those which are not bracketed are Heidegger's; unsigned notes in square brackets are the editor's; signed notes in square brackets are mine (Tr.). The same rules hold within a given footnote.

In translating as well as revising, my goal has been to produce readable texts, but also to take Heidegger's language seriously. To this end, some words have had to remain untranslated. However, since Heidegger was keenly aware that the philosophical import of his words was not always clear even in German, untranslated words are always circumscribed either in their immediate context (cf. *Ge-Stell* in chapter 17) or through the development of an entire chapter (cf. chapter 11 on *Ereignis*). One exception to this is the German *Seyn*, an archaic spelling of *Sein* which Heidegger uses extensively to express a more originary meaning of Being. To retain this reference, I have therefore transliterated it as "Beyng," following the practice of many current translators.

I would like to thank John Sallis for the initial impetus and continued support for this translation. In addition to the many colleagues who gave advice throughout the process—and they are too numerous to name here— Robert Metcalf and David Dusenbury provided comments and suggestions that ended up greatly enhancing the book. Through my time spent on the selections presented here, and in pursuing their connections, I have come to recognize their importance in understanding Heidegger's thought. I am confident that readers of this volume will share this experience.

Jerome Veith
Chestnut Hill, Massachusetts
February 2009

EDITOR'S PREFACE

This reader gathers together texts from which an exploration of Heidegger's thought is possible. It should aid in orienting its audience within the context of this thinking, and thereby also increase the accessibility of texts that are especially important for understanding Heidegger. The exemplarity of these texts will only prove itself in their use—in that they serve as starting points for the exploration of Heidegger's thought.

The introduction traces the contexts of the selections: the history of Heidegger's thought. It strives for clarity, but does not offer simplifications at any cost. Philosophy is unusual thinking. One does not come upon its peculiar perspective without concentration and patience. Then, however, it can reveal life and the world in incomparable ways. Heidegger's texts have become classic examples of this.

My sincerest gratitude goes to Dr. Hermann Heidegger, who supported the development of this reader in every respect. I would also like to thank his wife Jutta, Dr. Hartmut Tietjen, and Katrin Sterba for the editorial and proofreading support.

Günter Figal

Introduction

—⟨⟩⟨⟩⟨⟩—

Paths of Thought

A philosopher's significance, like that of an artist, lies not in his or her originality, but rather and especially in his or her power to adapt and to transform. No one starts from scratch, and no one develops ideas that are simply and solely their own. It is therefore decisive how successfully one makes that which is given and taken over unmistakably one's own. For this to occur, one must take up questions and problems, methods and concepts, and set them within a new context so that, in a favorable case, they are understood differently, perhaps even better. In this sense, every significant work of philosophy is at the same time both a summation and an opening of new possibilities of thought.

All footnotes in the introduction are the editor's. Except where publication details are given, all page references are to Heidegger's *Gesamtausgabe* (hereafter GA). English titles indicate sections of the GA that exist in translation, while German titles indicate sections which have not yet been translated. For publication details of GA volumes and English translations alike, the reader should refer to supplement 4 at the back of the volume, under GA 1, GA 2, etc.—Trans.

Martin Heidegger's thinking is significant in precisely this sense. In the philosophy of modernity, it belongs ranked with the thought of Kant, Hegel, and Schelling. The conviction that modernity is an upheaval—the closure of tradition and at the same time the possibility of finding new paths in a reflective treatment of it—connects Heidegger to Nietzsche. Yet in his comprehensive erudition and conceptual rigor, Heidegger is Nietzsche's superior. Heidegger has thought through the entirety of philosophy in a new way, and has thus become for the twentieth and the beginning twenty-first centuries what Hegel was for the nineteenth.

One recognized the significance of Heidegger's thought fairly quickly. The effect set in early, and has grown steadily since the publication of *Being and Time*. Meanwhile, an engagement with Heidegger has become a necessary condition for understanding philosophy. His philosophy demonstrates possibilities for every philosophical work that understands itself from out of, and in reflective relation to, tradition. This is also true for philosophers who engage Heidegger critically. To critique is to differentiate; a critique determines in what respect, and to what extent, one wishes to follow someone. In this way, critique confirms a philosopher's significance. With respect to Heidegger, we can trace this in Jean-Paul Sartre, Maurice Merleau-Ponty, Emmanuel Lévinas, Jacques Derrida, Hannah Arendt, and Hans-Georg Gadamer. These, as well as others who started from Heidegger, lead back to him even where they depart from him.

In the meantime, Heidegger's effect is immense. Thousands of treatises have been and are being written about him; the conferences, seminars, and lectures on his philosophy are countless. All this despite the fact that the results of his work are not even available in their completion. The *Gesamtausgabe* that he himself planned, and which encompasses 102 volumes, is not yet completed. But we can already state that the *Gesamtausgabe* represents a new foundation for the occupation with Heidegger's thought. Heidegger's decision against a historical-critical edition has accelerated the publication of his writings; 70 volumes have appeared in 31 years. This has radically changed the engagement with Heidegger's thinking. Most of the research contributions from before 1975—the year in which the first volume of the *Gesamtausgabe* appeared—are only of historical value anymore. Heidegger's thought has first become accessible in its individual parts through the *Gesamtausgabe*.

Nonetheless, the sheer volume of material is overpowering. Heidegger begins anew in almost every work or lecture, and he thus usually gains a new aspect for his thought. He often uses his concepts in a new fashion, in different circumstances, and thereby expands their meaning. In this way no one who takes Heidegger seriously can circumvent a thorough study of the *Gesamtausgabe*. There is no short path through which Heidegger's thought could be opened up. "Paths, not works"—that is the motto with which Heidegger prefaced the *Gesamtausgabe*. However, one must tread paths on one's own in order to come to know them. The same goes for the many paths of Heidegger's thought.

Yet in order to be able to move within the landscape of Heidegger's thought, one must obtain an overview. One should be able to view the whole, if one is to know where a certain path is, and where it leads. One should also be acquainted with possible points of departure; it is not imperative to begin with the earliest texts. Starting points in a landscape are places that are connected by paths. One can therefore move forwards or backwards from places that are not chronologically at the beginning or the end. Nevertheless, much is already present in the beginning that only takes shape later on. Furthermore, the beginning discloses the origin; by understanding how someone found their way into thought, one can more easily see what motivates their thinking.

Beginnings

Heidegger's philosophical development is quite inconspicuous at first. His studies in Freiburg—he had begun with theology and philosophy in 1909, but dropped theology in 1911—end with his 1913 thesis[1] that still belongs well within the realm of Neo-Kantianism, the dominant academic philosophy of the time. His *Habilitationsschrift*, dedicated to a medieval topic, presented in 1915 and published in 1916,[2] is also a solid contribution to scholarship, but nothing more. However, in the years following World War I, a distinct philosophical profile becomes recognizable. In the meantime, Heidegger had become the assistant to Edmund Husserl, who in 1916 had moved from Göttingen to Freiburg to succeed Heinrich Rickert, until then Heidegger's most important teacher. Heidegger was already acquainted

---

1. Martin Heidegger, "Die Lehre von Urteil im Psychologismus. Ein kritisch-positiver Beitrag zur Logik," in *Frühe Schriften: GA 1*, 59–188.

2. Martin Heidegger, "Die Kategorien- und Bedeutungslehre des Duns Scotus," in *Frühe Schriften: GA 1*, 189–411.

during his years of study with Husserl's major early work, the *Logical Investigations* (1900).[3] According to an autobiographical account, the volumes sat on his desk from the first semester onwards.[4] Now, however, Heidegger makes Husserl's phenomenology into his own subject-matter. He thereby already deviates distinctly from Husserl's philosophy, and basic outlines of his own approach become apparent.

This occurs in the lecture "The Idea of Philosophy and the Problem of the World-view" from 1919. Heidegger here picks up the main thought of Husserl's, that things are not to be taken philosophically in their real existence, but rather as "phenomena," which means: as they show themselves to consciousness apart from their coincidental givenness, so that they can be pondered and studied in their own showing of themselves. In this change from the "natural" to the phenomenological attitude, the factual existence of something is "bracketed," so that the essence, rather than the respective coincidental givenness of the thing, can show itself and come into view. Husserl calls this bracketing *epochê*.[5] In this sense, it is a "withdrawal" from the realism of the natural attitude, such that the focus is no longer on the object, but on its pure givenness in appearing. Only in this way can one see how the givenness of things is built up in consciousness, and thus one understands their inner composition, their structure.

Heidegger now gives this notion a peculiar turn. As he understands it, the phenomenological *epochê* does not deactivate the ordinary orientation among "factually" given things, but rather the scientific attitude that "objectifies" that which is. The scientific attitude is not deactivated to the extent that it is still caught up in the natural attitude, but only as a scientific attitude. Heidegger's phenomenology is a critique of science; it directs itself against the "general rule of the theoretical"[6] and thus also against philosophy, insofar as it is theoretical as well. Heidegger's phenomenology is based on the conviction that a true philosophy must be fought for and won against the commitments of the ruling philosophy. His phenomenology stands in opposition to the Neo-Kantian understanding of philosophy, but no less against the theoretical approaches of Husserl's phenomenological program.

---

3. Edmund Husserl, *Logical Investigations*, 2 vols., trans. J. N. Findlay (New York: Routledge, 1970).

4. Cf. Martin Heidegger, "My Way into Phenomenology," in *On Time and Being*: GA 14, 81.

5. Cf. Edmund Husserl, *Ideas Pertaining to a Pure Phenomenology and to a Phenomenological Philosophy*, trans. F. Kersten (Boston: Martinus Nijhoff, 1982).

6. Martin Heidegger, "The Idea of Philosophy and the Problem of World-view," in *Towards the Definition of Philosophy*: GA 56/57, 87.

A philosophy that proceeds in an objectifying fashion, that conceives of everything as thing-like, existing only to be observed, researched, and determined, misses the original access to things, according to Heidegger. This access does not consist in scientific observation, but rather in the experience of things in their originary context; it lies in life, insofar as this is the experience of the world.

Heidegger shows what this means more specifically in his first lecture after the war, in his phenomenological description of the "environmental experience" *(chapter 1)*. The description is at once difficult and vivid. Heidegger's extraordinary linguistic capacity is already at work here, but it must still struggle for the ability to make things evident. Heidegger is grappling for a language adequate to his thoughts; much still seems as if it were packed into the words and concepts, compact and undeveloped. At the same time, however, Heidegger's phrases are filled with the subject-matter that he is concerned with. This subject-matter is clear before his eyes, and one senses its presence precisely through the fact that it does not come to expression easily.

This text is a key to Heidegger's thinking; "world" remains a central concept all the way into the last writings. World is the context of things in which they are "meaningful," which means: in which they have a *meaning* and are thereby in some way *important* for the one experiencing, and for their life. The "meaningful," Heidegger says, is the "primary" (p. 35; GA 56/57, 73), which means: there are not first things which are then meaningful in each experience in a secondary sense, but rather things exist as meaningful. Meaningfulness is the way things exist. They exist by being given as something definite *in* experience and in the context of one's own behavior, as things that we more or less know what to do with.

Self-World and the Question of Being

If one follows the considerations as Heidegger develops them in this early lecture, then "world-experience" is the starting point of phenomenology. Heidegger understands phenomenology as a "primordial science"[7] that goes "along with experience."[8] This does not mean, however, that it is oriented by whatever is experienced, and is thus a purely coincidental description. The description is only phenomenological in that it aims at the

---

7. GA 56/57, 15.
8. Ibid., 117.

structure of world-experience and thus attempts to grasp "the meaningful" as such. Following Husserl, Heidegger is convinced that the meaningful as such is revealed not in an orientation toward things, but toward the experience of them. Things are meaningful in their cohesion for world-experience, and thus the cohesion of the world cannot exist without world-experience.

If this is so, then "world-experience" must be described with the emphasis on "experience." This, in turn, is only possible if a shift can be accomplished in life itself from what is experienced environmentally (*umweltlich Erlebten*) to an expressed experience of environment (*Umwelterleben*). This is, as Heidegger expresses it in the lecture-course of the winter semester 1919–1920, a shift from the "life-world" to the "self-world." Phenomenology in Heidegger's sense cannot exist without "the focus of factical life on the self-world."[9] The possibility of phenomenology lies in the self-world; the "focus" on it is equivalent to an *epochê* performed in life itself, which, because it exists in life itself, can also be grasped philosophically.

In the lectures of the early 1920s, Heidegger attempts to grasp in more detail both the anchoring of philosophy in life, as well as the peculiar movement that the concept of the "self-world" indicates. He seeks a "historical paradigm"[10] by which phenomenology, as he understands it, can orient itself. Heidegger is convinced that the philosophical tradition has missed what is decisive, namely "history" and "life";[11] the experiential character of life and its enactment, bound to certain situations and times, has remained concealed to the tradition. Thus Heidegger at first finds what he seeks outside of philosophy: in early Christian religiosity. But the attempt made in his lecture-course in the winter of 1920–1921 on the "Phenomenology of Religion"[12] fails: Heidegger reaches the conclusion that religious experience is only religiously accessible; it permits of no conceptual determination. If this is so, then philosophy cannot rely on religious experience as its source. For this reason, Heidegger begins anew and seeks the life-anchoring of philosophy in philosophy itself. This leads him to that philosopher whom he will thereafter view as the key figure for the understanding of philosophy as such, and to whom he owes the question that determines the rest of his thinking: Aristotle.

Heidegger's critical engagement with Aristotle begins with the lecture-

---

9. Martin Heidegger, *Grundprobleme der Phänomenologie:* GA 58, 172.

10. Ibid., 61.

11. Ibid., 146.

12. Martin Heidegger, "Introduction to the Phenomenology of Religion," in *The Phenomenology of Religious Life:* GA 60, 1–156.

course of the winter semester 1921–1922;[13] it continues with his lecture-course in the summer semester 1922,[14] and finds concentration in a text from the fall of 1922, one that documents Heidegger's thinking of this time like no other. This text was written for presentation to the philosophy faculties of Marburg and Göttingen, both universities where Heidegger had prospects of being named to a professorial position. However, he had not published anything since his *Habilitationsschrift* of 1916, so many desired to hear about his more recent research. This text, which has become known as the "Natorp-Report"—after the Marburg professor Paul Natorp (1854–1924)—sketches a work on Aristotle that Heidegger planned, but never wrote. Instead, his sketch of the introduction to this work *(chapter 2)* developed in the following years into that book for which Heidegger would quickly become famous: *Being and Time*.

The sections—not reprinted here—of Heidegger's programmatic text that deal deeply with Aristotle are especially significant, because they show how Heidegger finds a possibility of describing in more detail the way that life sharpens toward the "self-world." Aristotle's conception of practical reason (φρόνησις) offers him this possibility. Φρόνησις, as Heidegger picks it up, is "circumspection" (*Umsicht*) (p. 44; GA 62, 353); it is the accessibility of the world from the view of one's own possible behavior; the "full moment of factical life" is revealed in it.[15] With his description of φρόνησις, Aristotle discovered a kind of reason that remains bound within the accomplishment of life. He thus also opened the possibility of a philosophy that does not face life in a theoretical stance, but rather follows it understandingly and explicates its structure. For Heidegger, Aristotle's conception of practical reason initiates a phenomenology of life which, as understanding and explicating, is simultaneously *hermeneutic*.

However, as the portion of Heidegger's text reprinted here indicates, Aristotle does not hold onto this truth of life. As a Janus-faced figure, he is not only the discoverer of the truth of life, but also the father of the theoretical philosophy so criticized by Heidegger. This, for Heidegger, is the source of Aristotle's incomparable significance: In order to reach "the pri-

---

13. Martin Heidegger, *Phenomenological Interpretations of Aristotle*: GA 61.

14. Martin Heidegger, *Phänomenologische Interpretationen ausgewählter Abhandlungen des Aristoteles zur Ontologie und Logik*: GA 62.

15. Martin Heidegger, "Phänomenologische Interpretationen zu Aristoteles (Anzeige der hermeneutischen Situation). Ausarbeitung für die Marburger und die Göttinger philosophische Fakultät," in *Phänomenologische Interpretationen ausgewählter Abhandlungen des Aristoteles zur Ontologie und Logik*: GA 62, 384.

mordial motive sources," the practical wisdom of life, "in a dismantling return," one must take apart, "destroy" (*destruieren*) the self-evidence of the philosophical tradition schooled by and indebted to Aristotle (p. 55; GA 62, 368). However Heidegger's thought may develop and change, the notion that the truth of the philosophical tradition lies in its beginning remains determinative for his thinking from now on. Only in his later writings does Heidegger take distance from this notion.[16]

Heidegger's interaction with Aristotle is decisive in yet another sense. Only now does he find his way to the question that determines his further thinking: the question of "Being." This occurs through Heidegger's appropriation of Aristotle's thought that there must be a "guiding, basic meaning"[17] in all the various usages of the expressions "is" and "existing." Aristotle had seen this basic meaning in "beingness" (οὐσία), which he determines in book 7 of the *Metaphysics* as the immanent form (εἶδος) of every being.[18] Over against this, Heidegger answers the question about the guiding meaning of "existing" with reference to the "Being of factical life" (p. 52; GA 62, 364), which is now also called "Dasein" (p. 40; GA 62, 348). This means: everything *is* in the way that it appears in and for Dasein itself. Understood from the standpoint of "circumspection," however, Dasein is the openness for anything showing itself at all. So the Being of Dasein is that Being which understands itself in its own Being, and from which all other Being is to be understood and determined. The ontology of Dasein is therefore also the ontology of all ontologies; it is, as will be stated in *Being and Time*, "fundamental ontology."[19]

On the one hand, Heidegger's turn to the question of Being comes as a surprise. In his lecture-course of the winter semester 1919–1920, he had still made the ontological direction of traditional philosophy since Aristotle responsible for the neglect of the "decisive problem" of "history" and "life."[20] On the other hand, once Heidegger, through his understanding of the philosophical tradition, has bound himself so tightly to Aristotle, his ontological turn is resolute: If there exists an ontology of life or of Dasein, Aristotle's ontology can be understood as its problematic abbreviation. Only then is the ontological direction of the philosophical tradition not a

16. Cf. Martin Heidegger, "The End of Philosophy and the Task of Thinking," in *On Time and Being*, trans. Joan Stambaugh (Chicago: University of Chicago Press, 1972), 55–73.

17. Martin Heidegger, "My Way into Phenomenology," in *On Time and Being*: GA 14, 81–90.

18. Aristotle, *Metaphysics* 7, 11, 1037a29–30.

19. Martin Heidegger, *Being and Time*: GA 2, 18.

20. Martin Heidegger, *Grundprobleme der Phänomenologie*: GA 58, 146–147.

detour, but rather the covering over of the originary beginning which, as such, can be regained in the "destruction."

For Heidegger, Aristotle's ontology fails to convince because of its orientation toward individual things. It is, in the language of *Being and Time*, an ontology of the "present-at-hand"[21] (*Vorhandenen*), one which has turned away from the accomplishment of life or Dasein, and that faces things in a theoretical attitude. That this is the case, however, can only become evident if the turning as such is made understandable. Why does one, in Dasein, turn away from one's own Being, and toward beings?

Heidegger's programmatic essay answers this question by emphasizing the uncertainty and finitude of Dasein: We do not know how we will be, or whether we will be at all. Dasein is *temporal*; in its temporality, it has always already been in the world; and it is futural in the sense that it can be in the world. In Dasein lies the possibility of acting one way or another, and this action in turn stands under the basic provision of Being or non-being. Generally, one tries to escape this provision; one denies one's own finitude and seeks a stable Being not determined by the possibility of non-being. The presence-at-hand of things, made possible by their form (εἶδος), is this kind of Being. The presence (*Gegenwart*) of form is "presence" (*Anwesenheit*) and only this; it lacks the past as well as the future. However, once one sees through the temporal essence of presence, one must attempt to explicate it—and with it the Aristotelian understanding of Being—from out of time, more precisely out of the temporality of Dasein.

This is the basic notion of the book that would develop from Heidegger's programmatic essay. The "intention" of *Being and Time* is "the concrete development of the question about the meaning of 'Being,'" and "its preliminary goal is the interpretation of *time* as the possible horizon of every understanding of Being whatsoever."[22]

The question of time had concerned Heidegger from early on. He gives the lecture portion of his *Habilitation* on the "Concept of Time in the Science of History." The structure of time, as it is elaborated in *Being and Time*, had first gained distinct contours in Heidegger's lecture-course on the phenomenology of religion: Early Christian religiosity, as Heidegger interprets it, is determined by the acceptance of faith, and thus by something past; it is futural in its awaiting of Christ's return.[23] Heidegger finds the

21. Martin Heidegger, *Being and Time:* GA 2, 83.
22. Ibid., 1.
23. Cf. Martin Heidegger, *The Phenomenology of Religious Life:* GA 60, 175–180.

same structure in φρόνησις in the programmatic essay of 1922. As "readiness to deal with something," φρόνησις is equally determined by the pregivenness of what needs to be done and by its status as something to be realized.[24] Insofar as φρόνησις is the model for Heidegger's determination of Dasein as "care," as one's own Being-in-the-world as a circumspective worry, it only takes a generalizing step to reach the conception of *Being and Time*.

But this book is not yet within Heidegger's horizon during the composition of the programmatic essay. This situation only gradually changes in the years that begin with Heidegger's appointment to Marburg. In the lecture-courses of the Marburg years, Heidegger intensifies his occupation with Aristotle. At the same time, *Being and Time* takes on ever more distinct shape; in developing it, Heidegger returns to his lectures. If not causing this development, outside pressures certainly help to accelerate it. In 1925 Heidegger—who had until then held the position of associate professor—is recommended by the faculty for the primary chair of philosophy, in succession of Nicolai Hartmann. In order to qualify for the appointment, he prepares a publication based on the material of his lectures. *Being and Time* appears in 1927 in volume 8 of the *Yearbook for Philosophy and Phenomenological Research*, edited by Husserl.

What appears there is naturally only a fragment, more precisely an incomplete first part of two planned ones. The third section of the first part, which—under the title *Time and Being*—was to accomplish the step from ontology of Dasein to fundamental ontology, was never completed, just like the second part which was to deal with Kant, Descartes, and Aristotle.

It is not easy to say why *Being and Time* was not finished; various difficulties of continuing what was elaborated may have arisen. However, as the closing pages of *Being and Time* show, all of these difficulties have to do with the transition from the analysis of Dasein to the development of fundamental ontology. The vanishing point of the elucidations of *Being and Time* is "the fundamental-ontological question about the meaning of Being as such," and with respect to this, Heidegger underlines that the "emphasis on the constitution of Being [is] only *one* way."[25] When Heidegger adds that the "*thematic* analytic" of Dasein needs, "for its part, some of the light of the previously clarified idea of Being as such,"[26] he means that a clarification of

---

24. Martin Heidegger, "Anzeige der hermeneutischen Situation": GA 62, 384.
25. Martin Heidegger, *Being and Time*: GA 2, 575.
26. Ibid., 575.

"Being as such" cannot be won from the "constitution of Dasein." What Heidegger had discussed in *Being and Time* was Dasein in its everydayness, pre-philosophical Dasein. The understanding of Being that is characteristic of this Dasein reveals each own Being of Dasein to itself, but it does not lead to a concept of "Being as such."

World-Projection

The period after *Being and Time* remains determined, for Heidegger, by the question about "Being as such," and it is a time of constant searching. To be sure, with the years, a conclusive connection of thoughts crystallizes, and these can serve as answers to the questions that remain open after *Being and Time.* However, these thoughts no longer find the precise form that *Being and Time,* in all of its incompleteness, had offered. *Being and Time* remains the single large, systematic book that Heidegger ever published himself. Afterwards, his thought expresses itself in lecture courses, essays, and speeches, and in works that he never publishes. The great reflective treatises *Contributions to Philosophy* (GA 65) and *Mindfulness* (GA 66) only appear, according to Heidegger's instructions, after most of his lectures are made accessible. Heidegger's public effect in later years is still due to *Being and Time,* as well as a few self-published lecture-courses[27] and a series of collections.[28] One only sees today how what is articulated in these writings fits together into a dense fabric of thoughts. It is precisely so evident because one can closely follow the development of Heidegger's thinking through his lectures.

After the completion of *Being and Time,* the occupation with the possibilities and limits of the book are central to Heidegger's work. The lecture-course of the summer semester 1927, *Basic Problems of Phenomenology* (GA 24), is an attempt to continue the book; Heidegger takes the latter's discussion of temporality (*Zeitlichkeit*) and tries to modify it in relation to the time of "Being as such," to temporality (*Temporalität*). This attempt, already announced in *Being in Time,* is broken off. Instead, Heidegger now concentrates on the concept of Dasein and begins to elucidate this concept

---

27. Martin Heidegger, *An Introduction to Metaphysics:* GA 40; *Die Frage nach dem Ding:* GA 41; *Nietzsche I:* GA 43; *Nietzsche II:* GA 44; *The Principle of Reason:* GA 10; *What Is Called Thinking?:* GA 8.

28. Martin Heidegger, *Off the Beaten Track:* GA 5; *Pathmarks:* GA 9; *Vorträge und Aufsätze:* GA 7; *On the Way to Language:* GA 12.

in light of the concluding considerations of *Being and Time*, those of "Being as such." Dasein under the viewpoint of philosophy, or, as Heidegger himself says, the "metaphysics of Dasein" (p. 63; GA 26, 171), now takes on central importance.

The lecture-course of the summer semester of 1928, Heidegger's last course in Marburg, is especially revealing for this metaphysics; after the winter semester of 1928–1929, he teaches again in Freiburg as a successor to Husserl. The last Marburg course contains a comprehensive self-interpretation and self-correction on Heidegger's part *(chapter 3)*. Like many of the self-interpretive texts in which Heidegger attempts to clarify and further develop his earlier thoughts, this text is exceptionally difficult. Here Dasein is taken in its "neutrality," not in its individual peculiarity, but rather in the "positivity and potency of the essence" (p. 63; GA 26, 172), which means: in the way that Dasein's "there" as such rises to importance. This occurs in a "metaphysical projection" (p. 67; GA 26, 177), which should be understood as "transcendence" (p. 68; GA 26, 238). This, for Heidegger, is the possibility, essential to Dasein, of going beyond beings and understanding the world as a unified coherence of beings. The freedom of projecting the world is thereby determined as the "for-the-sake-of" (*Umwillen*) of Dasein. The "for-the-sake-of," the purpose of Dasein, is a freely projected, individually determined world.

The notion of world-projection, which is also discussed in the work "On the Essence of Ground,"[29] is a good example of the re-interpretive power of Heidegger's thought. In order to develop this notion, Heidegger returns to central concepts of *Being and Time* and gives these new meaning. "Projecting" is now no longer the immediate grasping of one's own, worldly possibilities, but the release of a world as such; the "for-the-sake-of" no longer designates the respective possibilities of being *in* a world, but the determined world itself.

It is no surprise that Kant's philosophy becomes central for Heidegger in these circumstances. In the winter semester of 1927–1928, Heidegger had held a lecture-course on the *Critique of Pure Reason*;[30] in 1929, he publishes a book on Kant that is also meant as a public self-interpretation of *Being and Time*.[31] The notion of world-projection makes especially evident how close Heidegger is to Kant in this period; the notion is a variation of the Kantian

---

29. Martin Heidegger, "On the Essence of Ground," in *Pathmarks: GA* 9, 123–175.
30. Martin Heidegger, *Phenomenological Interpretation of Kant's Critique of Pure Reason: GA* 25.
31. Martin Heidegger, *Kant and the Problem of Metaphysics: GA* 3.

thought "that reason only intuits what it itself brings forth in its projections."[32] Intuition is here no passive reception, but rather a structuring and shaping. Whatever one intuits, one has oneself brought into a cohesion, an order. However, interpreting Kant through *Being and Time*, Heidegger thinks that one must first experience the openness toward structuring and ordering itself, in order for this to occur. This openness is no merely "subjective" capacity, but is the possibility of beings themselves and, in this sense, is Being. Dasein can only understand the unified cohesion of beings on the basis of its understanding of Being. Thus, world-projection factors into the difference between Being and beings; the "ontological difference"[33] makes this projection possible.

Heidegger's first thoughts on the "metaphysics of Dasein" are not easy to follow; they lack the clarity that was so formative for the analyses of *Being and Time*, for all of its systematic intentions. However, to the degree in which the new ideas gain clarity, Heidegger regains his vividness and descriptive power. With regard to the notion of world-projection, this occurs first in the lecture-course of the winter semester 1931–1932. Here *(chapter 6)*, world-projection is elaborated in relation to the basic possibilities of science and art. A scientific theory or a work of art does not primarily discover individual things anew, but rather lets things as a whole, or at least a region of things, be seen anew. In order that such a sight can even be opened, however, the openness of all things, the openness of the world as such, must be experienced. It is an experience in which all that exists is "bracketed," set in an *epochê*. Here, what matters is no longer what shows itself, but only the possibility of something showing itself, and therefore also of other, unknown self-showings. The basic motif of phenomenology thus also resides in Heidegger's conception of world-projection.

Of course, projection cannot bring about the openness of the world in which it is accomplished. For a world-projection to be possible, Dasein must already be transposed into the openness of the world. Heidegger had already shown the conception of this displacement in *Being and Time*: it arises in attunements or "moods." Attunements are like the weather; they cannot be tied to anything in particular; there is often no determinate reason for them, but they cast a peculiar light on everything. This is especially true of those attunements that Heidegger calls "basic moods." Anxiety is described as one

---

32. Immanuel Kant, *Critique of Pure Reason*, B xiii.

33. Martin Heidegger, *The Metaphysical Foundations of Logic*: GA 26, 193. Heidegger uses this concept for the first time in his lecture-course *The Basic Problems of Phenomenology*: GA 24, 454.

such "basic mood" in *Being and Time*.[34] In it, the world is deprived of all significance for Dasein. The immersion in situations, the certainty of possibilities for action, the assuredness that one's own acting has a meaning—all of this disappears at once; it no longer matters. But precisely in this way, one's acting in the world becomes incontrovertible. Through the attunement of anxiety, "being-in-the-world as such" becomes evident.[35]

Heidegger takes up these analyses again in the lecture-course of the winter semester 1929–1930 *(chapter 5)*. In doing so, he explains the attunements' meaning for Dasein much more clearly than in *Being and Time*. What now interests Heidegger about the question of a "basic attunement" is also no longer the "facticity" of being-in-the-world, but instead the openness of the world that is possible and that makes possible world-projection—or as it is called here, "world-formation." The attunement that Heidegger describes from this viewpoint is boredom, and his development of it in this lecture-course belongs among Heidegger's most impressive analyses. Heidegger starts from the boredom encountered in daily life and finally penetrates to what he calls "profound boredom." It is an attunement that is no longer bound to any specific occasion, but is rather nothing but the openness of passing time, openness beyond any disappointment or fulfillment.

But Heidegger is concerned with more than description and analysis. The stated goal of this lecture-course is to "awaken" the fundamental attunement that is described and analyzed. The enactment of thinking should transpose one into the open and nullify all current, supposedly orienting "cultural-philosophical" interpretations of life and the world. Heidegger calls upon the only authentic interpretation of his present time: One should permit the openness of Dasein that is its "*sole* obligation" (p. 99; GA 29/30, 116), and thus reach the possibility of "letting [the world] be at work"[36] in projection. In order for this to occur, philosophy becomes involved in the world.

Politics

A few years later, the opportunity for such an involvement will appear even more favorable and urgent to Heidegger. On 21 April 1933, he is—almost

34. Martin Heidegger, *Being and Time*: GA 2, 244–253.
35. Ibid., 247.
36. Martin Heidegger, *The Fundamental Concepts of Metaphysics*: GA 29/30, 530.

unanimously—elected rector of the University of Freiburg. On 3 May, back-dated to 1 May, he joins the NSDAP. In the speech that he delivers at the celebratory reception of his rectorship (*chapter 7*), he places his philosophy in the service of the national "beginning," but also attempts to bind this "beginning" to philosophical insight. The speech is ambiguous: Heidegger makes it very clear that he sees the National Socialist takeover as an epochal historical opportunity. Conversely, he avoids any adaptation to the National Socialist ideology; there is no direct mention of National Socialism or the "Führer" Adolf Hitler, something that could not have been absent in any announcement loyal to the party. The "Self-Assertion of the German University," as Heidegger understands it, is also a self-assertion over against ideological monopolization. Instead of the people, biologically understood, being decisive, it should rather be the beginning "of our intellectual-historical Dasein," and that means: "the onset of Greek philosophy" (p. 110; GA 16, 108). The closing quotation from Plato's *Republic* makes clear that such an appeal has no certainty of being followed. Heidegger translates that everything great is "in the storm," and closer to the Greek wording this means: It leans toward falling—it can fail. In the *Republic* as well as for Heidegger, this bears upon the relationship of politics and philosophy.

Hölderlin, Art, and Truth

Heidegger did not need much time to experience this failure. In a letter dated 12 April 1934, he expresses his wish of resignation to the appropriate minister. The occasion for this was that the culture minister of Baden had, for political reasons, not accepted two deans that Heidegger appointed (Wilhelm von Möllendorff and Erik Wolf), and pressured him to lay them off. Over and above this, the reason for Heidegger's resignation is more likely the realization of the failure of his philosophical-political attempt. In a still unpublished record from 28 April 1934, on the "end of the rectorship," he states that "responsibility [was] no longer possible" in his official position, and he adds, with obvious reference to the National Socialists: "Long live mediocrity and noise!" "Obedience to a minister" and the "responsibility toward history" were not to be reconciled, and thus the attempt to subsume the National Socialist revolution under philosophical insight had failed all along the line: "My rectorship made the great mistake of bringing *questions* to my colleagues' attention, from which they are better left *closed off* for *their* own prosperity—and ruin."[37]

Thus, even the understanding of philosophy, especially in its capacity of effecting change, is affected by this failure, such that the political crisis is also a philosophical one for Heidegger. Only hesitatingly does he find his way back into philosophical work; in a letter to Karl Jaspers on 1 July 1935, he calls what he has managed to achieve a "thin stammering," while "the mandatory expression in the lectures" moves "in interpretations."[38]

Heidegger makes thoughtful progress with one of these interpretations, however. In the winter semester of 1934–1935 he lectures on Hölderlin; in a talk given in Rome in 1936 (*chapter 8*), he brings together the main ideas of this lecture-course. Heidegger's occupation with Hölderlin will last into his late years. He develops essential thoughts in dialogue with the poet, who for him reveals modernity in its essence. In Hölderlin's poetry, as Heidegger understands it, the world of modernity is projected. It is a godless world, its time is one "of need" "because it stands in a double lack and a double nothing: in the no-longer of the gods who have fled and in the not-yet of what is to come" (p. 128; GA 4, 47).

In the "double lack" of needful time, we can recognize the tension of temporality that Heidegger had developed as the essence of early Christian religiosity in his early lecture-course on the phenomenology of religion, and later on in his determination of φρόνησις. But now this tension is one of a historical situation. The present appears as a transitional time; the religion that had determined life and thinking all the way into modernity loses its impressional power. The religious does not disappear on account of this, however. The gods—that is, all gods who have been, including those that were effective in the tradition of Greek mythology—are still there. They are kept present in poetry, and in an especially urgent way, insofar as they are present as gods who have fled. Therein lies Hölderlin's epochal significance for Heidegger: in holding the gods fast as those who have fled, his poetry shows what it is time for. What is needed is neither a seamless continuation of history up until now, nor the free "design" of a new world, but rather the enduring of the loss and thus simultaneously the openness, in the opening of Dasein, for the possibility of a new encounter with the divine. By poetiz-

37. Martin Heidegger, "Überlegungen und Winke III," part of the "Black Notebooks," no. 113. I am grateful to Dr. Hermann Heidegger for indicating the record and for the permission to cite it here.

38. Martin Heidegger and Karl Jaspers, *Briefwechsel 1920–1963*, ed. Walter Biemel and Hans Saner (Frankfurt am Main: Vittorio Klostermann, 1990), 157.

ing the divine in its absence, the relationship to the divine is "founded." That is a "founding of Being" (p. 124; GA 4, 42). "Being," as Heidegger now understands it, exists through the saying power of poetry: "The poet names the gods and names all things with respect to what they are" (p. 123; GA 4, 41).

What Heidegger says about Hölderlin is not only meant as a determination of his poetry. If the task reserved for Hölderlin is to put "the essence of poetry itself into poetry" (p. 118; GA 4, 34), then the engagement with his poetry aims at the essence of poetry in general and, insofar as it deals with the art-character of poetry, at the essence of art. It is therefore logical that Heidegger turns to the question of the essence of art around the time of the first Hölderlin lecture. This occurs in a text on the "Origin of the Work of Art" *(chapter 9)*, which represents the first of three total versions. This first version is written more lightly and is more lively than the final version that Heidegger adopts for the *Holzwege* collection. Its development of ideas is more free, and this allows better access to them.

Heidegger's discussion of the artwork is uncommon from the outset: the artwork is not to be determined from the experience of art, nor in orientation to the presenting artist. The artwork is not to be understood in relation to something or someone, because it itself opens relationships. The work "itself first creates the space that it pervades," it determines "the place at which it comes to be erected" (p. 135; *Heidegger Studies* 5, 10). By being revealed as such, the work gives determination to the space in which it stands and the place at which it is erected.

When Heidegger describes the space of the artwork as "world," he is not only giving new meaning to this concept that has been central since the lecture-course of 1919. He also newly determines the place that the earlier concepts of world-projection and world-formation had occupied. The artwork now brings about the openness of a world; the world needs the work in order to be opened, to endure, and to "remain as worlding" (p. 135; *Heid. Stud.* 5, 9). This does not just apply to the world, but to Dasein as well. By conceiving of the openness of the world as arising from the artwork, Heidegger departs from his earlier notion of world-formation and no longer conceives of the world strictly from the aspect of life or Dasein. He now sees that the significance of things that can be discovered as worldly, just as the structure of human possibilities of being, has a counterweight. The artwork is not only the "setting-up" (*Aufstellung*) of a world, but also the "setting-forth" (*Herstellung*) of "earth" (p. 137; *Heid. Stud.* 5, 9–12). This is to be taken literally: "setting-forth" is not to be understood as production, but as setting apart and setting down. What would be nothing other than formed material in a result of production—stone, wood or paint, sounding tone, voiced word—rises to importance, as such, in the artwork. Insofar as these are not experienced as media or material, they belong to the earth in Heidegger's sense. This is not some "deposited mass of materials" (p. 137; *Heid. Stud.* 5, 11), but rather that which does not obey the significance of the world; it is that which exists *from itself*, not from worldly Dasein. By setting up the world and presenting the earth—and thus enacting the "strife" (p. 138; *Heid. Stud.* 5, 12) between world and earth—the artwork makes evident that the openness of the world cannot exist without the self-concealment of earth. This is important for the notion of openness itself. It cannot be thought without concealment.

In this piece on the origin of the artwork, Heidegger has two terms for the inextricability of openness and concealment: He calls them "truth" and "Beyng" (*Seyn*), so that the essence of art can be determined as the "setting-into-work of truth" (p. 144; *Heid. Stud.* 5, 17) and as the "founding of Beyng" (p. 146; *Heid. Stud.* 5, 18).

The question of truth concerns Heidegger very early on. It is already discussed in detail in his 1921 lecture-course on Augustine and Neoplatonism;[39] there the focus is on the relation to truth and the escape from it.[40] The question gains significance in Heidegger's involvement with Aristotle. He takes up Aristotle's notion that reason, in its various "modes of accomplishment," is an enactment of truth, understood in the Greek as ἀληθεύειν.[41] Truth is not something that occurs primarily "in judgment" as "'correspondence' of thought with the object,"[42] but is rather to be understood as "unconcealment" in the sense of the Greek ἀλήθεια;[43] the "true" is what is "no longer concealed."[44] It is what is discovered as that which it is and what therefore shows itself as that which it is. The truth itself, however, is the possibility of this discovery and self-showing. Truth in this sense is the central theme of phenomenology; it is the condition of possibility of phenomena.

Until the early 1930s Heidegger still grasps this notion entirely in Husserl's sense, phenomenologically understanding what appears through its

---

39. Martin Heidegger, "Augustine and Neo-Platonism," in *The Phenomenology of Religious Life: GA 60, 160–299*.

40. Ibid., 198–201.

41. Martin Heidegger, "Anzeige der hermeneutischen Situation": GA 62, 376.

42. Ibid., 377.

43. Cf. Martin Heidegger, *Being and Time:* GA 2, 290–299.

44. Martin Heidegger, *Plato's Sophist:* GA 19, 16.

appearance in consciousness—though Heidegger puts Dasein in the place that consciousness had occupied in Husserl. Thus, in the programmatic essay of 1922, he thinks truth as accomplishment; it is the discovery and sheltering of everything that, as discovered and sheltered in this discovery, can even be made into an object of assertion.[45] In *Being and Time*, truth is then understood as the openness of Dasein for its own possibilities and for the world in which these can be realized. In connection with the notion of the projection of Being, Heidegger ultimately identifies truth with freedom, that openness in which the projection of Being takes place.[46]

With regard to all of this, the essay on the work of art is a turning point; it corrects the notion that truth can be thought from Dasein. If truth must be set into the work, it is conditioned by the work. "Dasein" is now no longer humanity's Being-determination, insofar as humanity relates to itself and thus to its Being; rather, Dasein is the apprehension of the "there" as a determined openness. To be there now means: to take over, for oneself, the "there" opened by the artwork; humanity "takes over the task of being this 'there'" (p. 147; *Heid. Stud.* 5, 19).

With this re-interpretation, Heidegger also dissolves the notion of Being from human Dasein. Being (*Sein*)—or, as Heidegger writes in order to indicate the shifted meaning, "Beyng" (*Seyn*)—is now the openness in which that which shows itself and that which conceals itself can exist. It is, as Heidegger also says, the "clearing" into which "beings as such stand and show themselves" (p. 143; *Heid. Stud.* 5, 16); it is like an open spot in the forest, where light can fall in and bring something to appearance or place it in shadows. It is what happens to humanity, and what should be taken over historically as this happening by a people (*Volk*) (p. 147; *Heid. Stud.* 5, 19).

Turn to Φύσις

The turn that is presented with special concision and liveliness in the first version of "On the Origin of the Work of Art" is the turn from the accomplishment of Being (*Seinsvollzug*) to the occurrence of Being (*Seinsgeschehen*). It shapes Heidegger's thinking from this point onwards. Again and again, even in the latest writings, he attempts to clarify this turn, to think about its consequences, and especially to unfold it in its various moments. If this turn is to remain the central theme as such of Heidegger's

---

45. Martin Heidegger, "Anzeige der hermeneutischen Situation": GA 62, 376.
46. Martin Heidegger, "Vom Wesen der Wahrheit," in *Sein und Wahrheit*: GA 36/37, 81–264.

thought, then this means: The earlier conception, guided by the accomplishment of Being, is not simply replaced with the later way of thinking, developed from the occurrence of Being. The first remains present; what is described and conceptually contained in it remains in view, but it is now determined by the occurrence of Being. Both, together, form a subject-matter determined by the occurrence of Being.

At first, this is determinative for the internal development of Heidegger's thought. He continually reinterprets himself and attempts, with all readiness for self-criticism, to demonstrate the coherence of his "paths of thought." The understanding of Dasein that is developed in *Being and Time*, but that reaches back to the programmatic essay of 1922 and is basically valid until the early 1930s, is presented as a necessary condition for the later conception, and is thus also re-interpreted according to this conception.

An example of Heidegger's self-interpretation is the letter to Fr. William J. Richardson (*chapter 20*), in which Heidegger responds to Richardson's ambitious project of presenting Heidegger's thought thoroughly for the first time,[47] and answers several of the author's inquiries. Heidegger's letter dates from 1962, in his later productive period—Heidegger's own last publication collects texts from 1962 to 1964.[48] However, the decisive considerations of this letter to Richardson already apply to the mid-1930s. When Heidegger states that the inquiry of *Being and Time* is "supplemented" in his later thinking (p. 303; GA 11, 150), and thus brought into a whole, he designates precisely the intention of his first essay, "On the Origin of the Work of Art." The "adequate determination of Da-sein" as "the essence of the human as thought in terms of the truth of Being as such," which is gained for the first time with this "supplementation" (p. 303; GA 11, 150), is present in this essay. Already here, the subject-matter of the "turning" (*Kehre*), which Heidegger places in correspondence with his turn (*Wendung*) from Being-accomplishment to Being-occurrence, is put into thought: The work of art lets one experience that the openness of Being does not in the first instance belong to the self-relation of Dasein, but is rather something that begins and appears in Dasein. The experience of Being extends beyond the merely human.

Heidegger for the first time clarifies what this means in more detail in the lecture-course of the summer semester of 1935, *Introduction to Meta-*

47. William J. Richardson, *Heidegger: Through Phenomenology to Thought* (The Hague: Martinus Nijhoff, 1974).

48. Martin Heidegger, *On Time and Being: GA 14.*

physics. Here "the Being of beings" is understood in the sense of "truth" or "Beyng," and is determined as that "which opens of itself," the "self-opening unfolding"; in a third variation of the notion, it is called the "coming-to-appearance and the resting within it, in short the opening-remaining being-at-work."[49] Insofar as "truth" (or Beyng) occurs *of its own accord,* without any additional action and without the necessity of being retraced in its occurrence to a cause, it can be denoted with one word, one that Heidegger is convinced was decisive for early Greek poetry and thought: Truth is φύσις, "nature," as it is usually translated. Here, however, the word indicates the occurrence of openness itself in which something can show itself.

Heidegger has unfolded the notion of φύσις in a detailed as well as unique discussion of the determination of φύσις in Aristotle.[50] He also takes the idea up in a text on Hölderlin's hymn "As When on a Holiday . . ." *(chapter 10),* which was delivered "several times in 1939 and 1940"[51] and which thus belongs in the same period as the Aristotle-interpretation. The interpretation of Hölderlin's hymn makes more clear than the Aristotle-interpretation, however, what relative importance Heidegger attributes to the notion of φύσις—or, as he also says here with Hölderlin, "nature." Heidegger thinks that the attitude toward φύσις decides the fate of the West. The aim is to correspond to "nature," and thus the poets once again have special importance: They are "the future ones whose essence will be measured according to their adaptation to the essence of 'nature'" (p. 159; GA 4, 55). On the one hand, the essence of "nature" is thus poetized "according to the concealed truth of the originary basic word," i.e., φύσις. On the other hand, Hölderlin poetizes "something different" in the word "nature," something that is no longer φύσις, but rather stands "in a concealed relation" to φύσις (p. 160; GA 4, 57).

Heidegger here articulates the center of his historical thinking as it is developed in the latter half of the 1930s. The distinction between φύσις and "nature" corresponds to the difference between the first and second beginning of thinking as it is described in the *Contributions to Philosophy (chapter 11).* In both instances, Heidegger stresses the essential relatedness of the present to early antiquity, and both times he concludes that early Greek thinking and poetry cannot be taken over into the present. Heidegger

---

49. Martin Heidegger, *An Introduction to Metaphysics:* GA 40, 16.
50. Cf. Martin Heidegger, "On the Essence and Concept of
51. Martin Heidegger, *Elucidations of Hölderlin's Poetry:* GA 4, 203.

thereby corrects a conviction that had been dominant for him in the 1920s—the conviction that, on the path of "deconstruction," the Greek beginning could be laid bare and "repeated," brought back. He now holds, poetically as well as philosophically, that "the re-grasping of the beginning"[52] (as he had phrased it in 1925) is impossible—and thus the attempt at a "beginning" in his rectorship address comes to be questionable. The same goes for the assumption in his essay on the artwork that the poet can, out of his own completeness of language, speak the openness of Beyng to a people and thus enable its history. Instead, Heidegger takes up a thought from his Hölderlin lecture. In an obvious allusion to the "time of need" in which the old gods have fled and no new god is revealed, the *Contributions to Philosophy* speak of a time of crossing, of a "first bridge-building of a crossing." Heidegger clarifies that the bridge to be built "swings toward a shore that is yet to be decided."[53] This corresponds to the notion of the poets as "those to come." Poets do not reveal truth here and now, but instead prepare it in the sense of a new beginning. This, so Heidegger believes, occurs in Hölderlin's poetizing φύσις as "nature" and this as something "holy" into which the divine that has fled can return.

A dual insight is at play in the shift of Heidegger's historical thinking: In treating a repetition of the Greek beginning as impossible, he takes the stubbornness of history, especially that of the philosophical tradition, into account. By virtue of this tradition devolving from its beginning in the thinking of φύσις and becoming "metaphysics," an understanding of Being takes shape that cannot simply be incapacitated through a repetition of the beginning. This understanding of Being, furthermore, determines the present; it even reaches an extreme form in the present. For this reason, so Heidegger now thinks, an understanding of the philosophical tradition is dependent on a fundamental, new reflection on the possibility of the question of Being, one that is set out at the immediate beginning of the *Contributions to Philosophy*: This understanding is dependent on the reflection of what exists today.

Technological World, Will to Power

Heidegger's engagement with an unusual book is decisive for his reflection on the present. The book is Ernst Jünger's *The Worker*, which appeared in 1932; Heidegger immediately recognizes this book's importance. From 1934

52. Martin Heidegger, *History of the Concept of Time, Prolegomena:* GA 20, 184.
53. Martin Heidegger, *Contributions to Philosophy:* GA 65, 169.

onwards—possibly immediately after the failure of his rectorship, and in the face of the necessity of accounting for his own situation—Heidegger initiates a discussion with Jünger's essay, documented in many sources, that diagnoses the present (*chapters 12 and 13*). Heidegger instantly recognizes what is new and clear-sighted in Jünger's descriptions: Jünger saw like no other that the technologizing of the world has brought about an epochal shift that makes movements like "nationalism" and "socialism" appear anachronistic; they belong, as Heidegger states in agreement with Jünger, "to the civil pre-War era" (p. 191; GA 90, 237). Technology is not a continuation of manual labor in a larger fashion but rather a new form of the world, the institution of which Jünger associates with a new type of human, the "worker." This designates that person, according to Heidegger, who "goes over and beyond the human so far—the 'last' human—into another form" (p. 205; GA 90, 257).

As this reference to the "last human," taken from Nietzsche's *Thus Spoke Zarathustra,* indicates, Heidegger reads Jünger from a Nietzschean perspective. In Jünger's foresighted description of a thoroughly technologized world, Heidegger sees the clear image of a world determined by the "will to power," in other words, the absolutely set dynamism of restless change, increase, and overbidding of the real in new realities which are to be immediately overcome again. Nietzsche is the thinker that Heidegger continually returns to in the 1930s, and he dedicated no fewer than five lecture-courses to him.[54] He thereby discovers Nietzsche—who had until then been admired by poets and considered more of a "poet-philosopher"—as first and foremost a philosopher belonging in the same line as Plato, Aristotle, Leibniz, Kant, and Hegel. Nietzsche's notion of the "will to power," which Heidegger unfolds especially forcefully in the last of his Nietzsche-lectures (*chapter 15*), thus appears as the last and only possible remaining form of metaphysics.

Unlike Nietzsche, Jünger is no philosopher to Heidegger; he is "a pointer with his own stature" (p. 199; GA 90, 247–48), a "describer" (p. 206; GA 90, 259). However, as such, he makes evident to which reality the concept of the "will to power" applies. Furthermore, if Nietzsche's thought is "the end of that beginning in which the most ancient Greek thinkers

---

54. Martin Heidegger, *Nietzsche I: The Will to Power as Art:* GA 43; *Nietzsche II: The Eternal Recurrence of the Same:* GA 44; *Nietzsche III: The Will to Power as Knowledge:* GA 47; *Nietzsche: Der europäische Nihilismus:* GA 48; *Nietzsches Metaphysik* (prepared and announced for the winter semester 1941–1942, but not delivered): GA 50, 1–133. Cf. also Martin Heidegger, *Zur Auslegung von Nietzsches II. Unzeitgemäßer Betrachtung* (seminar in the winter semester 1938–1939): GA 46.

(Anaximander, Heraclitus, Parmenides) questioned Being" (p. 202; GA 90, 253), then Jünger's description offers the technologized world that image through which the end of metaphysics, and ultimately metaphysics itself, can be thought. This does not mean, for Heidegger, that Jünger thought about the world in this way. Jünger is for Heidegger a diagnostician who remains unaware of his own historical position. By coming to this conclusion, as a comparison of the selected texts shows, Heidegger's position toward Jünger becomes more critical. Jünger did not think the "metaphysics" in the end of which he belongs as a "pointer" and "describer." Heidegger's image of metaphysics is completely and solely his own. For him, metaphysics is a way of thinking that fails to experience φύσις because it attempts to comprehend "what opens of itself" by means of the model of production, of artificial presentation. This occurs in the contrasting assignment of determinations at play in the art of presentation (τέχνη): What must be created in art through a producer—who is oriented by an exemplary model (εἶδος)—surely occurs on its own in φύσις, but it occurs just as in the producing arts.[55]

   The significance of production as a philosophical model had occurred to Heidegger very early. Already in the programmatic essay of 1922, he notes that Aristotle thinks Being as being-produced (p. 59; GA 62, 373). The observation is accurate insofar as Aristotle indeed describes the meaning of "Being" with the model of production. By showing that in production, the εἶδος of something must already be present in order for anything to be produced, he simultaneously shows that the Being of the produced thing is essentially determined by the εἶδος. The "beingness," the οὐσία of the being, is the εἶδος that is present in it.[56] If, as Heidegger does, one holds to this notion and—in what is surely not an unproblematic generalization— understands all "metaphysics" in relation to it, then metaphysics can be understood as the essential condition for the development of modern technology. Modern technology is then, conversely, the "outermost possibility"[57] of metaphysics, because it is unceasing production and thus refuses to orient itself by a constantly present, decisive model. Thus it is, as Heidegger formulates with considerable clarity in one of his late texts,[58] the outermost form of metaphysics and at the same time its end.

---

55. Martin Heidegger, *Contributions to Philosophy*: GA 65, 190–191.

56. Aristotle, *Metaphysics* 7, 11, 1037a29–30.

57. Cf. Martin Heidegger, "The End of Philosophy and the Task of Thinking," in *On Time and Being*: GA 14.

58. Ibid.

This constellation is determinative for Heidegger's thinking. His philosophical work is the discussion of metaphysics with respect to technology, as well as the discussion of the technologized world and its metaphysical prehistory. While the first accentuation of the question arises especially in Heidegger's confrontation with Nietzsche, the text "The Age of the World Picture" (*chapter 14*), given as a talk in 1938, is an especially concise example of the second. Here Heidegger has made Jünger's descriptions his own and formulated them anew through his own concepts. Now, modern technology appears more clearly in its scientific form; it is "research" in its essence, and proves to be a projection of "beings as a whole" according to which these "solely and initially exist insofar as they are set in place (*gestellt*) by the human that presents and produces (*vorstellend-herstellenden Menschen*)" (p. 218; GA 5, 89). This setting-in-place (*Stellen*), which prefigures Heidegger's later determination of the essence of technology as "*Gestell*,"[59] is especially the securing of further production possibilities. As such, it is dependent on the "world picture"—a knowledge of the world that fixes beings in place and makes them available. By making the world into a picture, one is "in the picture" about it; the world now stands "in the way it stands to us, before us" (p. 218; GA 5, 89).

Language

However thoroughly and emphatically the world is fixed in place through the picture, Heidegger sees this placement as bringing about the end of the Western tradition of thought; it has exhausted itself in its "outermost possibility," no matter how powerfully the realization of this possibility reigns over the world. The end of metaphysics, however, leaves open the possibility of that "other beginning," which Heidegger speaks of in the *Contributions to Philosophy* and which he finds as the "holy" in Hölderlin's poem on "nature." In this, Hölderlin's significance for Heidegger is incomparable: As poet of the flown gods and the possible return of a god, Hölderlin brings to language a measure of Being in the world that is beyond technical-scientific notions of control; even if the gods have "fled," poetry allows them to remain present in relation to human Dasein. However, the otherness of a possible beginning beyond metaphysics does not lie, for Heidegger, solely in grasping the divine, but rather already in the essence of poetry itself. Poetry is close like no other to the order and placement of technical-

---

59. Cf. chapter 17 of the present volume.

scientific thinking—and it is, like no other, radically different from this. Poetry itself, and art in general, has the character of placing (*Stellens*); it is, as Heidegger had developed in the essay on the origin of the artwork, a "setting-up" and "setting-there." But the placing of art is essentially different from that of technology: It does not fix in place, but rather sets forth; it shows and lets be seen. This is because the essence of art, as Heidegger sees it, is language. In its linguisticality, art is literally phenomenological.

The question of language had already occupied Heidegger in his philosophical beginnings. The theories of judgment that he engages with in his dissertation always articulate a certain understanding of language; they view speech as expression, so that language is revealed more or less according to the model of a proposition. Heidegger sees this understanding of language as too narrow. He indirectly sets another understanding of language over against it, by describing philosophy in the emergency-semester lecture-course of 1919 as "hermeneutical"—as interpretive and communicative. This corresponds to the understanding of language as "discourse" in *Being and Time;* discourse is the possibility of communication in which Dasein is revealed as "being-with."

However, by stressing the communicative character of language in *Being and Time,* Heidegger at the same time limits its capacity for disclosure. *Being and Time* thus develops the idea that the structure of an expression is grounded in a "circumspective" understanding of the matter at hand. That something can be indicated "as something," for instance a hammer as heavy, one must first discover the heaviness of the hammer in its use, where it is experienced "as something" with which to hit nails. Or, to put it in Heidegger's terminology: The "apophantic as" is grounded in the "hermeneutical as."[60]

This notion is problematic. Even if speech about things belongs directly in connection with the dealings with them—if something that one deals with *can* be brought to language—then language must always already determine this dealing. Heidegger draws this consequence for the first time in the lecture-course of the summer semester 1931. Language, he states there, is "that in which the manifestness and discovery of the world in general breaks open and is."[61] The world can only be investigated in any which way because it is revealed in language.

Heidegger does not elaborate in more detail how the linguistic man-

60. Martin Heidegger, *Being and Time:* GA 2, 204–213.
61. Martin Heidegger, *Aristotle's Metaphysics*

ifestness of the world is to be thought until thirteen years later, in the lecture-course titled *Logic: Heraclitus' Teaching on Logos,* in the summer semester 1944 *(chapter 16).* Here Heidegger once again picks up the question of the relative placement of the proposition, in order to show that propositions only exist from out of the essence of language as "harvest" or "collection" (p. 251; GA 55, 268). Heidegger gleans this determination of language by returning, through an interpretation of Heraclitus, to the basic meaning of the Greek verb λέγειν. Λέγειν means "harvesting" in the sense of gathering-together, of the gathering. Various moments are connected in a proposition—for instance hammer and the heaviness that is attributed to it. Such a connection is only possible, however, because everything that is connected in the proposition is already gathered in the possibility of connection. Language, understood as gathering, holds everything together that is and that is not. It is, as Heidegger says with Heraclitus, the unity of all; all is one in it.

New Beginning: Thing and *Gestell*

The lecture-course on *logos* in Heraclitus is the last that Heidegger teaches for many years. The French [military] government bars him from teaching [in December 1946]—based partially on Karl Jaspers's extremely critical opinion. This ban is lifted in 1949, but Heidegger does not resume his teaching activity until his official retirement in 1951, with the lecture-course *What Is Thinking?* Before this, however, he had already made a new start. The "Club of Bremen," an "association of respected representatives of business and the Hanseatic upper class,"[62] had invited him in 1949, and he took this as a challenge. Especially in the first two of the Bremen lectures *(chapter 17),* he places new emphases and harmoniously brings together themes that he had previously developed independently of each other.

This applies above all to Heidegger's determination of the modern technological-scientific world. He finds new descriptions and powerful concepts. He elucidates the essence of technology as the removal of distances; here, the aim of forcing everything into a ready grasp is at work. Its essence is the "*Ge-Stell*" (p. 273; GA 79, 32), which means: the possibility of forcibly placing that precedes any specific technical process.

The removal of distances does not create nearness. Places can be

---

62. Heinrich Wiegand Petzet, *Auf Einen Stern Zugehen: Begegnungen und Gespräche mit Martin Heidegger, 1929–1976* (Frankfurt am Main: Societäts-Verlag, 1983), 59.

reached more quickly and comfortably, but still—or perhaps for this reason —remain matters of indifference; what can reached at any time and accessed without any difficulty does not demand understanding as things do that one holds distance from. What is new and surprising about the Bremen lectures is that Heidegger attributes to things the proximity that technology is designed to destroy. These things no longer occur as the "stuff" of *Being and Time*, which was accessible to Dasein in its use in the world. Things, as Heidegger now speaks of them, no longer belong in a world; rather, there would be no world without things. These are obviously conceived on the model of the work of art that Heidegger discussed in the 1930s; like the word conceived as λόγος, they gather together. In the pitcher that Heidegger selects as an example, the expanse and openness of the world, or "sky," is connected to its openly-placed concealing, the "earth." And insofar as the pitcher is a consecrational container, it lets humans, the "mortals," be connected to the "divine." As the openness that results from these distanced yet "close" connections, the world is a "fourfold." Its connections do not persist and are only realized in the use of the pitcher; without the thing that the pitcher is, the connections would not exist. Things are nodes of the world, as it were; places of connection through which humans belong in the world as well.

Like the Bremen lectures, many other of Heidegger's works after World War II are simultaneously retrospective and renewing. Heidegger finds a succinct simplicity in his train of thought, and his language becomes light in its own way, without losing exactitude or strictness. One basic trait remains the same: Heidegger's skepticism regarding the traditional language of philosophy and its conceptual assertions. However, Heidegger now no longer wishes to supersede the terms of the philosophical tradition by introducing his own terminology—as he had done in *Being and Time*. He dodges terminological writing by reflecting on spoken language, and making its translation into written language clear to himself. This is the case in a short text on "The Language of Johann Peter Hebel" (*chapter 19*), an author that Heidegger respected, among other things, for his ability to glean a linguistic form from spoken language. Hebel, as the author of the *Alemannic Poems*, "held himself listeningly toward the influx of the language-spirit of this dialect, in such a way that this language continually sprang together into single poems, in the way that crystals are formed" (p. 297; GA 13, 125). Heidegger's project as a thinker is related to this. New formations such as "fourfold" or "*Ge-Stell*" are developed out of the indicative possibilities of language in the description of phenomena; they are results of a path of thought that was discovered linguistically, and thus only make sense insofar as one pursues this path oneself. For this reason, they cannot simply be taken over without their determinative power being lost; to follow Heidegger's paths of thought, one still has to grasp his experiences in one's own words. Heidegger shows that thinking is also a discovery of words.

Occasionally, Heidegger openly displays the tension between the traditional language of philosophy and the possibilities that he developed of thinking in language. In these cases, traditional concepts are continually translated into non-terminological language until their meaning, as Heidegger understands it, is revealed. This is a late offshoot of "destruction" that is no longer identified as such. This transference occurs in especially impressive fashion in his speech "The Principle of Identity" *(chapter 18)*, which Heidegger delivered on the five hundredth anniversary of the University of Freiburg in 1957; an earlier version had been held as an extracurricular study in the same year. Like the Bremen lectures, this speech stems from Heidegger's insight into the essence of connection. This is not an addition to the connected moments; instead, these are to be thought from out of the connection. What goes for "sky" and "earth"—for the cohesion of the open and the concealed—also applies to the principle of identity. Its formal shape, "A = A," certainly shows on the one hand that something is itself and nothing else, it is itself alone. However, insofar as this can only be expressed in doubling, that which is the same must be thought from out of the relation that connects what is doubled. What is doubled cannot be differentiated according to the principle of identity. But it is only what it is in a relation or connection.

Heidegger explains this notion in light of a phrase by Parmenides, according to which thinking (νοεῖν) and Being (εἶναι) are the same (τὸ αὐτό). This sameness can be interpreted as "belonging together" (p. 287; GA 11, 36), and that in turn means that a "belonging to Being reigns within the human, a belonging that listens to Being" (p. 289; GA 11, 39). Thinking and Being are not like things persistent unto themselves; instead, they exist only in a connection that is one of listening. In listening, that which is heard is there, indistinguishable from listening, and the respective listening only exists through the presence of what is heard. What Heidegger said about φύσις and the language of poetry in the 1930s clearly resounds in this discussion of Being and its experience in thinking. Now, however, the connection or relation of Being to thinking is central as such. Heidegger adopts a word for this relation that had already supplied the appropriate subtitle for his *Contributions to Philosophy: Ereignis*. The word has multiple meanings for Heidegger. First, he indicates the old verb *eräugen* and reads in this "to catch sight of, to call something to oneself through looking" (p. 292; GA 11, 45). Understood as such, *Ereignis* is the sight of Being that is accomplished in thinking. Furthermore, the word reminds one of "property" (*Eigentum*), of "belonging" (*zu eigen sein*), and thus indicates that thinking, by belonging to Being, is "appropriated" (*übereignet*) to it (p. 289; GA 11, 39). Finally, in its common linguistic usage, the word describes the *occurrence* of the belonging-together of thinking and Being; this belonging does not simply exist, but rather continually "occurs" differently. Even the "*Ge-Stell*" is a possibility of the belonging-together of thinking and Being, a possibility of what Heidegger also calls the "history of Being"; in the *Ge-Stell*, "a peculiar ownership and appropriation" takes place (p. 291; GA 11, 45). Only, in technical-scientific forcing (*Stellen*), the belonging-together of thinking and Being is carried out without insight: it is not recognized as what it is. When the "thinking of *Ereignis* as appropriative event (*Er-eignis*)" (p. 292; GA 11, 46), the grasp of human existence and understanding of this existence in its connection succeeds, then the technical world has lost its unquestionableness and finality. A free or, as Heidegger also says, "released" relation to technology then emerges.[63]

Pure Shining

Insofar as Heidegger wishes to prepare such a relation, he fundamentally still understands his thinking as he did in the *Contributions to Philosophy:* as a crossing to the point at which "the now-inceptive world civilization one day overcomes the technical-scientific imprint as the only measure of humanity's residence on Earth."[64] However, Heidegger now thinks less often about an "other beginning," and more about what lies behind, and is distorted by, technical-scientific definitions. His attention to things, as voiced in the Bremen lectures, but also his increasingly intense involvement with art, belong to this theme. Heidegger discovers the peculiar essence of art, instead of understanding it (as he still did in "The Origin of the Work of Art") from poetry, and thus from Hölderlin, and therefore from the connection to a historical-philosophical project. One example of this is the text "Art and

---

63. On "releasement," cf. Martin Heidegger, Ἀγχιβασίν. *Ein Gespräch selbdritt auf einem Feldweg zwischen einem Forscher, einem Gelehrten und einem Weisen,* in *Feldweg-Gespräche:* GA 77, 1–159; and "Gelassenheit," in *Reden und andere Zeugnisse eines Lebensweges:* GA 16, 517–529.

64. Cf. Martin Heidegger, "The End of Philosophy and the Task of Thinking," in *On Time and Being,* trans. Joan Stambaugh (Chicago: University of Chicago Press, 1972), 67.

Space" *(chapter 21)*. Heidegger wrote this essay on stone, so that it could be lithographically printed together with the collages of the sculptor Eduardo Chillida. Sculptures open space; they "gather in," as Heidegger says. The first version of "On the Origin of the Work of Art" already made the point that art could open up space.[65] Now, however, space is not meant in the sense of a historical world, but in its perceptual spatiality; the sculptures make a space visible that the technical-scientific understanding of space misses. As a "confrontation with artistic space" (p. 306; GA 13, 204), art is no alternative to the technical-scientific arrangement of the world. However, it discovers this world differently, in such a way that it creates livable spaces. The artwork opens up a "free expanse" (p. 308; GA 13, 207) and thus provides the freedom without which the world would be unlivable. Living, which Heidegger had earlier attempted to think with respect to the "fourfold,"[66] is now determined differently, less schematically. Now it is the inhabiting of freedom.

If this freedom is discovered and opened up through art, thinking will always arrive too late: It can only thoughtfully pursue in words what occurs in art. And this pursuit reveals that freedom, understood as openness in the artwork, can actually not be separated from the artwork. The distinctions of thought must be guided by the simplicity of the artwork. Over against this simplicity, thinking restrains itself. Thought has its model in the simplicity of art.

Heidegger came to this conviction in a short text from his final years *(chapter 22)*. He had published a series of writings—on Paul Cézanne's art, among other things—in an edition of the journal *L'Herne* that was dedicated to the poet René Char. Char was a friend of Heidegger's. Through his stays with Char in Provence, Heidegger had become acquainted with Cézanne's landscape the "mountain of holy victory" (p. 311)—or *Mont Sainte-Victoire*—and had thus discovered Cézanne's art for himself. Heidegger worked over the writings on Cézanne again in 1974. In this last version, which is reprinted here, Heidegger takes back the distinction between Being and beings that had shaped his thinking since 1922, and what since 1926 was called the "ontological difference." When Cézanne, with regard to his art, speaks of "realization,"[67] this means "the appearance of the present in the clearing of coming-to-presence"—"such that the duality of both is bound up

---

65. Cf. p. 17 above.

66. Martin Heidegger, "Building Dwelling Thinking," in *Poetry, Language, Thought: GA* 7, 145–164.

67. On this term, cf. Rainer Maria Rilke, *Briefe über Cézanne*, ed. Heinrich Wiegand Petzet and Clara Rilke (Frankfurt am Main: Insel, 1977); also Gottfried Boehm, *Paul Cézanne. Montagne Saint-Victoire. Eine Kunst-Mongraphie* (Frankfurt am Main: Insel, 1988), 54–66.

in the simplicity of the pure shining of its images" (p. 311). If this creates for thinking "the question of twisting free of the ontological difference between Being and beings" (p. 311), this can only mean that thought should subordinate itself to the "pure shining" that the images are. In this notion of Heidegger's, a fundamental theme of his thinking returns: All reflections on discovery, truth as unconcealment, φύσις, and Being were part of the attempt to trace the mystery of phenomena that lies in their self-showing. Now, at eighty-five, Heidegger has found the clear and yet mysterious answer in the "pure shining" of images.

Günter Figal

ONE

The Environmental Experience

———— ∾∾∾ ————

1919

I bring a new experience to givenness not only for myself, but I ask you all—
each isolated I-self who is sitting here—to do the same. In fact, we wish to
enter into an experience that is to a certain degree unitary. You come into
this lecture hall as usual, at the usual hour, and go to *your* usual place. Focus
on this experience of "seeing *your* place," [71] or you can also put yourselves
in my own position: Stepping into the lecture hall, I see the lectern. We
dispense with a verbal formulation of this. What do "I" see? Brown surfaces,
at right angles to one another? No, I see something else. A large box with
another smaller one set upon it? Not at all. I see the lectern at which I am to

---

This chapter is largely based on a previous translation by Ted Sadler in *Towards the Definition of
Philosophy* (New York: Continuum Press, 2000), 59–64. Small changes have been made to certain
phrasings.

Bracketed numbers refer to the pagination of GA 56/57; the chapter opens at page 70.—Tr.

speak. You see the lectern from which you are to be addressed, and from which I have spoken to you before. In pure experience, there is no founding state of affairs—as it is called—as if I first of all see intersecting brown surfaces, which then reveal themselves to me as a box, then as a desk, then as an academic lecturing desk, a lectern, so that I attach lectern-hood to the box like a label. All of that is simply bad and misguided interpretation, diversion from a pure seeing into the experience. I see the lectern in one fell swoop, as it were, and not in isolation, but as adjusted a bit too high for me. I immediately see a book lying upon it as annoying to me (a book, not number of layered sheets covered in black marks); I see the lectern in an orientation, a lighting, a background.

Certainly you will say, that might be what happens in immediate experience, for me and in a certain way also for you, as you also see this arrangement of wood and boards *as* a lectern. This object, which all of us here perceive, somehow has the specific meaning "lectern." It is already different if we bring a farmer from deep in the Black Forest into the lecture hall. Does he see the lectern, or does he see a box, an arrangement of boards? He sees "the place for the teacher," he sees the object as fraught with meaning. If someone saw a box, then he would not be seeing a piece of wood, a thing, a natural object. But let us imagine a negro from Senegal suddenly transplanted here from his hut. What he would see, gazing at this object, [72] is difficult to say precisely: perhaps something to do with magic, or something behind which one could find good protection from arrows and thrown stones. Or, what is most likely—would he not know what to make of it at all, just seeing complexes of colors and surfaces, simply a thing, a something which simply is? So my seeing and that of a Senegalese negro are fundamentally different. All they have in common is that in both cases something is seen. *My* seeing is to a high degree something individual, which I certainly may not—without further ado—use to ground the analysis of the experience. For this analysis is supposed to yield universally valid scientific results in conjunction with the elaboration of the problem.

Assuming that the experiences were fundamentally different, that only my experience existed, I still assert that universally valid propositions are possible. This implies that these sentences would also be valid for the experience of the Senegalese negro. Let us put this assertion aside and focus once again on the experience of the Senegalese negro. Even if he saw the lectern simply as a bare something that is there, it would have a meaning for him, a moment of signification. There is, however, the possibility of showing that the assumption of the transplanted unscientific (not culture-less) negro seeing the lectern as simply something is nonsensical but not contra-dictory, i.e., not impossible in a formal-*logical* sense. The negro will see the lectern much more as something "which he does not know what to make of." The meaningful character of "instrumental strangeness," and the mean-ingful character of the "lectern," are in their essence absolutely identical.

In the experience of seeing the lectern, something is given *to me* from out of an immediate environment. This environmental milieu (lectern, book, blackboard, notebook, fountain pen, caretaker, student fraternity, streetcar, automobile, etc.) does not consist just of things, objects that are then [73] additionally conceived as meaning such and such; rather, the meaningful is what is primary, and is immediately given to me without any mental detours across thing-oriented apprehension. Living in an environ-ment, it signifies to me everywhere and always, it all has the character of world, "it worlds" [*es weltet*], which is something different from "it values" [*es wertet*]. (The problem of the connection between the two belongs to the notion of the eidetic genealogy of primary motivations and leads into difficult problem-areas.)

Let us bring to mind again the environmental experience, my seeing of the lectern. In my comportment toward seeing the lectern giving itself environmentally, do I find anything like an "I" in the pure sense of experi-ence? In this experiencing, in this living-toward, there is something of me: *My* "I" goes out completely beyond itself and resonates *along* in this "see-ing," as the self of the negro resounds in his own experience of "something which *he* cannot make out." *More precisely:* Only through this particular "I" resonating along does it experience something environmental, does it world. Wherever and whenever it worlds for me, *I* am somehow fully along with it. Let us compare this to the experience of the question.[1] I do not find myself in this. The "anything whatsoever," about whose "there is" I inquire, does not world. The world-like is extinguished here, when we grasp every possible environmental thing as anything whatsoever. This grasping, this firmly placing observation [*Fest-stellen*] of the object as such, occurs at the cost of forcing back my own "I." It belongs to the meaning of "anything whatsoever" that I *do not* resonate along in its determination, but rather that this resonating, this going-out-along-with [*Mitherausgehen*], is prevented. The object-being as such does not touch *me*. The "I" that firmly places [*fest-stellt*] is not *myself* anymore. Observation, as an experience, is only a rem-

---

1. [Based on what follows, Heidegger seems to be referring to the question: Is there anything whatsoever? — Tr.]

nant [74] of lived experience [*Er-leben*]; it is a de-living [*Ent-leben*]. What is objective, what is known, is as such removed, lifted out of the actual lived experience. The objectified occurrence, the occurrence as something objective and known, we call a *process* [*Vor-gang*]; it simply passes by my knowing "I," to which it is related only by being known, in a pale self-relatedness reduced to the minimum of experience. It is the essence of things and of their states of affairs to only give themselves precisely in knowledge, i.e., in the theoretical comportment and for the theoretical "I." In the theoretical comportment, I am directed toward something, but *I* do not live (as historical "I") toward this or that world-like thing. Let us once again contrast entire contexts of experience, so that it does not appear that the "opposition" pertains only to isolated experiences.

Let us place ourselves into the comportment of the astronomer, who in astrophysics investigates the phenomenon of sunrise simply as a process in nature, relating to it indifferently and letting it proceed along its course. Let us contrast this with the experience of the chorus of Theban elders, who in Sophocles' *Antigone* look at the rising sun on the first friendly morning after a successful defensive battle:

ἱακτὶς ἀελίου, τὸ κάλῳ
λιστον ἑπτατύλῳ φανὲν
Θήβᾳ τῶν προτέρων φάος

Sun's beam, fairest of all
That ever till now shone
On seven-gated Thebes[2]

[75] With this contrast, however, the problem of the *how* of the different modes of experience is not solved in any way, but instead first raised to begin with. (From here onwards, rework the end of the page with more substantial clarity!! Cf. supplement.)[3] For the time being, however, it will suffice for our purposes. As what do we see the experiences? The question of how such seeing is possible, of what it itself is, and whether it is not also theory (it is, after all, to become science), will be set aside for the moment.

---

2. Sophocles, *Antigone*, ll. 118–120. [Heidegger cites the German translation by Friedrich Hölderlin, "O Blik der Sonne, du schönster, der / Dem siebenthorigen Thebe / Seit langem scheint"; see Hölderlin, *Sämtliche Werke und Briefe*, ed. F. Zinkernagel (Leipzig, 1915), vol. 3, 374–375. The English rendering here is from *Greek Tragedies: Volume 1*, trans. David Grene (Chicago: University of Chicago Press, 1991), 185.—Tr.]

3. [This supplement has not been preserved.]

Let us in turn try to understand both experiences according to their own meaning—which one is irrelevant—and see if, in this understanding that turns toward experiences, we can regard these as processes, as objects that are presented [*vorgestellt*], observed [*festgestellt*] before us. But something does happen. In seeing the lectern I am fully present with my "I"; it resonates with the experience, as we said. It is an experience proper to me and that is how I see. However, it is not a process but rather an event [*Ereignis*] (non-process, a remainder of event in the experience of questioning). Lived experience does not pass in front of me like a thing that I place there, as an object; instead I myself appropriate [*er-eigne*] it to myself, and it occurs [*er-eignet sich*] according to its essence. And if, in looking at it, I understand it in this way, then I understand it not as process, as thing or object, but as something completely new—as an event. I see something thing-like just as little as I do an objectified sphere of things, a Being [*ein Sein*], either physical or psychical Being. Attending strictly to the experience, I do not see anything psychical. "Appropriating event" also does not mean that I appropriate the experience from the outside or from anywhere else; "outer" and "inner" have as little meaning here as "physical" and "psychical." The experiences are events of appropriation insofar as they live out of what is one's own, and life only lives in this way. (With this, the character of the event has not yet been fully determined.)

TWO

Indication of the Hermeneutical Situation

—◦◦◦—

1922

The following investigations serve a history of ontology and logic.[1] As *interpretations*, they fall under certain conditions of interpreting and understanding. The content of every interpretation,[2] that is, the thematic object in the How of its being interpreted, is only able to speak properly for itself when the given hermeneutical situation—to which every interpretation is relative—is made available in sufficient and clear distinction.

Previously translated by Michael Baur in *Man and World* 25 (1992): 355–393. This version has been edited for consistency within the present volume; it also incorporates the emendations and marginalia from Heidegger's original typescript, which the editor transcribed in preparation of the German edition of this volume.

Bracketed numbers refer to the pagination of GA 62; the chapter opens at page 346.—Tr.

1. [This is the beginning of the typed manuscript.]

2. [Handwritten note in the left margin:] Being-character of interpretation!—brings forth the being-*thus* [*Sosein*]—How. [Interpretation] is: having already grasped the *being*-historical!

Every interpretation, each according to a particular field and knowledge-claim, has the following:

(1) a *point of view*[3] that is more or less expressly appropriated and [347] fixed;

(2) a *direction of view* that is motivated by the point of view and within which the "as-what" and the "that-with-respect-to-which" [*woraufhin*] of the interpretation are determined. The object of the interpretation is grasped anticipatorily in the "as-what," and is interpreted according to the "that-with-respect-to-which";

(3) a *range of view* that is limited by the point of view and direction of view, and within which the interpretation's claim to objectivity moves.

The possible accomplishment of interpretation and understanding, as well as the appropriation of the object that thereby occurs, are transparent to the degree that the situation—*in* and *for* which an interpretation develops—is illuminated according to the aspects just mentioned. The hermeneutic of each respective situation has to develop the situation's transparency and has to bring this transparency, as hermeneutical, along into the approach of the interpretation.[4]

The situation of interpretation, as the understanding appropriation of the past, is always the situation of a living present. History itself, the past that is appropriated in understanding, grows in its comprehensibility with the primordiality of the decisive choice and the development of the herme-neutical situation. The past opens itself only according to the resoluteness and force of illumination that a present has available to it. The primordiality of a philosophical interpretation is determined by the specific certainty within which philosophical research maintains itself and its tasks. The con-ception that philosophical research has of itself and of the concretion of its problematic also already determines its basic attitude toward the history of philosophy. The direction of view, into which alone the past can be placed,

---

3. [Handwritten note in the lower margin:] *Having a view* is primary—predetermination of *that* which is to be interpreted at all, *what* it is, *as what* it is to be taken. Ontology (in what sense) of *life*, of beings—shaped as what, present how, and accessible as what?

4. [Handwritten note at the end of the paragraph:] The development of the hermeneutical situation is the *seizing* of the factical "conditions" and "prerequisites" of philosophical research. Actual prerequisites are not there to be "lamented" and "accepted by compulsion" as phenomena of in-completeness, but are instead to be *lived*; this does not mean to let them "unconsciously" rest with themselves, to move out of their way, but to *seize* them as *such*, and this means to thrust oneself into the *historical*.

determines what constitutes the object-field of philosophical problematics that is actually questioned [348]. Not only is this reading-into not contrary to the sense of historical knowing, but it is indeed the basic condition for bringing the past to expression. All interpretations in the field of the history of philosophy, as well as in those other fields that strive—over against problem-historical "constructions"—not to read anything into the texts, must admit that they too read into the texts, only they do so without orientation and with conceptual tools from the most disparate and uncontrollable sources. One takes one's lack of worry over what one "actually does," and a lack of knowledge about the means employed, for an elimination of any possible subjectivity.[5]

The clarification of the hermeneutical situation for the following interpretations, and thus for the demarcation of their thematic field, stems from the basic conviction that philosophical research, according to its Being-character, is something that an "age"—as long as it is not out of merely educational concern—can never borrow from another. But philosophical research—so long as it has understood itself and the meaning of its activity within human Dasein—is also something that will never want to claim the permission or ability to take away from future times the burden and the worry of radical questioning. With philosophical research that has become past, the possibility of its having an effect upon its future can never lie in the results as such, but is instead grounded in the primordiality of questioning that has been achieved and concretely developed, and through which such research—as a model that raises problems—is able to become the present ever anew.

The object of philosophical research is *human Dasein,* interrogated with respect to its Being-character. [349] This basic direction of philosophical questioning is not added on and attached externally to the questioned object—factical life—but is rather to be understood as the explicit grasping of a basic movement of factical life itself, which exists in such a way that in the concrete production [*Zeitigung*][6] of its Being, it is concerned with this

---

5. [Handwritten notes at the end of the paragraph:] (Cf. Mss. Hm., pp. 43–98). [This manuscript about hermeneutics could not be identified.] One interprets the insensibility and negligence concerning one's own hermeneutical situation, which is often muddled and recovered arbitrarily, as a lack of prejudice.

6. [Throughout this chapter, I have opted for the more straightforward translation of *Zeitigung* as "bringing forth" or "producing," in place of the more awkward "temporalizing." Nevertheless, one should not ignore the obvious temporal resonances in this word, which Heidegger clearly has in mind.—Tr.]

Being even when it avoids itself. Factical life has a character of Being such that it finds itself difficult to bear. The most unmistakable manifestation of this is factical life's tendency toward making things easy for itself. In this difficulty of bearing itself, life—according to the basic sense of its Being—*is* difficult, but not in the sense of an accidental quality. When factical life authentically is what it is, in this being-heavy and being-difficult, then the genuinely appropriate way of accessing and preserving it can only consist in making it difficult. Philosophical research must be held to this duty, if it does not want to fundamentally miss its object. Yet all making-easy,[7] all misleading currying of favors with regard to needs, all metaphysical reassurances based on what is usually just book-learning—all of this already amounts in its basic aim to a refusal to bring the object of philosophy within sight and within grasp, let alone to keep it there. Philosophy's own history is objectively present for philosophical research in a relevant sense if and only if it provides not diverse curiosities, but radically simple *things worthy of thought;*[8] i.e., if the history of philosophy does not distract the understanding present into seeking an enrichment of knowledge, but [350] rather forces the present back upon itself in order to increase questionability. Yet an appropriation of history with this concern means the following—and especially for a present within whose Being-character historical consciousness is constitutive: to understand radically what a particular past [form of] philosophical research posed, in *its* situation and *for* that situation, into its fundamental concern. *To understand* does not simply mean to cognitively confirm, but rather to *repeat* primordially what is understood in terms of its ownmost situation and for that situation. But this happens least of all in the borrowing of theorems, propositions, basic concepts, and principles, and in the revival of these—however that may be conducted. The understanding use of models, concerned about its own self, will fundamentally subject the models to the sharpest critique and shape them into a possible fruitful opposition.

Factical Dasein always only is what it is as completely its own, and not as the general Dasein of some universal humanity, concern for which is only

---

7. [Handwritten note over the beginning of the line:] Not to *gape at* thoughts that others have thought!

8. [Handwritten note in the top margin, with two arrows to the text:] "Tradition": precisely the unhistorical; past not present in it as what it is, i.e., as what is other and as the recoil of the present—but rather as an undecided present in the average indifferent "first" [*Zunächst*]. In tradition, [there is] no appropriated past (neither hermeneutical situation nor the past "what"-content). [Heidegger's second arrow points to "constitutive" in the following sentence.]

ever an illusory task. *Critique* of history is always only the critique of the present. Critique cannot be of the naive opinion that it can (may)[9] calculate for history how it should have taken place, if . . . ;[10,11] Rather, it must keep its view to the present and must see to it that it inquires in a manner appropriate to a primordiality within its own reach.[12] History is not [351] negated because it is "false," but rather because it still remains effective in the present, without being able to be a present that is authentically appropriated (or capable of being appropriated).[13]

The fixing of interpretation's basic historical attitude arises from the explication[14] of the sense of philosophical research. Its object was defined in an indicative fashion as *factical human Dasein as such*. The concrete specification of the philosophical problematic is to be derived from this, its object. For this reason, an initial preparatory highlighting of the specific objective character and Being-character of factical life becomes necessary. Yet this is not only because it is the *object* of philosophical research, but also because philosophical research itself constitutes a determinate *How* of factical life and, as such, brings along [*mitzeitigt*] in its accomplishment the concrete Being of life as it is in itself, and not first through some "application" after the fact. The possibility of such bringing-along is grounded in the fact that philosophical research is the explicit accomplishment of a basic movement of factical life and maintains itself always within factical life.

In this indication of the hermeneutical situation, the structures of the object—"factical life"—will not be concretely specified and grasped in their constitutive connections with one another. Rather, what is meant by the term "factical life" will be brought into view simply through the enumeration of the most important constitutive elements of facticity, and be made available as a *fore-having* [*Vorhabe*] for the concrete investigation.

The confusing ambiguity of the word "life" and of its application must not become grounds for simply getting rid of it. For then one renounces the

---

9. [Handwritten insertion above "can."]

10. [Handwritten insertion above the ellipsis:] it were certain with enough [?].

11. [Handwritten note in the lower margin:] One "does" history! instead of "*being*" it! One *is* not history, because this is "beautiful," "spiritually powerful," "respect for the past," piety, or a sign of a superior long view that does not naively absolutize itself! Where one "*does*" history, the historical has disappeared!

12. [Handwritten note in the top margin above this line:] for the past to recoil into existence, in order to show us *Dasein* as such, existence must not be *observed* [as] something, but be carried[?]!—as something that still drives itself into our Dasein, and leads the latter to fall.

13. [Handwritten insertion.]

14. [Handwritten note over the line:] of Being-character—again and *in* facticity.

possibility of investigating the directions of meaning that happen to belong to that word and that alone [352] make it possible to reach the objectivity that is meant in each instance. In connection with this, one must in principle keep in view that the term ζωή, *vita*, indicates a basic phenomenon upon which the Greek, the Old Testament, the New Testament Christian, and the Greek-Christian interpretations of human Dasein are all centered. The ambiguity of the term will have its roots in the intended object itself. For philosophy, this uncertainty of meaning can only be an occasion for eliminating it, or for making it into an expressly appropriated and transparent uncertainty, provided that it is indeed a necessary one based in the object. This focus on ambiguity (πολλακῶς λεγόμενον) is not an empty poking-about among isolated word-meanings, but instead the expression of the radical tendency to make the intended objectivity itself accessible and to make available the motivating source of the different meanings.[15]

The basic sense of the movement of factical life is *caring* (*curare*).[16] In the directed, caring "being-out-toward-something," the that-with-respect-to-which of life's care, the respective *world*, is there. The movement of caring has the character of factical life *dealing* with its world. The that-with-respect-to-which of care is the with-what[17] [*Womit*] of the dealings. The sense of the being-real and being-there of the world is grounded in and determined through the world's character as the with-what of the caring dealings. The world is there as always already somehow grasped (placed)[18] in care. The world articulates itself according to the possible directions of care as *world-environment, world-with,* and *self-world.* Correspondingly, caring is the care of livelihood, of profession, of enjoyment, of being undisturbed, of not dying, [353] of being-familiar-with, of knowing about, of being cognizant,[19] of making life secure in its final goals.

The movement of *concern*[20,21] shows manifold ways of accomplishment and of being related to the with-what of the dealings: tinkering with, preparing of, producing of, securing through, making use of, utilizing for, tak-

---

15. [Handwritten note at the end of the paragraph:] life—world—|Being|.

16. [Handwritten note in the lower margin:] *recuratio*: the historical!—therein the highest preservation of Being.

17. [Handwritten note in the lower margin:] the with-what never loses or gains the mere schematic character of a backdrop, if the Being-character of dealings (i.e., factical dealings) is understood (not, for instance, as lived-experience).

18. [Handwritten insertion above the line.]

19. [Handwritten insertion.]

20. [Handwritten note above the line:] emphasize the character of *Being.*

21. [Handwritten addition at "*concern*":] introduce.

ing possession of, safe-keeping, and forfeiting of. The with-what of the performative dealings—corresponding to each of these different ways of accomplishment—stands in each case within a particular knowledge and familiarity.[22] The caring dealings always have their with-what within a particular view; within the dealings, *circumspection* is alive, both guiding and bringing forth the dealings. Caring is looking around, and as circumspect it is at the same time concerned with the cultivation of circumspection, and with safeguarding and increasing familiarity with the object of one's dealings. In circumspection, the with-what of the dealings is grasped ahead of time as . . . , oriented toward . . . , interpreted as . . . . The objective exists as what is significant as such and such; the world is encountered in the character of significance. The caring dealings do not only have the possibility of giving up the care of orienting, but on the basis of a primordial tendency of movement within factical life, they have an inclination to do so. In this closing off of the tendency toward concerned dealings, the latter become a mere circumspecting without any inclination toward direction or orientation. The circumspecting acquires the character of a bare *looking at*.[23] In and for the care of looking, of curiosity (*cura, curiositas*), the world is there not as the with-what of the performative dealings, but merely with regard to its *appearance*. The looking is accomplished as an observing, addressing, and discussing[24] determination, [354] and can organize itself as *science*. This is thus a way of concerned, observing dealings with the world, a way that is brought forth by factical life. As such a movement of dealings, it is a way of being of factical life and co-constitutes its Dasein. The level of observing that is achieved at any given time (the determinateness of the objective connections of the world with respect to their appearance) coalesces with circumspection.[25] The circumspecting is actualized in the manner of *addressing* and *discussing* the objectivity of the dealings. The world is always encountered within a determinate way of being-addressed, of some address (λόγος).

In being released from the tendencies of directing, the dealings take a *pause*. Observing itself becomes an autonomous dealing, and as such it is a defining [kind of] *pausing* [*Sichaufhalten*] with what is objective by abstain-

---

22. [Handwritten insertion:] life, world.

23. [Handwritten note in the lower margin:] Life now has its Being in the *care* of observing. Possibility of one's own βίος.

24. [Handwritten insertion after "observing."]

25. [Handwritten note in the top margin:] With this, life appropriates its own state of Being, but at the same time new possibilities of its own questionability.

ing [*Sichenthalten*] from accomplishment. The objects are there as *signifi-cant*, and it is only in determinately directed and layered theorizing that what is objective (in the sense of what is simply object-like and thing-like) arises from the world's factical character of encountering (i.e., from what is significant).[26]

Factical life always moves within a determinate *interpretedness* that has been handed down, or revised, or re-worked anew.[27] Circumspection gives to life its world as interpreted according to those aspects in which the world is expected and encountered as the object of concern, is put to tasks, and is sought as refuge. These usually inexpressibly accessible aspects into which factical life *slips* [355] while on the path of habit—more than it expressly takes them on—map out the paths for the movement of care (for care and for circumspective addressing and discussion).[28] The interpretedness of the world is factically that interpretedness within which life itself stands. This interpretedness also establishes the direction in which life holds its own self in care; that means, however, that there is also established a determinate sense of the Dasein of life (the "as-what" and the "how"), within which human beings maintain themselves in their plans.[29]

The movement of care is not an *occurrence* of life that transpires for itself, over against the existing world. The world is there *in* life and *for* it, but not in the sense of merely being intended and observed.[30] How the world is there is only brought forth when factical life pauses within its concerned movement of dealings. This being-there of the world is what it is only as having grown from a particular *taking-pause* (as letting-encounter-in-Being)[31] and—as ac-tuality and reality, or even in the objectivity of nature (which is impoverished of all significance)—must for the most part provide the point of departure for

---

26. [Handwritten note at the end of the paragraph:] *Circumspection* deals with unthematized *world-life*—care and meaning—what is thematized is melted in; unthematized interpretation of life. Why interpretation? Circumspective, claiming world-*life*.

27. [Handwritten marginal comment:] Cf. supplementary material. [In GA 62 this is appendix 3b, 401ff.]

28. [Handwritten insertion.]

29. [Handwritten reference:] Cf. pp. 15f. [This is GA 62, 362–363.]

30. [Handwritten note in the top margin:] Life is precisely as a Being-like having of (one's) world. World is not something that does or does not open up to life after the fact; rather, life means *being* in a world, being in the sense of a caring dealing with it. The Being of life is *"falling prey"* to the Being of one's world. In dealings (in care), the world is somehow already made accessible; as somehow accessi-ble, it is at the same time *closed off* for life as circumspective care; the "already" is precisely, in terms of Being, the "not yet" of life's own movement of care.

31. [Handwritten insertion.]

the epistemological and *ontological* problematic. The taking-pause is, as *such*, in and for the basic movement of the *concerned* dealings.

However, concern is for its own part not just generally related to its world with primordial intentionality. The movement of concern is not an indifferent accomplishment, as if it were itself a process, and [356] only with it did anything even happen in life. There lives in the movement of caring an *inclination* toward the world as the *tendency* toward absorption in it, toward letting oneself be taken along by it. This tendency of concern is the expression of a basic factical tendency of life, a tendency toward *falling away* from oneself and thereby toward *falling prey* to the world, and thus toward one's own *falling apart*. Let the basic character of the movement of caring be terminologically fixed as factical life's *inclination toward falling* (or, in brief, the *falling-prey-to*[32]. . .); and with this, the *sense* of direction and the intentional that-with-respect-to-which of the tendency of caring is also indicated. The falling is to be understood, not as an objective event or as something that simply "happens" in life, but rather as an intentional How. This tendency [*Hang*] is the innermost *fate* [Verhängnis] that life factically bears. The How of this bearing in itself (as the way in which the fate "*is*") must be determined, along with the fate itself, as a constituent of facticity.

This character of movement is not a bad quality that surfaces from time to time, one that could be cultivated away in more advanced and happier times of human culture. This is so little the case that even such formulations of human Dasein as a heavenly naturalness or perfection to be reached are themselves only extensions of this very inclination of falling prey to the world. In closing one's eyes to life's ownmost character of Being, life becomes viewed as something worldly,[33] as an object of dealings that is producible in some ideal form, placed into care[34] as the that-with-respect-to-which of plain concern.

That factical life, in its inclination toward falling, arrives at such a world-laden interpretation of itself gives expression to a basic characteristic of this movement: [357] it is *tempting*[35] for life itself, insofar as it spreads possibilities across life's path; possibilities, drawn from the world, of an

---

32. [Handwritten note in the lower margin:] the expressly organized falling in the "philosophical" interpretation as "*hardening*." World—culture—"justice."

33. [Handwritten correction:] . . . to life's ownmost character of movement, life becomes viewed as something worldly.

34. [Handwritten insertion after the comma.]

35. [Handwritten addition in the top margin:] the falling Being-character of the knowledge that hurries ahead and evaluates ahead of time, by which life gets pulled along!

idealizing nonchalance and thus of passing oneself by. As tempting, the tendency toward falling is at the same time *comforting*[36] (in the public disposition),[37] i.e., it detains factical life in the locations of its fallenness, such that life addresses and caringly shapes these locations as quasi-situations of unworried security and of the most ideal effective possibilities.[38] (In contrast to *location*, the *situation* of factical life denotes life's taking-of-a-stance that is made transparent as falling and that is *apprehended* in the given concrete worry as the possible counter-movement to falling care.) As comforting, the tendency toward falling—which breeds temptation—is *alienating*.[39] This means that factical life becomes more and more alien to itself in its being absorbed in the world about which it is concerned, and the movement of caring—which is left up to itself and that appears to itself as life itself—increasingly takes away from factical life the possibility of seeing itself in worry[40] and thus the possibility of taking itself as the goal of appropriating return. In its three types of movement—temptation, comfort, and alienation—the tendency toward falling is the fundamental movement [358] not only of orienting, productive dealing, but also of circumspection itself and its possible autonomy, of observing and of the addressing and interpreting that define knowing. Factical life takes itself and cares for itself not only as a significant occurrence and as the importance of the world, but also speaks the *language* of the world, so long as it speaks with itself.

It is part of the inclination toward falling that factical life, which is actually always the factical life of the individual, is for the most part not lived as such. It moves instead within a certain *averageness* of caring, of dealing, of circumspection, and of grasping the world.[41] This averageness is the averageness of the *general public* in each case, of the surrounding area, of the dominating trend, of the "just like the many others, too." It is the *"they"*

---

36. [Handwritten addition in the lower margin:] The habit that falling develops for itself as protection and defense.

37. [Handwritten insertion.]

38. [Handwritten note in the left margin:] *Escalation!*

39. [Handwritten note in the left margin:] Dasein, precisely in its self-interpretation and disposition of belief, is most likely to think itself in the *world* and *otherwise historically.*

40. [Handwritten footnote, extant only in the typescript sent to Georg Misch in Göttingen:] Worry does not mean a mood with a sorrowful countenance, but the factical decidedness, the seizing of *existence* (cf. p. 13 [GA 62, 360–361]) as what is to be cared for. If one takes "care" as *vox media* (which, as category of meaning, has its origin in facticity's claim), then worry is the care of existence (*genetivus obiectivus*).

41. [Handwritten change to the end of the sentence:] of claiming and discussing and, in general, taking in the world.

who factically live the individual life—one cares about, one sees, judges, one enjoys, one does and asks. Factical life gets lived by the *"nobody,"* to which all life sacrifices its concern.[42] Life exists as always somehow bogged down in inauthentic tradition and habituation. Out of these there arise needs, and the ways of fulfilling the needs are pursued in concern. Within the world in which it is absorbed and within the averageness in which it goes about, life hides from itself. The tendency toward falling is life's evasion of itself. Factical life itself provides the keenest manifestation of this basic movement through the manner in which it stands toward *death.*

Just as factical life, in accordance with its Being-character, is not a process, so too death is not a ceasing that enters onto the scene at some time and that has the character of a snapping-off of this process. Death [359] is something that is *imminent for* factical life, something before which factical life stands as before something inevitable. Life *is* in such a way that its death is always somehow there for it; its death stands in view there for it, and this is so even if "the *thought of death"* is shut out and suppressed. Death presents itself as *the*[43] object of care, precisely in the fact that it is encountered as a *How* of life in the obstinacy of its imminence. The forced lack of worry about death within life's care is accomplished through flight into world-laden concerns. The looking-away from death, however, is so little a grasping of life in itself, that it becomes precisely life's own evasion of life and an evasion of life's authentic Being-character. The having of death as imminent—both in the manner of the concern that takes flight, as well as in the manner of the worry that takes hold—is constitutive for facticity's Being-character. In the *grasping* having of *certain* death, life becomes visible in itself. Death that exists in this way gives to life[44] a [kind of] sight, and continually brings life before its ownmost present and past—a past that comes from within life itself, burgeoning behind it.

When time and again one attempts to determine the *object*-character and Being-character of factical life, yet without determining the fundamental co-constituent of *death* and the "having of death" (a co-constituent that *guides the problematic*), the omission is such that it cannot be corrected again by merely adding further supplements. The pure and constitutive

---

42. [Handwritten note in the lower margin:] The "generality"—in philosophy, "general validity" is the logic of domination of the "they"! Likewise, Platonism [is the logic of domination] of the historical. The "general importunity" of all toward all!—toward interpreted Dasein.

43. [Undeciphered stenographical note.]

44. [Handwritten note after "life":] a Being and . . .

ontological problematic concerning the Being-character of death that is described here has nothing to do with a metaphysics of immortality or of the "what next?" As a constituent of facticity, the death that one has as *imminent*—and that one has in a manner, characteristic of death, such that life's present and past are made visible (historical)[45]—is at the same time the phenomenon out of which the specific "*temporality*" of human Dasein is to be explicatively highlighted. The fundamental sense of the *historical* is determined from the sense of *this temporality,*[46] [360] and never through the formal analysis of concept-formation within a coincidentally determined, directed[47] *writing* of history.

The constitutive characters of facticity that have been indicated—caring, the tendency toward falling, the How of the having of death—appear to run counter to what has been emphasized as the basic peculiarity of factical life, namely that it is a being which, in the manner of its bringing-forth (as a factical world-life),[48] depends on its own Being. But that only appears to be the case. In all of its self-evasion, life is factically there for itself; in "getting away from life," it precisely *surrenders* itself and chases after its absorption in world-laden concern. Like every movement of factical temporality, the "absorption-in" has in itself a more or less expressed and unacknowledged view *back* toward the thing from which it flees. The from-which of its fleeing, however, is life itself as the factical possibility of being expressly apprehended as an object of worry.

Any dealings have their own circumspection, and this—in the authenticity that is achievable at any time—brings the with-what of the dealings into the guiding fore-view. The Being of life in itself[49] that is accessible within facticity itself, is of such a kind that it becomes visible and reachable only by way of the *detour*[50] through the counter-movement against falling care. This counter-movement, as life's worrying [361] about not becoming lost, is the way in which the possible and apprehended authentic Being of

---

45. [Handwritten insertion.]

46. [Handwritten note in the top margin:] temporality—death, decisive uniqueness! This "once" is radically the "everything" of life.

47. ["Coincidentally" and "directed" are stenographical insertions.]

48. [Handwritten insertion.]

49. [Handwritten note in the left margin:] tendency and negation as fundamentally existential.

50. [Handwritten note in the left margin:] Take the *detour through* more sharply—retains its origins; i.e., life, in each of its ways of being, *is* historical; whatever "occurs" to it, "whatever it is," moves within the *tendency,* "gets stuck" in it; the *tendency toward* an attachment and being-caught.

life brings itself forth.[51] Let this Being, which is accessible in factical life and to factical life as the Being of factical life itself, be called *existence* [Existenz]. As worried about existence, factical life is *on a detour*. The possibility of apprehending the Being of life in worry is at the same time the possibility of missing existence.[52] The existence of factical life that is possible in each case, as in itself something that life can fail to see, is in principle questionable. The possibility of existence is always *that* of concrete facticity as a How of bringing forth this facticity in its temporality. It is impossible to ask in a direct and general manner what existence is. Existence becomes understandable in itself only through facticity's becoming questionable—that is, in the concrete *destruction* [Destruktion] of facticity with respect to its motives for movement, its directions, and its deliberate availabilities.[53]

The counter-movement to the tendency toward falling must not be interpreted as flight from the world (just as little as falling [should be interpreted] as becoming [362] worldly—bad).[54] It is typical of all flight from the world that it does not intend life in its existentiell [existenziellen] character, i.e., it does not apprehend life in the questionableness that lies at its roots.[55] It is typical of flight from the world rather to insert and shape life into a new comforting *world*. Through worry about existence, nothing is changed in the factical position of any given life. What is changed is the

---

51. [Handwritten note in the lower margin:] i.e., the well-known intentionality only reaches a "*first*"—in a falling observing and an observing pursuit of "experiences" (inner perception). Primordial phenomenon of which "intentionality" is an extension—still covered over; only accessible in radical interpretation of *full* facticity: *the fundamental existential*

the 'no' | the de-cision

| ← | - | →

factically = in motion = historical.

52. [Handwritten note in the top margin:] The seized possibility—existential questioning (am "I")—is life's placing itself on itself "into emptiness"; "am"—what fore-having [Vorhabe] of Being— from where? guaranteed how? To question *factically within* concrete care. World is "there" and precisely as such it has nothing to say.

The *abandonment* that is seized, and as being, *always* falling. Existential meaning = having given up ("having been abandoned by") in the *decision*. *Being* in worrying inquiry, i.e., looking interpretively to facticity as such, which expects nothing from the world. Not worldly abandonment of mood which, after all, wants a worldly comfort-pillow, cares for *it*.

53. [Handwritten note at the end of the paragraph:] destruction of its interpretedness that exists according to factical (existentiell) fore-having and preconception (the "what" in the "how" of this interpretation).

54. [Handwritten insertion.]

55. [This "existentiell" character, as Heidegger will come to clarify in *Being and Time,* means that "Dasein always understands itself in terms of its existence," and that "the question of existence never gets straightened out except through existing itself" (GA 2, 12; trans. Macquarrie and Robinson).—Tr.]

How of the movement of life, which as such can never become a matter for the general public or for the *"they."* The concern involved in the dealings is a concern that is worried about the self. For its own part, factical life's worrying about its existence is not a brooding about oneself in egocentric reflection; it is what it is only as the counter-movement to life's tendency toward falling, i.e., it takes place precisely in the concrete movement of dealings and of concern. Thus the *"against"*—as the *"not"*—expresses a primordial achievement that is constitutive of Being. With respect to its constitutive sense, negation has primordial primacy over position. And this is because the Being-character of the human is factically determined through a falling, through the worldly tendency. The sense of this primordial fact itself, and the sense of this factuality as such, can only be interpreted—if at all—in and relative to facticity as it is *apprehended.* The accomplishment of insight, and of insightfully addressing life with respect to its existentiell possibility, has the character of a worried interpretation of life according to its sense of Being. Facticity and existence do not mean the same thing, and life's factical Being-character is not determined by existence; the latter is only one possibility that brings itself forth *within that* Being of life that is characterized as factical. But this means that the possible radical problematic of life's Being is centered in facticity.

First of all, if philosophy is not a contrived preoccupation that merely runs alongside life, with just any "generalities" whatsoever and with arbitrarily posited principles, but exists rather as *questioning* [363] knowledge— i.e., as *research,* simply as the genuine explicit accomplishment of the tendency toward interpretation that belongs to life's own basic movements (within which life is concerned about itself and its own Being); And *secondly,* if philosophy intends to view and to grasp factical life in its decisive possibilities of Being—i.e., if philosophy has decided radically and clearly on its own (without sideways glances to the business of world-views) to make factical life depend on itself on the basis of its very own factical possibilities; That is, if philosophy is *fundamentally atheistic*[56] and under-

---

56. [Typewritten footnote:] "Atheistic" not in the sense of a theory of materialism or some such. Every philosophy that understands itself as what it is must know, as the factical How of interpreting life—precisely when it still has some "notion" of God—that the tearing-back of life toward itself, accomplished by philosophy, is religiously speaking an attack on God. Yet thereby alone does philosophy stand honestly before God, i.e., according to the possibilities available to it as such; atheistic here means holding oneself free from tempting care that merely speaks of religiosity. Is not perhaps already the idea of a philosophy of religion, even if it takes its account without human facticity, a pure contradiction?

stands this—then it has decisively chosen factical life in its facticity and has made this an object for itself. The How of philosophy's research is the interpretation of this sense of Being regarding its basic categorial structures —i.e., the ways in which factical life brings itself forth and *speaks* with itself in such bringing-forth (κατηγορεῖν).[57] Philosophical research does not need the finery of world-views or the hurried care about not-coming-along-too-late and still-coming-along, within the confusions of a present moment. This is so as long as philosophy has understood, on the basis of its apprehended object, that with this object there is entrusted to philosophy the primordial Being-conditions of the possibility of any world-view as something to be questioned, as something that [364] becomes visible only in the rigor of research. These conditions are not "logical forms"; rather, as categorially understood, they are also already the possibilities of the factical bringing-forth of existence, grasped in their genuine availability.

The problematic of philosophy has to do with the *Being* of factical life. In this regard, philosophy is *principal ontology,* and in such a way that the determinate, singular, worldly regional ontologies receive the ground and sense of their own problems from the ontology of facticity. The problematic of philosophy has to do with the Being of factical life in the respective How of its being addressed and interpreted. This means that philosophy, as the ontology of facticity, is at the same time the categorial interpretation of the addressing and interpreting—that is, it is *logic.*

Ontology *and* logic are to be brought back into the original unity of the problematic of facticity, and are to be understood as[58] the extensions[59] of principal research, which can be described as the *phenomenological hermeneutics* of facticity.

Philosophical research has to make the ever more concrete interpretations of factical life—those of caring circumspection and of concerned insight—categorially transparent in their factical unity of life's bringing-forth. This is to be done with respect to their *fore-having* (into whose basic

---

57. [Handwritten note in the top margin:] The sense of how these categories bring forth Being— of "speaking": speaking is an ἀληθεύειν, world-giving, i.e., having cares, bringing forth care, i.e., the Being of life; speaking as unthematized speaking of world-life with itself, in certain *ways* of speaking about the *world;* every so-called "principle" in this field; questions of order; of *preference;* of the universal; of the general.

58. [Handwritten note:] (factical, historical extensions—not a genuinely radical shaping of the problem that was originally central).

59. [Handwritten note:] deposed and fallen, traditional ways of beginning and questioning; deposed paths (especially the logic of "seemingly" radical questioning).

sense of *Being* life places itself) and in relation to their *preconceptions* (within whose ways of addressing and discussing factical life speaks to itself and with itself). The hermeneutic is *phenomenological,* which means: its object-field, factical life with respect to the How of its Being and its speaking, is seen thematically and research-methodically as a *phenomenon.*[60] The structure of the object [365] that characterizes something as a phenomenon, *full intentionality* (being-related-to, the that-with-respect-to-which of the relating as such, the accomplishment of the relating, the bringing-forth of the accomplishment, the preservation of the bringing-forth) is none other than that of an object having the Being-character of factical life. Intentionality, taken simply as being-related-to, is the first phenomenal character of the basic movement of life (i.e., of caring) that can be brought into relief *immediately.*[61] Phenomenology is radical philosophical research itself, just as it already *was* in its first breakthrough in Husserl's *Logical Investigations.* One has not apprehended phenomenology in its most central motives if one sees in it—as is sometimes the case within phenomenological research itself—only a philosophical pre-science for the purpose of preparing clear concepts, with whose help alone some *actual* philosophy is then supposed to be set in motion. As if one could descriptively clarify basic philosophical concepts without the central and always newly appropriated basic orientation toward the object of the philosophical problematic itself!

Thus is indicated the *point of view* that the following phenomenological interpretations, as investigations into the history of ontology and logic, will take. The idea of the phenomenological hermeneutic of facticity includes within it the tasks of: formal and material logic and a theory of their objects; the theory of science; the "logic of philosophy"; the "logic of the heart"; the "logic of fate";[62] the logic of "pre-theoretical and practical" thought. And it includes these within itself not as some unifying [366] collective concept, but rather according to its own effective force as the principal approach of the philosophical problematic.

But it has still *not become understandable* what kind of role historical investigations are supposed to play for such a hermeneutic, just why *Aristotle* is being placed within the theme of the investigation, and further how

---

60. [Handwritten note in the left margin:] purely indicative! without direction from the problematic of facticity.

61. [Handwritten note in the lower margin:] *"Intentionality"*: the determined, formalized Being-character of dealings; to be removed from "psychological," "consciousness"-theoretical, or "experience"-thematizing plans!

62. [Handwritten insertion.]

the investigation is to be carried through. The motivations for the particular *directions of view* (the possession and the path of the view)[63] emerge from the *concrete* apprehension of the point of view. The very idea of facticity implies that only *authentic* [eigentliche] facticity—understood in the literal sense of the word: one's *own* [eigene] facticity—that of one's own time and generation, is the genuine object of research. On account of its inclination toward falling, factical life for the most part lives in what is inauthentic—i.e., in what is handed down, in what is reported to it, in that which it appropriates in its averageness. Even what is primordially cultivated as one's own authentic possession falls prey to averageness and publicness. It loses the specific sense of origin that belonged to its primordial situation and it arrives, freely floating, in the ordinariness of the "they." This falling affects all of factical life's dealings and circumspection, not least of all life's own actualizing of interpretation according to its plans and preconceptions. *Philosophy*, in its way of taking objects, its manner of asking questions, finding answers, and having answers,[64] also stands within this movement of facticity—since philosophy is simply the explicit interpretation of factical life.

Accordingly, the philosophical hermeneutic of facticity necessarily makes its own beginning within its factical situation, doing so within an already given particular interpretedness of factical life that first sustains the philosophical hermeneutic itself and that can never be completely eradicated. According to what has been said about the tendency toward falling that affects every interpretation, it follows that precisely *"what is obvious"* about this interpretedness—what is not discussed about it, what is assumed not to require any further clarification—will be *that* which *inauthentically* (i.e., without explicit [367] appropriation on the basis of its origins) maintains the dominating effective force in presenting the problems and in guiding the inquiry.

The addressing and self-interpreting that are accomplished by factical life itself receive their path of view and manner of speaking from what is objective as world-laden. Where human life (Dasein, the human) is the object of an interpretatively defining kind of questioning, this objectivity stands within [one's] plans as a world-laden occurrence, as "nature."[65] (The mental is understood as nature, and the same goes for spirit and life,

---

63. [Handwritten insertion.]
64. [Handwritten insertion.]
65. [Handwritten note:] (but this not yet in the modern, *theoretical* sense).

which are understood in an analogous categorial articulation.) There are intellectual-historical motives for the fact that we today still speak of the "nature" of the human, of the soul, and in general of the "nature of the thing"; and for the fact that we talk about this objectivity categorially—i.e., in categories that stem from a particular explication, from "nature" as seen in a particular way. Even where the objects are fundamentally no longer approached as "substances" in a crude sense (an approach, by the way, from which Aristotle was far removed, contrary to what is often taught) and where the objects are not interrogated according to their occult qualities, the interpretation of life nevertheless moves within basic concepts, within questioning approaches, and within tendencies of explication that have arisen from experiences of objects, experiences that we today no longer have available to us.

For the most part, the philosophy of today's situation moves inauthentically within the *Greek* conceptuality—indeed one that has passed through a chain of diverse interpretations. The basic concepts have lost their original functions of expression that are particularly suited to particularly experienced regions of objects. Yet in all the analogizing and formalizing that these concepts have undergone, there remains a particular character of origin: they still carry with them a part of the genuine tradition of their original meaning, insofar as there is still detectible in them the direction [368] of meaning that goes back to their objective source. By beginning with the idea of the human, the ideals of life, and representations of the Being of human life, the philosophy of today's situation moves within offshoots of basic experiences that have been brought forth by Greek ethics and above all by the Christian idea of the human and of human Dasein. Even anti-Greek and anti-Christian tendencies persist fundamentally within the same directions of view and ways of interpreting. Thus the phenomenological hermeneutic of facticity—insofar as it wants to help today's situation along through interpretation toward a radical possibility of appropriation, and this in the manner of a making-attentive that first provides concrete categories—sees itself as called upon to loosen up the handed-down and dominating interpretedness in its hidden motives, unexpressed tendencies, and ways of interpreting; and to push forward by way of a *dismantling return* toward the primordial motive sources of explication. *The hermeneutic carries out its task only on the path of destruction.* So long as it has understood the manner of objectivity and the manner of Being of its thematical that-with-respect-to-which (the facticity of life), philosophical research is *"historical"* knowing in the radical sense. For philosophical research, the destructive confrontation with philosophy's history is not a mere appendix for the purposes of illustrating how things were earlier; it is not an *occasional* review of what others "did" earlier; it is not an opportunity to design entertaining world-historical perspectives. The destruction is rather the authentic path upon which the present must encounter itself in its own basic movements—and in such a way that the continual question thereby springs forth from history to face the present: To what extent is it (the present) itself worried about the appropriations of radical possibilities of basic experiences and about their interpretations? The tendencies toward a radical logic of origins and the approaches to ontologies thereby gain a principal critical elucidation. Thus the critique that simply and already arises from the concrete accomplishment of the destruction [369] does not apply to the bare fact *that* we stand within a tradition, but applies rather to the *How*. What we do not originally interpret and express is what we do not possess in authentic safe-keeping. Insofar as it is factical life (and that also means the possibility of an existence that lies within it) that is to be brought into a safe-keeping that brings forth, this life renounces—with the originality of interpretation—the possibility of rootedly possessing itself, *of being* itself.

The intertwining of the decisive constitutive effective forces of the Being-character of today's situation is to be described briefly, with reference to the problem of facticity, as the *Greek-Christian interpretation of life*. The anti-Greek and anti-Christian tendencies of interpretation—which are determined by, and relative to, the Greek-Christian interpretation of life— shall also be determined through this description. The idea of the human and of human Dasein that is set up within such an interpretation determines the philosophical anthropology of *Kant* as well as that of German Idealism. *Fichte, Schelling,* and *Hegel* start from *theology* and borrow from it the basic impulses for their speculation. This theology is rooted in Reformation theology, which succeeded to only a very small extent in achieving a genuine explication of *Luther's* new basic religious position and of its immanent possibilities. For its own part, this basic position resulted from his originally appropriated interpretations of Paul and of Augustine, and from his simultaneous confrontation with late Scholastic theology (Duns Scotus, Ockham, Gabriel Biel, Gregory of Rimini).

The late Scholastic doctrines concerning God, the Trinity, the situation before the Fall, sin, and grace all operate with the conceptual means that Thomas Aquinas and Bonaventure provided for theology. But that means that the idea of the human and of the Dasein of life that is determined in advance within all of these theological problem-areas is based on Aristotelian physics, psychology, ethics, and ontology; and thus the basic Aristotelian doctrines are treated according to a particular selection and interpretation. [370] At the same time, Augustine is crucially influential as well, and through him, so too is Neo-Platonism; and through Neo-Platonism, *Aristotle* is once again influential, and this to a greater extent than is ordinarily assumed. These connections are more or less familiar in their bare literary-historical filiations. What is missing completely is an authentic interpretation with its central foundation in the basic philosophical problematic of facticity, as it has been expounded. The research of the Middle Ages, in its leading respects, is constrained within the schematism of a Neo-Scholastic theology and within the framework of a Neo-Scholastically molded Aristotelianism. First of all, it is necessary in general to understand the scientific structure of medieval theology, as well as its exegeses and commentaries, as particularly mediated interpretations of life. Theological anthropology must be traced back to its basic philosophical experiences and motives, in such a way that one can understand the influential forces and the manner of reformulation that originated from the basic religious and dogmatic attitude of the time.[66] The hermeneutical structure of commentary on the *Sentences* of Peter Lombard—which bore the authentic development of theology up until Luther—is not only *not* laid bare as such: the very possibility of *questioning and approaching* it is lacking. Even *those* things that were brought into Lombard's *Sentences* in the manner of and in selections from Augustine, Jerome, and John Damascene,[67] are already important for the development of medieval anthropology. In order to have any standard for these reformulations at all, there must be available an interpretation of Augustinian anthropology [371] that does not simply excerpt propositions on psychology from his works, in the manner of some textbook on psychology or moral theology. The center of such an interpretation of Augustine with respect to the basic ontological-logical constructions of his life's teaching should be taken from his writings on the Pelagian controversy and from his teachings on the church. The idea of the human and of Dasein that are

---

66. [Typewritten footnote:] The hymnology and music of the Middle Ages, as well as its architecture and sculpture, are only accessible in a sense of intellectual history based on an original phenomenological interpretation of the philosophical-theological anthropology of this age, an anthropology that spread environmentally and communally through sermon and school. As long as this anthropology is not explicitly taken up, the "Gothic person" will remain a mere phrase.

67. [John Damascene (c. 676–c. 754), whose *Expositio Fidei* was later called *Sententiae Damasceni* in allusion to the *Sententiae* of Peter Lombard, written c. 1150.]

effective here point back to Greek philosophy, to patristic theology—which is founded upon Greek thinking—to Pauline anthropology and that of John's gospel.

Within the context of the task of the phenomenological destruction, the important thing is not merely to point out, in a pictorial manner, the different currents and dependencies. The important thing is rather to highlight the central ontological and logical structures within each of the decisive turning points of the history of Western anthropology by way of a primordial return to the sources. This task can be achieved only if a concrete interpretation of the Aristotelian philosophy is made available, one that is oriented according to the problem of facticity—i.e., according to a *radical phenomenological anthropology.*

In light of the problem of facticity that has been formulated, *Aristotle* is only the fulfillment and the concrete refinement of the philosophy that had gone on before. At the same time, however, Aristotle gains in his *Physics* a principal new basic approach from which his ontology and logic stem, and in turn the history of philosophical anthropology—which has been schematically and retrospectively described above—is infiltrated by this ontology and logic. The central phenomenon, whose explication is theme of the *Physics,* is being in the How of its being-moved.

At the same time, the literary form in which Aristotelian research has been handed down (treatises in the style of thematic exposition and investigation) offers the only basis that is suitable for the particular methodical intentions of the following interpretations. Only by going back from Aristotle, does Parmenides' doctrine of Being become determinable and understandable as the crucial [372] step that decided the sense and destiny of Western ontology and logic.

The researches that aim at carrying out the task of the phenomenological destruction take as their object late Scholasticism and Luther's early theological period. Thus this framework also encompasses tasks whose difficulty is not easily over-estimated. Therefore the basic comportment toward history, and the direction of view with respect to Aristotle, are determined by the point of view (i.e., by the starting point and the exposition of the problem of facticity).

Every interpretation must, according to both its point and direction of view, *over-illuminate* [*überhellen*] its thematic object. The thematic object becomes appropriately determinable only when one succeeds in seeing the object not arbitrarily, but rather too sharply on the basis of its accessible content; and then, by scaling back the illumination, in coming back to a demarcation that is as appropriate for the object as possible. An object that is only ever viewed in half-darkness becomes graspable precisely in *its* half-dark givenness only by passing through an over-illumination. As over-illuminating, however, the interpretation must not question too far nor claim for itself a general, fantastic objectivity in the sense of historical knowledge—as if it reached an "in-itself." To even ask about the "in-itself" is to misjudge the object-character of the *historical*. To arrive at relativism and skeptical historicism because of the unavailability of such an "in-itself" is just the reverse side of *this same* misjudging. The translations of the inter-preted texts and above all the translation of the decisive basic concepts arose from the concrete interpretation and contain the latter *in nuce* [in a nutshell]. The coining of terms stems not from a desire for innovation, but rather from the content of the texts.

The starting point of the Aristotle-interpretation, which is determined by the point of view, must now be made understandable, and the first part of the investigations must be sketched in summary fashion. The guiding question of the interpretation must be: *As what objectivity of which Being-character is being-human, "being-in-life," experienced and interpreted?* What is the sense of [373] Dasein within which the interpretation of life places the human as an object in advance? In brief, within what *plan of Being* does this objectivity stand? Further: How is this Being of the human conceptually explicated? What is the phenomenal ground of the explication and which categories of Being develop as the *explicata* of what is thus seen?

Is the sense of Being that in the end characterizes the Being of human life drawn genuinely from a pure basic experience of just this object and its Being, or is human life taken as a being within a more comprehensive field of Being, that is to say, is it subject to a sense of Being that is fixed as something archontic? What does Being even mean for Aristotle? How is it accessible, graspable, and determinable? The object-field that provides the original sense of Being is the object-field of those objects that are *produced* and used in dealings. Thus the that-with-respect-to-which, toward which the original experience of Being is directed, is not the Being-field of *things* as a kind of object that is grasped in a *theoretical* and fact-like manner, but rather the world that is encountered in the dealings that produce, perform, and use. That which is completed in the movement of the dealings of production (ποίησις), that which has arrived at its presence-at-hand and is thus available for a tendency of use, is that which *is*. Being means *being produced* and, as something produced, it means something that is significant relative to some tendency of dealings: It means being available. Insofar as it is the object of circumspection or the object even of an independent, observing kind of grasping, the being is addressed according to its *appearance* (εἶδος). The observing grasping is explicated in addressing and discussing (λέγειν). The addressed "what" of the object (λόγος) and its appearance (εἶδος) are the same in a certain way. But this means that what is addressed in the λόγος is, as such, the authentic being. In the object being addressed, the λέγειν brings into safe-keeping the being in its appearing Beingness (in its οὐσία). But οὐσία has the primordial meaning—at work in Aristotle himself and also even later on—of what is in the household, in one's possession, that which is available [374] for use within one's surroundings: It means *possessions*. That about the being which, as the being's Being, comes into safe-keeping—i.e., that which characterizes the *being* as *possession*—is the being's *being-produced*. In production, the object of the dealings comes to its appearance.

The field of Being belonging to the objects of dealings (ποιούμενον, πρᾶγμα, ἔργον κινήσεως) and the way of addressing that belongs to dealings—a *logos* that is characterized in a particular way or, more precisely, the object of dealings in the How of its being addressed—indicate the plan from which the basic ontological structures, and thus the ways of addressing and determining that concern the object "human life," are to be drawn.

How do the ontological structures develop? As the *explicata* of an addressing, observing determination, i.e., on the path of a *research* that takes the field of Being—brought into the particular plan by way of a basic experience—according to particular respects and articulates it in these respects. Therefore the researches, whose object is experienced and intended in the character of being-moved, within whose "what" something like movement is given in advance, must mediate the possible access to the authentic motive source of Aristotelian ontology. Such research is present in the *Physics* of Aristotle. This research is to be taken interpretationally-methodically as a *full phenomenon* and is to be interpreted: with respect to its object in the How of the researching dealings with the object; with respect to the basic experience within which the object is pre-given as the starting point for the research; with respect to the constitutive movements of the accomplishment of the research; and with respect to the concrete ways in which the object is intended and conceptually articulated. In this way, the being that is in movement becomes visible according to its categorial structure, and the ontological constitution of the archontic sense of Being also becomes visible. Yet for the phenomenological interpretation of this research, one also needs an understanding of *that* sense in which Aristotle generally understood research and its accomplishment. Research is a way of observing dealing (ἐπιστήμη). Research has its particular genesis in concerned and directed dealing, and [375] only on the basis of this genesis does it become understandable with respect to the manner of its dealing—i.e., the manner of its questioning something with respect to that thing's "in what way" (αἴτιον) and its "whence" (ἀρχή). Insight into the genesis of the research is provided through the preliminary interpretation of *Metaphysics*, book A, chapters 1 and 2.[68] Understanding that observes and defines (ἐπιστήμη) is only *one* way in which beings come into safe-keeping: beings that, necessarily and for the most part, are what they are. Another possible way of dealings that are concerned, that orient things, and that think things over exists with respect to *those* beings that can also be other than what they are at the moment: the beings that are managed, handled, or produced first of all within the dealings themselves. This mode for the safe-keeping of Being is [τέχνη].[69] Aristotle interprets the different ways of illuminating the dealings—corresponding to the different regions of Being (circumspection, insight, regard)—as ways of accomplishing pure *beholding* that provides a view in the first place. He interprets these within an original problem-context and does so with respect to their possible basic achievement of the appropriation of Being and safe-keeping (*Nicomachean Ethics,* book Z). Through the interpretation of this section, the phenomenal horizon shall be won in advance; this is the phenomenal horizon into which research and theoretical knowing are to be placed as ways of οἷς ἀληθεύει ἡ ψθχή (1139b15). The first part of the investigations thus includes the interpretations of:

1) *Nicomachean Ethics,* book Z;
2) *Metaphysics,* book A, chapters 1 and 2;
3) *Physics,* books A and B, and book Γ, chapters 1–3

---

68. [This passage citation is missing in the typescript, and was appended by the editor.]
69. [This Greek term, missing in the original typescript, was inserted by the editor.]

THREE

The Problem of *Being and Time*

━━━━━━━━━━━━━━━━━━━━

1928

The understanding of Being forms the fundamental problem of metaphysics as such. What does "Being" mean? This is the fundamental question of philosophy *par excellence*. The aim here is not to present the formulation of this problem and its "retrieval" in *Being and Time*. We wish instead to make an external presentation of its guiding principles and thereby pin down the "problem of transcendence."

a) First, a general description. Fundamental ontology, as the analysis of the existence of Dasein, constitutes the approach to the problem. The analysis proceeds solely with the purpose of a fundamental ontology; the

---

This chapter is based on a previous translation by Michael Heim, in *The Metaphysical Foundations of Logic* (Bloomington: Indiana University Press, 1984), 136–141. It has been emended in minor ways to cohere with the translations in the present volume.

Bracketed numbers refer to the pagination of GA 26; the chapter opens at page 171. — Tr.

approach, execution, limit, and mode of concretizing certain phenomena are governed by this purpose. The understanding of Being is to be brought to light by way of Dasein's mode of Being, which is primarily existence. The constitution of Dasein's Being is such that the intrinsic possibility of understanding Being, which belongs essentially to Dasein, becomes demonstrable. The issue is therefore neither one of anthropology nor of ethics, but of this being in its Being as such, and thus of a preparatory analysis concerning it; the metaphysics of Dasein itself is not yet the central focus.

b) The guiding principles:

1. Instead of the term "human," the neutral term *Dasein* was chosen for that being which is the theme of the analysis. This designates the being for which its own proper mode of being is, in a definite sense, not indifferent.

2. The peculiar *neutrality* of the term "Dasein" is essential, because the interpretation of this being must be carried out prior to every [172] factual concretion. This neutrality also indicates that Dasein is neither of the two sexes. But this sexlessness is not the indifference of an empty void, the weak negativity of an indifferent ontical nothingness. In its neutrality, Dasein is not the indifferent nobody and everybody, but the primordial positivity and potency of the essence.

3. Neutrality is not the nothingness of an abstraction, but instead precisely the potency of the *origin*, which bears in itself the intrinsic possibility of every concrete factual humanity.

4. This neutral Dasein is never the one that exists; Dasein only ever exists in its factical concretion. But neutral Dasein is surely the primal source of intrinsic possibility that springs up in every existence and makes it intrinsically possible. In Dasein, the analysis always speaks only about the Dasein of those existing [*Existierenden*], not to the Dasein of existences [*Existenzen*]; the latter would be nonsense, since one can only speak to those that are existing. The analysis of Dasein is thus prior to all prophesying and heralding world-views; nor is it wisdom, something available only in the structure of metaphysics. The philosophy of life has a prejudice against this analysis as a "system of Dasein." The prejudice arises from a fear of the concept, and shows a misunderstanding of the concept and of "systematicity" as an architectonic that is thoughtful while nevertheless historical.

5. This neutral Dasein is thus also not the egocentrically singular, ontically isolated individual. The egoicity of the individual does not become the center of the entire problematic. Yet Dasein's essential content, to belong to itself in its existence, must be taken up along with the approach. To be sure, the approach that begins with neutrality implies a peculiar isolation

of the human, but not in the factical existentiell sense, as if the one philosophizing were the center of the world. Rather, it is the *metaphysical isolation* of the human.

6. [173] Dasein as such harbors the intrinsic possibility for being factically dispersed into bodiliness and thus into sexuality. The metaphysical neutrality of the human, isolated in its innermost core as Dasein, is not the empty abstraction from the ontic, a neither-nor, but instead the properly concrete aspect of the origin, the not-yet of the factical dispersion [*Zerstreutheit*]. As factical, Dasein is, among other things, always divided up [*zersplittert*] into a body and concomitantly in each case split [*zwiespältig*] into a particular sexuality. Division and splitting [*Zersplitterung und Zerspaltung*] sound negative at first (much like "destruction" [*Zerstörung*]), and negative concepts such as these, taken ontically, are associated with what is worthless. But here we are dealing with something else, with a description of the multiplication (not "multiplicity") that is present in every factically individuated Dasein as such. We are not dealing with the notion of a large primal being in its simplicity becoming ontically split into many individuals, but with the clarification of the intrinsic possibility of multiplication which, as we shall see more precisely, is present in every Dasein and for which embodiment presents an organizing factor. However, the multiplicity is also not mere formal plurality of determinations, but belongs to Being itself. In other words, in its metaphysically neutral concept, Dasein's essence already contains a primordial *strewing* [Streuung] that is, in a definite respect, a *dispersion* [Zerstreuung]. A blunt indication on this point: As existing, Dasein never merely relates to a particular object; if it relates solely to one object, it does so only by turning away from other beings that always appear prior to, and along with, the object. This multiplication does not occur through many objects existing, but rather the other way around. This also holds for Dasein's comportment to itself—namely according to the structure of historicity in the broadest sense, insofar as Dasein occurs as stretching along in time. Another essential possibility of Dasein's [174] factical dispersion is its spatiality. The phenomenon of Dasein's dispersion in space is seen, for example, in the fact that all languages are shaped primarily by spatial meanings. This phenomenon, of course, can only first be elucidated when the metaphysical problem of space is posed, a problem that first becomes visible after running through the problem of temporality (radically put: the metontology of spatiality; cf. appendix).[1]

---

1. [For this appendix see GA 26, 195ff.]

7. The transcendental dispersion belonging to the metaphysical essence of neutral Dasein, as the binding possibility of each factical existential dispersion and division, is based on a primordial feature of Dasein: on *thrownness*.

8. This thrown dispersion into a multiplicity, which is to be taken metaphysically, is the precondition, for example, for Dasein being able to let itself in each case be factically governed by beings that it is not, but with which it nevertheless identifies on account of its dispersion. Dasein can be governed, for example, by what we call nature in the broadest sense. Only what is essentially thrown and entangled in something can be governed and enfolded by it. This also holds for the emergence in nature of primitive, mythic Dasein. In being governed by nature, mythic Dasein has the peculiarity of not being conscious of itself with regard to its mode of Being (which is not to say that mythic Dasein lacks self-awareness). However, it belongs essentially to factical dispersion that thrownness and captivation remain deeply hidden from themselves, and precisely in this way the simplicity and "care-lessness" of an absolute sustenance arise in Dasein.

9. The essentially thrown dispersion of Dasein, still understood as completely neutral, announces itself in Dasein's *being-with* Dasein. This being-with . . . does not emerge on account of factically existing together; it is not explained solely on the basis of the supposedly more primordial species-Being of sexually [175] differentiated bodily creatures. Instead, the species-like unification and joining-together presupposes the dispersion of Dasein as such, that is, being-with in general. But this basic metaphysical characteristic can never be deduced from the species-like organization, from living with one another. Rather, factical bodiliness and sexuality are always explanatory only—and even then only within the bounds of the essential arbitrariness of all explanation—to the extent that a factical Dasein's being-with is pushed precisely into this particular factical direction, where other possibilities are shielded off or remain closed.

10. Being-with as an authentic comportment to existence is possible only on the basis that each co-existing Dasein can be, and is, authentically itself. This freedom of the with-one-another, however, presupposes the possibility of the self-determination of a being with the character of Dasein as such, and it is a problem how Dasein can exist as essentially free in the freedom of the factical ties of being-with-one-another. Insofar as being-with is a metaphysically fundamental determination of dispersion, it is clear that the latter ultimately has its ground in the freedom of Dasein as such. The basic metaphysical essence of metaphysically isolated Dasein is centered in

freedom. But how is this concept of freedom to be grasped metaphysically? It seems too empty and too simple. Nevertheless, ontic inexplicability does not preclude an ontological-metaphysical understanding! Freedom is the term for central problems (in-dependence, bindingness, regulation, standards), some of which we touch upon in treating the concept of world (§11c).[2]

The above puts into theses what we treated in the analysis of Dasein. We still need two further guiding statements to make clear how the analysis is carried out.

11. This metaphysics of Dasein, initially an analysis, can be attained only in the free projection of the constitution of Being itself. Precisely because Dasein always exists as itself, and since being [176] oneself, like existing, only ever exists in its accomplishment, the projection of the fundamental ontological constitution of Dasein must arise by constructing one of the most extreme possibilities of Dasein's authentic and total capability of being. The projection is directed toward Dasein as a whole as well as toward the fundamental determinations of its wholeness, even though Dasein is in each case only as something existing. To put it differently: Attaining the metaphysical neutrality and isolation of Dasein as such is only possible on the basis of the extreme existentiell *involvement* of the one who projects.

This involvement is necessary and essential for the metaphysical projection, for metaphysics as such, but is precisely for that reason, as an individual existentiell act, not authoritative and obligatory within the many concrete possibilities of each factical existence. For the metaphysical projection itself reveals the essential finitude of Dasein's existence, which can only be understood existentially in the inessentiality of the self that only becomes concrete—as can be proven metaphysically—through and in the service of each possible totality, a whole which becomes manifest in a rather special way in metaphysical inquiry. Nevertheless it remains a problem in its own right as to what extent there is an existentiell guidance, an indirect guidance, in the metaphysical projection and in the existentiell involvement of the person who philosophizes.

12. The ontological interpretation of Dasein's structures must be concrete with regard to the metaphysical neutrality and isolation of Dasein. Neutrality is in no way identical with the indeterminacy of a vague concept of a consciousness as such. Real metaphysical generalization does not exclude *concreteness,* but is rather in one respect the most concrete—as Hegel

---

2. [See GA 26, 238.]

had seen, though he exaggerated it. Yet concreteness in the analysis of Dasein-phenomena that give direction and content to the metaphysical projection of Dasein easily [177] misleads one, first, into taking the concrete phenomena of Dasein by themselves and, second, into taking them as existentiell absolutes in their extreme, fundamental-ontological conceptualization. The more radical the existentiell involvement, the more concrete the ontological-metaphysical projection. But the more concrete this interpretation of Dasein is, the easier it becomes to misunderstand in principle by taking the existentiell involvement for the essential and only thing, whereas this involvement itself precisely becomes manifest in the projection, with all its indifference to the particularity of the person.

The existentiell involvement of fundamental ontology brings with it the semblance of an extremely individualistic, radical atheism—this is the world-view interpretation one gropes for. Yet that interpretation must be tested for its legitimacy and, if it is correct, it must be examined for its metaphysical, fundamental-ontological sense. One may nevertheless not lose sight of the fact that with such a fundamental-ontological clarification nothing has yet been decided, and what furthermore ought to be shown is that nothing is decidable in this manner. However, there is also always the factical necessity of the "presupposition" of a factical situation.

These guiding principles should indicate briefly the sort of intent behind the analysis of Dasein and the requirements for carrying out the analysis. The basic intent of the analysis is to show the intrinsic possibility of the understanding of Being, which means at the same time the possibility of transcendence.

FOUR

Transcendence

—❧—

1928

Dasein, we can say, exists for the sake of something; and now we must still ascertain, in terms of content, that for the sake of which Dasein exists. What is the final purpose for which humans exist? Here we would seem to have the decisive question. But only seemingly, for the question is ambiguous. It appears to address the whole directly, yet the question is premature. It assumes that it can be somehow decided objectively while, ultimately, the sense of the [239] question itself is such that, in each case, only the questioner alone can pose the question in its real sense and answer it. But if this is the case, then we must show why it is so. In other words, it must become clear from the metaphysics of Dasein why, in conforming to the essence of

---

This chapter is based on a previous translation by Michael Heim, in *The Metaphysical Foundations of Logic* (Bloomington: Indiana University Press, 1984), 185–195. Some phrasings have been altered.

Bracketed numbers refer to the pagination of GA 26; the chapter opens at page 238.—Tr.

its Being, Dasein must itself take over the question and answer concerning the final purpose: why searching for an objective answer is in itself a, or the, misunderstanding of human existence in general.

In contrast to truth about things present at hand, truth about existing things is truth for existing things. The latter truth consists only in being-true qua existing. And questioning, too, must be understood accordingly, not as an inquiry-about but as a questioning-for, where the questioner's situation is included in the question.

Before one sets out prematurely, then, to give an answer to the question about the final human purpose—an answer which would at bottom be none at all—before we try to fill in the content of the formal for-the-sake-of [Umwillen], we must first examine more closely this for-the-sake-of itself, so as to avoid an inadequate construal of for-the-sake-of as the constituent of worldhood.

The existence of Dasein is determined by the for-the-sake-of. It is Dasein's defining characteristic that it is concerned with this being, in its Being, in a specific way. Dasein exists for the sake of Dasein's Being and its capacity-for-being. But, one might immediately object, here we have just provided a determination of the contents of the for-the-sake-of, and we have pinned down the final purpose of Dasein: It is Dasein itself. Not only that, we have provided a determination of the final purpose of Dasein that is one-sided in the greatest degree. It is an extreme egoism, the clearest delusion to assert that all beings—including nature and culture and whatever else there might be—only exist in each case for the individual human being and his egotistic goals. In fact, if this [240] were the sense of the claim of the ontology of Dasein, then it would indeed be madness. But then neither would it be explicable why one would need an analysis of Dasein in order to assert such outrageous nonsense. On the other hand, after all, Kant has said: Humans exist as ends in themselves.

But things are ultimately not so simple if, within a metaphysics of Dasein, the statement is made concerning essence: It belongs to Dasein's essence to be concerned about its own Being. It would be completely superfluous to correct the statement and indicate that many people precisely do sacrifice themselves for others and find fulfillment in friendship and community with others. The correction is superfluous because it tries to correct something that it cannot. After all, the statement is not an ontic assertion claiming that all existing humans in fact use, or even should use, everything around them solely for their own particular egotistic aims. The ontological statement—that it belongs to Dasein's essence that its own

Being resides in its for-the-sake-of—so little excludes that humans precisely are factically concerned with the Being of others, that the ontological statement precisely provides the metaphysical grounds of possibility that something like Dasein can even be with others, for them, and through them. In other words, if the statement—that it belongs to Dasein's essence that, in its Being, it is concerned with this Being itself—stands at the outset of an ontological analysis of Dasein and in immediate connection with the statement of transcendence, then it is a simple imperative of even the most primitive methodology to at least ask whether or not this ontological statement of essence does, or could, present an ontic claim from a world-view that preaches a so-called individualistic egoism.

This statement and everything connected to it does not deal with an existentiell, ethical egoism, but rather deals with the ontological-metaphysical description [241] of the egoicity [*Egoität*] of Dasein itself. Dasein can only exist factically for another Dasein, and exist with it as a thou, because Dasein is primarily determined by egoicity. The thou is not an ontic replicate of a factical ego; but neither can a thou exist as such and be itself as thou for another ego if it is not at all Dasein, i.e., if it is not grounded in egoicity. The egoicity that belongs to the transcendence of Dasein is the metaphysical condition of the possibility for a thou to be able to exist and for an I-thou relationship to be able to exist. The thou is also most immediately thou if it is not simply another ego, but rather a "you yourself are." This selfhood, however, is its freedom—and this freedom is identical with the egoicity on the basis of which Dasein can, in the first place, ever be either egoistic or altruistic.

Indeed, in the very fact that we can make the I-thou relation into a problem at all indicates that we transcend each factual ego and factual thou and that we grasp the relation as a relation of Dasein as such—i.e., we grasp the relation in its metaphysical neutrality and egoicity. Of course, we usually do so without suspecting anything of these presuppositions we take for granted. However rich and interesting the analysis of possible I-thou relationships may be, it cannot solve the metaphysical problem of Dasein, because it cannot even pose the problem. Instead, with its first approach, such an analysis already thoroughly presupposes, in some form, the entire analysis of Dasein and constantly employs it. Today, for various reasons, the problem of the I-thou relation is of great interest to world-views. There are sociological, theological, political, biological, and ethical problems that ascribe a prominence to the I-thou relation; however, this conceals the philosophical problem.

Here we see, then, a new difficulty characteristic of the problem of subjectivity and of every ontology of Dasein. The first difficulty concerned the unjustified isolation of the closed-off subject from all objects, the mis-guided [242] view that the most presuppositionless approach is the one starting from a worldless subject. The current difficulty, however, is with regard to the view that an approach beginning with a subject—though in the end a transcending subject—is an even more individualistic, more ego-tistical subjectivism; that the more radically one makes an ontology of Dasein into a problem and task, the more extremely must one embrace individualism—or, more correctly: the more such individualism seems to obtrude, along with the difficulty of holding and maintaining the ontologi-cal intent.

If we say that Dasein is in each case essentially mine, and if the task is to define this characteristic of Dasein ontologically, this does not mean we should investigate the essence of my self as this factical individual, or of some other given individual. The object of inquiry is not the individual essence of my self, but the essence of mineness and selfhood as such. Likewise, if the "I" is the object of the ontological interpretation, then this is not the individual I-ness of my self, but I-ness in its metaphysical neutrality: we call this neutral I-ness egoicity [*Egoität*]. But here, too, there is danger of a misunderstanding. One could ask whether thou-ness must not also be-come a topic of inquiry in the same fashion, and be taken as equiprimordial together with I-ness. That is certainly a possible problem. But the I-ness as counter-phenomenon to thou-ness is still not metaphysical egoicity. Here it becomes clear that the term "I" always pushes in the direction of the isolation of my self in the sense of a corresponding severance from the thou. Against this, I-ness does not mean the factical ego distinguished from the thou. Egoicity rather means the I-ness also at the basis of the thou, which precisely prevents understanding the thou factically as an alter ego. But why is a thou not simply a second ego? Because being an ego, in contradistinc-tion to being a thou, does not at all pertain to the essence of Dasein, because a thou is what it is only qua itself, and likewise for the [243] "I." Therefore I usually use the expression *selfhood* [Selbstheit] for metaphysical I-ness, for egoicity. For the "self" can be said equally of the I and the thou: "I-myself," "you-yourself," but not "thou-I."

Pure selfhood, understood as the metaphysical neutrality of Dasein, is simultaneously an expression of the metaphysical isolation of Dasein in on-tology—an isolation that must never be confused with an egoistic-solipsistic exaggeration of one's own individuality. We suggested earlier (§10, heading

11)[1] how individuality nevertheless necessarily has a function in involvement. Since selfhood is the fundamental character of existence, but since to exist means, in each case, a capability to be, one of the possibilities of existence must serve the concrete exposition of ontological selfhood, and for this reason the approach using an extreme model was chosen (cf. *Being and Time* §64). I have not at any time been of the opinion that this problematic and its inherent task would be quickly comprehended today, or that it would even have to be comprehended by the multitude. What Hegel says in the preface to his *Phenomenology of Spirit* is even more accurate today than it was in his time: "It is not a pleasant experience to see ignorance—and a crudity without form or taste, which cannot focus its thought on a single abstract proposition, still less on a connected chain of them—be convinced at one moment that it is freedom and tolerance of thought, and at the next moment that it is genius."[2]

To be for its own sake is an essential determination of the Being of that being we call Dasein. This constitution that we will now, for brevity, call the for-the-sake-of, provides the intrinsic possibility for this being to be itself—i.e., for *selfhood* to belong to its Being. To exist as a self [244] means to be fundamentally toward oneself. Being toward oneself constitutes the Being of Dasein and is not something like an additional capacity to observe oneself over and above just existing. Being toward oneself is precisely existing, only the former must be understood in the original metaphysical scope and must not be restricted to some activity or capability, or to any mode of apprehension such as knowledge or apperception. Moreover, being toward oneself as being a self is a presupposition for the various possibilities of ontic relations to oneself.

Furthermore this being, as factical, can in each case only expressly choose itself as a self because it is, in its essence, defined by selfhood. Yet the "can" here also includes its flight from choice. What then is implied by this possibility grounded in selfhood—this possibility of choosing oneself expressly or of fleeing the choice? What is essentially chosen along with the express choice of oneself?

Here, however, is the origin of "possibility" as such. Only through freedom, only a free being can, as transcending, understand Being—and it must do so in order to exist as such, i.e., to be "among" and "with" beings.

---

1. [See GA 26, 171ff.]

2. *Collected Works*, ed. J. Schulze (Berlin, 1832), vol. 2, p. 54. [G. W. F. Hegel, *Phenomenology of Spirit*, trans. A. V. Miller (New York: Oxford University Press, 1977), 42. Translation modified.—Tr.]

We have mentioned several times how all of these metaphysical, ontological statements are exposed to the continual misunderstanding of Being
taken ontically and existentielly. One main reason for this misunderstanding lies in not maintaining one's grasp on the proper metaphysical horizon
of the problem. There is a particular danger of this at the present stage of
our exposition. We said that Dasein chooses itself. One inadvertently then
fills in the term Dasein with the common concept of the isolated, egoistic
subject, and then interprets Dasein's choosing itself as a solipsistic-egoistic
contraction into oneself, whereas in the genuine metaphysical sense, precisely [245] the reverse is the case. Dasein—and only Dasein qua Dasein—
should choose itself (Dasein). Many times, even *ad nauseam,* we pointed
out that this being qua Dasein is always already with others and always
already with beings not of Dasein's nature. In transcending, Dasein transcends every being, itself as well as every being of its own sort (Dasein-
with) and every being not of Dasein's sort. In choosing itself, Dasein actually chooses precisely its being with others and precisely its being among
beings of a different character.

Complete commitment of one's self essentially lies in the express choice
of one's self, not toward somewhere it might not yet be, but to where and
how it always already is, qua Dasein, insofar as it exists. To what extent this
factically succeeds in each case is not a question of metaphysics but a
question and affair of the individual person. Dasein can only be committed
to others because it can expressly choose itself on the basis of its selfhood;
and Dasein can in turn only listen to a thou-self because, in being toward
itself as such, Dasein can understand something like a "self." Something like
human community is only possible because Dasein, constituted by the for-
the-sake-of, exists in selfhood. These are primary existential-ontological
statements of essence, and not ethical claims about the relative hierarchy of
egoism and altruism. The phenomenon of authentic self-choice, conceived
existentially-ontologically, highlights most radically the metaphysical selfhood of Dasein—and this means transcendence as transcending one's own
Being, transcending Being as being with others, and transcending beings in
the sense of nature and items of use. Again, methodologically this suggests
an extreme existential-ontological model.

N.B. In Kierkegaard, there is much talk of choosing oneself and of the
individual, and if it were my task to say once again what Kierkegaard has
said, [246] then it would not only be a superfluous endeavor, but would be
one which necessarily and substantially lagged behind him with regard to
his purpose. His purpose is not ours, but differs in principle—which does

not prevent us from learning from him, but rather obliges us to learn what he has to offer. But Kierkegaard never pushed onward into the dimension of this problematic because it was not at all important for him, and his work as an author had a completely different fundamental aim which also required different ways and means.

The statement that the for-its-own-sake belongs to the essence of Dasein is an ontological statement: It asserts something about the essential constitution of Dasein in its metaphysical neutrality. Dasein is for its own sake and herein, in the for-the-sake-of, lies the ground of the possibility for an existentiell, egoistic or non-egoistic, for-my-own-sake. But herein lies, just as primordially, the ground of a for-his-or-her-sake and for every kind of ontic reason-for. As constituting the selfhood of Dasein, the for-the-sake-of has this universal scope: in other words, it is *that toward which* Dasein, as transcending, transcends.

In the context of the inquiry about transcendence, we began with the problem of world and came, by way of the realm of ideas and the ἐπέκεινα τῆς οὐσίας, up against for-the-sake-of as the basic character of world. This for-the-sake-of is to be understood as the metaphysical structure of Dasein, but not with regard to a factual existent's setting up particular egoistic goals. We must pursue this for-the-sake-of more sharply—the metaphysical constitution and fundamental structure of world—so that we can have an understanding of being-in-the-world as transcendence.

The for-the-sake-of is in, and for, a will. But the latter does not mean the existentiell-ontic act of will, but rather the metaphysical essence, the intrinsic possibility, of willing: *freedom.* In freedom, such a for-the-sake-of has always [247] already emerged. This self-presentation of the for-the-sake-of resides in the essence of freedom. Something like for-the-sake-of does not exist somewhere for freedom to then simply draw upon it. Rather, freedom is itself the origin of the for-the-sake-of. But again, not in such a way that there would first be freedom and then also the for-the-sake-of. Instead: freedom is one with the for-the-sake-of. It is unimportant here to what extent something defined as free is, in fact, free—or to what extent it is aware of its freedom. Nothing is said here regarding the extent to which it is free or only latently free, bound or enthralled by others or by beings not of Dasein's kind. Only a free being can be unfree.

Here we also have to remove freedom from the traditional perspective where emphasis is primarily placed on self-initiating spontaneity, *sua sponte* [on its own will], in contrast to a compulsive mechanical sequence. However, this initiative "from itself" remains indefinite without selfhood. And this means that one must take transcendence back into freedom; one must seek the fundamental essence of transcendence in freedom.

In other words, the world primarily described by the for-the-sake-of is the primordial totality of what Dasein, as free, intimates of itself. Freedom intimates itself; it is the primal understanding, i.e., the primal projection of what freedom itself makes possible. In the projection of the for-the-sake-of as such, Dasein gives itself the primordial *commitment* [*Bindung*]. Freedom makes Dasein responsible [*verbindlich*] to itself in the ground of its essence. To be exact, freedom gives itself the possibility of commitment. The totality of the commitment residing in the for-the-sake-of is the world. As a result of this commitment, Dasein commits itself to a capability of being toward itself as able to be with others in the ability to be among extant things. Selfhood is free responsibility for and toward oneself.

As free, Dasein is world-projection. But this projecting is only projected in such a way that Dasein holds itself in it [248] and the free hold binds Dasein—i.e., so that the hold puts Dasein, in all its dimensions of transcendence, into a possible space for choice. Freedom holds this commitment over against itself. In freedom, the world is held over against freedom itself. The world is the *free counter-hold* [*Widerhalt*] of Dasein's for-the-sake-of. Being-in-the-world is accordingly nothing other than freedom, the latter no longer understood as spontaneity but as the indicated constitution of its metaphysical essence (which, to be sure, is thus not yet fully determined).

As transcendence, however, the free counter-hold of the for-the-sake-of has the character of leaping over each factical and factual being, as was pointed out earlier. The world, as the totality of essential intrinsic possibilities of Dasein as transcending, *surpasses* all actual beings. These reveal themselves whenever and however they are encountered—and precisely when encountered as themselves—but always only as a restriction, as one possible realization of the possible, as the insufficient of an excess of possibilities within which Dasein always maintains itself as free projection.

Dasein in itself is *excessive*, i.e., determined by a primary insatiability for beings—both metaphysically as such and also existentially, in factical individuation. This primary insatiability can be seen in a definite, ontic, existentiell comportment. Only on the basis of insatiability can there be any relaxation-with, any existentiell peace of mind or dissatisfaction. The latter should not be confused with insatiability in a metaphysical sense. The essence of freedom, which surpasses every particular factical and factual being (its surpassive character) can also be seen particularly in despair, where one's own lack of freedom engulfs a Dasein absorbed in itself. Even this completely factical lack of freedom is itself an elemental testimony to transcendence, for despair lies precisely in the despairing [249] person's vision of the impossibility of what is possible. The person still witnesses the possible, inasmuch as he despairs of it.

The surpassing of factical beings that is peculiar to the world as such, and thereby to transcendence and freedom, corresponds to the ἐπέκεινα [beyond]. In other words, the world itself is surpassive [*übertrifftig*]; beings of Dasein's character are distinguished by upswing [*Überschwung*]. World is the free surpassive counter-hold of the for-the-sake-of.

Only insofar as Dasein in its metaphysical essence, freely presenting its own for-the-sake-of, overshoots itself [*überschwingt*], does Dasein become, as upswing [*Überschwingende*] toward the possible, the occasion (from a metaphysical viewpoint) for beings to emerge as beings. Beings of Dasein's nature must have opened themselves as freedom—i.e., world must be held out in the upswing, beings must be constituted as being-in-the-world, as transcending—if these beings themselves as beings in general are to become apparent as such. Thus factically existent Dasein, seen metaphysically from this being-in-the-world, is nothing other than the existent possibility for beings to gain *entry to world*. Only when, in the totality of beings, a being attains more Being in the existence of Dasein—i.e., when temporality comes about [*Zeitlichkeit sich zeitigt*]—do beings have the opportunity to enter the world. Entry into world, furthermore, provides the possibility for beings to be able to be revealed.

Before proceeding to clarify transcendence in its intrinsic possibility, so as to see the rootedness of the essence of ground in transcendence, we must first make transcendence more intelligible by briefly characterizing the entry into world.

So far as we have succeeded in clarifying transcendence, one thing must be clear—namely that the world does not mean beings: neither individual objects nor the totality of objects standing over against a subject. Whenever one wishes to express transcendence as a subject-object relation, especially as in the movement of philosophical [250] realism, the claim is frequently made that the subject always already presupposes the "world" and, by this, one means existing objects. Now we should note that this thesis is far from even seeing the real phenomenon of transcendence. But we will not go further into this.

What is it supposed to mean that the subject "presupposes" objects that are—"presupposes" that these object are? There is no sensible meaning to connect with this statement, not to mention the fact that we never run across any such presupposing. Is it supposed to mean that "we" make the assumption in advance that objects are? On account of some agreement? By what right do we make that assumption? How did we come to it in the first place? Only on the supposition of the isolated subject. And do those beings as such ever show themselves to us—those beings that we permit to exist, as it were, only out of kindness? There is nowhere the trace of any such presupposition. And only one thing is apt in all the talk about presupposing the "world," presupposing objects, and that is that factically existing Dasein always already comes across available things, has always already in advance come across beings. But these beings, and the fact that they already exist in advance, do not rest upon a presupposition; nor, as it were, upon a metaphysical fraternizing: Let us presuppose that beings are, and then we want to try to exist among them. The very encounter with available things sharply contravenes our having presupposed their availability. It implies on the contrary that, as existents, we have no prior need to presuppose objects beforehand.

Yet beings (things present at hand) could never be encountered had they not the opportunity to enter a world. We are speaking therefore of the possible and occasional entrance of beings into a world. When and how is this possibility realized? Entry into a world is not a process that available things go through, in the sense that beings undergo a change thereby and through this change break into the world. The available's entry into a world [251] is "something" that happens to it. Entry into a world has the characteristic of happening, of history. World-entry happens when transcendence happens, i.e., when historical Dasein exists. Only then is the being-in-the-world of Dasein existent. And only when the latter is existent have available things, too, already entered a world, i.e., become intraworldly. And only Dasein, qua existing, provides the opportunity for world-entry.

Accordingly, intraworldliness is not a present-at-hand property of available things in themselves. Available things are beings as the kind of things they are, even if they do not become intraworldly—even if world-entry does not happen to them and there is no occasion for it at all. Intraworldliness does not belong to the essence of available things as such, but it is only the transcendental condition, in the primordial sense, for the possibility of available things being able to emerge as they are. And that means it is the condition for existing Dasein's experience and comprehension of things as they are. World-entry and its occurrence is the condition not for available things to first become available and enter into that which manifests itself to us as its availability and which we understand as such. Rather, entry into a

world and its occurrence is solely the condition for available things announcing themselves in their not requiring world-entry regarding their
own Being.

As being-in-the-world, transcending Dasein in each case factically provides beings with the opportunity for world-entry, and this provision on the
part of Dasein consists in nothing other than transcending.

If, however, intraworldliness is not a property of intraworldly available
things as available, where does it belong, and how is it itself? It obviously
belongs to world and only is along with it; it only happens insofar as being-
in-the-world happens. There is world only insofar as Dasein exists. But then
is world not something "subjective"? In [252] fact it is! Only, one may not at
this point reintroduce a common, subjectivistic concept of "subject." Instead, the task is to see that being-in-the-world, which as existent supplies
available things with an entry to a world, precisely transforms the concept
of subjectivity and of the subjective from the ground up.

When Dasein exists, world-entry has simultaneously also already occurred together with it, and it has happened in such a way that available
things entering there in principle undergo *nothing*. They remain so completely untouched that it is on account of world-entry that existing Dasein
can, on its part, approach, encounter, and touch them. But if what enters a
world undergoes nothing in the occurrence of world-entry, is then the
world itself nothing? Precisely: The world is nothing—if "nothing" means:
not a being in the sense of something available; also "nothing" in the sense
of no-thing, not one of the beings Dasein itself as such transcends; but
Dasein transcends itself as well. The world: a nothing, no being—and yet
something; nothing of beings—but Being. Thus, the world is not nothing in
the sense of *nihil negativum*. What kind of *nihil* is the world and then
ultimately being-in-the-world itself?

With this, we come upon the question about the intrinsic possibility of
transcendence itself, of being-in-the-world as the upswing [*Überschwungs*]
to a surpassive counter-hold, wherein Dasein makes itself known to itself in
its metaphysical essence, so as to bind itself primordially as freedom in this
self-understanding. I maintain that the intrinsic possibility of transcendence
is time, as primordial temporality!

FIVE

Description of the Situation
Fundamental Attunement

—⦿—

1929–1930

The fundamental task now consists in awakening a fundamental attunement [*Grundstimmung*] in our philosophizing. I intentionally say: in *our* philosophizing, not in some arbitrary philosophizing, nor even in philosophy itself, for there is no such thing. It is a matter of awakening *a* fundamental attunement that is to sustain our philosophizing, and not *the* fundamental attunement. Accordingly, there is not merely a single one, but several. Which one concerns us? From where are we to derive such an attunement? We are faced with a choice concerning which fundamental attunement to

---

The translation of this chapter is based on that of William McNeill and Nicholas Walker, in *The Fundamental Concepts of Metaphysics* (Bloomington: Indiana University Press, 1995), 59–82. Some minor emendations have been made, and some key terms and phrases have been changed to coincide with terminology throughout the present volume.

Bracketed numbers refer to the pagination of GA 29/30; the chapter opens at page 89.—Tr.

awaken here. Yet we are faced not only with this choice, but also with the much more difficult question of the way in which we are to awaken this or that fundamental attunement in our philosophizing.

Attunements—are they not something we can invent least of all, something that comes over us, something that we [90] cannot simply call up? Do they not form of their own accord, as something we cannot forcibly bring about, but into which we slip unawares? If so, then we cannot and may not forcibly bring about such an attunement artificially or arbitrarily, if we are going to allow it to be an attunement. It must already be there. All we can do is *to ascertain it*. Yet how are we to ascertain a fundamental attunement of philosophizing? Can an attunement be ascertained as continuously at hand, can it be demonstrated as a universally admitted fact? Is attunement in general something we take note of as something at hand, just as we notice, for instance, that some people are fair and others dark? Is attunement something that one simply has or does not have? Of course, people will say, attunement is perhaps something other than a person's hair or skin color, yet still something that can be ascertained with regard to humans. How else should we know about such attunements? Then a survey must be able to provide the fundamental attunement we are seeking. Assuming this could be carried out, even just within the circle of those present here and now—are we really so sure that each person we ask is in a position to inform us about the existence [*Dasein*] of this fundamental attunement "in them"? Perhaps such a thing as the fundamental attunement we are seeking is precisely something that cannot be ascertained in this way by an inquiry. It could be that in order to ascertain an attunement, one must not only have it, but also be correspondingly attuned to it.

We can already see that any so-called objective ascertaining of a fundamental attunement is a dubious, indeed impossible endeavor. Accordingly, it is also meaningless to ask in general about the pervasiveness and universality of attunement, or to worry about the universal validity of something ascertained in this way. In other words, it is not necessarily an objection to our claim of the existence of a fundamental attunement if one of you, or even many, or all of you, assure us that you are unable to ascertain such an attunement in yourselves whenever you observe yourselves. For [91] in the end there is nothing at all to be found by observation—no matter how astute, even if it were to call upon psychoanalysis for help.

Thus we shall not speak at all of "ascertaining" a fundamental attunement of our philosophizing, but of *awakening* it. Awakening means making something wakeful, *letting* whatever is sleeping *become wakeful*.

"That which sleeps" is in a peculiar way absent and yet there. If we awaken an attunement, this means that it is already there. At the same time, it expresses the fact that in a certain way it is *not* there. How strange: Attunement is something that is simultaneously there and not there. If we wanted to continue philosophizing formally in the customary manner, we could say immediately: Something that is simultaneously there and not there has that kind of being that intrinsically contradicts itself. For being-there [*Da-sein*] and not-being-there is a straightforward contradiction. But whatever is contradictory cannot be. It is—and this is an ancient proposition of traditional metaphysics—intrinsically impossible, just as a round square cannot exist. We shall see that we must not only put in question this venerable principle of old metaphysics, which is based on a very specific conception of Being, but also shake it from the ground up.

After all, what we generally know about things, we know in terms of an unambiguous either/or. Things are either at hand or not at hand. Is this not valid for humans as well? Certainly—either someone is there or not there. Yet at the same time one must recall that the state of affairs here is quite different from the case of a stone. For we know from experience of ourselves as humans that something can be at hand in us and yet not be, that there are processes that belong to [92] us that nevertheless do not enter our consciousness. Humans have a consciousness, and something can be at hand in them of which they know nothing. In that case it is presumably at hand in them, but not at hand in their consciousness. A stone either has a property or does not have it. We, on the contrary, can have something and at the same time not have it—that is, not know of it. We speak, after all, of the unconscious. In one respect it is at hand, and yet in another respect it is not at hand, namely insofar as it is not conscious. This strange "at hand and yet at the same time not at hand" arises from the possibility of being conscious of something unconscious. This distinction between not being there in the sense of the unconscious and being there in the sense of what is conscious also seems to be equivalent to what we have in mind with awakening, specifically with the awakening of whatever is sleeping. Yet can we straightforwardly equate sleep with the absence of consciousness? After all, there is also an absence of consciousness in being unconscious [*Ohnmacht*]—which cannot be identified with sleep—and especially in death. This concept of the nonconscious, therefore, is much too broad, irrespective of the question as to whether it is at all suitable. Furthermore, sleep is not simply an absence of consciousness. On the contrary, we know that sleep precisely has a peculiar, and in many cases extremely animated, consciousness, namely that of dreams, so that here the possibility of characterizing something using the distinction "conscious/unconscious" indeed breaks down. Waking and sleeping are not equivalent to consciousness and unconsciousness.

Thus it is already clear that we will not get by with the distinction between "unconscious" and "conscious." To awaken an attunement cannot mean simply to make conscious an attunement which was previously unconscious. To awaken an attunement means, after all, to let it *become awake* and as such precisely to let it *be*. If, however, we make an attunement conscious—come to know of it and explicitly make the attunement itself into an object of knowledge [93]—we achieve the contrary of an awakening. The attunement is thereby precisely destroyed, or at least not intensified, but weakened and altered.

And yet the fact remains: Whenever we awaken an attunement, this entails that it was already there, and yet not there. On the negative side, we have seen that the distinction between being there and not being there is not equivalent to that between consciousness and unconsciousness. From this, however, we may conclude something further: If attunement is something that belongs to humans, is "in them," as we say; or if humans have an attunement, and if this cannot be clarified with the aid of consciousness and unconsciousness; then we will not come close to this matter at all so long as we take the human as something distinguished from material things by the fact that it has consciousness, that it is an animal endowed with reason—a rational animal—or an ego with pure life-experiences that has been tacked onto a body. This conception of the human as a living being—a living being that in addition has reason—has led to a complete failure to recognize the essence of attunement. Both the awakening of attunement and the attempt to broach this strange task in the end coincide with the demand for a complete transformation of our conception of humans.

In order not to make the problem all too complicated here at the outset, I shall not enter into the question of what sleep properly is. For in a methodological respect, one could say that we will acquire information about the essence of awakening only if we clarify what sleeping and waking mean. I shall mention here merely that the task of clarifying such phenomena as sleeping and waking cannot be addressed extrinsically as one particular question. Rather, such clarification can only occur on the presupposition that we possess a fundamental conception of how a being must be structurally determined such that it can sleep or be awake. We do not say that the stone is asleep or awake. Yet what about [94] the plant? Here already we are uncertain. It is highly questionable whether the plant sleeps, precisely because it is questionable whether it is awake. We know that the animal sleeps. Yet the question remains as to whether its sleep is the same as that of the human, and indeed the question as to what sleep in general is. This problem is most intrinsically bound up with the question concerning the structure of Being pertaining to these various kinds of beings: stone, plant, animal, human.

In contrast to the many misinterpretations of sleep in modernity, we see already in the philosophers of antiquity that the fundamental character of sleep shows itself to have been grasped in a much more elementary and immediate manner. Aristotle, who wrote a treatise specifically on waking and sleeping (Περὶ ὕπνου καὶ ἐγρηγόρσεως), a treatise that has a peculiar character of its own, noticed something remarkable in saying that sleep is an ἀκινησία. He does not connect sleep with consciousness or unconsciousness. Rather, he says that sleep is a δεσμός, a being-bound [Gebundenheit], a peculiar way in which αἴσθησις is bound—and not only a way in which perception is bound, but also our essence, in that it cannot take in other beings which it itself is not. This characterization of sleep is more than an image, and opens up a broad perspective that has by no means been grasped in its metaphysical intent. For fundamental metaphysical reasons we must forego entering into the problem of sleep, and must attempt to clarify on *another path* what it means to awaken an attunement.

When we speak of the simultaneous being-there and not-being-there, it is by no means a matter of the [95] distinction between consciousness and unconsciousness in the case of humans. This becomes clear from an occurrence that happens when we are quite awake, if for the moment we posit wakefulness as conscious life in contrast to unconscious life (sleep). How often it happens, in a conversation among a group of people, that we are "not there"—how often we find that we were *absent,* albeit without having fallen asleep. This not-being-there, this being-away [Weg-sein], has nothing at all to do with consciousness or unconsciousness in the usual sense. On the contrary, this not-being-there can be highly conscious. In such being-absent we are precisely concerned with ourselves, or with something else. Yet this not-being-there is nonetheless a *being-away.* Think of the extreme case of madness, where the highest degree of consciousness can prevail and yet we say: The person is deranged [ver-rückt], displaced, away and yet there. Nor are being-there and being-away identical with waking and sleeping. Why we nevertheless rightly conceive of them in these terms will become apparent later.

We see that this *potential* to be away ultimately belongs to the way in which humans are in general. Yet the human *can* only be away in this manner if its Being has the character of being-there [*Da-sein*]. *We call the Being of the human Da-sein,* in a sense yet to be determined, and in distinction to the being at hand of the stone. In the end, being-away pertains to the essence of existence [*Dasein*]. It is not something that happens arbitrarily from time to time, but is an essential characteristic of the human's very Being, a *how* according to which the human is, so that a human being—insofar as it exists—is, in its being there, also always already and necessarily away in some manner. All this transpires in such a way that the distinction between "conscious" and "unconscious" turns out not to be a primary one, but can be ascertained both in being-there and in being-away.

An attunement is to be awakened. Yet this means that it is there and not there. If attunement is something that has the character of "there and not there," then attunement itself has to do with the innermost essence of human Being, with its [96] Dasein. *Attunement belongs to the Being of the human.* The possibility and manner of this "there and not there" has now already been brought closer to us, although we do not yet see it correctly by any means. For as long as we speak in this way—that attunement is there and not there—we take it as something that both appears and does not appear in humans. Yet the being-there and being-away of humans is something completely different from being at hand or not being at hand. We speak of being at hand or not being at hand, for example, with respect to a stone (e.g., roughness is not at hand in this erratic stone), or in a particular conception relating to a physical process, or indeed even to a so-called emotional experience. Being at hand and not being at hand are decisive concerning being and non-being. Yet what we have designated as being-there and being-away are something in the Being of man. They are possible only if and so long as humans *are. Being away is itself a way of being.* Being-away does not mean: not being at all. It is rather a *way* of being-there. The stone, in its being away, is precisely *not* there. Humans, however, must be *there* in order to be able to be away, and only so long as they are there do they have the possibility of an "away" in general.

Accordingly, if attunement indeed belongs to the Being of humans, we may not speak of it or take it as though it were at hand or not at hand. Yet people will reply: Who will deny us that? Attunements—joy, contentment, bliss, sadness, melancholy, anger—are, after all, something psychological, or better, psychical; they are emotional states. We can ascertain such states in ourselves and in others. We can even record how long they last, how they rise and fall, the causes that evoke and impede them. Attunements or, as one also says, "feelings," are events occurring in a subject. Psychology, after all, has always distinguished between thinking, willing, and feeling. It is not by chance that it will always name feeling in the third, subordinate [97] position. Feelings are the third class of lived experience. For naturally the human is in the first place the rational living being. Initially, and in the first instance, this rational living being thinks and wills. Feelings are certainly also at hand. Yet are they not merely, as it were, the adornment of our thinking and willing, or something that obfuscates and inhibits these? After all, feelings and attunements constantly change. They have no fixed subsistence; they are that which is most inconstant. They are merely radiance and shimmer, or else something gloomy, something hovering over emotional events. Attunements—are they not like the utterly fleeting and ungraspable shadows of clouds flitting across the landscape?

One can certainly take attunements this way, as shades and side-effects of other emotional events. Indeed hitherto they have basically always been taken this way. This characterization is indisputably correct. Nevertheless, one would not wish to claim that this ordinary conception is the sole possible one, or even the decisive one, simply because it lies closest and can most easily be accommodated within the ancient conception of the human. For attunements are not mere emotional events or states in the way that a metal is liquid or solid, given that attunements indeed belong to the Being of man. Therefore, we must now ask: How are we to grasp attunement *positively* as belonging to the essence of the human, and how are we to relate toward the human itself if we are to awaken an attunement?

Before pursuing this question, let us review what has been said thus far regarding the task of our lecture-course. We are confronting the task of awakening a fundamental attunement in our philosophizing. Attunements are something that cannot be straightforwardly ascertained in a universally valid way, like a fact that we could lead everyone to see. Not only can an attunement not be ascertained, it ought not to be ascertained, even if it were possible to do so. For all ascertaining entails bringing to consciousness. [98] With respect to attunement, all making conscious means destroying, altering; whereas in awakening an attunement, we are concerned to let this attunement be as it is, as this attunement. Awakening means letting an attunement be; one which, prior to this, has evidently been sleeping, if we may employ this image to begin with in accordance with linguistic usage. Attunement is in a certain way there and not there. We have seen that this distinction between being-there and not-being-there has a peculiar character, and is by no means equivalent to the distinction between a stone's being at hand or not being at hand. The not being at hand of the stone is not a particular manner of its being at hand, but the complete opposite of the latter. By comparison, being-away—absence in its various forms—is not something like the exclusive opposite of being-there. Rather, all being-away presupposes being-there. We must be there [*da-sein*] in order to be able to be away. Only as long as we are there [*da-sind*] can we be away at all, and vice-versa. Hence being-away, or this "there and not there," is something peculiar—and attunement is connected in some as yet obscure way with this peculiar manner of being.

We also touched upon the fact that it is fundamentally misleading to say that an attunement is there, for in such a case we take attunement as something like one existing property that appears amongst others. In contrast to this conception, which denies that attunements are existing things, we brought common opinion to bear, as found in psychology and in the traditional view of things. Attunements are feelings. Alongside thinking and willing, feeling is the third class of experience. This classification of experiences is carried out on the basis of the conception of the human as a rational living being. This characterization of feelings is not something to be disputed in the first instance. But we concluded with the question [99] as to whether this characterization of attunements, which is correct within certain limits, is decisive, and whether it is the essential one. By contrast, we saw that first, attunements are not beings, not things that somehow simply appear in the soul; second, attunements are just as little the most inconstant and most fleeting things, contrary to what people think. It is a matter of showing what is *positive*, by way of contrast with our negative thesis. We must bring attunements and their essence a few steps closer to us in order to counter-pose our positive thesis to these two negative ones.

A human being we are with is overcome by grief. Is it simply that this person has some state of lived experience that we do not have, while everything else remains as before? If not, what is happening here? The person overcome by grief closes himself off, becomes inaccessible, yet without showing any harshness toward us; it is simply that he becomes inaccessible. And yet we may be with him as before, or perhaps even more frequently, and may be more accommodating toward him. He does not alter anything about his comportment toward things or toward us either. Everything remains as before, and yet everything is different, not only in this or that respect but—irrespective of the sameness of *what* we do and *what* we engage *in*—the *way* in which we are together is different. Yet this is not some subsequent effect of the attunement of grief being at hand in him, but belongs rather to his grief as part of it.

What does it mean to say that he is attuned in this way, inaccessible? The manner and way in which we can be with him, and in which he is with us, has [100] changed. It is the grief that constitutes this way (the way in which we are together). He draws us into the manner in which he is, although we do not necessarily feel any grief ourselves. Our being with one another, our being-there, is different; its attunement has shifted. Upon closer consideration of this context—which we shall not pursue any further now—we can already see that attunement is not at all inside, in some sort of soul of the other, and that it is not at all somewhere alongside in our soul. Instead we have to say, and do say, that the attunement imposes itself on everything. It is *not* at all *"inside"* in some interiority, only to appear in the flash of an eye; but for this reason it is *not at all outside either.* Where and how is it, then? Is this attunement, grief, something concerning which we may ask where it is and how it is? Attunement is not some being that occurs in the soul as an experience, but the how of our being-there with one another [*Miteinander-Daseins*].

Or let us consider other possibilities. A human being who—as we say— is in good humor brings a lively atmosphere with them. Do they, in so doing, create an emotional experience that is then transmitted to others, in the manner in which infectious germs wander back and forth from one organism to another? We do indeed say that mood is infectious. Or another human being is with us, someone who through their manner of being makes everything depressing and puts a damper on everything; nobody steps out of their shell. What does this tell us? Attunements are *not side effects,* but are something that in advance determine our being with one another. It seems as though an attunement is in each case already there, so to speak, like an atmosphere in which we first immerse ourselves, and that then attunes us through and through. It does not merely seem so, it is so; and faced with this fact, we must dismiss the psychology of feelings, experiences, and consciousness. It is a matter of *seeing* and *saying* what is happening here. It is clear that attunements are not something merely at hand. They themselves are precisely a fundamental manner [101] and fundamental way of being, indeed of being-there—and this always directly includes being with one another. Attunements are ways of being-there, and thus ways of being-away. An attunement is a way, not merely a form or a mode, but a way [*Weise*]—in the sense of a melody that does not merely hover over the so-called proper being at hand of the human, but that sets the tone for such being, i.e., attunes and determines the manner and way of its Being.

Thus we have the positive correlate of our first negative thesis, namely that attunement is not a particular being. In positive terms, attunement is a fundamental manner, the *fundamental way in which Dasein is as Dasein*. We now also have the counter-thesis to our second negative thesis that attunement is not something inconstant, fleeting, merely subjective. Rather, because attunement is the originary way in which every Dasein is as it is, it is not what is most inconstant, but that which gives Dasein *subsistence and possibility* in its very foundations.

From all of this, we must learn to understand what it means to take so-called "attunements" in the correct way. It is not a matter of taking up an opposite stance to psychology and delimiting more correctly a kind of emotional experience—thus improving psychology—but rather a matter of first opening up a general perspective upon the *Dasein* of the human. Attunements are the fundamental ways in which we *find* ourselves *disposed* in such and such a way. Attunements are the *how* according to which one is in such and such a way. Certainly—for reasons we shall not go into now— we often take this "one is in such and such a way" as something different, in contrast to *what* we intend to do, *what* we are occupied with, or *what* will happen to us. And yet this "one is in such and such a way" is not—is never— simply a consequence or side effect of our thinking, doing, and acting. It is—to put it crudely—the presupposition for such things, the "medium" within which they first happen. And precisely *those* attunements to which we pay no heed at all, the attunements we least observe, those attunements which attune us in such a way that we feel as though there is no attunement there at all, [102] as though we were not attuned in any way at all—these attunements are the most powerful.

At first and for the most part, we are affected only by particular attunements that tend toward "extremes," like joy or grief. A faint apprehensiveness or a buoyant contentment are less noticeable. The *lack of attunement* in which we are neither out of sorts nor in a "good" mood is apparently not there at all, yet it is there. Yet even in this "neither/nor" we are never without an attunement. We take the lack of attunement as not being attuned at all, however, for quite essential reasons. When we say that a human being who is good-humored brings a lively atmosphere with them, this means only that an elated or lively attunement is brought about. It does not mean, however, that there was no attunement there before. A lack of attunement prevailed there which is seemingly hard to grasp, which seems to be something apathetic and indifferent, yet is not like this at all. We can see once more that attunements never emerge in the empty space of the soul and then disappear again; rather, Dasein as Dasein is always already attuned in its very grounds. There is only ever a change of attunement.

We stated in a provisional and rough manner that attunements are the "presupposition" for, and "medium" of, thinking and acting. That means as much as to say that they reach more primordially back into our essence, that in them we first meet ourselves—as a Da-sein. Precisely because the essence of attunement is that it is no mere side effect, precisely because it leads us back into the foundation of Dasein, the essence of attunement remains concealed or hidden from us. For this reason, we initially grasp the essence of attunement in terms of what confronts us at first, namely the extreme tendencies of attunement, those that irrupt and then disappear. Because we take attunements in terms of their extreme manifestations, they seem to be one set of events among others, and we overlook this [103] peculiar attunedness: the primordial, pervasive attunement of the whole Dasein as such.

From this it becomes clear that awakening attunements is a manner and means of grasping Da-sein with respect to the specific "way" in which it is— of grasping Da-sein as Da-sein, or better: of letting Da-sein be as it is, or can be, as Da-sein. Such awakening may perhaps be a strange endeavor, difficult and scarcely transparent. If we have understood our task, then we must now see to it that we do not suddenly start to deliberate *about* attunements again or even *about* awakening, but inasmuch as this awakening is an acting, we must *act* in accordance with it.

Yet even if we keep to this, we shall still meet difficulties that are necessary and that merely make clear to us, as we run through them, that this awakening of a fundamental attunement is not something that one can simply undertake like picking a flower, for instance.

To awaken a fundamental attunement, then! The question immediately arises as to *which* attunement we are to awaken or let become wakeful in us. An attunement that pervades *us* fundamentally? Who, then, are *we*? What do we mean here in referring to "*us*"? We, this number of individual humans assembled here in this room? Or [104] "us" insofar as we, at this university, stand before certain tasks in the study of the sciences? Or "us" insofar as we, in belonging to the university, are also drawn into the process of the education of spirit [*Bildung des Geistes*]? And this history of spirit—is it merely a

German occurrence, or is it Western and indeed European? Or should we draw the circle in which we stand even wider? We mean "us," but in what situation, and how are we to demarcate and delimit this situation?

The broader the perspective we have on this situation, the fainter our horizon becomes, and the more indeterminate our task. And yet we sense that the broader the perspective we take, the more passionately and decisively it will take hold of us—of each one of us.

At this point, however, a clear task also imposes itself that we can evidently no longer evade. If we are to awaken a fundamental attunement in ourselves, and wish to do so, then to this end we must *make sure of our situation.* Yet which attunement are we to awaken for *ourselves today?* We can answer this question only if we know *our* situation well enough to gather from it which fundamental attunement pervades us. Since something essential and ultimate is evidently at issue in awakening the fundamental attunement and in our intention to do so, this situation of ours must be seen in its greatest possible breadth. How are we to satisfy this demand? If we examine things more closely, then not only does the demand to characterize our situation prove not to be a new one, but this task has already been fulfilled in a manifold sense. For us it will merely be a case of bringing a unitary character to the description of our situation, and of retaining its *pervasive fundamental trait.*

If we look around for the explicit characterizations (interpretations, depictions) of our contemporary situation that come into question, then we may concentrate upon and very briefly acquaint ourselves with *four* [105] of them. In such cases the choice is never free from arbitrariness. Such arbitrariness, however, is rendered innocuous by what we gain.

The best-known interpretation of our situation, one that was provocative for a short period, is the one that has come to be expressed in the slogan "decline of the West."[1] What is essential for us is what underlies this "prophecy" as its fundamental thesis. Reduced to a formula, it is this: the decline of life in and through spirit. What spirit, in particular as reason (*ratio*), has formed and created for itself in technology, economy, world trade, and in the entire reorganization of existence symbolized by the city, is now turning against the soul, against life, overwhelming it and forcing culture into decline and decay.

---

1. Oswald Spengler, *Der Untergang des Abendlandes,* vol. 1 (Vienna and Leipzig: Wilhelm Braumüller, 1918), vol. 2 (Munich: Beck, 1922). [See *The Decline of the West,* trans. H. Werner (New York: Oxford University Press, 1991). —Tr.]

The *second* interpretation moves in the same dimension, except that the relation of soul (life) to spirit is seen differently. Commensurate with this different vision, it does not settle for a prediction of the decline of culture through spirit, but comes to repudiate spirit. Spirit is seen as the adversary of the soul.[2] Spirit is a sickness that has to be exorcised in order to liberate the soul. Freedom from spirit here means: Back to life! Life, however, is now taken in the sense of the obscure simmering of drives, which is simultaneously grasped as the breeding ground of the mythical. This is the opinion proffered by the popular philosophy of Ludwig Klages. It is essentially determined by Bachofen and above all by Nietzsche.

A *third* interpretation likewise keeps to the dimension of the first two, but sees neither a process of the decline of spirit in life, nor does it seek to uphold a struggle of life against spirit. Instead it attempts to find a balance between life and spirit, and [106] regards this as its task. This is the view represented by Max Scheler during the final period of his philosophizing. It is expressed most clearly in his lecture at Lessing College, "Man in the Epoch of Balance."[3] Scheler sees humans in the epoch of balance between life and spirit.

A *fourth* interpretation basically moves within the orbit of the third, and simultaneously includes the first and second within it. Relatively speaking, it is the most unoriginal and philosophically most fragile. We mention it only because it introduces a historical category for characterizing our contemporary situation, and looks toward a new Middle Ages. "Middle Ages" is here not supposed to mean a renaissance of the particular historical epoch that we know and indeed conceive of in very different ways. Rather, the title moves in the same direction as the third interpretation. What is meant is a middle or mediating epoch that is to bring about a new sublation of the opposition between "life and spirit." This fourth interpretation is represented by Leopold Ziegler in his book *The European Spirit*.[4]

This is only a formulaic, summarizing indication of what one is acquainted with today, what one talks about, and what has in part already been forgotten again. They are interpretations that are partly borrowed second- and third-hand and shaped into an overall picture, views that subsequently penetrate into the higher journalism of our age and create the

2. Ludwig Klages, *Der Geist als Widersacher der Seele*, vols. 1 and 2 (Leipzig, 1929).

3. Max Scheler, "Der Mensch im Weltalter des Ausgleichs," in *Philosophische Weltanschauung* (Bonn, 1929), 47ff. [See *Philosophical Perspectives*, trans. O. A. Haac (Boston: Beacon Press, 1958).—Tr.]

4. Leopold Ziegler, *Der Europäische Geist* (Darmstadt, 1929).

spiritual space—if one may say such a thing—in which we move. If one were to take this pointer concerning the four interpretations of our situation as more than what it is, namely a mere pointer, then it would necessarily be unfair, because it is too general. And yet, the essential thing that matters to us is the fundamental trait of these interpretations—or rather, the perspective from which they all see our contemporary situation. Expressed formulaically [107] once more, this perspective is that of the relation between life and spirit. It is no accident that we find this fundamental trait of these interpretations of our situation in the distinction and opposition provided by this formula.

In view of this distinction and of these two catchwords, it will initially be said that this simply invokes something that is already well known. How can this help us grasp what is peculiar about the contemporary and future situation of humans? Yet it would be a misunderstanding if one were to take these two terms merely as though they designated two components of the human, as it were: soul (life) and spirit—two components that have always been ascribed to humans and whose relation has always been one of conflict. Rather, these terms arise from certain basic orientations of the human. If we take the expressions in this way, then we can easily see that what is at issue here is not some theoretical elucidation of the relation between spirit and soul, but what Nietzsche means by the terms *Dionysian* and *Apollonian*. Thus, all four interpretations also point back to this common source—to Nietzsche and to a particular conception of Nietzsche. All four interpretations are only possible given a particular reception of Nietzsche's philosophy. This hint is not meant to question the originality of the interpretations, but is merely intended to indicate the place and source where the actual engagement must occur.

We cannot here enter into the concrete details of how Nietzsche conceives of this fundamental opposition. We shall characterize it only to the extent necessary for us to see what is at stake. The extent to which we can forego this task of interpreting the four [108] depictions of our situation and their source will be seen more clearly later.

This opposition of Dionysos and Apollo sustains and guides Nietzsche's philosophizing from early on. He himself knew this. This opposition, taken from antiquity, inevitably revealed itself to the young classical philologist who wanted to break with his discipline. Yet he also knew that however much this opposition is maintained in his philosophizing, it became transformed for him and through this philosophizing. Nietzsche himself knew: "Only whoever transforms himself is related to me." I would like deliberately to draw on the final interpretation, which he gave in his major and decisive work, in that work that he was never to complete in the form in which he harbored it within him: *The Will to Power.* The heading of the second section of the fourth book reads: "Dionysos."[5] Here we find peculiar aphorisms, and the whole work is in general a cluster of essential thoughts, demands, and valuations. To begin with, I shall provide evidence of how clearly Nietzsche, around this period shortly before his breakdown, saw that this opposition had been determinative for him from early on. Even before his doctorate, Nietzsche was called to Basel in 1869 as *professor extraordinarius.*

> *Around 1876* I had the horror of seeing everything I had hitherto wanted *compromised* as I understood where Wagner was now heading: and I had very strong ties with him, through all the bonds of a deep unity of need, through gratitude, through the lack of any substitute and through the absolute depriva- tion that I saw before me.
>
> Around the same time, I appeared to myself as though inescapably *incarcer- ated* in my philology and teaching activity—in a contingent and stopgap period of my life: I no longer knew how to escape, and was tired, exhausted, worn out.
>
> [109] Around the same time, I understood that my instinct was heading in the opposite direction to that of Schopenhauer: toward a *justification of life,* even in its most frightful, most ambiguous, and most deceptive aspects—for this I held the formula "Dionysian" in my hands.[6]

Later, we then read:

> Apollo's illusion: the *eternity* of beautiful form; the aristocratic legislation *"thus it shall be always!"*
>
> Dionysos: sensuousness and cruelty. Transitoriness could be interpreted as enjoyment of productive and destructive energy, as *constant creation.*[7]

There follows a section in which Nietzsche then interprets this opposition in what is probably its most beautiful and decisive form, and connects it with its source:

> The word *Dionysian* expresses an urge for unity, a reaching beyond the person, the everyday, society, reality, beyond the abyss of passing away: a pas-

---

5. Friedrich Nietzsche, *Der Wille zur Macht,* in *Gesammelte Werke (Musarionausgabe)* (Munich, 1920), vol. 19, 336ff. [See *The Will to Power,* trans. Walter Kaufmann and R. J. Hollingdale (New York: Random House, 1968).—Tr.]

6. Ibid., 337, no. 1005.

7. Ibid., 359–360, no. 1049.

sionate and painful swelling over into more obscure, more full, more lingering states; an enraptured yes-saying to the overall character of life as that which is the same, of the same power, of the same bliss in the midst of all change; the grand pantheistic shared joyfulness and compassion that approves and sanctifies even the most frightful and questionable aspects of life; the eternal will to creation, to fruitfulness, to return; the feeling of unity in the necessity of creating and destroying.

The word *Apollonian* expresses the urge for complete being-for-oneself, for the typical "individual," for everything that simplifies, sets in relief, makes things strong, clear, unambiguous and typical: freedom under the law.

The further development of art is just as necessarily linked to the antagonism of these two forces of nature and art as is the further development of humankind to the antagonism [110] of the sexes. The fullness of power and moderation, the highest form of self-affirmation in one cool, noble, aloof beauty: the Apollonianism of the Hellenic will.[8]

There then follows his characterization of the origin of this interpretation, and thereby his most profound analysis of the Greek world:

This opposition of the Dionysian and the Apollonian with the Greek soul is one of the greatest enigmas that I felt attracted by, in view of the essential nature of the Greeks. I was fundamentally concerned with nothing other than surmising why precisely the Greek Apollonianism had to grow out of a Dionysian underground: the Dionysian Greek needed to become Apollonian: that is, to shatter his will for the immense, for the multiple, the uncertain, the horrifying, upon a will for measure, for simplicity, for classification in rules and concepts. The immeasurable, the desolate, the Asiatic lies at his foundation: the courage of the Greek consists in the struggle with his Asiatic nature: beauty is not bestowed upon him, just as little as logic, or as the naturalness of morals—it is captured, willed, fought for—it is his *conquest*.[9]

One final point, in order to indicate how this opposition became decisively transformed into "The Two Types: Dionysos and the Crucified":

[. . .] Here I locate the *Dionysos* of the Greeks: the religious affirmation of life, of life as a whole, not denied or divided; (typical—that the sexual act awakens profundity, mystery, reverence).

Dionysos versus the "Crucified": there you have the opposition. [. . .] The God on the cross is a curse on life, a sign to redeem oneself thereof—Dionysos

---

8. Ibid., 360–361, no. 1050.
9. Loc. cit.

dismembered is a *promise* of life: it will be eternally born again and come home out of destruction.[10]

It does [111] not require many words to see that here in Nietzsche an opposition was active that in no way came to light in the four interpretations of our situation, but only had a residual effect as material that was taken over, as a literary form.

It is not to be decided here which of the four interpretations is the more correct in Nietzsche's sense. Nor indeed can we show here that none is correct, because none can be correct, insofar as they all mistake the essence of Nietzsche's philosophy, which for its part rests on strange foundations. These foundations indeed show themselves to be based on a quite ordinary and metaphysically highly questionable "psychology." Yet Nietzsche can afford that. Nevertheless, this is no *carte blanche*.

We know only that Nietzsche is the source of the interpretations we have mentioned. We are not saying this in order to accuse the interpretations of being derivative, or to detract from their originality in any way, but in order to designate the direction from which an understanding is to be gained, and to show where the place of the confrontation proper lies (cf. the [Stefan] George-circle, psychoanalysis).

All these questions are secondary for us. We are not even asking whether all of these interpretations of our situation are correct or not. In such cases, most of it always tends to be correct. And yet it is essential to mention them. For what is going on in these interpretations? We are claiming that what is going on is a *diagnosis* of culture in which, with the aid of the aforementioned categories of life and spirit, one passes through and beyond world history in a single stroke. In this way, what is contemporary is indeed meant to be located in its *setting*, its *situation* is supposed to be determined. Yet we ourselves are not at all concerned, let alone affected by this world-historical determination of where we are, [112] by the settling of accounts with our culture. On the contrary, the whole affair is something sensational, and this always means an unconceded, yet once again illusory appeasement, albeit of a merely literary and characteristically short-lived kind. This whole approach of cultural diagnosis, which is non-binding and is interesting for just this reason, then becomes even more exciting by being developed and reconstituted, whether explicitly or not, into *prognosis*. Is there anyone who

---

10. Ibid., 364–365, no. 1052.

does not wish to know what is coming, so that they can prepare themselves for it, so as to be less burdened, less preoccupied and affected by the present? These world-historical diagnoses and prognoses of culture do not involve us, they *are no attack upon us*. On the contrary, they release us from ourselves and present us to ourselves in a world-historical situation and role. These diagnoses and prognoses of culture are the typical marks of what is called "philosophy of culture" and that is now making an impact through many weaker or even more fantastic variations. This philosophy of culture does not grasp us in our contemporary situation, but at best sees only what is contemporary—yet a contemporaneity which is entirely without us, which is nothing other than what belongs to the eternal yesterday. We have deliberately characterized these interpretations of our situation using foreign words—diagnosis, prognosis—because their essence does not grow out of anything original. They lead a literary existence—albeit one that is by no means accidental.

But if philosophy of culture, in its interpretation of our contemporary situation, precisely fails to *take hold of us* or even *grip us*, then we would be mistaken if, in the considerations we made, we thought that in order to grasp our fundamental attunement we first had to be certain of our situation in this way.

It could, however, be said that perhaps it is only this particular kind of interpretation of our situation that is inadequate—a claim for which, [113] moreover, we would first require evidence, something that we have so far not provided as such. In any case, we will need some kind of pointers to let us see *where* we now stand. *Culture,* surely, is precisely the expression of our soul—indeed, it is a widespread opinion today that both culture and humans in culture can only be properly and philosophically comprehended through the idea of expression or symbol. We have today a philosophy of culture concerned with expression, with symbol, with symbolic forms. The human as soul and spirit, coming to expression in forms that bear an intrinsic meaning and which, on the basis of this meaning, give a sense to Dasein as it expresses itself: This, roughly speaking, is the schema of contemporary philosophy of culture. Here too, almost everything is correct, right down to what is essential. Now we must ask anew: Is this view of the human an essential one? What is happening in these interpretations, quite apart from the classification of the human in culture as provided by the philosophy of culture? The human, perhaps even the contemporary one, is thus presented in terms of the expression of his or her achievements. And yet the question remains whether presenting the human in this way *hits upon and grasps its Da-sein,* or indeed brings it into being; whether this presentation that is oriented toward expression not only factically misses the essence of the human, but *must* necessarily miss it, quite irrespective of all aesthetics. In other words, such philosophy only attains the *presentation* of the human, but never reaches its *Da-sein.* Not only does it factically fail to reach it, but it is of necessity unable to, because in itself it blocks the path to doing so.

Perhaps—precisely if and because we are striving to awaken a fundamental attunement—we must indeed proceed from an "expression" in which we are merely presented. Perhaps this awakening of a fundamental attunement indeed looks like a firmly fixing observation [*Fest-stellung*], yet is something other than presenting or ascertaining. Accordingly, if we cannot escape the fact [114] that everything we are saying looks like a presentation of our situation and seems as though it is ascertaining an attunement that underlies this situation and ex-presses itself in the situation—if we cannot deny this appearance and even less cast it aside—then this is saying merely that *ambiguity* is precisely now setting in for the first time. Is this surprising? If our introductory characterization of the essential ambiguity of philosophizing, of *our* philosophizing, was not some hollow cliché that was intended merely to say something peculiar about philosophy, then *ambiguity* must impose its power now at the *beginning.* We deny that such ambiguity is to be remedied in the slightest by our declaring or asserting in advance that there exists a theoretical difference between presenting our spiritual situation and awakening a fundamental attunement. That does not relieve us of anything at all. The more proper our beginning is, the more we shall leave this ambiguity in play, and the harder the task will be for each individual to decide for him- or herself whether he or she understands or not.

If the kind of interpretation of our situation provided by philosophy of culture leads us onto an erroneous path, then we are not to ask: *Where do we stand?*—but must ask: *How do things stand with us?* Yet if things stand in some way or other—in this way or that—with us, then this does not take place in a void: We are still standing somewhere. We would do well to infer from *where* we are standing *how* things stand with us. Thus we must, after all, first present our own situation; perhaps we merely have to characterize it differently than the aforementioned interpretations. Yet this is not necessary at all. We already know enough about our situation without going into those interpretations in more detail or adding another one. Nor do we have to reject them as incorrect. We already know enough about our situation merely by observing *that these interpretations exist*—the prevalence of philosophy of culture—and that they determine Dasein in many ways, even if these are not verifiable.

[115] We now ask anew: What does the fact that these diagnoses of culture find an audience among us—albeit in quite different ways—tell us about what is happening here? What is happening in the fact that this higher form of journalism fills or even altogether delimits our "spiritual" space? Is all this merely a fashion? Is anything overcome if we seek to characterize it as "fashionable philosophy" and thus to belittle it? We may not and do not wish to resort to such cheap means.

We said that this philosophy of culture at most presents what is contemporary about our situation, but does not take hold of *us*. What is more, not only does it not succeed in grasping us, but it unties us from ourselves in imparting us a role in world history. It unties us from ourselves—and yet does so precisely as anthropology. Flight and disorientation, illusion and lostness become more acute. The *decisive question* is now: What lies behind the fact that we give ourselves this role and indeed *must* do so? Have we become too *insignificant* to ourselves, that we require a role? Why do we find no meaning for ourselves any more, i.e., no essential possibility of being? Is it because an *indifference* yawns at us out of all things, an indifference whose grounds we do not know? Yet who can speak in such a way when world trade, technology, and the economy seize hold of humans and keep them moving? And nevertheless *we* seek a *role for ourselves*. What is happening here?—we ask anew. Must we first make ourselves interesting to ourselves again? Why *must* we do this? Perhaps because we ourselves have become *bored* with ourselves? Is the human being itself now supposed to have become bored with itself? Why so? *Do things ultimately stand in such a way with us that a profound boredom draws back and forth like a silent fog in the abysses of Dasein?*

We do not ultimately need any diagnoses or prognoses of culture in order to make sure of our situation, because they merely provide us with a role and untie us from ourselves, instead of helping us to want to find ourselves. Yet [116] how are we to find ourselves—in some vain self-reflection, in that repugnant sniffing out of everything psychological that today has exceeded all measure? Or are we to find ourselves in such a way that we are thereby *given back* to ourselves, that is, given back to *ourselves,* so that we are *given over* to ourselves, given over to the task of becoming what we are?

We may not, therefore, flee from ourselves in some convoluted idle talk about culture, nor pursue ourselves in a psychology motivated by curiosity.

Rather, we must find ourselves by binding ourselves to our Dasein and by letting such *Da*-sein become our *sole* obligation.

But will we find ourselves via this indication of that *profound boredom,* which perhaps none of us know at first? Is this questionable, profound boredom actually supposed to be the *sought-after fundamental attunement* that must be *awakened*?

[117] By drawing attention to this profound boredom, it now seems as though we have done what we were attempting to avoid from the outset— namely ascertaining a fundamental attunement. Yet have we ascertained a fundamental attunement? By no means. We cannot ascertain one at all; indeed, we are quite unable to do so, since it is entirely possible for everyone to deny that such an attunement is there. We have not ascertained one at all—indeed everyone will say we have arbitrarily asserted that such an attunement is at hand. Yet what is at issue is not whether we deny it or assert it. Let us simply recall what we asked: Do things actually stand in such a way with us that a profound boredom draws back and forth like a silent fog in the abysses of Dasein?

Nevertheless, so long as this boredom remains questionable, we cannot awaken it. Or can we perhaps do so after all? What does it mean to say that this boredom is questionable for us? Initially this amounts to saying in formal terms that we do not know whether this attunement pervades us or not. Who—"we"? *We* do not know this. This not knowing and not being acquainted with this boredom—does it not precisely also belong to the way in which we are, to *our* situation? Why do we not know about it? Because it is perhaps not there at all? Or—because we *do not want* to know about it? Or do we know about it after all? Are we "merely" lacking courage concerning what we know? In the end, we [118] do not want to know of it, but constantly seek *to escape* it. If we constantly seek to escape from it in this way, we ultimately have a bad conscience, and are consoled by persuading ourselves and proving to ourselves that we do no know of it—therefore it is not there.

How do we escape from this boredom [*Langeweile*] in which we find, as we ourselves say, that *time* becomes drawn out, becomes long [*lang*]? Simply by always making an effort, whether consciously or unconsciously, to pass the time; by welcoming highly important and essential preoccupations for the sole reason that they take up our time. Who will deny this? Yet do we then still need to first ascertain the fact that this boredom is there?

Yet what does it mean to say that we *drive away* and *shake off* boredom? We constantly cause it to *fall asleep.* For evidently we cannot annihilate it by passing the time, however intensively. We "know"—in a strange kind of knowing—that boredom can return at any time. Thus it is already there. We shake it off. We succeed in making it fall asleep. We wish to know nothing of it. This does not at all mean that we do not wish to be conscious of it, but rather that we do not wish to let it be awake—it, this boredom that ultimately is already awake. With open eyes it looks into our Da-sein (albeit entirely from a distance), and with this gaze already penetrates us and attunes us through and through.

Yet if it is already awake, then surely it does not need to be awakened. Indeed not. Awakening this fundamental attunement does not mean making it awake in the first place, but *letting it be awake, guarding against it falling asleep.* We can easily see from this that our task has not become any easier. Perhaps this task is essentially more difficult, similar to the way in which we can experience at any time that it is easier to wake someone up by startling them than to guard against them falling asleep. Yet whether our task is difficult or easy is not what is essential here.

[119] We already face a much more essential difficulty: Not to let boredom fall asleep is a strange or almost insane demand. Is it not entirely opposed to what all natural and sound human comportment is concerned with every day and every hour, namely to pass the time and precisely not to let boredom arise—that is, to shake it off and make it fall asleep whenever it approaches? And *we* are supposed to let it be awake! Boredom—who is not acquainted with it in the most varied forms and disguises in which it arises, in the way it often befalls us only for a moment, the way it torments and depresses us for longer periods, too? Who does not know that we have already set about suppressing it and are concerned to drive it away as soon as it approaches; that this does not always succeed, that indeed precisely when we set upon it with all the means at our disposal it becomes stubborn, obstinate; that it then really does persist and returns more frequently, slowly propelling us to the threshold of melancholy? Even when we succeed in shaking it off—do we not then know at the same time that it may well return? Do we not have the strange knowledge that what we have fortunately seen driven away and made to vanish could at any time be there once again? And does this belong to it, if it shows itself to us in this way?

Yet where does it vanish to, and from where does this insidious creature that maintains its monstrous essence in our Dasein return? Who is not acquainted with it—and yet, who can safely say freely what this universally familiar phenomenon actually is? What is this boredom such that, when faced with it, we set ourselves the demand to let *it*, this very attunement, be awake? Or is this boredom that is familiar to us here in this way, and of which we now speak so indeterminately, a mere shadow of our actual boredom? We indeed asked and are repeatedly asking: Have things ultimately gone so far with us that a *profound* boredom draws back and forth like a silent fog in the abysses of Dasein?

[120] This *profound boredom* is the *fundamental attunement*. We pass the *time*, in order to master it, because time becomes long in boredom. Time becomes long for us. Is it supposed to be short, then? Does not each of us wish for a truly long time for ourselves? And whenever it does become long for us, we pass the time and ward off its becoming long! We do not want to have a long time, but we have it nonetheless. Boredom, long time: Especially in Alemannic usage, it is no accident that "to have long-time" [*lange Zeit haben*] means the same as "to be homesick" [*Heimweh haben*]. If someone has long-time for . . . , this means he is homesick for . . . . Is this accidental? Or is it only with difficulty that we are able to grasp and draw upon the wisdom of language? Profound boredom—a homesickness. Homesickness—philosophizing, we heard somewhere, is supposed to be a homesickness.[11] Boredom—a fundamental attunement of philosophizing. *Boredom—what is it?*

Boredom—whatever its ultimate essence may be—shows, particularly in our German word, an almost obvious *relation to time:* a way in which we stand with respect to time, a feeling of time. Boredom and the question of boredom thus lead us to the problem of time. We must first let ourselves enter the problem of time, in order to determine boredom as a particular relation to it. Or is it the other way around—does boredom first lead us to time, to an understanding of *how time resonates in the ground of Da-sein* and how it is only because of this that we can "act" and "maneuver" in our customary superficial way? Or are we failing to ask correctly concerning either the first relation—that of boredom to time—or the second—that of time to boredom?

Yet we are not in fact posing the problem of time, the question of what time is, but are posing the three quite different questions of what *world, finitude,* and *individuation* are. Our philosophizing is meant to be moving

---

11. [Heidegger has referenced this earlier in the lecture-course by citing a fragment from Novalis: "Philosophy is really homesickness, an urge to be at home everywhere" (GA 29/30, 6–8). This is fragment 21 in Novalis, *Schriften,* ed. J. Minor (Jena, 1923), vol. 2, p. 179.—Tr.]

and maintaining itself in the direction of and along the path of these [121] three questions. What is more, these three questions are supposed to spring *from a fundamental attunement* for us. This attunement, profound boredom —if only we knew what it is, or were even pervaded by this attunement! Yet even assuming that we were pervaded by this fundamental attunement, what in the world does boredom have to do with the question concerning world, finitude, and individuation? We can perceive that this fundamental attunement of boredom is tied up with time and the problem of time. *Or are the three questions ultimately tied up with the question of time?* Is there not an ancient conviction that the world and time both originated together—that both are equally old, equally original and related to one another? Is there not a less venerable, self-evident opinion according to which whatever is finite is temporal? Then finitude would be bound up with time just as much as world. Are we not acquainted with the ancient doctrine of metaphysics according to which something individual becomes this individual thing by virtue of its specific position in time, so that like the first two questions of world and finitude, the problem of individuation would also be a problem of time? Time, for its part, stands in a relation of boredom to *us*. Boredom is accordingly the fundamental attunement of our philosophizing, in which we develop the three questions of world, finitude, and individuation. Time is thereby itself something that determines us in the working out of these three guiding questions. If time is tied up with boredom, and on the other hand is somehow the basis for our three questions, then the fundamental attunement of boredom constitutes an exceptional possibility of answering the three questions. Perhaps all this is indeed the case. Yet if so, then what has been said after all remains only a precursory opening up of a broad and as yet obscure perspective. All this is meant merely to serve toward making more comprehensible [122] the state of helplessness we shall get into *if we are now to become involved in boredom with the intention of explicating the three metaphysical questions above.*

For what remains obscure to us is precisely the extent to which boredom is supposed to be our fundamental attunement, and evidently an essential one. Perhaps nothing at all rings a bell with us, and nothing is conjured up. Where might the reason for this lie? Perhaps we are not acquainted with *this* boredom because we do not at all understand boredom *in its essence.* Perhaps we do not understand its essence because it *has never become essential* for us. And in the end it cannot become essential for us, because it not only belongs at first and for the most part to those attunements that we shake off in our everyday lives, but to those attunements that we do not allow to attune us as attunements even when they are there. Perhaps that very boredom which often merely flashes past us, as it were, is more essential than *that* boredom with which we are explicitly concerned whenever this or that particular thing bores us by making us feel ill at ease. Perhaps that boredom is more essential which attunes us neither favorably nor unfavorably, and yet does attune us, but does so in a way that it seems that we are not attuned at all.

This *superficial boredom* is indeed meant to lead us into *profound* boredom or, to put it more appropriately, the superficial boredom is supposed to manifest itself as the profound boredom and to attune us through and through in the ground of Dasein. This fleeting, cursory, *inessential* boredom must become *essential*. How are we to bring this about? Are we explicitly and intentionally to produce boredom in ourselves? Not at all. We do not need to undertake anything in this respect. On the contrary, we are always already undertaking too much. This boredom becomes essential of its own accord—if only we are not opposed to it, if we do not always immediately react to protect ourselves, if instead we make room for it. This is what we must first learn: *not to resist straightaway* but *to let resonate*. Yet how [123] are we to make room for this initially inessential, ungraspable boredom? Only by not being opposed to it, but letting it approach us and tell us what it wants, what is going on with it. Yet even to do this, it is necessary in the first place that we remove from indeterminacy whatever we thus name and apparently know as boredom. We must do this, however, not in the sense of dissecting some psychological experience, but in such a way that we thereby approach ourselves. Whom? Ourselves—*ourselves as a Da-sein.* (Ambiguity!)

SIX

The Projection of Being in Science and Art

~~~

1931–1932

To become free means to bind oneself to what is genuinely clearing [*Lichtende*], to what makes free and lets through, to "the light"; but the light symbolizes the idea. The idea contains and gives Being. Seeing the ideas means understanding the what- and how-being, the *Being* of beings. Becoming free for the light means to a let a light come on,[1] to understand Being and essence, and to thus first experience beings as such. The understanding of Being releases beings themselves as such. Only in this understanding can beings first be beings. Beings in any possible region can only be encoun-

---

This chapter is based on a previous translation by Ted Sadler in *The Essence of Truth: On Plato's Cave Allegory and Theaetetus* (New York: Continuum, 2002), 45–48. I have made slight alterations to the text.

Bracketed numbers refer to the pagination of GA 34; the chapter opens at page 60. — Tr.

1. [Cf. Kant, *Critique of Pure Reason*, B xi.]

tered, draw near, or recede on the basis of the freedom that releases. The essence of freedom is thus, briefly stated, the *illuminating view*: to allow, in advance, a light to come on, and to bind oneself to this. Only from and in freedom (its essence understood as we have developed it) do beings become more beingful [*seiender*], because they are this or that. To become free means to understand Being as such, an understanding that first lets beings *be as* beings. Whether beings become more beingful or less beingful is therefore up to the freedom of humans.[2] Freedom is measured according to the primordiality, breadth, and decisiveness of the binding, i.e., this *individual* grasping itself as *Da-sein*, set back into the isolation and thrownness of its historical past and future. The more primordial the binding, the greater the proximity to beings.

[61] Understanding, as we said earlier,[3] means being able to stand before something, to have an overview of it, to see its blueprint. To understand *Being* means to project in advance the essential lawfulness and the essential construction of beings. Becoming free for beings, looking into the light [*Ins-Licht-sehen*], means to enact the *projection of Being* [*Seinsentwurf*] wherein a look (picture) of beings is projected and held up in advance, so that in viewing this look one can relate to beings as such. We shall briefly clarify with three fundamentally different examples *how* such freedom, as a modeling projection of Being, first allows us to come closer to beings.

1. What was the *discovery of nature* at the beginning of the modern period, accomplished in the works of Galileo, Kepler, and Newton, actually grounded in? It was not, as people usually think, in the introduction of experimentation. Ancient investigations of nature already "experimented" as well.[4] The basis was also not, as one often hears, the fact that instead of hidden qualities of things (Scholasticism), quantitative relations were now sought out, posited, and determined. The ancients and medievals alike already measured and counted. It was also not a matter of mathematization itself, but of what this presupposes. What was decisive, what actually happened, is that a projection was made which *delineated* in advance what was henceforth to be *understood* as nature and natural process: a spatiotemporally determined movement-context of mass-points. In principle, despite all progress and transformation, nothing about this projection of nature has changed to the present day. Only after this delineation, in the

---

2. [Cf. the saying of Protagoras in Plato, *Theaetetus* 152a.]

3. Cf. above, [GA 34,] p. 2.

4. Nevertheless, there is an essential difference between trial [*Versuch*] and experiment.

light of this concept of nature, could nature be interrogated with respect to the lawfulness of its particular processes, and be put to the test, as it were, through experiments. Certainly, whether this discovery of "nature" and what followed from it came closer to, or [62] became more removed from *nature,* is a question that natural science itself is quite unable to decide. It is a question in itself whether beings became more beingful through this science, or whether something intervened between the beings and the knowers by virtue of which the relationship to beings was crushed, the instinct for the essence of nature was driven out, and the instinct for the essence of humans was suffocated.

As stated, the projection has in principle remained the same until the present day. But something has indeed changed. Not so much the substantive possibilities or radical changes in method; first and foremost, rather, the projection has forfeited its original essential character of *liberation.* This is evident from the fact that the beings that are today the object of theoretical physics, and of physics in general, have not been made *more beingful* through this modern science, but just the reverse. We see this from the poverty of what today calls itself philosophy of nature. Enough—whatever our philosophical estimation of natural science and its history, this penetration into nature happened on the basis, and along the path of, a paradigmatic projection of the Being of these beings, namely of nature.

2. A second example can show something analogous in the world of a completely different science, that of *historiography,* the science of the *history* of humans and their works. A person of Jacob Burckhardt's stature is not considered a great and genuine historian, rather than a mere scholar, on account of his studious reading and copying of sources, nor because he found a manuscript somewhere, but because he allowed his projective essential view of the fate, greatness, and misery of humans, of the conditions and limits of human action, to have an effect: In short, because he let his anticipatory understanding of the *occurrence* of what we call history, of the *Being* of these particular beings, [63] work in itself. This view-to-the-essence [*Wesensblick*] illuminated the way for the research of so-called facts, which others had seen and described long before him.

If one hears it said from all sides today that through the progress of science, there has arisen such a great mass of materials and information that no individual can form a synthesis any longer, one must respond: First, even the fact of speaking about a synthesis proves that one has not grasped what it is about; certainly not summarizing, synthetic description! Second, the whole argument twists things around. The fact that the material has grown so extensive, and progress has been so great, is not the reason for the impossibility of a real relationship to history. On the contrary, it is already the consequence of the longstanding inner impoverishment and powerless-ness of human Dasein—precisely the incapacity to understand the *occur-rence* of history, i.e., the incapacity to *be* fundamentally historical instead of busying oneself with historicism or the commonality of "sociology." It would certainly be a misunderstanding to think that historical knowledge requires no effort. Quite the contrary! The question is only where it sets to work, and who has the right, and who can assume the right, to work historically.

3. Yet another example leads completely out of the region of the sciences just considered, but reveals all the more the inner power of human understanding of Being, the illuminating view [*Lichtblickes*]. I refer to *art* and in particular to *poetry*.

The essence of art is not the expression of lived experience, and does not consist in an artist expressing his "soul-life" such that, as Spengler thinks, later ages must inquire about how the cultural soul of an historical period announced itself in art. Neither does it consist in the artist depicting reality more accurately and more precisely than others, or producing [64] (presenting) something that gives pleasure to others, that provides enjoy-ment of a higher or lower type. Rather, the artist possesses the essential insight for the possible, for bringing the hidden possibilities of beings into the work, and thus for making humans see what it really is with which they so blindly busy themselves. What is essential in the discovery of reality happened, and happens, not through science, but through originary philos-ophy, as well as through great poetry and its projections (Homer, Virgil, Dante, Shakespeare, Goethe). Poetry makes beings more beingful. Poetry—not just any writing! But in order to understand what the work of art and poetry as such are, philosophy must first break the habit of grasping the problem of art as one of aesthetics.

From these examples it should be clear how freedom, as the self-binding to the anticipatory projection of Being (the "idea," the essential conception of beings), first makes possible a relationship to beings—in the allegory: how the illuminating view, the seeing-into-the-light, first opens and frees the look for beings.[5] On the basis of the indicated connections between idea and light, light and freedom, freedom and beings, we now attempt to take up the question concerning the nature of ἀλήθεια.

---

5. See [GA 34,] supplement 6.

SEVEN

Rectorship Address
The Self-Assertion of the German University

———— ❧ ————

27 May 1933

Assuming the rectorship means committing oneself to leading this university *spiritually*.[1] The teacher and student body under the rector's leadership will awaken and gain strength only by being truly and collectively rooted in the essence of the German university. This essence will only attain clarity, rank, and power, however, when the leaders themselves are first and foremost, and at all times, led by the inexorability of that spiritual mission which impresses onto the fate of the German people the stamp of their history.

This translation is based on a previous version by William S. Lewis in *The Heidegger Controversy*, ed. Richard Wolin (New York: Columbia University Press, 1991), 29–39. I have made minor corrections and altered some phrasings.

Bracketed numbers refer to the pagination of GA 16; the chapter opens at page 107.—Tr.

1. [The words *Geist* and *geistig* will be rendered here by "spirit" and "spiritual," respectively, though the German has further connotations of mind or intellect.—Tr.]

Do we know of this spiritual mission? Whether yes or no, the question remains unavoidable: *Are* we, the teachers and students of this advanced school, truly and collectively rooted in the essence of the German university? Does this essence truly have the power to shape our existence? It does, but only if we fundamentally *will* this essence. But who would wish to doubt this? One generally takes the predominant, essential character of the university to reside in its "self-governance"; this shall be preserved. But have we also fully considered what this claim to the right of self-governance demands of us?

After all, self-governance means: to set ourselves the task and to determine the way and means of realizing in order thus to be what we ourselves ought to be. But do we know *who we ourselves are,* this body of teachers and students at the highest school of the German people? *Can* we know this at all, without the harshest and most constant *self-reflection*?

Neither knowledge of the conditions that prevail today at the university, nor even familiarity with its earlier history, guarantee sufficient knowledge of the essence of the university—unless we first delimit, clearly and uncompromisingly, this essence for the future, *will* it in such self-limitation, and in this willing *assert* ourselves.

[108] Self-governance can exist only on the basis of self-reflection. Self-reflection, however, only occurs in the strength of the self-assertion of the German university. Will we carry this out, and how?

The self-assertion of the German university is the original, common will to its essence. We regard the German university as the advanced school which from science and through science[2] educates and disciplines the leaders and guardians [*Führer und Hüter*] of the fate of the German people. The will to the essence of the German university is the will to science as the will to the historical, spiritual mission of the German people as a people that knows itself in its state [*Staat*]. Science and German fate must come to power at *the same time* in the will to essence. And they will do this then and *only* then when we—the teachers and students—*on the one hand* expose science to its innermost necessity, and *on the other,* when we stand firm toward German fate in its urgent distress.

Yet we will not experience the essence of science in its innermost necessity as long as we—in speaking of the "new concept of science"—simply provide for the independence and presuppositionlessness of an all-

---

2. [I will use "science" throughout to translate *Wissenschaft,* though this clearly lacks the breadth of the German term. — Tr.]

too-contemporary science. This activity, which merely negates and scarcely looks back beyond the last decades, will gradually appear as a true effort to understand the essence of science.

If we wish to grasp the essence of science, then we must first ask ourselves the decisive question: Should science still continue to *exist* for us in the future, or ought we to let it drift off to a quick end? It has never been unconditionally necessary that science should exist. But if science should exist, and if it should exist *for* us and *through* us, then under what conditions can it truly exist?

Only when we submit to the power of the *beginning* of our spiritual-historical existence. This beginning is the onset of Greek philosophy. That is when, [109] from the culture of one people and by the power of that people's language, Western humans rise up for the first time against *beings as a whole* and question them and comprehend them as the beings that they are. All science is philosophy, whether it knows it and wills it or not. All science remains bound to that beginning of philosophy and draws from it the strength of its essence, provided that it still remains equal to this beginning.

Here we want to recover for *our* existence two distinguishing characteristics of the original Greek essence of science.

There circulated among the Greeks an old report that Prometheus had been the first philosopher. Aeschylus has this Prometheus speak an adage that expresses the essence of knowledge:

τέχνη δ'ἀνάγκης ἀσθενεστέρα μακρῷ

"But knowledge is far less powerful than necessity." That means: All knowledge of things remains beforehand at the mercy of overpowering fate and fails before it.

For precisely this reason, knowledge must develop its highest defiance, for which alone the entire might of the concealedness of beings will first rise up, in order really to fail. Thus beings reveal themselves in their unfathomable inalterability and confer their truth on knowledge. This adage about the creative impotence of knowledge is a saying of the Greeks, in whom we all too easily see the model for knowledge that is purely self-reliant and thus lost to the world; this knowledge is presented to us as the "theoretical" attitude. But what is θεωρία for the Greek? It is said that it is pure contemplation that remains bound only to its object in its fullness and its demands. The Greeks are invoked to support the claim that this contemplative behavior is supposed to occur for its own sake. But this claim is incorrect. For on the one hand, "theory" does not happen for its own sake, but rather out of the passion to remain close to beings [110] as such and to be beset by them. On the other hand, however, the Greeks struggled precisely to understand and carry out this contemplative questioning as a—indeed as *the*—highest mode of ἐνέργεια, of humans' "being-at-work." It was not their wish to bring practice into line with theory, but conversely to understand theory as the supreme realization of genuine practice. For the Greeks, science is not a "cultural treasure," but the innermost determining center of their entire existence as a people and a state. Science, for them, is also not merely the means of making the unconscious conscious, but instead the force that keeps all of existence in focus and embraces it.

Science is the questioning that stands firm in the midst of beings as a whole as they continually conceal themselves. This active perseverance knows of its impotence in the face of fate.

That is the essence of science in its beginning. But does this beginning not already lie two and a half thousand years behind us? Has human progress not changed science as well? Certainly! The subsequent Christian-theological interpretation of the world, as well as the later mathematical-technical thinking of modernity, have removed science from its beginnings both temporally and with regard to its objects. But that by no means relegates the beginning itself to the past, let alone destroys it. For, assuming that the original Greek science is something great, then the *beginning* of this great thing remains its *greatest* moment. The essence of science could not even be emptied and used up—which it is today, all results and "international organizations" notwithstanding—if the greatness of the beginning did not *still* exist. The beginning still *exists*. It does not lie *behind* us as something long past, but rather stands *before* us. As the greatest moment, the beginning has in advance already passed over all that is to come and thus over us as well. The beginning has invaded our future; it stands there as the distant injunction that orders us to recapture its greatness.

Only if and when we resolutely obey [111] this decree in order to win back the greatness of the beginning will science become the innermost necessity of our existence. Otherwise, science will remain something in which we become involved purely by chance or will remain the calm, pleasurable comfort of an activity free of danger, which promotes the mere advancement of factual knowledge.

If, however, we obey the distant decree of the beginning, then science must become the fundamental event [*Grundgeschehnis*] of our spiritual existence as a people.

And if our ownmost existence [*Dasein*] itself stands on the threshold of a great transformation; if it is true what the last German philosopher to passionately seek God, Friedrich Nietzsche, said: "God is dead"; if we must take seriously this abandonment of today's human in the midst of beings: how does it stand with science?

Then the Greeks' initially wondering perseverance in the face of beings will be transformed into a completely unsheltered exposure to what is concealed and uncertain—that is, what is worthy of question. Questioning will then no longer simply be the surmountable, preliminary stage to the answer as knowledge, but questioning will instead itself become the highest form of knowledge. Questioning will then unfold its most proper power for disclosing the essence of all things. Questioning will then force us to radically simplify our gaze toward what is inescapable.

Such questioning will shatter the encapsulation of the various fields of knowledge into separate disciplines, return them from their scattering into boundless and aimless isolated fields and niches, and directly expose science once again to the fruitfulness and blessing of all the world-shaping forces of humans' historical existence, such as: nature, history, language; the people, custom, the state; poetry, thought, belief; sickness, madness, death; law, economy, technology.

If we will the essence of science in the sense of *the questioning, unsheltered standing-firm in the midst of the uncertainty of beings as a whole*, then *this* will to the essence will create for our people the world of its innermost and most extreme danger, i.e., its [112] truly *spiritual* world [*wahrhaft geistige Welt*]. For "spirit" is neither simply empty acumen, nor the noncommittal play of wit, nor the busy practice of never-ending rational analysis, nor even world-spirit [*Weltgeist*]. Rather, spirit is the originally attuned and knowing, determined resolve toward the essence of Being. And the *spiritual world* of a people is not its cultural superstructure—just as little as it is its arsenal of useful knowledge and values. Instead, it is the power of deeply preserving the forces that are rooted in the people's soil and blood; the power to arouse most inwardly and to shake most extensively our people's existence [*Dasein*]. A spiritual world alone will guarantee our people greatness. For it will transform the constant decision between the will to greatness and the toleration of decline into the law that establishes the pace for the march upon which our people has embarked on the way to its future history.

If we want *this* essence of science, then the teachers of the university must really advance to the outermost dangerous position of uncertainty concerning the world. If they stand firm there, i.e., if from there—in the essential, afflicting proximity to all things—there arises for them a common questioning and a commonly attuned discourse, then they will become strong enough to lead. For what is decisive in leading is not merely advancement but the strength to go alone, not out of obstinacy or the desire to dominate [*Herrschgelüste*], but by virtue of the most profound destiny and the broadest obligation. Such strength binds to what is essential, singles out the best, and awakens the genuine following of those who have new courage. But we do not need to first awaken such a following. The German students are on the march. And they seek *those* leaders through whom they intend to elevate their own destiny to a grounded, knowing truth and place it in the clarity of the interpretive-effective word and deed.

A will to the essence of the university comes out of German students' resolve to stand firm in the face of the extreme distress of German fate. This will is [113] a true will, insofar as the German students, through the new Student Law,[3] place themselves under the law of their essence and thereby first delimit this essence. To give the law to oneself is the highest freedom. The much-praised "academic freedom" is being banished from the German university because this freedom was false, as it was only negating.[4] It mostly meant lack of concern, arbitrariness in one's intentions and inclinations, lack of restraint in everything one does. The German student's notion of freedom is now being returned to its truth. The bonds and the service of German students will develop out of this freedom.

The first bond is the one that binds to the national community [*Volksgemeinschaft*]. It obligates one to share cooperatively in the toil, the striving, and the abilities of all classes and members of the nation. This bond will henceforth be secured and rooted in student life through *labor service.*

The *second* bond is the one that binds to the honor and the destiny of the nation in the midst of other peoples. It demands the preparedness, secured in knowledge and ability and firmed up through discipline, to follow one's duty to the end. This bond will in the future embrace and pervade all of student life in the form of *military service.*

The *third* bond is the one that binds students to the spiritual mission of the German people. This people shapes its fate by placing its history into the openness of the overpowering might of all the world-shaping forces of human existence, and by capturing its spiritual world ever anew. Thus exposed to the extreme questionableness of its own existence, this people

---

3. [This law, which went into effect on 1 May 1933, aimed at aligning universities with National Socialist goals by establishing leadership hierarchies among students. — Tr.]

4. [See Heidegger's comment on this sentence in supplement 1, p. 315. — Tr.]

has the will to be a spiritual people [*geistiges Volk*]. It demands of itself and for itself, and of its leaders and guardians, the harshest clarity that comes from the highest, broadest, and richest knowledge. A youth of students that ventures early into manhood and spreads its will over the destiny of the nation compels itself to thoroughly serve this knowledge. They will no longer permit *knowledge service* [Wissensdienst] to be the dull, quick training for a "distinguished" profession. [114] Since the statesman and the teacher, the doctor and the judge, the pastor and the master-builder lead the people in its existence and watch over this existence in its essential relations to the world-shaping forces of human Being and keep it focused, these professions and the education toward them are entrusted to the knowledge service. Knowledge does not serve the professions, but the other way around: The professions realize and administer the people's highest and most essential knowledge, that of its entire existence. But for us this knowledge is not the calm taking-note of essences and values in themselves; rather, it is the placing of one's existence [*Dasein*] in the most acute danger in the midst of overpowering beings. The questionableness of Being in general compels the people to work and struggle and forces it into its state, to which the professions belong.

The three bonds—*through* the people *to* the destiny of the state *in* its spiritual mission—are equiprimordial aspects of the German essence. The three forms of service that follow from them—labor service, military service, knowledge service—are equally necessary and of equal rank.

Cooperative knowledge about the people, knowledge of the destiny of the state that holds itself in readiness, and these together with the knowledge of the spiritual mission first create the original and full essence of science—the realization of which has been given us as our task—assuming that we obey what the beginning of our spiritual-historical existence [*Dasein*] decreed in the distant past.

It is *this* science that is meant when the essence of the German university is defined as the advanced school that, from science and through science, educates and disciplines the leaders and guardians of the fate of the German people.

This primordial concept of knowledge does not just commit one to "objectivity" but, first of all, to essential and simple questioning amidst the historical-spiritual world of the people. Indeed, it is only from here that objectivity can establish itself, i.e., find its character and limits.

[115] Science in this sense must become the force that shapes the body of the German university. This implies two things: First, the teachers and

students must each in their own way be *seized* by the idea of science and *remain* seized by it. At the same time, however, this concept of science must penetrate into and transform the basic forms in which the teachers and students collectively pursue their respective scholarly activities: It must transform from within the *faculties* and the *disciplines.*

The faculty will only be a faculty if it develops into a capacity for spiritual legislation [*geistiger Gesetzgebung*] that is rooted in the essence of that faculty's particular science, so that it can give shape to the forces of existence that beset *it* and fit them into the *one* spiritual world of the people.

The discipline will only be a discipline if it places itself from the very outset within the realm of this spiritual legislation, thereby bringing down disciplinary barriers and overcoming the musty and false character of higher education as superficial professional training.

At the moment when the faculties and disciplines get the essential and simple questions of their existence underway, the teachers and students will already be in the embrace of the *same* ultimate necessities and afflictions attendant to existence [*Dasein*] as a people and a state.

Giving form to the original essence of science, however, demands such a degree of rigorousness, responsibility, and superior patience that by comparison, for example, the conscientious observance or the zealous modification of fixed ways of doing things hardly matters.

If, however, the Greeks needed three centuries just to put the *question* of what knowledge is on proper footing and on a secure path, then *we* certainly cannot think that the elucidation and unfolding of the essence of the German university can occur in the present or coming semester.

But there is, to be sure, *one thing* that we do know which follows from the essence of science as indicated above, and that is that the German university can only attain form [116] and power when the three forms of service—labor service, military service, and knowledge service—come together primordially into *one* formative force.

That is to say, the teachers' will to essence must awaken to the simplicity and breadth of the knowledge of the essence of science and grow strong. The students' will to essence must force itself upwards into the highest clarity and discipline of knowledge, and must incorporate in a demanding and determining way the cooperative knowledge about the people and its state. Both wills must prepare themselves for mutual struggle [*Kampf*]. All capacities of will and thought, all strengths of the heart, and all capabilities of the body must be developed *through* struggle, must be intensified *in* struggle, and must remain preserved *as* struggle.

We choose the knowing struggle [*wissenden Kampf*] of those who question, and declare with Carl von Clausewitz: "I renounce the foolish hope for salvation by the hand of chance."

The community of teachers and students in struggle will, however, only transform the German university into the site of spiritual legislation and realize it in a concentrated center for the highest service to the people in its state if the teachers and students arrange their existence to be simpler, tougher, and more modest in its needs than that of all other comrades [*Volksgenossen*]. All leadership must allow its following to have its own strength. All following carries resistance [*Widerstand*] within it. This essential opposition between leading and following must neither be covered over nor, indeed, obliterated altogether.

Struggle alone will keep this opposition open and implant within the entire body of teachers and students that fundamental mood [*Grundstimmung*] out of which self-limiting self-assertion will empower resolute self-reflection to true self-governance.

Do we will the essence of the German university, or do we not will it? It is up to us whether and how extensively we endeavor, wholeheartedly and [117] not just casually, to bring about self-reflection and self-assertion, or whether we—with the best intentions—merely alter the old arrangements and add some new ones. No one will prevent us from doing this.

But neither will anyone ask us whether we will it or not when the spiritual strength of the West fails and the West starts to come apart at the seams—when this expended, illusory culture collapses into itself, pulling all forces into confusion and allowing them to suffocate in madness.

Whether such a thing does or does not occur depends solely on whether we as a historical-spiritual people will ourselves, still and again, or whether we will ourselves no longer. Each individual *has a part* in deciding this, even if, and precisely if, he evades this decision.

But it is our will that our people fulfill its historical mission.

We will ourselves. For the young and youngest power of the people, which is already reaching beyond us, *has* already *decided* this.

We can only fully understand the glory and greatness of this new beginning, however, if we carry within ourselves that deep and broad thoughtfulness upon which the ancient wisdom of the Greeks drew in uttering the words:

τὰ ... μεγάλα πάντα ἐπισφαλῆ ...

"All that is great stands in the storm . . ." (Plato, *Republic* 497d9)

EIGHT

Hölderlin and the Essence of Poetry

—⟨ɷɷⱺ⟩—

2 April 1936

In memory of
Norbert von Hellingrath
who was killed in action on
14 December 1916.[1]

The five guiding phrases:

1. Poetizing: "This most innocent of occupations." (III, 377)
2. "That is why language, the most dangerous of goods, has been given to humans . . . so that they may bear witness to what they are . . ." (IV, 246)
3. "Much has the human experienced.
   Named many of the heavenly ones,
   Since we have been a conversation
   And can hear from one another." (IV, 343)

Previously translated by Keith Hoeller in *Elucidations of Hölderlin's Poetry* (Amherst, N.Y.: Humanity Books, 2000), 51–65. Though I have consulted Hoeller's version in preparing the present chapter, much of it has been newly translated from the original. Throughout this chapter, Heidegger cites the historical-critical edition of Hölderlin's works begun by Norbert von Hellingrath and completed by Friedrich Seebass and Ludwig von Pigenot: *Hölderlins Sämtliche Werke*, 6 vols. (Berlin: 1923, 1943).

Bracketed numbers refer to the pagination of GA 4; the chapter opens at page 33.—Tr.

1. [Heidegger saw himself as extremely indebted to Hellingrath, who was one of the first to critically edit and compile Hölderlin's writings. Hellingrath died at age twenty-eight at the Battle of Verdun.—Tr.]

4. "But what remains is founded by the poets." (IV, 63)
5. "Full of merit, yet poetically, the human
   Dwells on this earth." (IV, 25)

Why choose Hölderlin's work in order to show the essence of poetry? Why not Homer or Sophocles, why not Virgil or Dante, why not Shakespeare or Goethe? After all, the essence of poetry has also been realized in the works of these poets, indeed even more richly than in Hölderlin's creation, which broke off so early and abruptly.

That may be. And yet Hölderlin, and he alone, is chosen. But can one even glean the general essence of poetry from the work of a single poet? We can only attain what is general, i.e., what is valid for many, through a comparative study. For this, one would need a presentation of the greatest possible diversity of poems and kinds of poetry. Hölderlin's poetry is only one among many others. In no way can it solely serve to [34] determine the essence of poetry. Thus our project is already mistaken from the outset. Certainly—as long as we understand the "essence of poetry" to mean that which is gathered together in a universal concept, and is then applicable in equal fashion to all poetry. But this sort of universal that is equally valid for every particular is always something indifferent, that "essence" that can never become essential. But we precisely seek this essentiality of the essence, that which will force us to decide whether we shall take poetry seriously in the future; whether—and how—we provide the conditions for standing within poetry's sphere of influence.

Hölderlin has not been chosen because his work, as one among many, realizes the universal essence of poetry, but rather for the sole reason that Hölderlin's poetry is sustained by the poetic vocation of putting the essence of poetry itself into poetry. For us, Hölderlin is in a preeminent sense *the poet's poet*. For that reason, he forces the decision.

But—to write poetry about the poet, is that not an indication of misguided self-reflection and at the same time the confession of a lack of worldly content? To write poetry about the poet, is that not clueless exaggeration, something remote and a dead end?

May what follows serve as an answer. Certainly, the path by which we reach the answer is an emergency route [*Notweg*]. Here we cannot, as one ideally should, interpret Hölderlin's individual poems at a continuous pace. Instead, we will merely ponder five of the poet's key phrases on poetry. The specific order of these phrases, as well as their inner connection, should present us with the essential essence of poetry.

[1]

In a letter to his mother dated January 1799, Hölderlin calls poetizing "this most innocent of all occupations" (III, 377). How is it the "most innocent"? Making poetry appears in the [35] unassuming form of *play*. It freely invents its world of images and remains lost in thought in the realm of the imagined. This play thus evades the seriousness of decisions, which make one guilty either way. Poetizing is thus completely harmless. And at the same time it is without effect, for it remains mere saying and speaking: that has nothing in common with the deed, which immediately intervenes in what is real and changes it. Poetizing is like a dream, not reality; a play with words, not the seriousness of action. Poetry is harmless and ineffectual. What is less dangerous than mere language? By taking poetry as the "most innocent of all occupations," however, we have not yet grasped its essence. Poetry creates its works in the realm and with the "material" of language. What does Hölderlin say about language? Let us listen to the second of the poet's phrases.

[2]

In a fragmentary draft from the same period as the letter just quoted (1800), the poet states:

> But the human dwells in huts, and wraps himself in the modest garment, for more intimate is / also more attentive, and it is his understanding that he maintains the spirit like the priestess does the heavenly flame. And that is why free will / and the higher power to command and to accomplish have been given to him, who is like the gods, and that is why the most dangerous of goods, language, has been given to humans, so that in creating, destroying, perishing, and returning to the everliving master and mother, he may bear witness to what he is / to have inherited, learned from her, her most divine gift, all-sustaining love. (IV, 246)

Language, the realm of the "most innocent of all occupations," is "the most dangerous of goods." How do these two fit together? Let us put this question aside for the time being, and consider three preliminary questions: 1. Whose good is language? 2. How is it the [36] most dangerous good? 3. In what sense is it a good at all?

First, let us note where this phrase about language is written: in the draft of a poem that is supposed to say who the human is, in contrast to the other beings of nature; the rose, the swans, the stag in the forest are mentioned (IV, 300 and 385). That is why, in distinguishing [us humans] from the other living beings, the fragment begins: "But the human dwells in huts."

Who is the human? The one who must bear witness to what he is. To bear witness means, on the one hand, to testify; but at the same time it means to stand, in the testimony, for what is testified. The human is *who* he *is* precisely in bearing witness to his own existence [*Daseins*]. This attestation does not mean a subsequent and additional expression of human being; rather, it forms a part of human existence. But what is the human supposed to testify to? His belongingness to the earth. This belongingness consists in the fact that the human is the inheritor, and the learner of all things. But these very things stand in opposition. What keeps things apart in opposition and at the same time joins them together, Hölderlin calls "intimacy." The attestation of belonging to this intimacy occurs through the creation of a world and through its rise, as well as its destruction and decline. The attestation of human being, and thus its proper accomplishment, occurs through the freedom of the decision. The latter takes hold of what is necessary, and places itself in the bindingness of the highest demand. Attesting to the belongingness to beings as a whole occurs as history. But in order for history to be possible, humans have been given language. It is a human good.

But how is language the "most dangerous of goods"? It is the danger of all dangers, because it first creates the possibility of danger. Danger is the threat to Being by beings. Now it is only by virtue of language that humans are even exposed to something manifest, which *as* beings beset and inflame the human in [37] his existence, and as nonbeings deceive and disappoint him. Language first creates the manifest site of the threat to Being and of confusion, and thus the first possibility of the loss of Being, i.e., danger. But language is not only the danger of dangers, it necessarily harbors within itself a continual danger to itself. Language is tasked with making beings as such manifest in works and with preserving them. In language, the most pure and most concealed, as well as the confused and common, can be expressed. Indeed even the essential word, if it is to be understood and become the common property of all, must make itself common. Accordingly, another of Hölderlin's fragments states: "You spoke to the divinity, but this you have all forgotten, that the first fruits belong to the gods, not the mortals. The fruit must first become more common, more everyday, then it will be suitable for mortals" (IV, 238). The pure and the common are both equally something said. As word, the word thus never offers an immediate guarantee as to whether it is an essential word or a deception. On the contrary—an essential word in its simplicity often looks like an inessential one. And on the other hand, what in its finery gives the appearance of the essential is only something recited and repeated. Thus language must constantly place itself in an appearance that it itself creates, and so endanger what is most its own: the genuine utterance.

In what sense, now, is this most dangerous thing a "good" for humans? Language is their property. It is at their disposal for the communication of experiences, decisions, and moods. Language serves to facilitate understanding. As a tool appropriate for this purpose, it is a "good." But the essence of language is not exhausted by being a means of understanding. This determination does not hit upon its proper essence, but rather merely points to a consequence of this essence. Language is not merely one tool among many others that the human possesses; rather, [38] language first grants the possibility of standing in the midst of the openness of beings. Only where there is language is there world—that is, the constantly changing cycle of decision and work, of act and responsibility, but also of caprice and noise, decay and confusion. Only where world holds sway is there history. Language is a good in a more primordial sense. It holds good for the fact—i.e., it guarantees—that humans can *be* historical. Language is not a tool at one's disposal, but instead that event [*Ereignis*] that has the highest possibility of human being at its disposal. We must first of all assure ourselves of this essence of language, in order to truly comprehend the domain of poetry and thus poetry itself. How does language occur? To find an answer to this question, let us ponder a third phrase of Hölderlin's.

[3]

We come across this phrase within a long and convoluted draft of the unfinished poem that begins "Conciliator, you who never believed . . ." (IV, 162ff. and 339ff.):

> Much has the human experienced.
> Named many of the heavenly ones,
> Since we have been a conversation
> And can hear from one another. (IV, 343)

From these verses, let us first select the one that immediately fits into the context so far: "Since we have been a conversation . . ." We—human beings —are a conversation. Human Being is grounded in language; but this first properly occurs in *conversation*. This, however, is not just one way in which language takes place; language is only essential as conversation. What we usually mean by [39] "language," namely a stock of words and rules of combination, is only a foreground of language. But what does "conversation" mean? Obviously, speaking with one another about something. In this, language mediates the coming-together. Yet Hölderlin says: "Since we have been a conversation and can hear from one another." Being able to hear is not merely a consequence of speaking with one another, but is instead the condition for this. Even being able to hear is itself in turn based upon the possibility of the word, and needs it. Being able to talk and being able to hear are equally originary. We are a conversation—and that means we are able to hear from one another. We are a conversation, and that also always means: We are *one* conversation. The unity of a conversation, however, consists in one and the same thing being manifest in the essential word, something we agree upon, and on the basis of which we are united and thus properly ourselves. The conversation and its unity support our existence.

But Hölderlin does not simply say "we are a conversation"—rather: "Since we have been a conversation . . ." Even where humans' ability to speak is present and exercised, the essential event of language—conversation— does not necessarily occur. Since when have we been a conversation? If there is to be *one* conversation, the essential word must remain related to what is one and the same. Without this relation, even an argument is impossible. But the one and the same can only be manifest within the light of something that remains and is constant. However, constancy and endurance come to appearance only when persistence and presence light up. But this occurs at the moment when time opens itself up in its extensions. Ever since the human placed himself in the presence of something enduring, he can expose himself to the changeable, to what comes and goes; for only the persistent is changeable. Only since "torrential time" has been torn open into present, [40] past, and future, has it become possible to agree upon something that lasts. We have been *one* conversation since the time when there "is time." Ever since time arose and was brought to stand, we *are* historical. Both—to be *one* conversation and to be historical—are equally ancient, belong together, and are the same.

Since we have been a conversation—humans have experienced much and named many of the gods. Ever since language has properly occurred as a conversation, the gods have spoken and a world has appeared. But again it is important to see that the presence of the gods and the appearance of the world are not a consequence of language's occurrence, but are instead simultaneous with it. And this to the extent that it is precisely in naming the gods and in the world becoming word that the authentic conversation, which we ourselves are, consists.

But the gods can only speak if they themselves address us and make a claim upon us. The word that names the gods is always a response to such a claim. This response always stems from the responsibility of a destiny. Only through the gods bringing our existence [*Dasein*] to language do we enter the realm of the decision whether to promise ourselves to the gods or deny ourselves to them.

Only now can we fully judge what it means to say: "Since we have been a conversation . . ." Since the gods have brought us into the conversation, there is time, since then the ground of our existence has been a conversation. The statement that language is the highest event [*Ereignis*] of human existence thus receives its interpretation and justification.

But at once the question arises: How does this conversation that we are begin? Who performs this naming of the gods? Who, in torrential time, takes hold of something enduring and brings it to stand in the word? Hölderlin tells us with the secure simplicity of the poet. Let us listen to a fourth phrase.

[4]

[41] This phrase forms the conclusion to the poem "Remembrance" and reads: "But what remains is founded by the poets" (IV, 63). This line sheds light upon our question concerning the essence of poetry. Poetry is a founding by the word and in the word. What is founded in this way? What remains. But can what remains even be founded? Is it not that which is always already present? No! Precisely what remains must be held in place to secure it against being torn away; what is simple must be wrested from chaos, measure must be opposed to excess. What supports and reigns through beings as a whole must come into the open. Being must be opened, so that beings might appear. But precisely this that remains is what is fleeting. "Thus everything heavenly is quickly passing; but not in vain" (IV, 163ff.). But that this may remain, it is "entrusted to the care and service of those who make poetry" (IV, 145). The poet names the gods and names all things with respect to what they are. This naming does not consist in something previously known being merely furnished with a name; rather, by speaking the essential word, the poet's naming first nominates beings to that

which they are. Thus they become known *as* beings. Poetry is the founding of Being in words. What remains is therefore never drawn from the transitory. What is simple can never be directly seized from the chaotic. The measure does not lie in excess. We never find the foundation in the abyss. Being is never a being. But because Being and the essence of things can never be calculated and derived from what is present at hand, things must be freely created, posited, and bestowed. Such free bestowal is founding.

Through the gods being named, and the essence of things coming to expression so that they first shine forth, humans' Dasein is brought into a firm relation and placed on a ground. The poet's saying is not only a founding in the sense of a free [42] bestowal, but at the same time in the sense of the firm grounding of human existence in its ground. If we comprehend this essence of poetry, that it is the founding of Being in words, then we can have an inkling of the truth of the words that Hölderlin spoke long after he had been taken away into the protection of the night of madness.

[5]

We find this *fifth* guiding phrase in the great and simultaneously vast poem which begins:

> In lovely blueness blooms the
> Steeple with its metal roof. (VI, 24ff.)

Here Hölderlin says (line 32ff.):

> Full of merit, yet poetically, the human
> Dwells on this earth.

Whatever humans bring about and pursue is gained and earned through their own efforts. "Yet," Hölderlin says in sharp opposition, all of this does not touch the essence of their dwelling on this earth, it does not reach into the ground of human existence [*menschlichen Daseins*]. Human existence is "poetic" in its ground. But we now understand poetry as the founding naming of the gods and of the essence of things. To "dwell poetically" means to stand in the presence of the gods and to be struck by the essential nearness of things. Existence [*Dasein*] is "poetic" in its ground, which simultaneously means that, as founded (grounded), it is not something earned, but is rather a gift.

Poetry is not just an ornamental accompaniment to existence, not just a temporary enthusiasm, and certainly not excitement or amusement. Poetry is the sustaining ground of history, and is therefore also not merely an appearance of culture, above all not the mere "expression" of a "cultural soul."

That our existence is poetic in its ground can also not mean, in the end, that it is really just a harmless game. But [43] does Hölderlin himself, in the first key phrase we cited, not call poetry "this most innocent of all occupations"? How does that fit together with the essence of poetry we have now unfolded? This brings us back to the question that we first put aside. By answering this question now, we shall try at the same time to summarize, to bring before our inner eyes, the essence of poetry and of the poet.

The first result was that the domain of poetry is language. The essence of poetry must therefore be grasped from the essence of language. But it later became apparent that poetry is the founding naming of Being and of the essence of all things—not an arbitrary saying, but that whereby everything first steps into the open, which we then discuss and talk about in everyday language. Hence poetry never takes language as a material at its disposal, but instead first makes language possible. Poetry is the primordial language of a historical people. Thus the essence of language must be understood out of the essence of poetry, and not the other way around.

The ground of human existence is conversation as the proper occurrence of language. But the primordial language is poetry as the founding of Being. Yet language is "the most dangerous of goods." Thus poetry is the most dangerous creation—and at the same time the "most innocent of all occupations."

In fact—only if we think these two conceptions together as one do grasp the full essence of poetry.

But is poetry even the most dangerous of creations? In a letter to a friend, written immediately before his departure for his last journey to France, Hölderlin writes:

> O friend! The world lies before me more brightly and more serious than before! I am pleased with what happens, I am pleased as when in the summer "the old holy father with calm hand shakes the holy lightning flashes out of the red clouds."[2] For among all that I can see of God, this sign has become my chosen one. I used to be able to rejoice over a new truth, a better view [44] of what is above us and around us, but now I fear that I shall end like old Tantalus, who received more from the gods than he could digest. (V, 321)

---

2. [Hölderlin appears here to be misquoting Goethe's poem, "Grenzen der Menschheit": "Wenn der uralte / Heilige Vater / Mit gelassener Hand / Aus rollenden Wolken / Segnende Blitze / Über die Erde sät."—Tr.]

The poet is exposed to the god's lightning flashes. This is spoken of in that poem that we consider to be the purest poem on the essence of poetry, and which begins:

> As when on a holiday, to see the field
> A countryman goes out, at morning ... (IV, 151ff.)

Here the last stanza states:

> Yet it behooves you, the poets, to stand
> Bare-headed beneath God's thunderstorms,
> To grasp the Father's ray, itself, with your own hands
> And to offer to the people
> The heavenly gift shrouded in song.

And one year later, after Hölderlin had returned to his mother's house as if struck by madness, he wrote to the same friend, recalling his stay in France: "The mighty element, the fire of the heavens and the stillness of humans, their life in nature and their confinedness and contentment, moved me continually, and as one says of heroes, I can well say of myself that Apollo has struck me" (V, 327). The excessive brightness drove the poet into darkness. Do we need any further testimony to the highest danger of his "occupation"? The poet's own proper destiny says it all. Hölderlin's verse in *Empedocles* sounds like a premonition:

> ... He must
> Leave on time, through whom the spirit spoke. (III, 154)

And yet poetry is the "most innocent of all occupations." So Hölderlin writes in his letter, not only to spare his mother, but because he knows that this harmless [45] exterior belongs to the essence of poetry, just as the valley belongs to the mountain; for how else could this most dangerous work be carried out and preserved, if the poet were not "cast out" (*Empedocles,* III, 191) of ordinary life and protected *from* it by the appearance of the harmlessness of his occupation?

Poetry looks like a game and yet is not. A game indeed brings people together, but in such a manner that each forgets himself. In poetry, conversely, humans are gathered into the ground of their existence. There they come to rest; not, of course, the illusory rest of inactivity and emptiness of thought, but to that infinite rest in which all powers and relations are quickened (cf. the letter to his brother, 1 January 1799, III, 368–369).

Poetry awakens the appearance of the unreal and of the dream over against the tangible and loud reality in which we believe ourselves to be at home. And yet, on the contrary, what the poet says and undertakes to be is truly real. Thus Panthea, with the clear knowledge of a friend, acknowledges of Empedocles (III, 78):

... To be himself, that is
Life and we others are only the dream of it.

Thus the essence of poetry seems to vacillate with the look of its own exterior, and yet stands firm. After all, it is itself, in its essence, a founding— that is: firm grounding.

To be sure, every founding remains a free gift, and Hölderlin hears it said: "Poets be free, like swallows" (I, 168). This freedom, however, is not unrestrained caprice and stubborn desire, but supreme necessity.

As the founding of Being, poetry is bound in a *twofold* sense. In viewing this most intimate law, we first grasp its essence in its entirety.

Poetizing is the originary naming of the gods. But the poetic word first obtains its naming power when the gods themselves bring us to speak. How do the gods speak? [46]

... and hints are,
From time immemorial, the language of the gods. (IV, 135)

The poet's saying is the intercepting [*Auffangen*] of these hints, in order to pass them on to his people. This intercepting of the hints is a reception, and yet at the same time a new giving; for in the "first signs" the poet already catches sight of the completed whole, and boldly puts what he has seen into his word, in order to predict what is not yet fulfilled. Thus

... the bold spirit flies, like the eagle
Ahead of the thunderstorm, prophesying
The coming of his gods. (IV, 135)

The founding of Being is bound to the gods' hints. And at the same time the poetic word is only the interpretation of the "voice of the people." That is what Hölderlin calls the tales [*die Sagen*] in which a people is mindful of its belongingness to beings as a whole. But frequently this voice falls silent and exhausts itself. It is not at all capable of saying by itself what is authentic—it needs those who interpret it. The poem titled "Voice of the People" has been preserved for us in two versions. Above all, the final stanzas are different, yet in such a way that they compliment each other. In the first version, the conclusion reads:

> Because it is pious, for love of the heavenly
> I honor the voice of the people, the calm,
> But for the sake of gods and humans,
> May it not always rest too willingly. (IV, 141)

We add the second version:

> ... and sayings
> Are indeed good, for they are a memory
> To the highest, yet there is also a need of
> One to interpret the holy sayings. (IV, 144)

Thus the essence of poetry is joined into the laws of the hints of the gods and the [47] voice of the people—laws that strive both apart from, and toward each other. The poet himself stands between the former—the gods—and the latter—the people. He is one who has been cast out—out into that *between*, between gods and humans. But only first in this between is it decided who the human is and where his existence settles. "Poetically the human dwells on this earth."

Unexposed and ever more safe, from the richness of the images pressing on him, and ever more simply, Hölderlin dedicated his poetic word to this realm of the between. This compels us to say that he is the poet's poet.

Can we still believe that Hölderlin is trapped in an empty and excessive self-reflection, owing to the lack of worldly content? Or do we recognize that this poet, because of an excess of impetus, poetically thinks through to the ground and center of being? It is to *Hölderlin* himself that we must apply the verse which he said of Oedipus in that late poem "In lovely blueness blooms...":

> Perhaps King Oedipus has
> One eye too many. (VI, 26)

Hölderlin puts into poetry the very essence of poetry—but not in the sense of a timelessly valid concept. This essence of poetry belongs to a specific time. But not in such a way that it merely conforms to that time as some time already existing. Rather, by founding anew the essence of poetry, Hölderlin first determines a new time. It is the time of the gods who have fled *and* of the god who is coming. It is the *time of need* because it stands in a double lack and a double nothing: in the no-longer of the gods who have fled and in the not-yet of what is to come.

The essence of poetry that Hölderlin founds is historical in the highest degree, because it anticipates an historical time. As an historical essence, however, it is the only true essence.

The time is needy, and thus its poet is overabundant—so abundant that he would often like to languish in the thought of those who have been, and in expectation of [48] the one who is coming, and would simply like to sleep in this apparent emptiness. But he holds firm in the nothingness of this night. By thus remaining with himself in the highest individuation of his vocation, he brings about truth vicariously and therefore truly for his people. The seventh stanza of the elegy "Bread and Wine" (IV, 123ff.) proclaims this. It states poetically what here can only be discussed thoughtfully.

> But friend, we come too late. Indeed, the gods are living,
> But above our heads, up in another world.
> Endlessly there they act and seem little to care
> Whether we live or not, so much do the heavenly spare us.
> For a fragile vessel is not always able to hold them,
> Only at times can the human bear divine fullness.
> Henceforth life is a dream about them. But wandering astray
> Helps, like sleep, and need and night make us strong,
> Until heroes enough have grown in the strong cradle,
> Hearts, as once, resemble the heavenly in strength.
> Thundering then they come. Meanwhile, I often think it is
> Better to sleep than so to be without friends,
> So to be always waiting, and what to do and say in the meanwhile
> I do not know and what are poets for in a time of need?
> But they are, you say, like those holy priests of the wine-god
> Who traveled from land to land in holy night.

NINE

On the Origin of the Work of Art

First Version

=⟋⟋⟍=

1935

What can be said here in the frame of an address about the origin of the artwork is little enough, much about it perhaps strange, but most of it exposed to misinterpretations. Beyond all this, however, only *one thing* should matter, namely: to prepare a transformed basic relation of our Dasein to art, while recognizing what has long been thought and said with regard to the determination of the essence of art.

We are familiar with artworks. Buildings and images, sound compositions and linguistic works are placed and housed here and there. The works stem from the widest-ranging ages; they belong to our own people and to foreign peoples. We usually also know the "origin" of artworks that are

---

This is the first published translation of this piece. For background information on this selection see Dr. Hermann Heidegger's note in supplement 3, "Sources for the Present Volume."

Bracketed numbers refer to the pagination of *Heidegger Studies* 5; the chapter opens at page 5. — Tr.

present [6] in such fashion; for where else should an artwork have its origin but through the artist's presentation [*Hervorbringung*]? The latter entails two processes: first the formulation of the artistic thought in the imagination, and then the transfer of the thought into the artistic product. Each is equally weighted, even if the formulation of the artistic thought remains the precondition for its execution and thus is "more original." The formulation of the thought is a purely intellectual process which, as a "mental experience," can be described. This contributes to the psychology of the presentation of artistic products. Such a contribution can be quite informative, but it *never* provides an illumination of the origin of the artwork. Why not? To begin with, because "origin" is here simply equated with "cause" of the presence-at-hand of artworks. One takes this direction of inquiry toward the "origin" as so self-evident, however, because one does not at all proceed from the *work* of art, but rather from the artistic product as a *piece of art*. To be sure, it remains correct to say that the artistic structure is created out of the "intellectual struggle" of the artist. The presentation is *his* competent achievement. This becomes the "expression" of his "personality," which "lives itself out" in the presentation and "frees itself from its storm of emotion." Thus, the artwork is always also the artist's creation. But this createdness does not constitute the work-being of the work. That is so little the case that the presentation's ownmost will yearns to let the work be. Especially in *great* art—and that is all we are speaking of here—the artist remains something trivial over against the reality of the work, almost like a passage that destroys itself in creating.

The question concerning the origin of the *work* must first of all insist on really beginning with the artwork as such. To this end, it is obviously necessary to seek out the artwork where it is already detached from the presentation and *present in itself*. We come across artworks in art collections and art exhibitions. They are housed there. We find artworks in public places and in individuals' homes. They are placed there. The works stand in the open; for the study of art history determines their historical heritage and membership. Art connoisseurs and art writers describe their content and explain their "qualities"—as one says—and thus make the works accessible for the communal and individual enjoyment of art. Those who like art and those who love it promote the collection of artworks. Officials take over the care and preservation of the artworks. Art commerce provides an economy. A diverse activity goes on around the artworks at hand, one which we simply and without any contemptuous meaning call the *art business*. It mediates the way to the artworks themselves. At least, insofar as they are now detached from the relation to presentation through artists. The mere ignoring of this relation, however, does not yet guarantee that we now experience the work-being of the work—for the art business, after all, [7] in turn places the works in another relation, namely that of the activity surrounding the works. The work encounters us here in the way that it is an *object* within the art business that cares, explains, and enjoys. But such *object-being* cannot in turn be equated with the work-being of the work.

Let us step before works of great art—before the Aegina sculptures in the Munich collection,[1] before the *Bärbele* of Strasbourg in Frankfurt's Liebighaus,[2] or into the realm of Sophocles' *Antigone*. The works are transposed from their proper location and space. Despite all status and so-called "quality" and impressiveness, their work-being is nevertheless no longer what matters. As well-kept and comprehensible as they may still be, the transposition into the collection, the appropriation into traditional preservation, has withdrawn them from their world. However, even if we make an effort to reverse or prevent such transpositions of the works—for instance by visiting the Temple of Paestum in its location, and the Bamberg Cathedral in its city square—the world of the preserved works has decayed. We can perhaps trace it and imagine additions to it through historical recollection, but world-withdrawal and world-decay can never be reversed. To be sure, we can experience the works as "expressions" of their age, as testimony to a former splendor and might of a people. We can "be inspired" by our "magnificent German cathedrals." And yet, world-decay and world-withdrawal have broken their work-being.

The object-being of the works in the art business and the createdness of the artist's works are both possible determinations of work-being. But the former is a consequence, the latter a co-condition of work-being. Not only do these not exhaust work-being: taken in themselves they even prevent the sight and knowledge of it.

As long as we do not grasp the work in its work-being, however, the question concerning the origin of the work of art remains without an adequately secured approach.

But why, then, is the determination of the artwork's work-being so difficult? Because the work-being determines itself out of that in which the work is grounded. And according to the work's essence and necessity, *this*

---

1. [The pedimental sculptures from the Temple of Aphaia at Aegina (c. 500 BC), housed at the Glyptothek in Munich since 1830.—Tr.]

2. [Nikolaus Gerhaert von Leyden's portrait bust, *Bärbele von Ottenheim* (1464).—Tr.]

ground alone is the origin of the work. The origin does not lie in the artist as the cause of the createdness of the work. The origin of the artwork is art. Art does not exist because there are artworks, but rather the contrary: because and insofar as art occurs, the necessity of the work exists. And the necessity of the work is the artist's initial ground of possibility.

For the time being, these are merely assertions. They place us in a strange position. The question about the origin of the art*work* has to proceed from the work-being of the work. But this work-being already determines itself out of the origin. What we seek—the origin—we must already have; and what we have, we must first seek. We are moving in a *circle*. But that may always count—at least in philosophy—as a sign that [8] the inquiry is in order. The difficulty—that we are ready to begin only at the end of the explanations—is unavoidable.

We can only join in the accomplishment of the circular movement of our inquiry through a leap [*Sprung*]. And in the end, this leap is the only way of knowing adequately about *the* origin [*Ursprung*] into which we inquire. So everything hinges on us making the right jumping-off [*Absprung*] for this leap. This jumping-off consists, according to the structure of these considerations, in gaining the adequate preconception of the art*work* in its work-being.[3]

The Artwork as a Work

The previous comments served to deter misinterpretations of the work-being of the work as either a being-produced by the artist or an object-being for the art business. Usually, both interpretations are even combined. In these cases, the artwork always still stands in relation to something else, and is not grasped from itself. But can we even apprehend anything about it, apart from any relation? At the very least, this apprehension is then always itself a relation. Let us leave out this fundamental question here. Another question is more essential now with regard to our task: Does not the attempt at *separating* the work out from all relation to other things outside of it act precisely contrary to the essence of the *work itself*? To be sure, for the work wants to be disclosed *as a work*. It is not disclosed as an afterthought; disclosedness is not simply intended *along with* the work, but rather work-being means being-disclosed. Yet the question is what disclosedness [*Offenbarkeit*] and publicity [*Öffentlichkeit*] mean here. Not the

---

3. [Reading *Werksein* instead of *Werkstein*.—Tr.]

audience that drifts around in the art business. In general, what the work "affects" by standing out into the open is never something at hand that it must simply hit like a fixed target. Rather, the work's publicity is first effected [er*wirkt*] in and through its disclosedness. Where an "audience" exists, the work's only relation to it is to destroy it. And the power for this destruction measures the greatness of an artwork.

To be sure, this relation to the open is essential to work-being; yet the relation, for its part, is grounded in the *basic trait* of work-being, which must now be brought to light incrementally.

We ask about the work—about how, in itself, it is with itself. The work is with itself insofar as it is at work. And the artwork is at work in its *setting-up*.

This term indicates a characteristic of the work-being of the work. Usually, with respect to the artwork, one speaks of "setting up" in the sense of housing a work in a collection or placing the work at an appropriate location. Setting-up in the sense of erecting [*Errichtung*] is essentially different from mere housing and installation: for instance, the building of a certain temple of Zeus; or the placement, the bringing-to-stand [9] of a certain statue of Apollo; or the performance of a tragedy that is simultaneously, but not only, the erecting of a poetic-linguistic work in the language of a people.

Such setting-up as *erecting* is dedication and praise. To dedicate means "to consecrate" in the sense that in the work-like presentation, the holy is opened as holy and the god is wrested into [*hereingerungen*][4] the openness of his presence. Praise belongs to dedication as appraisal of the dignity and splendor of the god. Dignity and splendor, which are opened in the work-like appraisal, are not properties beside, behind, and in addition to which the god stands; rather, he comes to presence in the dignity and splendor.

Every setting-up in the sense of the dedicating-praising erecting is always also establishment [*Erstellung*] as a kind of placement of the building and the statue, as a saying and naming within a language. However, the placing and housing of an "art product" is not, conversely, already a setting-up in the sense of establishing erecting; for this setting-up assumes that the work to be erected and set up *already* has *in itself* the essential characteristic of setting-up—is itself in its ownmost way something that *sets* up [*auf*stellend]. But how should we apprehend this actual "setting-up" that co-constitutes the work-being of the work?

The work in itself is a towering-up in which a world is broken open and

---

4. [In later versions of this essay, Heidegger emends this to "invoked" (*hereingerufen*).—Tr.]

placed to abide as opened. But what is this—a *world*? That can only be said in the roughest of intimations here. To begin on the defensive: World is not the accumulation of things at hand as the result of an accomplished, or merely thought, counting-over of these things. The world is just as little a sum of what is at hand as it is merely an imagined and thought *frame* for what is at hand. The world worlds—it surrounds our Dasein as an accompaniment wherein the leisure and haste, the remoteness and proximity, the expanse and narrowness of all beings remain open for us. We never encounter this accompaniment as an object, but instead it guidingly holds our doing and leaving-be entranced [*entrückt*] in a structure of references, out of which the beckoning grace and striking fate of the gods arrive—and remain absent. Even this absence is a way in which the world worlds. This guiding accompaniment can succumb to confusion and thus be a *non*-world [Un*welt*]. However, whether world or non-world, this guiding accompaniment—in all of its non-objectivity [*Ungegenständlichkeit*]—always remains more existent [*seiender*] than any graspable thing at hand in which we ordinarily believe ourselves to be at home. World is what is always out of the ordinary; in knowing it, we do not know what we know. (However, world [is] never an object that *stands* before us, but rather the non-object that we investigate.)

Now the work, as work, sets up, i.e., breaks the world open, and brings the opened to stand, to remain as worlding [*weltenden Verbleib*]. Work is at work in such a setting-up. An art product in the broader sense, which lacks this essential characteristic of setting up world, *is* no artwork, but rather a piece of art that is not at work on anything but simply flaunts an empty know-how and perhaps even makes some kind of "impression."

[10] On account of the fact that the real work toweringly omits a world and keeps it in reserve, it entails a superior refusal of what is commonly present-at-hand. The unordinary that surrounds every work is the seclusion into which the work sets itself back, setting up only its own world. Solely on the basis of this solitude, the work can loom out into the open—in the process of opening it—and bring about its own publicity. All things that are then incorporated into its realm become as if something inexhaustible and unavoidable had come over them.

On account of the fact that the work *is* a work—that it brings its world to an open towering—it first effects the task that it serves, first creates the space that it pervades, and first determines the place at which it comes to be erected. The setting-up as dedicating-praising erecting always grounds in the setting-up as the towering omission of a world. The latter can refuse the former, and the latter can get stuck in the inessential, mere installation of art products. The erected work, however, can fall into the fate of world-withdrawal and world-decay. To be sure, the work remains available, but it is no longer there—it is on the run. Yet this absence is not nothing, but instead the flight remains in the work that is present-at-hand—provided that it is a work—and this flight even still remains in the fragment (whereas the im-maculate preservation of a product does not yet make it a work).

Setting-forth [Herstellung] belongs, together with setting-up, to the work-being of the work. Yet at the outset, we specifically eliminated the presenta-tion through the artist, as work-being cannot be grasped from createdness, but createdness must rather be grasped from work-being. However, setting-forth and presenting do not mean the same thing. To distinguish the essen-tial characteristic of work-being that is named in this word, we begin with its ordinary meaning, as we did with "setting-up." Every work is, insofar as it exists, made of stone, wood, metal, color, tone, or language. This is the matter used in fabrication. It is brought into a form. This division of the artwork according to matter and form then goes on to produce further distinctions according to content, proportion, and shape. The use of these determina-tions of matter and form is possible at any time with respect to the artwork, is easy to grasp by anyone, and has therefore been generally accepted for centuries. And yet the determinations are not at all self-evident. They stem from the very precisely oriented explanation of beings that Plato and Aris-totle brought to bear at the end of Greek philosophy. According to this explanation, all beings each have their own look [Aussehen] that shows itself in their form. A being stands in such a form insofar as it is fabricated out of something into something. It can make itself into that which it is, as all growing things do; it can be produced. Beings as beings are always fab-ricated, things at hand. This interpretation of the Beyng [Seyn] of beings,[5] however, is not only not self-evident, it is also not even obtained from the experience of the artwork as a work of art, but rather [11] at most from the experience of the artwork as a produced thing. Thus, the division according to matter and form is applicable to the work at any time, but it is certainly also equally untrue any time one is supposed to grasp the work-being of the work through it.

If we thus distinguish the work-being of the work through a second

---

5. [Heidegger uses this term Seyn, an archaic spelling of Sein, from the 1930s onward. It denotes the difference between beings and their Being or beingness, and serves to call to mind a more originary meaning of Being than has been addressed in the history of metaphysics.—Tr.]

essential characteristic, which we call setting-forth, then this cannot mean that it is made out of a material. Instead, we mean that the work sets forth in its work-being, in a literal sense. But what does the work as such set forth, and how is it productive [*herstellend*]? Just as the work towers into its world, so it sinks back into the massiveness and weight of stone, into the hardness and gleam of metal, into the durability and flexibility of wood, into the luminosity and darkness of color, into the sounding of tone, and into the naming power of the word. Is all of this initially and only matter that is simply snatched up somewhere, used and exhausted in manufacture, and then disappears as mere matter through formation? Do not all of these things first come to light in the work? Are weight, gleam, luminosity, and sounding just materials that are "brought under control"? Or is it not the weight of the rock and the gleam of metals, the uprightness and pliability of the tree, the light of day and the dark of night, the rush of the flood and the murmuring in the boughs? What can we call it? Certainly not material as means to the production of something. We call the unison of this unsurpassable plenitude the *earth,* and do not mean by this a deposited mass of materials nor the planet, but rather the harmony [*Einklang*] of mountain and sea, of storms and air, of day and night, of trees and grass, of eagle and horse. This earth—what is it? That which unfolds constant plenitude, and yet always takes what is unfolded back into itself and retains it. The stone burdens, shows its weight, and thus precisely retreats into itself; the color lights up, and yet remains closed off; the tone rings out, and yet does not step into the open. What does step into the open is precisely this closing off, and that is the *essence of the earth.* All of its things flow together in mutual unison and yet: The same self-ignorance is in each of the things that closes itself off.

The work sets forth the earth, sets it into the open as that which closes itself off. The work does not consist of [*besteht nicht aus*] earth as if of a material, instead it endures [*besteht*] the earth, it withstands its closing-off. By supplying the earth, the work itself thus sets itself back into the earth as into its closing-off ground on which it rests; a ground which, since it is essential and always closing itself off, is an abyss. Both essential characteristics of the work-being of the work—setting-up as towering opening of a world, and setting-forth as retreating preservation of the earth that closes itself off—are not incidentally joined in the work, but stand in an essential interrelation. However, both characteristics are only what they are by being grounded in the actual basic trait of work-being, which needs to be named now.

[12] The world that the work toweringly keeps in reserve turns toward the earth as an opening accompaniment and does not tolerate anything closed off and hidden. The earth, however, which lets the work crowd in and set forth, wants, in its closing-off, to be everything and take everything back into itself. But precisely for this reason, the earth cannot dispense with the opened world, if the earth is itself to gleam forth in the full rush of the closing-off and retention of all things. And neither can the world disappear from the earth, if the world is to play itself *toward* something guidable as a worlding *accompaniment*. World is against earth and earth against world. They are in *strife*. But this strife is the intimacy of their mutual belongingness. In setting up the world and setting forth the earth, the work is the accomplishment of this strife. Here accomplishment does not mean suppression and conquest of the strife, but on the contrary means to bear out the strife as such, indeed to *be* this strife itself. The strife, however, is not just the *consequence* of the fact that world and earth come to oppose each other in setting-up and setting-forth. Rather, since the work is such contestation in the ground of its determination, it provokes and preserves this strife. Since contestation is the basic trait of work-being, setting-up and setting-forth are the essential traits of this being. Yet why must the work be such contestation in the ground of its Beyng? Wherein is the work-being of the work grounded, that it should relate to the work in this way? That is the question concerning the origin of the artwork. We will pursue it as soon as we have sufficiently established, first, *how* the work is entirely with itself as contestation, and second, *how it is actually at work*.

How does the contestation of this conflict happen? The dark harshness and the luring weight of the earth, its unresolved crowding-in and lighting-up, its unspoken concealment of all things—to sum up: The self-squandering hardness of its closing-off is only endured in again another hardness, and that is the hardness of the boundary in contour [*Umriß*], elevation [*Aufriß*], and layout [*Grundriß*].[6] Since that which secludes itself must be torn into the open, whatever performs this tearing must itself become the rift, the drawing boundary and jointure [*Fuge*]. Here, in the basic trait of work-being as contestation, lies the ground of necessity of what we call "form." Without pursuing the origin of "form" as such any further, we now ask something more urgent: What is accomplished in this contestation of the conflict?

---

6. [As it appears that Heidegger is alluding to the various dimensions of hard contours, I deviate here from Hofstadter's phrasing of "sketch" and "design" in his translation of the later version of this essay.—Tr.]

Insofar as the work is contestation, it removes the earth, while opening it, into a world. As a directing accompaniment, this world never moves into the earth. But the inserting removal moves the work forward and opens an openness that is the middle of *that* space in which the earth is closed off in a world-like manner, and the world is open in an earth-like manner. The work first grounds this space by opening it. The space is the openness of the there, into which things and humans come to stand in order to endure it.

The building which, as a temple, contains the shape of the god, simultaneously allows the latter to stand outward through the open portico into the area that is thereby first established as holy. Towering into a world and reaching back into the earth, the temple opens the there in which a people comes to itself, i.e., enters the decreeing power [*fügende Macht*] of its god. The earth first becomes world-like through the work, and as [13] such becomes a home [*Heimat*]. Similarly, there occurs in the work of language the naming and saying through which the Beyng of things first comes to be expressed, and through which the unspeakable enters the world with the speakable. In the poet's naming of this kind, a people's great concepts of beings as a whole are prefigured. The work of building, saying, and shaping exacts the there, the diffuse and rooted center in which, and out of which, a people grounds its historical dwelling—one becomes unhomely [*unheimisch*] among beings in order to get down to the uncanniness [*Unheimlichen*] of Beyng.

The essence of the work-being lies in the contestation of the conflict of setting-up and setting-forth, a contestation that, in itself, establishes the open closeness of earth and world.

With this essential determination of the work-being of the work, we have reached a standpoint that allows for a decision concerning the long-standing and familiar conception of the artwork as a *representation of something*. To be sure, the notion that the work is the imitation of something present at hand, in the sense of a depiction and copying, has gradually lost support. This by no means, however, overcomes the conception of the work as a representation, but rather only hides it. For whether the work is taken as "sensualization of the invisible" or, conversely, as symbolization of the visible, there lies in each of these determinations the unquestioned, assumed prejudice that the fundamental achievement of the work is to represent something.

The error in this interpretation of work-being stems from the same source as the one-sided and premature characterization of the work as a manufactured thing. According to this notion, the work is *initially*—and that always means "genuinely" here—a formed material like a shoe or a box. But at the same time, the work is now supposed to say something above and beyond what it initially is (ἄλλο ἀγορεύειν); the manufactured thing is thus brought together with something else (συμβάλλειν). Allegory and symbol provide the framing conceptions according to which, in many variations, the artwork is determined as a higher, manufactured structure.

Determinations that stem similarly from the distinction between matter and form lend further confusion to this idea of the artwork that is already errant in its beginning, for matter is equated with the *sensual*. As the "element of art," the non-sensual and supernatural come to be represented in it. If matter is the sensual, then it is taken to be what is *due* to the senses, what becomes accessible through them and their tools. Nothing is thereby said about the matter itself and its mode of belonging to the work-being. Furthermore, this determination of access to the supposed material is untrue; for the weight of a stone, the dullness of a color, the sound and stream of a series of words are certainly not experienced without the senses, but are never solely or genuinely experienced through them. The earth in its closing-off plenitude is just as sensual as non-sensual, if these characterizations say anything at all.

[14] Introducing the determination "sensual" hits just as little upon something essential about the work-being of the work as the determination of the material that goes along with this. But both are, within certain limits, correct and clear. Thus, the distinction between the sensual and the supernatural forthwith became the guiding thread for various allegorical and symbolic attempts to interpret the work, and art in general. Already in Plato—where the distinction between matter and form first becomes decisive for the entire subsequent Western position toward beings—matter, as the sensual, counts as inferior over against the higher, non-sensual idea. In the realm of Christian thinking the sensual, as inferior, at times becomes the adverse that must be overcome. The work thus provides the defeat of the sensual, as well as the elevation to the superior that is represented in it. Now whether this demotion of the sensual is accomplished or refused by the work, its achievement is always to represent something. But the artwork does not represent anything—and this for the simple and sole reason that there is nothing that it is supposed to represent. Since the work, in the contestation of the conflict between world and earth, opens each of these in their own way, it first exacts the open: the clearing in whose light we encounter beings as such, as if on the first day or—if they have already become everyday beings—in a changed manner. The work cannot represent

anything, because it basically never sets upon anything already standing and objective—provided, of course, that it is an artwork and not simply a product imitating one. The work never represents, but rather sets *up* the world and sets *forth* the earth, because it is the contestation of this conflict. By nature of this, the work remains at work, it *is* simply just itself—and nothing else.

But then how *is* the work genuinely? What kind of actuality does it possess?

Despite all sorts of variations, the interpretation of the actuality of the artwork to which Plato gave rise has remained dominant until today. In this development, the predetermination of the artwork as a manufactured thing was again decisive. Over against that which is present-at-hand from itself and which grows "from nature," what is manufactured by human hands is always something supplementary, especially when it imitates natural things. After all, these things are for their part already depictions of those exemplars that Plato calls "ideas." What is manufactured, and thus also the artwork, becomes an after-image of a depiction of an exemplar. And since the ideas represent what genuinely exists, what things in truth are, the work is merely a reverberation and actually not real. But if one tries, in opposition to Plato, to reverse this demotion of the actuality of the work in some way, then one must, over against the sensual make-up of the work, still deal with the argument that it represents a non-sensual, "intellectual" [*geistigen*] content. By virtue of this representation, then, the artwork is still "more ideal," more intellectual than the palpable things of everyday life. It raises itself out of their surroundings and is enveloped "by an air of spirit" [*Geisteshauch*]. In this way, the artwork withdraws from the actuality of the present-at-hand. The realm of the work is one of [15] appearance. This is not supposed to mean "of crude deception," a notion that is indeed close at hand; for the shaped marble block of a statue pretends to be a living body, when in actuality it is merely cold stone. The work is an appearance [*ein Schein*] because it is not itself what it represents; but it is an entitled appearance because in its representation, it brings to light something non-sensually intellectual.

In these interpretations of the artwork's actuality, the latter is shifted from one unreality into another. Sometimes the work is not yet as real as the things at hand, sometimes it is no longer as real as they are. Every time, the presence-at-hand of everyday things is decisive as the true reality; measured by this, the artwork is always unreal, no matter which way it is interpreted. And yet, the opposite of all this is true. The temple that towers up on a promontory or in a rocky valley, the statue that stands in the holy area, these works are not merely also present-at-hand, if need be, among all that remains: sea and land, springs and trees, eagles and snakes. Rather, they occupy the center in the cleared space of the appearance of things—they are more real than any thing, because each of these can first reveal itself as existing in the openness established by the work. Even if barely suspected of it, Hölderlin's poetry stands more actually in the language of our people than all theaters, movies, and rhymes—more actual, for example, than the buildings that house bookstores and libraries in which the palpable volumes of his collected works exist. The poetry is more actual than all of this because in it the un-tread center of the Germans' world and earth is prepared for them, and great decisions are kept in reserve.

Indeed, that is precisely the ownmost essence of the work-being—that it can never be measured by whatever is present-at-hand and supposedly genuinely real, but is instead itself the standard of what exists and does not exist. There are thus no current works that would be works of art, for only those works are works of art that are at work in such a way as to make and transform their time according to *themselves*. The work, as the opening center of the existence of historical Da-sein, is more actual than all remaining beings.

The solitude of every artwork is the indication that, in contesting the conflict, it towers into its world in the resting-back into its earth. Its standing-there is the restrained unobtrusiveness of standing-back-into-itself. That does not mean, however, that the work is extracted from common reality; this is impossible, because it is moved into this reality as its shattering [*Erschütterung*] and refutation. The more a work achieves what we call "effect," however, the more secluded it must be able to remain. If it lacks this power, then it is not a work of art.

These few, coarse remarks should indicate the work-being of the work from afar. The goal was to gain a preconception of the [16] artwork as a work. This preconception should guide us as we attempt a step upon the path of the question concerning the origin of the artwork.

Art as Origin of the Work

The characterization of the contestation of the conflict between world and earth as the fundamental characteristic of the work-being of the work has driven us to the question: *Why is contestation the essence of work-being?* We will presently take up this question, which has been put off until now. The anticipatory answer is: The work-being of the work has the basic trait of contestation because, and insofar as, the work is a work "of" art. Art "itself"? Where and how does it exist? Does art "itself" exist for itself at any time or any place? Yet before we ask *whether* and *how* art "itself" exists, we must clarify *what* it even is. Does the word "art" always merely remain an empty collective name for all that happens in the art business, or is it simply just each work itself? Neither. After all, we now no longer place the question "What is art?" into a vacuum. By asking, "Wherein does the work-being of the work have its ground?," we seek what actually happens in the contestation. The question is: What is primarily and finally at work in the work? By asking in such a manner, we know that we are moving in a circle.

The work—remaining with itself, stepping back into itself, and thus persisting—opens the "there," the center of the open, into whose clearing beings as such stand and show themselves. This open unites the breaking-open of a world and the self-secluding of the earth which, as secluding itself, steps into the open. World becomes unconcealed and earth closes itself off, but in the open. By virtue of the fact that this closeness of the open opposition of self-*concealing* and self-*revealing* [*Sichverbergenden und Sichentbergenden*] happens, what has been taken to be the real is revealed as something that does not exist. It comes to light—i.e., into the open—that concealment, disguise, and distortion of beings had prevailed. What thus happens in the contestation—the opening of the openness of the opposition between what is unconcealed and concealed, the discovery of veiling and disguise—this nested occurrence is the happening [*Geschehen*] of what we call *truth*. For the essence of truth does not consist in a statement's correspondence to a subject-matter. Rather, truth is this basic occurrence of opening up the openness of beings as such. Therefore, the concealed and the self-concealing (the mystery) are just as essential to truth as veiling and disguise and distortion—the un-truth.

In the work as such, the happening of truth is at work, i.e., the truth is set to work in the work. *The setting-into-work of truth, that is the essence of art.* *Truth,* we must always keep in mind, does not here mean some *single* truth, a singular true thing, such as a thought or principle, an idea or a value, that is somehow "represented" by the work. Instead, truth means the essence of what is true, the openness of all that is open. Of course, [17] we have hereby only made a first indication of the essence of art on the basis of the work-being. In art, truth occurs as the disclosure of beings. But it is not *yet* demonstrated that, and how, art is the *origin* of the work. In a preconception, we call an origin that type of ground that necessitates the work-being of the work in its dire necessity.

Art is the setting-into-work of truth. Then it is as follows: on the one hand, a work is present, and on the other, truth. And the latter is transplanted into the former through art. This is not at all the case; for the work does not exist prior to the truth, nor the latter prior to the work. Rather, by coming to work, truth happens. However—and this the decisive question— *why must truth come to work in order to occur?*

If truth first comes to work *with* the work and *in* the work, and is not at hand somewhere beforehand, then it must *become*. Whence does the opening-up of the openness of beings arise? Out of nothingness, perhaps? Indeed, if by non-being we mean that which is present-at-hand, which the work then refutes and shatters, so to speak, as the supposedly true being. Truth is never read off from that which is already at hand. Rather, the openness of beings occurs by being projected, by being *poetized*. All art is in essence poetry, i.e., the breaking-open of that open in which everything is otherwise than usual. By virtue of the poetic projecting, what prevailed until now and was usual becomes non-existent. Poetry is no wandering contrivance of something random, no drifting-off into the unreal. The open that poetry, as a project, opens up (projects ahead) and holds open, first allows beings as such to enter and brings them to shine [*Leuchten*].

Truth, as the openness, occurs in projecting—in poetry [*Dichtung*]. Art, as setting-into-work of truth, is essentially poetry. But is it not pure arbitrariness to trace architecture, visual art, and music back to "poetry" [*Poesie*]? It would be, if we wanted to interpret these arts from the standpoint of the art of language and as derivations from it. Yet the art of language, "poetry" [*Poesie*], is itself *only one* way of projecting, of poetry [*Dichtens*] in this determinate but *broader* sense. Nevertheless, the work of language—poetry in the narrower sense—has an *exceptional* place in the whole of art. One is accustomed to identifying a "language of forms" in artists and their works, in architecture and painting, for example. Why "language" in a building? Well language is, after all, "expression." And art is "expression," too. And therefore all art is "language." And since the art of language is called "poetry" [*Dichtung*], all art is poetry. The determination of the essence of art could not be more coarsely misinterpreted than through such "explanations." A demonstration of their untenability might clarify the actual sense of the statement that art is poetry.

Let it be admitted at the outset that the determination of art as expression has its correctness. The notion that art is expression is just as indisputable as the statement that the motorcycle is something that makes noise. Every mechanic would [18] laugh at such a determination of the essence of the machine. But no one laughs when it has been said for a long time that art is expression. Certainly, the Acropolis is an expression of the Greeks, and the Naumburg Cathedral is an expression of the Germans, and the "baa" is an expression of the sheep. Indeed, the artwork is simply a special expression, i.e., its own "baa"—probably. The work, however, is not a work because it is an expression. Rather, it is an expression because it is a work. The characterization of the work as expression not only contributes nothing to the determination of the work-being, but instead already forestalls any actual inquiry into this Beyng.

However, this characterization of art as expression, which is infinitely correct and yet lacking an essence, is not even applicable to language. To be sure, language serves the purposes of communication, conversation, and agreement. But it is not merely, and not in the first place, an oral and written expression of what needs to be shared: true or untrue things, i.e., evident or disguised beings *as* evident or disguised. Language does not only communicate what is manifest and just convey this further. Rather, genuinely and initially, it is the essence of language to first elevate beings into the open as beings. Where there is no language—as with stones, plants, and animals—there is also no openness of beings and thus also no openness of non-beings, un-beings, or emptiness. By first naming objects, language brings beings to word and to appearance. This naming and saying is a projecting in which it is *announced* what beings are open as. This projective announcing is at the same time a *rejection* of all dull confusion. The projective saying is poetry, the myth [*Sage*] of the world and earth, and thus of the space of proximity and distance of the gods. The primordial language [*Ursprache*] is such a myth as the primordial poetry of a people, in which their world arises and their earth begins to close itself off *as* theirs. Poetry is the essence of language, and only as a *result* of this can it *also* become "expression." Art and the artwork, however, are not one kind of language, but rather the opposite: The work of language is the basic form of art because the latter is poetry. Poetry in the narrower sense, poesy [*Poesie*], remains the basic form of art (poetry in the broader sense), because in poetic *saying, that* open is projected and becomes a property of human existence wherein beings are displayed and preserved as beings. Building and shaping, conversely, always occur in the already-open of the myth and the saying and are thus, as paths of art, never language, but are each their own poetry.

However, the determination of the essence of poetry as projecting *does not exhaust* its essence. Without a glimpse into the *full* essence of poetry— i.e., of art—we also do not grasp the becoming of truth. We particularly do not grasp how something like the work is necessary for the becoming of truth. (The ground of the necessity of each work is its origin.)

The full essence of poetry comes to light in the statement: Poetry—the essence of art—is *founding of Beyng* [Stiftung des Seyns]. So it is not the bringing-forth of [19] beings. But what does Beyng mean, in contrast to the beings that we name after it? We grasp this being there, the organ, and we grasp it in contrast to, say, a cat. The organ *is*. We grasp this Beyng with difficulty, however, even though we are also certain that the organ is, and is not nothing, just as we know that it is an organ and not a cat. But we would rather take the organ and the cat, and leave Beyng to the philosophers. Yet what, despite all this common sense and its proximity to life, is closer to us than Beyng? What would the organ and the cat and everything else "*be*" without Beyng? In order that this does not remain a mere word, which despite its ungraspability it never is, an instruction may serve as an expedient: We have a sense of Beyng and its concept when we grasp that frequently mentioned openness that appears in the poetizing projecting. Beyng is that which is open and concealed to us, and how each being is open and concealed to us. Beings are only *in themselves* by virtue of the fact that *we* are essential *for* Beyng.

To desire to say directly, in one statement, what the essence of Beyng is, is already to misunderstand this essence. Beyng needs the *founding of Beyng* precisely because it can never be shown like something present-at-hand.

Founding is a *unity*, in itself, of *three things*. For one, founding is a giving: the free gift. Founding is also erecting, setting something on a ground: *grounding*. And finally, founding is setting something afoot: beginning. We must listen for giving, grounding, and beginning, and understand them as a whole, when we call art the poetizing founding of Beyng.

Now founding as giving, as free gift, means that which we earlier already introduced as a characteristic of poetry, the projecting of the open as the "otherwise than usual." The projecting releases something that not only never arises out of the present-at-hand and usual, but that the present-at-hand can also never make up for. Projecting is founding as giving. Now, what does founding as grounding and beginning mean, and how does this essentially belong together with the projecting?

Truth as openness is always the openness of the there into which all beings and non-beings stand, and from which, as secluding themselves, they withdraw. Thus, the "there" itself remains rooted in this dark abyss. This "there," however—in what way does it exist? Who takes over the task of being this "there"? Answer: the human—not as an individual, also not as a community. Both of these ways of being human are only possible at all if humans first take over the there: i.e., stand amongst beings *as* amongst beings and non-beings; i.e., stand toward Beyng as such. This way of being the there is called history. By being the there—i.e., by being historical—humans become a people. In the poetizing projecting, the "otherwise than usual" is not simply opened, but rather, since the openness always remains an openness of the there, it is always thrown ahead of the there—or of whoever is the there. That is, the poetizing projecting is thrown toward historical Da-sein. The there only exists in its [20] openness if it is taken over and endured from within the removal into something relinquished and the preservation of what is handed down, i.e., from within history. The there only exists if a people takes over the task of being the there, [and thus] becomes historical. This there itself is never something general, but is rather always this one, singular there. The people is always already thrown into its there (Hölderlin the poet). This throw exists if it is truly poetry. But if the projection is poetry, then the throw will never simply be an arbitrary demand, but rather the opening of that into which Dasein, as historical, is already thrown. Wherever a people is thrown, there is always the earth, their earth, the closing-off ground on which the thrown there rests. The projection that is essentially a throw only *projects* if it elevates its open up out of the concealed ground, if that which is given up in it is fundamentally handed down as a determination that is concealed and thus to be unconcealed. The "otherwise than usual" steps into the open in the projection, but this "otherwise" is fundamentally not something foreign, but rather only the ownmost [*Eigenste*] of historical Dasein that was concealed until now. The projection comes from nothingness insofar as it does not stem from the usual and from what has existed until now; it does not come from nothingness because, as what is throwing, it raises up the concealed and deposited determination, lays it down *as* a ground, and grounds it. Founding, as giving projecting, is essentially at the same time this grounding. Openness can only be openness of the there—i.e., truth as such can only occur—if the projection is a grounding one. It grounds by engaging with that which secludes itself, with the earth. This latter must come into the open *as* that which secludes itself, i.e., in its opposition to the projected world. Since art, as poetry, is founding and projecting grounding, it must found and place openness, i.e., truth, in such a way that the latter comes to stand in that which enacts the conflict between earth and world—and that is the work. The essence of art as the founding of Beyng is the ground of the necessity of the work. The Beyng of the work does not consist in its being present-at-hand as a produced being, but rather, as contestation, in bringing about the openness of the there and letting humans historically take over Beyng. (Indeed, for this reason, the work bears the characteristic trait of toweringly resting back into itself and drawing itself out of all that is simply present-at-hand.)

The essence of art is the origin of the artwork. Art does not exist on account of works, but rather a work must exist if, and insofar as, art exists. But how and why must art exist? It has its essence not in speaking the truth philosophically in the concept, not in bringing it to action and composure in the essential act, but in setting it into the work. Art lets truth originate in its own way, it is a letting-originate: an origin. Art in its innermost essence is origin, and only this. It is not something else beforehand and then also origin. Rather, because it is essentially a letting-originate of truth, it is simultaneously the ground for the necessity of the work. Art is only the origin and sense of the ground for the possibility and necessity [21] of the work because it is origin in the "original" sense.

Yet *must* truth, the openness of the there, occur in such a way that it originates in the origin as art? Indeed it must, for truth, as the openness of beings, is always at the same time concealment and reservedness of earth. Truth is essentially earth-like. Yet the work necessitated by art—and only this work—originally places the earth, as closing itself off, in conflict with the projected world; and for this reason the work—i.e., art—is necessary in the occurrence of truth. The most concealed ground for the necessity of the artwork, its most authentic origin, is the essence of truth itself. If truth is to occur—i.e., if history is to exist—then a work must exist—i.e., it must be art as the founding of Beyng.

For *founding* is not only a free-ing projection, and not only the grounding that elevates the closed-off ground, but is simultaneously a *beginning*. It provokes the origin. An origin [*Ursprung*], however, can only begin as a leap [*Sprung*]. The beginning of art is unmediated, which entails, rather than rules out, that it is the longest-prepared and most concealed. The leap, as a beginning, is always that leap forward in which everything that is to come is already leaped over, even if it is still covered up. The beginning is never beginner-like in the sense of the primitive, which is only called this because it is not capable of producing anything that follows. Yet indeed the beginning is always inceptive, not out of any inadequacy on the part of what is reached, but out of the plenitude that is reserved in it. As every origin has its beginning, so every beginning has its inception. The latter is that in the course of which the always-sudden beginning arises, as if with something found. For the beginning to be the one that it is, there is need of an occasion. And the occasion is always a coincidence, namely in the light and the breaking-open region of the beginning as the leap of an origin, i.e., as such a leap wherein the truth originates as openness of beings. Where this occurs, history begins. The beginning of a people's art is always the beginning of their history, and the same goes for the end. That is why there is no prehistoric art, for history already began with art, and art can only be or not be as historical. There is no such thing as "art" in itself. However, in prehistory there is pre-art, whose formations are neither just thing-works (tools), nor yet artworks. There is, however, just as little gradual crossing-over from pre-art to art as there is from prehistory to history. There is always the leap of the beginning, which one grasps precisely when one refrains from making this leap understandable in the end, i.e., from leading it back to what is familiar. The leap of the origin, according to its essence, remains a mystery, for the origin is one mode of that ground whose necessity we must call freedom.

The essence of art as the setting-into-work of truth is the origin of the artwork. This origin is so originary, and thus so inaccessible, that we always remain exposed—even in these passages—to the non-essence of [22] the essence. The more originary the essence of something is, the more firm the non-essence in turn is, with its sneaking obtrusiveness and obstinacy.

Knowledge of the essence is just knowledge as decision. In inquiring about art, the decision is: Is art essential for us, is it an origin and thus a founding *leap forward* into our history? A leap forward, or only still an *addendum* that is carried along as an "expression" of the present-at-hand and carried on for embellishment and amusement, for recreation and excitement?

Are we in proximity to the essence of art as origin, or are we not? And if we are not in the proximity of the origin, do we know this, or do we not know this and just stagger about in the art business? If we do not know it, then the first thing should be to raise it to our awareness. For the clarity concerning who we are and who we are not is already the decisive leap into the proximity of the origin. Such proximity alone guarantees a truly grounded historical Dasein as genuine rootedness on this earth. For—and these words of Hölderlin's should provide the ending—

Reluctantly
that which dwells near its origin abandons the site. (*Die Wanderung*)

Supplements
(Unincorporated marginal comments)
1. [To *Heidegger Studies* 5, pp. 19–20:]
Setting on the ground, thus setting-forth [*her-stellen*]; the setting-up not production [*Herstellung*].

There must be conflict—i.e., there must be a work.

From the essence of art as poetry.

When must a work be? When earth and world into the open there, when truth.

2. [To *Heidegger Studies* 5, pp. 20–21:]
Why must a work exist? Because the essence of art is poetry, but the projection can only exist as a *grounding* one, as a setting-forth of the ground and a setting of the open back into this.

But why must the essence of art as poetry be such? Because poetry is an occurrence of truth and because truth "is" always earth-like; and such that poetry is a way that truth springs *forth*.

Art *an* origin of *truth*. Basic mode of its becoming. Art is history. Doing and thinking. *Originating*.

Art the ground, because itself essentially a primordial leap. Preconception only inauthentic. Primordial leap—what kind of ground?

TEN

"As When on a Holiday . . ."

———⟨∿⟩———

1939–1940

Wie wenn am Feiertage, das Feld zu sehn
Ein Landmann geht, des Morgens, wenn
Aus heißer Nacht die kühlenden Blize fielen
Die ganze Zeit und fern noch tönet der Donner,
In sein Gestade wieder tritt der Strom,
Und frisch der Boden grünt
Und von des Himmels erfreuendem Reegen
Der Weinstock trauft und glänzend
In stiller Sonne stehn die Bäume des Haines:

Previously translated by Keith Hoeller in *Elucidations of Hölderlin's Poetry* (Amherst, N.Y.: Humanity Books, 2000), 67–99. Though I have consulted Hoeller's version in preparing the present chapter, and taken over Heidegger's footnotes from that version, much of it has been translated anew from the original. Throughout the chapter, Heidegger cites the historical-critical edition of Hölderlin's works begun by Norbert von Hellingrath and completed by Friedrich Seebass and Ludwig von Pigenot: *Hölderlins Sämtliche Werke*, 6 vols. (Berlin: 1923, 1943).

Bracketed numbers refer to the pagination of GA 4; the chapter opens at page 49. — Tr.

So stehn sie unter günstiger Witterung
Sie die kein Meister allein, die wunderbar
Allgegenwärtig erziehet in leichtem Umfangen
Die mächtige, die göttlichschöne Natur.
Drum wenn zu schlafen sie scheint zu Zeiten des Jahrs
Am Himmel oder unter den Pflanzen oder den Völkern,
So trauert der Dichter Angesicht auch,
Sie scheinen allein zu seyn, doch ahnen sie immer.
Denn ahnend ruhet sie selbst auch.

Jezt aber tagts! Ich harrt und sah es kommen,
Und was ich sah, das Heilige sei mein Wort.
Denn sie, sie selbst, die älter denn die Zeiten
Und über die Götter des Abends und Orients ist,
Die Natur ist jezt mit Waffenklang erwacht,
Und hoch vom Äther bis zum Abgrund nieder
Nach vestem Geseze, wie einst, aus heiligem Chaos gezeugt,
Fühlt neu die Begeisterung sich,
Die Allerschaffende wieder.

Und wie im Aug' ein Feuer dem Manne gläntz,
Wenn hohes er entwarf: so ist
Von neuem an den Zeichen, den Thaten der Welt jezt
Ein Feuer angezündet in Seelen der Dichter.
[50] Und was zuvor geschah, doch kaum gefühlt,
Ist offenbar erst jezt,
Und die uns lächelnd den Aker gebauet,
In Knechtgestalt, sie sind bekannt, die
Die Allebendigen, die Kräfte der Götter.

Erfrägst du sie? im Liede wehet ihr Geist,
Wenn es von der Sonne des Tags und warmer Erd
Entwacht, und Wettern, die in der Luft, und andern
Die vorbereiteter in Tiefen der Zeit
Und deutungsvoller, und vernehmlicher uns
Hinwandeln zwischen Himmel und Erd und unter den Völkern.
Des gemeinsamen Geistes Gedanken sind,
Still endend in der Seele des Dichters.

Daß schnellbetroffen sie, Unendlichem
Bekannt seit langer Zeit, von Erinnerung

Erbebt, und ihr, von heilgem Stral entzündet,
Die Frucht in Liebe geboren, der Götter und Menschen Werk
Der Gesang, damit er beiden zeuge, glükt.
So fiel, wie Dichter sagen, da sie sichtbar
Den Gott zu sehen begehrte, sein Bliz auf Semeles Haus
Und Asche tödtlich getroffene gebahr,
Die Frucht des Gewitters, den heiligen Bacchus.

Und daher trinken himmlisches Feuer jezt
Die Erdensöhne ohne Gefahr.
Doch uns gebührt es, unter Gottes Gewittern,
Ihr Dichter! mit entblößtem Haupte zu stehen,
Des Vaters Stral, ihn selbst, mit eigner Hand
Zu fassen und dem Volk ins Lied
Gehüllt die himmlische Gaabe zu reichen.
Denn sind nur reinen Herzens
Wie Kinder, wir, sind schuldlos unsere Hände.

Des Vaters Stral, der reine versengt es nicht
Und tieferschüttert, eines Gottes Leiden
Mitleidend, bleibt das ewige Herz doch fest.

As when on a holiday, to see the field
A countryman goes out, at morning, when
Out of the hot night the cooling lightning flashes had fallen
The whole time and the thunder still sounds in the distance,
The river enters its banks once more,
And the fresh ground becomes green
And with the gladdening rain from heaven
The grapevine drips, and gleaming
In quiet sunlight stand the trees of the grove:

So in favorable weather they stand
Whom no master alone, whom she, wonderfully
All-present, educates in a light embrace,
The powerful, divinely beautiful nature.
So when she seems to be sleeping at times of the year
Up in the heavens or among plants or the peoples,
The poets' faces are also mourning,
They seem to be alone, yet are always anticipating.
For anticipating, too, she herself is resting.

But now day breaks! I awaited and saw it come,
And what I saw, may the holy be my word,
For she, she herself, who is older than the ages
And above the gods of Occident and Orient,
Nature is now awakening with the clang of arms,
And from high aether down to the abyss,
According to firm law, as once, begotten out of holy Chaos,
Inspiration, the all-creative,
Again feels herself anew.

And as a fire gleams in the eye of the man
Who has conceived a lofty design, so
Once more by the signs, the deeds of the world now
A fire has been kindled in the souls of the poets.
And what came to pass before, though scarcely felt,
Only now is manifest,
And they who smiling tended our fields for us,
In the form of servants, they are known,
The all-living, the powers of the gods.

Do you ask about them? In the song their spirit blows,
When from the sun of day and warm earth
It awakens, and storms that are in the air, and others
That more prepared in the depths of time
And more full of meaning, and more perceptible to us,
Drift on between heaven and earth and among the peoples.
The thoughts of the communal spirit they are,
Quietly ending in the soul of the poet.

So that quickly struck, for a long time
Known to the infinite, it quakes
With recollection, and kindled by the holy ray,
Its fruit conceived in love, the work of gods and men,
The song, so that it may bear witness to both, succeeds.
So, as poets say, when she desired to see
The god, visible, his lightning flash fell on Semele's house
And ashes mortally struck gave birth to
The fruit of the thunderstorm, to holy Bacchus.

And hence the sons of the earth now drink
Heavenly fire without danger.

Yet us it behooves, you poets, to stand
Bare-headed beneath God's thunderstorms,
To grasp the Father's ray, itself, with your own hands,
And offer it to the people
The heavenly gift wrapped in song,
For only if we are pure in heart,
Like children, are our hands innocent.

The Father's ray, the pure, does not sear it
And deeply shaken, sharing a god's suffering,
The eternal heart yet remains firm.

[51] The poem was written in 1800. It only became known to the Germans 110 years later. Using the handwritten drafts, Norbert von Hellingrath[1] first gave the poem a form and published it in 1910. Since then another age has passed. During these decades, the open upheaval of modern world history has begun. Its course will force the decision concerning the future character of the reign of humans, now absolute, which subjugates the planet as a whole. Hölderlin's poem, however, still waits to be interpreted.

The text that serves as our basis here, and that has been repeatedly checked against the original manuscripts, rests upon the following attempt at an interpretation.

The poem lacks a title. It is divided into seven stanzas. Each stanza, with the exception of the fifth and seventh, consists of nine lines. The fifth stanza lacks the ninth line. According to von Hellingrath's edition, the seventh stanza contains twelve lines. Zinkernagel's edition adds some fragments from an earlier draft as an eighth stanza.[2]

The first stanza delivers us into a countryman's sojourn in the fields on a holiday morning. Work has ceased there. And the god is nearer to the human. The countryman wants to see how the fruit has held up in the thunderstorm, which came out of the hot night and threatened the crop. The distant, withdrawing thunder still reminds of the alarm. But no flood endangers the field. The land blooms fresh and green. The grapevine delights in the blessing of the heavenly drink. The forest stands in the still light

---

1. [See the dedication of chapter 8 and corresponding note. — Tr.]

2. [Though Heidegger relies on Hellingrath's edition in this chapter, he refers here to the critical-historical edition of Hölderlin's works compiled by Franz Zinkernagel: *Friedrich Hölderlins Sämtliche Werke und Briefe*, 8 vols. (Leipzig: Insel, 1914). Rather than "clean up" Hölderlin's texts and obscure the writing process, Zinkernagel published facsimiles of the poems that included handwritten variations and additions. — Tr.]

of the sun. The countryman knows of the weather's constant threat toward his possession, and yet finds everywhere the peacefulness of the delightful. He waits confidently for the future gift of the field and the grapevine. Fruits and humans are protected in the benevolence that permeates earth and heaven, and that grants something that remains [*ein Bleibendes*].

The first stanza names all of this as if it wanted to describe a picture. Its last line, naturally, ends with a colon. The [52] first stanza opens itself to the second. The "So . . ." with which the second stanza begins corresponds to the "As when . . ." at the outset of the first. The "As when . . . : So . . ." indicates a comparison that, like a brace, holds the initial stanza in unity with the second, or even to all of the following ones.

Like a countryman on his walk, lingering in the fields, happy about the protection of his world, "So in favorable weather they stand"—the poets. And what benevolence permits them to detect the favorable? The favor of being those

> Whom no master alone, whom she, wonderfully
> All-present, educates in a light embrace,
> The powerful, divinely beautiful nature.

The inner movement of these three lines strives toward the final word "nature," and echoes off in it. What Hölderlin still calls "nature" here resonates throughout the entire poem up to its last word. Nature "educates" the poets. Mastery and teaching can only "inculcate" something. By themselves they can achieve nothing. In contrast to human zeal and human activity, something of a different nature must educate differently. Nature "educates" "wonderfully all-present." She[3] is present in all that is real. Nature comes to presence in human work and in the destiny of peoples, in the stars and in the gods, but also in stones, plants, and animals, as well as in streams and in thunderstorms. The omnipresence of nature is "wonderful." She can never be found somewhere within the real, like an isolated actual thing. The all-present is also never the result of combining isolated real things. Even the totality of what is real is at most the consequence of the all-present. This latter itself withdraws from any explanation on the basis of what is real. The all-present cannot be hinted at by something real. Already present, it imperceptibly prevents any particular intrusion upon it. When human deeds

---

3. [Although the feminine *Natur* is usually rendered as a neutral "nature" in English, I have retained the feminine pronoun throughout, in the interest of staying close to Hölderlin's personification, as well as maintaining the readability of Heidegger's interpretation.—Tr.]

attempt this intrusion, or when divine activity is directed to it, they only destroy the simplicity of what is wonderful. The wonderful [53] withdraws from all producing, and yet pervades everything with its presence. That is why nature educates "in a light embrace." The all-present knows nothing of the one-sided heaviness of what is merely real: that which at one time attracts humans, at another time repels them, and at another abandons them, each time delivering them into the distortion of all that is random. However, nature's "light embrace" also does not suggest an impotent weakness. The "all-present," after all, is called "powerful." But where does nature draw her power from, if she is present prior to everything? Nature does not have to borrow her power from somewhere else. She is herself that which empowers. The essence of power is determined by the omnipresence of nature, which Hölderlin calls "powerful, divinely beautiful." Nature is powerful because she is god-like in beauty. So nature resembles a god or a goddess? If this were the case, nature, which permeates everything, including the gods, would be measured according to the divine, and would no longer be "nature." The latter is called "beautiful" because she is "wonderfully all-present." The completeness of her presence does not mean the quantitatively complete containment [*Umgreifen*] of all that is real, but rather the manner of permeating even those real things that, according to their kind, seem to mutually exclude each other. This omnipresence holds the most extreme oppositions, of the highest heaven and the deepest abyss, over against each other. In this way, the things that stand over against each other remain stretched apart in their obstinacy. Only thus can the opposed things come forth into the extreme sharpness of their otherness. What thus appears in an "extreme" way is what most appears. What appears in this way is what captivates [*Berückende*].[4] At the same time, however, omnipresence displaces [*entrückt*] the opposites into the unity of their belonging together. This unity does not allow obstinacy to disappear into a faint equilibrium, but rather takes it back into that [54] peace that lights up as a quiet brilliance from the fire of strife, in which the one pushes the other into appearance. This unity of omnipresence is that which displaces [*das Entrückende*]. All-present nature captivates and displaces [*berückt und entrückt*]. The coincidence of captivation and wonder, however, is the essence of the beautiful. Beauty lets one opposite come to presence in its opposite,

---

4. [Heidegger's note from the second, 1951 edition:]

ἐκφανέστατον
ἐρασμιώτατον   τὸ καλόν

lets their relation to each other come to presence in its unity, and thus lets everything come to presence in all else from the purity of what differs. Beauty is omnipresence. And nature is called "divinely beautiful" because in their appearance, gods or goddesses come closest to awakening the look of captivation and wonder. But in truth they are not capable of pure beauty after all, for their particular appearing remains a semblance; since mere captivation ("epiphany") resembles wonder, and mere wonder (displacement into mystical immersion) manifests itself as captivation. But the god is nevertheless capable of the highest look of the beautiful, and thus comes closest to the pure appearance of omnipresence.

Nature that is powerful because it is divinely beautiful, because it is wonderfully all-present, embraces the poets. They are drawn into this embrace. This inclusion transposes the poets into the fundamental characteristic of their essence. Such transposition is education. This characterizes the poets' destiny:

> So when she seems to be sleeping at times of the year
> Up in the heavens or among plants or the peoples,
> The poets' faces also are mourning,
> They seem to be alone, yet are always anticipating.

Sleep is kind of being-away, of absence. But how could "nature" take on the look of being absent, if she did not come to presence in the heavenly ones, in the earth and its growth, in the peoples and their history? "At times of the year" the all-present appears to be sleeping. Here "the year" means, at one and the same time, the year of the "seasons" and "the years of the peoples," the ages of the world. Nature appears to be sleeping, and yet does not. She is awake, but awake in the manner of [55] mourning. This mourning withdraws from everything into the remembrance of the one [das Eine]. But the remembrance of mourning remains close to what has been taken from it and what appears to be distant. Mourning does not sink into the current that pulls one to what is merely lost. It lets what is absent always come again. Thus it also appears as if the mourning poets were confined to their isolation and imprisoned within it. They are not "alone." In truth, "they are always anticipating." Anticipation [Ahnung] thinks forward into what is distant, which does not withdraw but rather is coming. But because what is coming itself still rests and remains in its incipience, the anticipation of what is coming is at once a thinking-forward and a thinking-back. Thus the poets persist in their belonging to nature:

For anticipating, too, she herself is resting.

Nature is at rest. Her rest in no way signifies cessation of movement. To rest is to gather oneself toward the beginning that is present in all movement, and toward its coming. That is why nature, too, is at rest anticipating. She is with herself by thinking ahead to her coming. Her coming is the coming to presence of omnipresence, and is thus the essence of the "all-present."

Only because there are those who anticipate are there those who belong to nature and correspond to it. Those who co-respond [*Ent-sprechenden*] to the wonderfully all-present—to the powerful, divinely beautiful—are "the poets." Which poets does Hölderlin mean? Those who stand in favorable weather. They alone persist in correspondence to anticipating, resting nature. The poet's essence will be decided anew from this correspondence. "The poets" are not all poets in general, also not certain indeterminate ones. "The poets" are those future ones whose essence will be measured according to their adaptation to the essence of "nature." And what this word "nature"— known for a long time, and long since worn out in its ambiguity—names here must be determined solely on the basis of this single poem.

One usually encounters "nature" in the familiar distinctions of "nature and art," "nature and spirit," "nature and [56] history," "natural and supernatural," "natural and unnatural." Thus "nature" always means a particular realm of beings. But if one wanted to posit "nature," as named in this poem, as "identical" with "spirit"—in the sense of "identity" in which Hölderlin's friend Schelling thought of it at about the same time—then this would also be an erroneous interpretation of nature. Even the sense that Hölderlin himself gave to the word "nature" up until this hymn, in *Hyperion* and in the first drafts of *Empedocles,* falls short of what is now named "the wonderfully all-present." At the same time, "nature" now becomes an incongruous word in reference to what is coming, which it is supposed to name. Nevertheless, the fact that this word "nature" is still permitted as a guiding word of this poem is due to the resonance of a saying-power whose origin reaches far back.

Nature, *natura,* is called φύσις in Greek. This word is the fundamental word of thinkers at the beginning of Western thought. But the translation of φύσις by *natura* (nature) already transposes subsequent elements into the beginning, and replaces what is solely proper to the beginning with something foreign to it.

Φύσις, φύειν, means growth. But how do the Greeks understand growth? Not as a quantitative increase, nor as "development," nor even as the succession of a "becoming." Φύσις is an emerging and opening [*Hervorgehen und Aufgehen*]: a self-opening that, in opening, at the same time turns back into the emergence and thus fuses with it, giving each present thing its presence. Thought as the fundamental word, φύσις means the opening into the open: the lighting of that clearing into which something in general can enter and appear, present itself in its outline, show itself in its "look" (εἶδος, ἰδέα), and thus be present as this or that. Φύσις is the opening returning-to-itself; it names the coming to presence of that which resides in the opening as the open. The clearing of the open, however, becomes most purely discernible in letting the transparency of brightness shine through: in "light." Φύσις is the opening of the clearing of what is cleared, and is thus the hearth and the site [57] of light. The shining of the "light" belongs to the fire; it is the fire. Fire is above all brightness and blaze [*Helle und Glut*]. Brightness clears, first provides the open for all appearing, and gives discernability to all that appears. The blaze glows and, in its glowing, sparks all that is emerging into its appearing. Thus fire, as brightening-glowing "light," is the open that already comes to presence in everything that emerges and disappears within the open. Φύσις is what is present in all. But then must "nature"—if it is φύσις, and as the "all-present"—not also be that which sets everything aglow? That is why, in this poem, Hölderlin also names "nature" the "all-creative" and the "all-living."

In this poem, Hölderlin's word "nature" poetizes its essence according to the concealed truth of the originary, fundamental word φύσις. But Hölderlin was not acquainted with this originary word's sustaining capacity, which even today has barely been ascertained. Likewise, with what he names "nature," Hölderlin does not just want to bring what was experienced in ancient Greece back to life again. With the word "nature," Hölderlin poetizes something different, something that stands in a concealed relation to what was once named φύσις.

Nature, which in a "light embrace" keeps everything within its openness and clearing, seems at times to be sleeping. At these times, what has been lighted has retreated into itself in mourning. The mourning that seals itself off is impenetrable and it appears as darkness. But this mourning is not merely an arbitrary darkness, but rather an anticipating rest. The darkness is the night. Night is the resting anticipation of the day.

But now day breaks! I awaited and saw it come,
And what I saw, may the holy be my word.

The exclamation with which the third stanza begins names the opening of the blazing glowing brightness. Daybreak is the arrival of the anticipating nature that has been at rest. Dawn is nature herself in her coming. The exclamation "But now day breaks!" sounds like an invocation of nature. But the call actually calls to something that is coming. The poet's [58] word is the pure calling of what those poets who are always anticipating wait and long for. What has been called itself compels, from its essence, the poet to speak—and the poetic naming states just this. Compelled in this way, Hölderlin names nature "the holy." In the hymn "At the Source of the Danube," written only shortly afterward, Hölderlin says:

> We name you, compelled by the holy, we name you
> Nature! And new, as from a bath
> From you emerges all that is divinely born.[5]

Yet in a pencil revision, the poet subsequently crossed out precisely these lines; Hellingrath points to this (IV^2, 337ff.) with the remark that from now on, the name "nature" no longer suffices for Hölderlin. But as the fundamental poetic word, the name "nature" is already overcome in the hymn "As When on a Holiday . . ." This overcoming is the consequence and sign of a saying that begins from a more primordial point.

Hölderlin names daybreak as the lightening of the clearing that is present in everything. The awakening of the clearing light, however, is the stillest of all events. But since it is named—indeed demands to be named—the awakening of "nature" arises in the sound of the poetic word. The essence of what is named unveils itself in the word. For by naming what is essential, the word separates the essence from the non-essence. And because the word separates them, it decides their strife. The word is a weapon. Hence Hölderlin, in the same hymn ("At the Source of the Danube") speaks of the "weapons of the word" as the "sanctuaries" that preserve the holy.

Because the breaking day, the lightly embracing and wonderfully all-present has now become the single thing to be said and is within the word, nature "is now" "awakening with the clang of arms . . ." But why must "the holy" be the poet's word? [59] Because the one who stands "under favorable weather" must name only that to which he anticipatingly belongs: nature. In awakening, nature unveils her own essence as the holy.

---

5. [Heidegger's note from the second, 1951 edition:] Nature as the *holy*—compels us into naming. The *holy* is the "whence" (cf. Beissner II, 2, 695ff.).

> For she, she herself, who is older than the ages
> And above the gods of Occident and Orient,
> Nature is now awakening with the clang of arms

Nature is older than those ages [*Zeiten*] that are measured out to humans and to peoples and to things. But nature is not older than "time" [*Zeit*]. After all, how could nature be older than "time"? As long as she remains "older than the ages" she is, of course, "older"—therefore earlier, thus more timely [*zeitiger*], thus precisely more time-like [*zeithafter*]—than "the times" with which the sons of the earth calculate. "Nature" is the oldest time, and not at all "supratemporal" in the metaphysical sense, and definitely not "eternal" in the Christian sense. Nature is more timely than "the times" because, as the wonderfully all-present, she has already bestowed the clearing on everything real, the clearing in whose openness everything that is real can first appear. Nature is prior to everything real and to all action, even prior to the gods. For she, "who is older than the ages," is also "above the gods of Occident and Orient." Nature is not by any means "above" the gods as if in an isolated domain of reality "above" them. Nature is above "the" gods. She, "the powerful," is capable of something other than the gods: As the clearing, in her everything can first be present. Hölderlin calls nature the holy, because she is "older than the ages and above the gods." Thus "holiness" is in no way a property borrowed from a determinate god. The holy is not holy by virtue of its divinity; rather, the divine is divine because it is "holy" in its way—for Hölderlin also calls "chaos" "holy" in this stanza. The holy is the essence of nature. As the breaking day, nature unveils her essence in awakening.

> And from high aether down to the abyss,
> According to firm law, as once, begotten out of holy Chaos,
> [60] Inspiration, the all-creative,
> Again feels herself anew.

This "and" which follows "awakening" did not lead to anything that would perhaps take place apart from it, for instance, as its consequence. The "and" initiates the unveiling of the essence of what nature, as awakening, is. In awakening, nature comes to herself. Inspiration, the all-creative, again feels herself anew. And that is now the name for all-present nature. That which is clear lets everything emerge into its appearance and glowing, so that everything real, sparked by it, stands in its own contour and measure. In this way its own essence is distinguished, and everything that appears is pervaded by spirit [*Geist*]: in-spired [*be-geistert*]. As the all-present, all-creative one, nature in-spires everything. She herself is "inspiration." She can in-spire only because she is "spirit." Spirit reigns as the sober but daring confrontation [*Auseinandersetzung*] that sets everything present into the well-delineated boundaries and structures of its presence. Essential thinking is such a confrontation. "Thoughts" are what is most proper to "spirit"; through them everything precisely belongs together because it is set apart [*auseinandergesetzt*]. Spirit is the unifying unity. It lets the togetherness of everything real appear in its collectedness. The spirit is therefore essentially, in its "thoughts," the "communal spirit." It is spirit in the form of inspiration, which draws everything that appears into the unity of the all-present. This all-present itself has in its inspiration the kind of presence that opens and awakens. In awakening, nature comes to herself and resonates with herself. Since nature is primordial and prior to everything, when she feels herself again, she can only feel in a primordial way—i.e., "anew."

The open—within which everything has its coming-to-presence and endurance—toweringly pervades the realm of all domains. That is why the awakening reigns "from high aether down to the abyss." "Aether" is the name for the father of light and the all-enlivening, lightening air. "Abyss" names that which encloses everything and that is borne by [61] "mother earth." Above all, "aether" and "abyss" name the most extreme domains of reality, but also the supreme divinities. Both are thoroughly pervaded by inspiration. Inspiration does not stray into arbitrariness like a blind intoxication. It is

According to firm law, as once, begotten out of holy Chaos

Nature fits everything that is real into the characteristics of its essence. By "spirit" appearing in what is real, and the spiritual being reflected in the spiritual, the fundamental characteristics of the all are unfolded. For this to occur, immortals and mortals must meet, and both must maintain their relation to the real in their own way. All individualized real things, in all their connections, are possible only if, before all else, nature grants the open within which immortals and mortals and all things can encounter each other. The open mediates the relations between all real things. It only consists of this mediation and is thus something mediated. What is mediated is therefore only possible by virtue of mediation. Thus, mediation must be present in everything. Yet the open itself, which first provides for mutuality and collectivity the realm in which they belong to each other, does not stem from any mediation. The open is itself the immediate. Nothing mediated, be it a god or a human, can ever immediately reach the immediate. Peering into this essential depth of the all, Hölderlin thoughtfully recognizes the significance of an early fragment by Pindar (Schröder no. 169):

νόμος ὁ πάντων βασιλεὼς
θνατῶν τε καὶ ἀθανάτων
ἄγει δικαιῶν τὸ βιαιότατον
ὑπερτάτᾳ χειρί . . .

In Hölderlin's translation (V², 276):

Das Gesez,
Von allen der König, Sterblichen und
Unsterblichen; das führt eben
Darum gewaltig
Das gerechteste Recht mit alterhöchster Hand.

The law
Of all, the king, mortals and
Immortals; which for that very reason
Powerfully steers
The most just right with the uppermost hand.

[62] Hölderlin titles this fragment "The Highest." On the basis of his own reflection, he says about it:

> The immediate, strictly speaking, is as impossible for the mortals as for the immortals; the god, according to his nature, must distinguish different worlds, since heavenly goodness, for its own sake, must be holy, pure. The human, as the knowing one, must also distinguish different worlds, because knowledge is only possible through opposition. For this reason the immediate, strictly speaking, is as impossible for the mortals as for the immortals. Strict mediatedness, rather, is the law.

That which is first present in everything gathers everything isolated together into a single presence and mediates appearance to each thing. The immediate all-presence is the mediator for everything mediated, that is, for the mediate. The immediate is itself never something mediate; on the other hand, the immediate, strictly speaking, is the mediation—that is, the mediatedness of the mediated—for it renders the latter possible in its essence. "Nature" is the all-mediating mediatedness, is "the law." Because nature remains the primordial, that which is originally unshakeable prior to everything, she is the "firm law." By awakening to herself, nature originates in accordance with her essence: "according to firm law."

But nature is nevertheless "begotten out of holy Chaos." How do "*chaos*" and "*nomos*" ("law") go together? "Chaos," after all, means for us lawlessness and confusion. Hölderlin himself says: "And holy wilderness, preparing much, has grown roots" ("The Titans," IV², 208); he speaks of the "holy wildernesses" (IV², 250, 341), also of the "clumsy wilderness" (IV², 216), and of the "primeval confusion" ("The Rhine," IV², 180). Nevertheless, χάος first of all means the yawning, gaping chasm, the open that first opens itself, wherein everything is engulfed. The chasm prevents all criteria for anything distinct or grounded. Therefore, for all experience that only knows what is mediated, chaos seems to be undifferentiated and thus mere confusion. The "chaotic" in this sense, however, is only the inessential aspect of what "chaos" means. Thought in terms of "nature" (φύσις), chaos remains that gaping out of which the open opens itself, so that it may grant its bounded presence to all that is differentiated. That is why Hölderlin calls "chaos" and "confusion" "holy." Chaos is the holy itself. Nothing that is real precedes this opening, but rather always only enters into it. All that appears is already surpassed each time by it. "As once" [*wie einst*], nature is prior to and above everything. She is the former [*das Einstige*]—and that in a double sense. She is the oldest of every former thing, and always the youngest of subsequent things. By awakening, nature's coming, as what is most futural, comes out of the oldest of what has been, which never ages because it is each time the youngest.

What is always former is the holy [*Heilige*]. For as the primordial, it remains in itself unscathed and "whole" [*heil*]. Yet the originary whole, through its omnipresence, gives to each real thing the wholeness of its abiding presence. But what is whole and grants wholeness, as the immediate, seals all fullness and any structure into itself, and is thus precisely unapproachable for any individuated being, be it a god or a human. The holy, as the unapproachable, renders useless any immediate intrusion of the mediate. The holy removes all experience from its habits, and so deprives it of its place. Displacing [*ent-setzend*] in this way, the holy is the awesome [*Entsetzliche*] itself. But its awesomeness remains concealed in the mildness of its light embrace. Because this light embrace educates the future poets, they, as the initiated ones, know the holy. Their knowledge is divination. Divining concerns what is coming and what is rising, the dawn. "But now day breaks!" What happens now, when the holy itself comes?

And as a fire gleams in the eye of the man
Who has conceived a lofty design, so
Once more by the signs, the deeds of the world now
A fire has been kindled in the souls of the poets.

[64] Just as the lofty design of a thoughtful man is reflected in his glance, so when the holy unveils itself in its coming, a light shines in "the souls of the poets." A brightness extends to the individual souls of those poets who, embraced by the holy, belong to it. Because they mourn with divining nature, they too must come into the clearing when nature awakens, and must themselves become a brightness. These poets then stand openly in the open that clears itself "from high aether down to the abyss." The openness of the open then joins what we call "a world." Solely for this reason, the signs and the deeds of the world step into the light for these poets; for they are not without a world. Although poets, according to their being, belong to the holy and think the reality of everything real, that is, "spirit"—and although they are thus especially "spiritual" themselves—they must at the same time also remain immersed and captive within what is real.

The poets, even
The spiritual, must be worldly. ("The Only One," first version)

Thus it is that the signs and deeds of the world can become an occasion for the glowing of the rising brightness to catch fire. The "worldly" "sensations," "activities," and "successes" are nothing more than an occasion; for at no time can something worldly by itself make the holy appear. Moreover, only those who already see the arrival of what is to come are capable of interpreting something in the world as a sign of what is coming, and of estimating it as a deed for what is coming. Above all, it is never the signs and the deeds of the world that should actually step into the open. "What came to pass before, though scarcely felt," "only now" comes into manifestation, and so too into the realm of human perception. "Before" here means that oldest of times, in advance of everything real, that was formerly perceptible only in its first glimmering: the very first, originary opening of what has since become present in all, but since then has also [65] been susceptible to inversion and even forgottenness: "nature" (φύσις). But how did this originary advent reign, prior to the awakening that now arises and becomes known "anew"?

And they who smiling tended our fields for us,
In the form of servants, they are known,
The all-living, the powers of the gods.

The nature that is "all-present" and "all-creative" is now called the "all-living." To be sure, this word is applied to the powers of the gods, the powers by which gods are capable of their actions, and by which they themselves are what they are. But these powers do not derive from the gods. Rather, the gods themselves have their being by virtue of them, the powers that, as "all-living," hold everything, even the gods, in "life." "Before," nature, "smiling," tended "the fields" for humans. With a fleeting hint back to the first stanza, the word "fields" stands here for everything on which and from which humans live. Formerly, the whole of the holy was "smiling," all-present, tireless, friendly, quite untroubled if humans "scarcely felt" what was then happening. In their hurry toward the tangible, humans took what was granted by divinely beautiful nature solely for their own use and service, and reduced the all-present to the form of a servant. But she permitted this, "smiling" in the tranquil releasement of the primordial, unconcerned with successes; she left it to humans to misconstrue the holy. When "nature" is misconstrued in that way, each thing "is" no more than what it accomplishes. In truth, however, each thing always accomplishes only that which it is. But everything, even every humanity, only "is" according to the "way" in which nature, the holy, coming to presence through itself, remains present within it.

But if it is only the poets who are lightly embraced by all-present nature, how are "the people" ever to stand in the presence of the holy? How are "the sons of the earth" ever to experience the "all-living powers," the holy, if the fire remains locked up "in [66] the souls" of the poets? Even the poet is never capable of attaining the holy through his own reflection, or indeed of exhausting its essence and forcing it to come to him through his questioning.

Do you ask about them? In the song their spirit blows . . .

In "song," and only in song, "spirit" joins itself to the structure of the holy that is capable of being pursued in thought. But the spirit does not blow in every "singing." That only occurs in a song,

When from the sun of day and warm earth
It awakens . . .

The original text clearly reads "awakens" [entwacht], and not "grows [entwächst], as most editions now read. Song must spring from the awakening of nature "from high aether down to the abyss." If it shares in this way in the "awakening inspiration," then the breath of the coming of the holy drifts in it. The origin of song is thus quite different from its usual conception. Its awakening happens in "storms" that "drift on between heaven and earth and among the peoples." It is necessary that the whole realm in which nature previously seemed to be sleeping experiences an upheaval. This upheaval of the all stems from a shock that is "more prepared in the depths of time." The awakening reaches back into the oldest time, from which all that is to come has already been prepared. Therefore, the shocks of the all are also "more full of meaning . . . to us"—namely, to the poets who share in the awakening. The richness of the primordial grants their word such an excess of meaning as can scarcely be uttered. Hence, "a load of logs" is laid on their shoulders. That is why for them too, there is "much to be retained" ("Ripe are . . ." IV², 71); "much is to be said" (IV², 219, 221), for "there is still much to be sung" ("At the Source of the Danube," IV², 161). Yet because the shocks stem from the oldest depths of awakening nature, and because the poets are lightly embraced by nature, inspiration thus must be more present and so "more perceptible" to them. [67]

> The thoughts of the communal spirit they are,
> Quietly ending in the soul of the poet.

Hölderlin deliberately placed a comma after the "are." Just as an inconspicuous tap of the sculptor's chisel imparts a different form to the figure, so this comma places a special emphasis on the "are." "Awakening nature," "inspiration," is present. The manner of its presence is to be coming. The holy keeps everything together in the unscathed immediacy of its "firm law." Separating everything, "spirit" remains attached to everything, pervading and joining everything through thought. As "spirit," it is always "communal spirit." And as for the presence of the inspiration of spirit, permeating everything and maintaining everything in its unity—what sort of presence is that? "Quietly ending in the soul of the poet." "Inspiration" does not end by vanishing and ceasing. On the contrary, inspiration is admitted in and preserved—to be sure, "quietly." The shock is stilled and preserved into rest. The awesome power of the holy rests in the mildness "of the poet's" soul. The holy is quietly present as what is coming. That is also why it is never represented and grasped as an object. Elsewhere in this poem, Hölderlin speaks of the poets in the plural (lines 10–11, 16–17, 31, 56). But here he speaks of a single poet, the one who says, "I awaited and saw it come." The certainty of his words stems from his knowledge:

> The thoughts of the communal spirit they are,
> Quietly ending in the soul of the poet.

According to the count, the fifth stanza lacks a line. Thus we must insert an intervening thought, so that there is a clear transition to the next stanza.

Now that day breaks, "the" poet, too, has awoken. Pervaded by the resonance of awakening inspiration, a "spiritual one" is now ordained to be the sole poet. After all, there has to be a poet if a word of song is to be formed. The single poet preserves the stilled shock of the holy in the stillness of his silence. Since a song of the authentic word can only [68] spring from silence, everything is now prepared:

> So that quickly struck, for a long time
> Known to the infinite, it quakes
> With recollection, and kindled by the holy ray,
> Its fruit conceived in love, the work of gods and humans,
> The song, so that it may bear witness to both, succeeds.

The Pindaric structure of these lines is sustained by this single thought: Because the holy is quietly preserved in the soul of the poet, its song will succeed—i.e., the word will convey the holy. However, this success does not only consist in the fact that a song results, but that "it," the soul of the poet, has good luck insofar as the work does not miscarry in composition. These emphasized words, that the song succeeds, mean to say: The threat of an essential misfortune is withstood. But where would the threat of misfortune arise from? Where else than from the possibility of not finding good fortune? The good fortune, that is, of the favor which is necessary for the birth of the song. For even if the poet's soul may preserve in itself the presence of what is coming, the poet by himself is never immediately capable of naming the holy. The embers of the light, quietly preserved in the soul of the poet, need to be kindled. Only a ray of light that emanates again from the holy itself is strong enough for that. Therefore, someone higher—who is nearer to the holy and yet still remains beneath it, a god—must throw the kindling lightning-flash into the poet's soul. In doing so, the god takes upon himself that which is "above" him, the holy, and brings it together into the sharpness and force of the sole ray through which he is "allotted" to the human, in order to bestow it.

Since neither humans nor gods by themselves can ever achieve an immediate relation to the holy, humans need the gods and the heavenly ones need mortals: [69]

> The heavenly
> Are not capable of everything. For
> The mortals reach sooner into the abyss. ("Mnemosyne")

There is only love between gods and humans because the gods must be gods and the humans must be humans, and because nevertheless, the one can never be without the other. Through the mediation of this love, however, they precisely do not belong to themselves but to the holy, which for them is the "strict mediateness," "the law." Yet the holy ray strikes the poet suddenly. Instantaneously, divine fullness blesses him. "Struck" in this way, he would be tempted to follow only this good fortune and to lose himself in the sole possession of the god. But that would be misfortune, because it would mean the loss of his poetic essence; for the essential condition of the poet is grounded not in the reception of the god, but in the embrace by the holy.

But the poet now stands in favorable weather, so that he remains familiar with what already comes to presence in everything finite, that is, with the "infinite." And because all-present nature is "older than the ages," his belonging to her is likewise "long familiar." Now when the holy ray strikes the poet, he is not carried away into the blaze of the ray, but is fully turned toward the holy. To be sure, the poet's soul "quakes" and so lets the quieted shock awaken within itself; but it quakes with recollection, that is to say, with the expectation of that which happened before: this is the opening up of the holy. The shaking breaks the stillness of silence. The word comes to be. The word-work that originates in this way lets the belonging together of god and human appear. The song bears witness to the ground of their belonging together, bears witness to the holy. "Only now" that the thoughts of the communal spirit are first manifest, does the song of the poet's soul succeed. But not always, when a work succeeds, is there also good fortune.

So, as the poets say, when she desired to see
The god, visible, his lightning flash fell on Semele's house,
[70] And ashes mortally struck gave birth to
The fruit of the thunderstorm, to holy Bacchus.

The desire to see the god in a human manner carried Semele away into the single blaze of the released lightning-flash. She who received forgot about the holy.[6] It is true that fruit was born, Bacchus, the god of the "vine," who

---

6. [Following an affair with Zeus, Semele was tricked by Hera into asking Zeus to visit Semele in his full divine splendor. Having promised to fulfill Semele's wishes, Zeus destroyed her with his "lightning-flash." He managed, however, to save the unborn Dionysos/Bacchus and bear him in his thigh until birth. —Tr.]

Bears witness to earth and heaven, when it, drenched
By the high sun, rises from the dark soil . . . (Last draft of *Empedocles*)

But the fruit was not born to her who conceived, for in conceiving the fruit, she was reduced to ashes. Semele's fate reveals in contrast how only the presence of the holy guarantees that the song truly succeeds. The recollection of Semele's fate, spoken by Euripides (*The Bacchae*) and by Ovid (*Metamorphoses* 3, 293), is only introduced into the poem as a counter-theme. That is why the beginning of the following (seventh) stanza is not joined to the end of the sixth, but is connected to the middle part of the stanza:

And hence the sons of the earth now drink
Heavenly fire without danger.
Yet us it behooves, you poets, to stand
Bare-headed beneath God's thunderstorms . . .

Although the word "drink" does indeed remind one of the wine-god, it means the reception of the other fruit—the perception, by humans, of the spirit that pervades the successful song. What they perceive in the song is the awakening inspiration, the glowing brightness: "heavenly fire." This word, which henceforth recurs in the hymns ("The Rhine," line 100; "The Titans," line 271), does not mean the lightning-flash, but rather that "fire" which, prior to the birth of the song, is "now kindled in the souls of the poets": that is, the holy. This fire is called "heavenly" because it is mediated by a "heavenly one." "Now" that "day breaks," "now" that "nature awakens with the clang of arms," "now" that "what came to pass before, only now is manifest": "now" the holy has lost its danger for the sons [71] of the earth. The shock of chaos that offers no support, the terror of the immediate that frustrates every intrusion; the holy is transformed, through the quietness of the protected poet, into the mildness of the mediated and mediating word.

Since the song was successful because it came from the holy, "the sons of the earth" and especially "the poets" are transported into a new kind of essence, but in such a way that the essential constitution of the sons of the earth and that of the poets drifts apart more decisively than ever before. While the sons of the earth now simply receive that which is without danger ("And hence . . . drink . . ."), the future poets ("Yet . . . it behooves . . .") are placed into extreme danger. Now they must stand where the holy opens up more preparedly and more primordially. The poets must leave to the immediate its immediacy, and yet also take upon themselves its mediation as their only task. That is why it is their duty and obligation to remain in relation to those higher mediators. Now that day breaks, the "load of logs" is not lessened, but rather intensified to the point of hardly being bearable. Even if the immediate is never perceived immediately, it is still necessary to grasp the mediating ray "with our own hands," and to endure the "storms" of the primordial that opens. In the knowledge of what thus obligates them, the poets belong together. "We poets"—they are those unique and future ones, of whom Hölderlin himself, as the first, foretells all that is to be said. These poets are capable of the task that has been entrusted to them when the grasping and offering of their hands is permeated by a "pure heart." "Heart" is that wherein the unique essence of these poets gathers itself: the quietness of their belonging within the embrace of the holy. For Hölderlin, "pure" always means the same as "original"—that is, decisively remaining in a primordial determination. This is characteristic of children. The "pure heart" is not meant here in a "moralistic" sense. The phrase indicates a way of relating, a manner of correspondence to "all-present" nature. If the poets [72] remain within the all-presence of this powerful and beautiful "nature," this excludes any possibility of their merely boasting about what is their own, and of their mis-measuring what the law is. Their hands are "innocent." Their supreme decisiveness, poetic saying, then appears as the "most innocent of all occupations."

In terms of content, line 62 concludes the seventh stanza, but also according to the number of lines chosen for the stanzas. The comma that Hellingrath and Zinkernagel placed after the word "hands" at the end of line 62 does not appear in the original manuscript. With line 63, a thought begins that returns to the saying of the holy and introduces the consummation of the poem. That is why in the present text, a period has been placed at the end of line 62, which Hölderlin has left without a punctuation mark. The seventh stanza treats of two matters: The poets give the gift of the song, mediated by a "heavenly one," to the sons of the earth; the poets themselves, however, are placed beneath "God's thunderstorms." But this poem as a whole cannot close with the naming of the sons of the earth and the poets. For what this poem, in its completion, is actually tasked with saying is what the poem itself says in the third stanza, which sustains everything else:

> But now day breaks! I awaited and saw it come,
> And what I saw, the holy be my word.

The final word of this poem must return to the holy. The poem speaks of the poets and of the gift of the song only because the holy is the terror of complete shock and is the immediate. Hence the sons of the earth need the mediation of the holy through the gift of the unthreatening song. But precisely the fact that the holy is entrusted to a mediation by the god and poets, and is born in a song, threatens to invert the essence of the holy into its opposite. The immediate thus becomes something mediated. Because song awakens only with the awakening of the [73] holy, even the mediated itself arises out of the immediate. This origin of song—the "clang of arms," "with" which nature awakens—is thus the shock that reaches into the essential depths of the holy. By the holy becoming word, its innermost essence begins to vacillate. The law is threatened. The holy risks losing its firmness. But

> The Father's ray, the pure, does not sear it
> And deeply shaken, sharing a god's suffering,
> The eternal heart yet remains firm.

This phrase, "the eternal heart," is unique in all of Hölderlin's poetry. And what this phrase signifies is said only in this single poem.

In its origin, the holy is the "firm law": that "strict mediatedness" in which all relations of all real things are mediated. Everything only is because it is gathered into the all-presence of the inviolable, and remains within this.

All is intimate.

Thus begins a late draft (IV², 381). Everything only is by shining forth out of the intimacy of the all-present. The holy is intimacy itself; it is "the heart."

But the holy, "above the gods" and humans, is "older than the ages." The former [das Einstige], which is the first before all things and the last subsequent to all things, is what precedes everything and maintains everything in itself: the primordial and, as this, the enduring. Its remaining is the eternity of the eternal. The holy is the former intimacy, "the eternal heart." The endurance of the holy, however, is threatened by mediation through the word of the song, the mediation that stems from the holy itself and is demanded by its coming. But it is not only the human word that threatens. Rather, and still more surprising, it is the "holy ray" of the father, sent into the kindling and conception of the word, that threatens to deprive the holy of its immediateness and, by placing it in the mediated, to [74] surrender it to essential annihilation. For even in the "Father's ray," the holy is already exteriorized into the mediated, if indeed even the immortals have only a mediate relation to the holy. But

The Father's ray, the pure, does not sear it . . .

—"it," the eternal heart. To "sear" means, according to the phrase *sengen und brennen,* the same as to annihilate; instead of "does not sear it," Hölderlin first wrote, "does not kill it." In abrupt, excited strokes of the pen, the following remark is found in the inner margin of the concluding lines:

The / sphere / that is / higher than /
That of the human / this is the god.

The hint that the poet wants to preserve for himself with these words means here: The higher sphere, the holy ray, threatens even the holy still more deeply with the loss of its essence. But even this sphere is only "higher" and not "the highest." Thus, what sprang from the origin cannot affect the origin. And hence the "eternal heart," although "deeply shaken," "yet remains firm." The shock is, of course, grounded in that depth out of which the holy "shares a god's suffering." How does the god suffer, who, as the lightning-flash, advances in the holy ray? In an explicit addition, this ray is called "the pure" because it holds to the decisiveness of belonging to the holy; for "heavenly goodness, for its own sake, must be holy" (notes to the Pindar fragment "The Highest," V^2, 276). This insistent belongingness is suffering, not mere endurance. But the manner in which Hölderlin thinks the essence of this suffering unveils itself in a subsequent alteration of the later version of that hymn entitled "The Only One," which states that the Christian God is not exactly the only one. Here (IV^2, 379) Hölderlin speaks of a

. . . Wasteland full of
Faces, so that to remain innocent
Truth is a suffering.

[75] Because the intimacy that once was, the remaining within the undamaged "law," is a suffering, the eternal heart suffers from its essential beginning. That is why it also "shares a god's suffering." By offering itself to the decisiveness of the ray that is a suffering, the holy nevertheless abides, radiating in the truth of its essence, and so it suffers primordially. Yet since this originary suffering is not a sacrificial tolerance, but instead the intimacy that gathers everything to itself, it does not share the god's suffering in a pitying and compassionate way. Suffering means to remain steadfast in the beginning. To the beginning, opening and bestowal are never equivalent to loss or completion, but are always only a more magnificent beginning, a

more primordial intimacy. The holy is to be spoken in its firmness. Its remaining, however, is never the empty endurance of something present at hand; rather, it is the coming of the beginning. Before this, as what is former, nothing more primordial can be thought. As arrival, abiding is the primordiality of the beginning before which nothing else can be thought.

But what remains is founded by the poets. ("Remembrance")

The poem is incomplete in many respects. It remains indeterminable what particular arrangement of the conclusion Hölderlin himself may have chosen. But all incompleteness here is only the result of the profusion that flows from the innermost beginning of the poem, and demands a concise conclusion. Every attempt to retrace the structure of the final stanza can only strive to awaken those who have the capacity to hear what the "word" of this poem is.

But now day breaks! I awaited and saw it come,
And what I saw, may the holy be my word.

"Now"—when is this "now"? Is it the point in time around 1800 when the poem was written? Indeed the "now" clearly names that point in time in which Hölderlin himself says: "But now the day breaks!" The "now" certainly names Hölderlin's age and no other. Yet [76] Hölderlin's age is solely that time attuned by his words. Hölderlin's age is, to be sure, his age in the strictest sense. But this age of his is precisely not that which was merely simultaneous and contemporary with him in the usual sense.

The "now" names the coming of the holy. This coming alone specifies the "age," in which it is "time" for history to confront its essential decisions. Such a "time" can never be specified ("dated") and is not measurable by dates of the year and divisions of centuries. "Historical dates" are merely projected guidelines on which the occurrences are strung by human calculation. These occurrences can never occupy more than the foreground of history that is accessible to exploration (ἱστορεῖν). But this "historiographical" element is never history itself. History is rare. History only occurs when the essence of truth[7] comes to be decided on primordially.

In its coming, the holy—"older than the ages" and "above the gods"— grounds another beginning of another history. The holy primordially decides in advance concerning humans and gods: whether they are, and who they are, and how they are, and when they are. What is coming is said in its

---

7. [Heidegger's note from the first, 1941 edition:] Beyng itself.

coming through a calling. Beginning with this poem, Hölderlin's word is now the calling word. Hölderlin's word is now *hymnos* in a newly characterized and unique sense. We usually translate the Greek word ὑμνεῖν by the words "to praise" and "to celebrate." We easily understand by this translation a song a celebration of praise that is drunk with words. But now the poetic word is a founding saying. The word of this song is no longer a "hymn to" something—neither a "Hymn to the Poets" nor a hymn "to" nature. Rather, it is the hymn "of the holy." The holy bestows the word and itself comes into this word. This word is the primal event of the [77] holy. Hölderlin's poetry is now a primordial calling that, called by what is coming, says this and only this as the holy. The hymnal word is now "compelled by the holy," and because compelled by the "holy" also "sobered by the holy." So says a fragment from the year 1800 that is entitled "German Song":

> . . . then sits in the deep shade
> When above his head the elm tree rustles,
> By the stream that breathes out coolness the German poet
> And sings, when of the water sobered by the holy
> Enough he has drunk, listening far out into the stillness
> To the song of the soul.
> (Fragment no. 10, IV², 244)

The "deep shade" saves the poetic word from the excessive brightness of the "heavenly fire." The "stream that breathes out coolness" protects the poetic word from an excessively strong blaze of the "heavenly fire." The coolness and shade of sobriety correspond to the holy. This sobriety does not deny inspiration. Sobriety is the sensibility that is always ready for the holy.

Hölderlin's word conveys the holy, thereby naming the singular space of time, time of the primordial decision for the essential structure of the future history of gods and humanities.

This word, though still unheard, is preserved in the Occidental language of the Germans.

ELEVEN

Ereignis

1936–1938

The *Contributions* inquire along a path . . .

The *Contributions* inquire along a path that is first prepared through the *crossing* to the other beginning, the one that Western thinking now enters. This path brings the crossing into the open space of history and establishes it as a sojourn that may last a very long time. In the accomplishment of this sojourn, the other beginning of thinking always only remains intimated, but is indeed already decided.

Thus, though they already and exclusively speak of the essence of Beyng [*Seyn*]—i.e., of the "event" [*Er-eignis*]—the *Contributions* cannot yet join together [*fügen*] the free articulation [*freie Fuge*] of the truth of Beyng

---

In translating this chapter, I consulted the previously published translation by Parvis Emad and Kenneth Maly, *Contributions to Philosophy (From Enowning)* (Bloomington: Indiana University Press, 1999), as well as an unpublished draft translation by Dennis Schmidt, David Krell, and Richard Rojcewicz.

Bracketed numbers refer to the pagination of GA 65; the chapter opens at page 4.—Tr.

out of the latter itself. If this ever succeeds, then the essence of Beyng will, in its trembling, determine the framework [*Gefüge*] of the philosophical work itself. This trembling will then strengthen into the power of the released mildness of an intimacy proper to that *divinization* of the god of gods, from which the *assignment* of Da-sein to beyng occurs as the grounding of its truth.

Nevertheless, we must already attempt here that thoughtful discourse of philosophy in the other beginning, as if in a preparatory exercise. This discourse does not describe nor explain, does not proclaim or teach; here, discourse does not stand over against what is to be said, but is rather the latter itself as the holding-sway of Beyng.

This discourse gathers Beyng to an initial sounding of its essence, and itself indeed only sounds forth from out of this essence.

The preparatory exercise voices an inquiry that is neither a purposive activity of an individual nor a limited calculation of a community, but is instead, and prior to all this, the further hinting of a hint that arises from, and remains assigned to, what is most worthy of question.

Detachment from any "personal" accomplishment will only succeed on the basis of the intimacy of the earliest belonging. No grounding is granted that would not be guaranteed by such a detachment.

[5] The age of "systems" is past. The age of constructing the essential form of beings on the basis of the truth of Beyng has not yet come. In the meantime, in the crossing to the other beginning, philosophy must have achieved something essential: the projection, i.e., the founding opening of the temporal field of the truth of Beyng. How is this sole task to be accomplished? Here we remain without precedent and without a foothold. Mere modifications of what came before, even if they were to arise with the help of the greatest possible mixture of historically familiar ways of thinking, cannot get us to budge. And ultimately, any kind of world-view-theory stands outside of philosophy, because it can only exist through a denial that Beyng is worthy of question. In valuing this question-worthiness, philosophy has its own underived and incalculable dignity. All decisions concerning philosophy's activity take place from out of the preservation of this dignity, and *as* preservations of this dignity. In the realm of what is most worthy of question, however, this activity can only be a sole questioning. If any of philosophy's hidden ages call for it to decide upon its essence out of the clarity of its knowing, then it must do so in the crossing to the other beginning.

The other beginning of thinking is called such not because it is merely different in form from any given previous philosophies, but rather because it must be the only other beginning arising *in relation to* the one and only first beginning. This assignment of the one beginning to the other also already determines the character of thoughtful reflection in the crossing. It is as *historical* reflection that transitional thinking achieves the founding projection of the truth of Beyng. History is not thereby the object or sphere of an observation, but instead that which first awakens thoughtful inquiry and effects it as the scene of its decisions. In the crossing, thought puts in dialogue the earliest past of the Beyng of truth and the most remote future of the [6] truth of Beyng, and in this dialogue brings to words the hitherto unquestioned essence of Beyng. In the knowledge of transitional thinking, the first beginning remains decisive as the first, but is nevertheless overcome as a beginning. For this thinking, the clearest respect for the first beginning—one that first discloses this beginning's uniqueness—must be accompanied by the recklessness of departure involved in another inquiry and discourse.

The outline of these "contributions" to the preparation of the crossing is taken from the still-unmastered contours of the historicality of the crossing itself:

the sounding [*der Anklang*]
the passing play [*das Zuspiel*]
the leap [*der Sprung*]
the founding [*die Gründung*]
the future ones [*die Zukünftigen*]
the last god [*der letzte Gott*]

This outline does not provide a list of various observations regarding various objects; it is also not an introductory ascent from the low to the high. It is a preliminary sketch of the temporal field that the history of the crossing first creates as its realm, in order to decide, on the basis of its lawfulness, about the futureless ones—i.e., those who are always merely "eternal"—and the future ones—i.e., those who only are once. [. . .]

On the Event

[10] Everything depends here on the sole *question* concerning the truth of Beyng: on *questioning*. In order that this attempt might become an

impetus, the *wonder* of questioning must be experienced in its accomplishment and must be made effective as awakening and strengthening the power to question.

Inquiry immediately arouses the suspicion of being an empty, obstinate attachment to the uncertain, the undecided, and the undecidable. It appears as a restraint of "knowledge" into idle reflection. It seems to be narrowing, hampering, if not even nullifying.

And yet: questioning entails the driving, affirmative assault on what is unmastered, the expansion into what is still unexplored yet needs to be considered. Here, what reigns is the self-surmounting into what surpasses us. Questioning is liberation toward what hiddenly compels us.

In its seldomly experienced essence, questioning is so completely different from what the appearance of its non-essence indicates, that it often robs the discouraged of their last remnant of fortitude. Thus, they then also do not belong to the invisible circle enclosing all whose questioning is answered by the hint of Beyng.

The questioning pursuit of the truth of Beyng cannot be calculated from what preceded it. And if it is to prepare the beginning of another history, the accomplishment must be originary. Just as all engagement with the first beginning of the history of thought is unavoidable, so the questioning itself must certainly forget about everything that surrounds it and merely ponder its own dire need.

History only *comes to be* in the immediate leap over what is "historiological."

The inquiry concerning "meaning"—i.e., according to *Being and Time* the question about the founding of the projective area, in short the question about the *truth of Beyng*—is and remains *my* question and is my *only question*, since after all it concerns what is most *unique*. [11] In the age of *complete lack of inquiry*, it suffices to even initially ask *the* question of all questions.

In the age of endless need—which arises out of the hidden dire need of *needlessness*—this question must necessarily appear as the most useless idle talk, the kind that one has opportunely already passed over.

Nevertheless, the task remains: *the restoration of beings from out of the truth of Beyng.*

The question concerning the "meaning of Beyng" is the question of all questions. The accomplishment of this question's unfolding determines the essence of what one calls "meaning," as well as that in which the question takes place as reflection, and opens the inquiry as an inquiry: the openness for self-concealment, i.e., for the truth.

The question of Being is *that* leap into Beyng that the human accomplishes as a seeker of Beyng, insofar as he is a *thoughtfully* creative one. The seeker of Beyng with the ownmost abundance of seeking energy is the poet, who "institutes" [*stiftet*] Beyng.

We of the current age, however, have the sole duty of preparing that thinker through the anticipatory founding of a secure readiness for what it most worthy of question.

For the Few—for the Rare

For the few who *question* again from time to time, i.e., that put the essence of truth up for decision anew.

For the rare who are endowed with the greatest courage for solitude, in order to think the nobility of Beyng and to speak of its uniqueness.

Thought in the other beginning is originally historical in a unique way: the acquiescent authority over the holding-sway of Beyng.

We must risk a projection of the holding-sway of Beyng as the *appropriative event because* we do *not* know the task of our history. Would that we could fundamentally experience the holding-sway of this unknown in its self-concealing.

[12] Would that we wanted to develop this knowledge, so that what is abandoned and unknown leaves our will in solitude, and thus forces the persistence of Da-sein into the greatest restraint over against what conceals itself.

Nearness to the last god is reticence, which must be put into works and words in the style of restraint [*Verhaltenheit*].

To be in the nearness of the god—even if this nearness is the furthest distance of undecidability concerning the flight or arrival of the gods— cannot be considered "good fortune" or "misfortune." The persistence of Beyng itself carries its own measure in itself, if it is still in need of measure at all.

But to whom among us of today is this persistence granted? Its necessity is something for which we have hardly *prepared* ourselves, nor is there even an *indication* of this preparedness as the inception of another course of history.

Reversions to the demands and deadlocked ways of thought of metaphysics will for a long time still disturb and impede the clarity of the path as well as the determinateness of discourse. Nevertheless, the historical moment of the crossing must be accomplished on the basis of the knowledge that all metaphysics (founded upon the guiding question: What are beings?) was incapable of bringing humans into the basic relations to beings. After all, how is it supposed to achieve this? Even the will to do so will fall on deaf ears as long as the *truth* of Beyng and its uniqueness have not become a *dire need*. Yet how is thought to succeed in what was previously denied the poet (Hölderlin)? Or must we merely wrest his path and work from being buried, and direct them toward the truth of Beyng? Are we equipped for this?

The truth of Beyng only becomes a dire need through those who question. They are actually *believers,* because they persist toward the foundation —by opening the essence of truth (cf. The Founding, 237. Faith and Truth [GA 65, 368]).

The *questioners*—alone and without the aid of enchantment—establish the new and highest degree of urgency [13] in the center of Beyng, in the holding-sway of Beyng (the event) as the center.

The questioners have relinquished all curiosity; their seeking loves the abyss in which they know the oldest foundation.

If we are to be granted a history once again, a creative exposure to beings from a belongingness to being, then *this* determination is inescapable: to *prepare* the temporal space of the last decision—whether, and how, we experience and found this belongingness. This entails founding the knowledge of the appropriative event in thought, through the founding of the essence of truth as Da-sein.

However the decision concerning historicality or lack of history may fall, the questioners who prepare this decision in thought must *be;* may each of them bear solitude into his greatest hour.

What discourse does the highest silence of thought achieve? What procedure is most likely to bring about reflection on Beyng? Discourse on truth; for truth is the "between" for the holding-sway of Beyng and the beingness of beings. This between founds the beingness of beings in Beyng.

However, Beyng is not something "earlier"—existing in itself, for itself. Rather, the event is the spatio-temporal simultaneity for Beyng and beings (cf. The Passing Play, 112. The "A priori" [GA 65, 222]).

In philosophy, propositions are never subject to proof; and this not only because there are no *highest* propositions from which others could be derived, but rather because what is true here are not at all "propositions," nor simply the things they speak about. All "proving" assumes that the one who understands, coming to the content of the proposition with his presentations, remains the same, unchanged in the course of understanding the presentational structure of the proof. And only the "result" of the proof can demand an altered mode of presentation—or rather the presentation of something previously unnoticed.

[14] In philosophical knowledge, on the other hand, there begins with the first step a transformation of the one who understands, and not in the moral-"existential" sense, but with respect to Da-sein. In other words, the relation to Beyng—and prior to that always to the truth of Beyng—changes into Da-sein itself in the mode of displacement. Since, in philosophical knowing, everything is displaced at the same time in each case—the being of humans in its stance in truth, this truth itself, and thus the relation to Beyng—and since an immediate presentation of something present-at-hand is thus never possible, philosophical thinking remains strange.

Especially in the other beginning, the leap into the "between" must be accomplished instantly—according to the inquiry about the truth of Beyng. The "between" of Da-sein overcomes the χωρισμός not by building a bridge between Beyng (beingness) and beings, as if they were equally available banks, but rather by transforming Beyng and beings at the same time into their simultaneity. The leap into the between first originates [*erspringt*] Da-sein and does not come to occupy a space that already stood available.

The basic attunement of thinking in the other beginning resonates among the moods that can only distantly be called:

horror
restraint (cf. Prospect, 13. Restraint [GA 65, p. 33])   } presentiment

awe (cf. Prospect, 6. The Basic Attunement [GA 65, p. 20])

The inner relation among these is only experienced by thinking through the individual junctures into which the founding of the truth of Beyng and the holding-sway of truth must fit. The word for the unity of these moods is lacking, and yet it would be necessary to find it in order to avoid the easy misunderstanding that everything here is based upon a cowardly weakness. The blustering "heroism" might judge it so.

[15] *Horror:* It is most easily clarified in contrast to the basic attunement of the first beginning, to *wonder.* But a clarification of an attunement never guarantees that it actually *attunes,* instead of merely being presented.

To be horrified is to be taken aback from customary actions in the familiar, back into the openness of the onrush of what conceals itself, the openness in which the previously familiar proves to be at once disturbing and gripping. The most familiar, however, and therefore most unknown, is the abandonment by Beyng. Whereas before, beings were simply beings, horror lets humans be taken aback by the fact that beings *are,* and that Beyng has abandoned and withdrawn from all "beings" and whatever appeared as such.

Yet *this* horror is no mere shrinking back, nor the perplexed giving up of the "will." Rather, since the self-concealment of Beyng opens up precisely in this horror, and beings themselves and the relation to them want to be preserved, an ownmost "will" arises out of and joins the horror, and this is what we here call *restraint.*

Restraint (cf. Prospect, 13. Restraint [GA 65, 33]): the preliminary attunement of readiness for the refusal as gift. Without alleviating the horror, there reigns in restraint a turn toward the hesitating self-refusal as the holding-sway of Beyng. Restraint is the *center* (cf. below) for horror and awe. These only characterize more expressly what *originally* belongs to restraint. Restraint determines the style of inceptive thinking in the other beginning.

According to what has been stated, *awe* is not to be confused with shyness or even understood in that direction. Such a view is out of the question to the extent that the awe intended here actually even exceeds the "will" of restraint, and does so out of the depth of the foundation of the unitary basic attunement. From the latter, and from awe in particular, stems the necessity of reticence, which is the letting-hold-sway of Beyng as event that [16] resonates throughout the whole comportment among beings and all relation to them.

Awe is the way of approaching and staying near what is most distant as such (cf. The Last God [GA 65, 403ff.]), which in its intimation—and if held in awe—nevertheless becomes the closest and gathers all relations of Beyng into itself (cf. The Leap, 115. The Guiding Attunement of the Leap [GA 65, 227]).

Yet who is capable of attuning this basic attunement of horrified-awed restraint in essential humans? And how many still will realize that *this* attunement-by-Beyng does not justify an avoidance of beings, but rather the opposite: the opening of the simplicity and greatness of beings, and the originally urgent necessity of sheltering the truth of Beyng in beings in order thus to once again give historical humans a goal: *to become the founder and preserver of the truth of Beyng,* to *be* the there as the foundation that the very essence of Beyng requires: *care,* not as a trivial worry about random things, and not as renunciation of joy and power, but more originally than all of this, as uniquely care *"for the sake of Beyng,"* not the beyng of the human, but the Beyng of beings as a whole.

The oft-repeated indication that "care" is only to be thought in the inceptive realm of the question of Being, and not as an arbitrary, personally accidental, "world-view" or "anthropological" outlook on humans, will remain without effect in the future as long as those who merely "write" a "critique" of the question of Being do not experience—and do not want to experience—any of the dire need stemming from the abandonment of Beyng. For in the age of a wretchedly flaunted "optimism," the very words "care" and "abandonment by Beyng" already sound "pessimistic." Now that precisely those moods indicated by these names, as well as their opposites, have become fundamentally *impossible* in the realm of inceptive questioning —since they presuppose the thought of value (ἀγαθόν), the previous [17] interpretations of beings, and the customary understanding of the human— the question arises as to who could reflect enough in order to at least permit all of this to become a question.

Especially in inceptive thought, realms of the truth of Beyng must be traversed in order to retreat again into concealment when beings flare up. This stepping aside belongs essentially to the indirectness of the "effects" of all philosophy.

In philosophy, what is essential must retreat into what is inaccessible (to the many) after having had its impact, even though it is almost completely concealed. This is the case because what is essential is unsurpassable and *therefore* must withdraw into making the beginning possible. For one must always begin again with Beyng and its truth.

All beginnings are in themselves what is unsurpassably complete. They escape historiology not because they are supra-temporally eternal, but because they are greater than eternity: *the pulses* of time that grant Being the openness of its self-concealment. One's own founding of this temporal space is called Da-*sein.*

In restraint—the attuning center of horror and awe, the fundamental *characteristic* of the basic attunement—Da-*sein* attunes itself to the *stillness* of the passing-by of the last god. Existing creatively in this basic attunement of Dasein, the human becomes a *guard* for this stillness.

Thus the inceptive reflection of thinking necessarily becomes genuine thought—that is to say, thought that sets *goals.* It does not set just any goal, and not *the* goal in a general sense, but rather the unique and only goal of our history. This goal is *seeking* itself, the seeking of Beyng. It is itself the deepest discovery, and occurs when humans decisively become preservers of the truth of Beyng, the guards for that stillness.

Being *seeker, preserver,* and *guard*—that is what *care* as the basic trait of Dasein means. Its name gathers in itself the determination [18] of the human, insofar as the latter is understood from out of its foundation—i.e., out of Da-sein. This Da-sein is reciprocally appropriated to the *event* as the essence of Beyng, and only due to this origin as the founding of the temporal space ("temporality") can it become capable of transforming the dire need of abandonment by Beyng into the necessity of creating as the retrieval of beings.

And by fitting into the juncture of Beyng, we are *at the disposal of the gods.*

Seeking itself is the goal. And that means: "goals" are still emphasized too much and still stand in front of Beyng—and cover over what is necessary.

At the disposal of the gods—what does this mean, if the gods are what is undecided, since the open place of divinization is still refused? It means: to be at disposal for use in the opening of this open place. And the most needed are those that must determine in advance the openness of *this* open place, and achieve the attunement to it by thinking of, and calling into question, the essence of truth. At the "disposal of the gods" means: standing far away from, and outside of, the common-ness of "beings" and their interpretations; belonging to the most distant ones, to whom the flight of the gods remains nearest in its furthest withdrawal.

We are already moving, even if only transitionally, in another truth (in the more originally transformed essence of "true" and "correct").

Of course, the founding of this essence requires an exertion of thought of the kind that had to be accomplished in the first beginning of Western thinking. This exertion is foreign to us because we have no sense of what mastering the *simple* entails. Those of today, who are hardly worthy of mention even in turning away from them, remain excluded from the knowledge of the way of thinking; they flee to "new" contents and, by introducing the "political" and the "racial," supply [19] themselves with a previously unknown façade for the old gear of academic philosophy.

One relies on the shallow pools of "lived experiences," incapable of measuring the expansive structure of the space of thought, or of thinking the depths and height of Beyng in this opening. And wherever one believes oneself to be above "lived experience," one invokes an empty sagacity.

Whence, then, should the education to essential thinking come? From thinking ahead and pursuing decisive paths.

Who, for instance, follows the long path of founding the truth of Beyng? Who surmises something of the *necessity* of thinking and questioning—of that necessity which does not require the crutches of "why" and the support of "wherefore"?

The more necessary the thoughtful discourse about Beyng is, the more inescapable becomes the silencing of the truth of Beyng through the *course* of questioning.

The poet, more easily than others, veils truth in the image and thus presents it to the gaze for preservation.

Yet how does the thinker preserve the truth of Beyng, if not in the heavy slowness of his inquisitive steps and their attendant consequences? As inconspicuously as the sower who, in a lonely field under a giant sky, paces off the furrows with heavy, halting, momentarily restraining steps and measures and shapes the concealed space of all growth and ripening with the scattering toss of his arm. Who is still capable of accomplishing this in thought, as the most inceptive part of his power, and as his greatest future?

If a thoughtful question is not simple and prominent enough to determine the intention or style of thought for centuries by assigning it the highest tasks, then it is best that the question remain unasked. For, in merely being parroted, it only adds to the incessant market of [20] colorfully changing "problems," those "reproaches" that concern nothing and no one.

In this regard: how does it stand with the question of Beyng as the question about the truth of Beyng, the question that simultaneously and reciprocally inquires about the Beyng of truth? How long must the path become on which one merely encounters the question of truth?

Whatever may truly and in the future be called philosophy has as its primary and only task to first find the place of thoughtful posing of the newly inceptive question, i.e., to found *Da-sein* (cf. The Leap [GA 65, 225ff.]).

The thoughtful question concerning the truth of Beyng is the moment that carries the crossing. This moment is never actually determinable, even less calculable. It first marks the time of the event. The sole simplicity of this crossing will never be historiographically graspable, because the public historiological "history" has long surpassed the crossing when the latter can be shown to it in a mediate fashion. There thus remains for this moment a long futurity, provided that beings' abandonment by Beyng can once again be broached.

In Da-sein and *as* Da-sein, beyng appropriates truth and reveals it as a refusal, as that realm of hinting and of withdrawal—of stillness—in which the arrival or flight of the last god is first decided. The human cannot achieve anything *toward this end,* least of all if he is tasked with preparing the founding of Da-sein in such a way that this task once again determines the essence of the human.

TWELVE

On Ernst Jünger (1)

———❧———

1939–1940

We would like to attempt something very simple here: to read together in texts that can serve as direct impulses for reflection.

In doing so, we would like to avoid two things: merely educated and scholarly discussions of solitary concepts, but also loose conversation about what is merely public and current.

The genuine and reflective reading of essential books can only ever aim at approximating what is *not* written in the books and what can never be written in books.

The original and experienced relation to *what* is to be grasped [*begriffen*] is more important than the tidiness of concepts [*Begriffe*] and the security of a strict adherence to a particular reflective plane. This in turn

---

Bracketed numbers in this chapter refer to the pagination of GA 90; the chapter opens at page 235. — Tr.

demonstrates, of course, that the *actual concept* is something distinct from a mere grasping-tool of abstract thought, one that can be changed according to whim and separated from what is "grasped." The philosophical concept is always an embodying totality [*Inbegriff*], insofar as it envelops [*einbegreift*] the one who thinks, thereby attacks [*angreift*] them and challenges their Da-sein. That is why this reading and discussion will only succeed if we inquire from the nearest possible proximity, voice concerns, attempt answers, and set out on our project from different angles.

On this voyage I would like, at most, to take the position of a helmsman who seeks to maintain a course toward the approximate. The captain of the vessel that we ourselves are is the secret of the story that awaits us.

Perhaps our aim can gain clarity, and some questions perhaps already arise, if we first say something about Jünger himself. These comments are not intended as "biography," for in the age of newspapers', radio's, and television's reckless, public manipulation of all human achievements and failures, we will [236] more easily see that essential kinds of history, works, and humanity can only exist from out of the passion for the great stillness of Being—a passion that never knows itself.

Ernst Jünger

World War I determines his writing, thinking, and saying. This, of course, goes for everything that materialized as human-historical acting and think-ing in the time after the war—or, as we more accurately say now, the time between the wars. However, Jünger fought through the full length of the war, from being a volunteer marksman to a second lieutenant of infantry and assault detachment leader. He was injured seven times, and awarded the House Order of Hohenzollern and the Pour le Mérite. But this also applies to others who may have fallen prematurely or, if they made it through, remain silent.

Indeed, the writing of "war books" based on such experiences cannot distinguish Jünger either, not even if one esteems him especially highly as a writer. The *Rumänisches Tagebuch*[1] by Hans Carossa; the war journal of the young Bernhard von der Marwitz ("Stirb und Werde");[2] Friedrich

---

1. Hans Carossa, *Rumänisches Tagebuch* (Leipzig, 1924). [Translated as *Roumanian Diary* by Agnes Neill Scott (New York: A. A. Knopf, 1930).—Tr.]
2. Bernhard von der Marwitz, "Stirb und Werde," in *Briefe und Kriegstagebuchblätter*, ed. H. von Koenigswald (Breslau, 1931).

Franz von Unruh's story *Verlorener Posten,*[3] about the sovereign of Baden's own regiment and its several days of battle at the Loretto Heights—all of these writings have their own incomparable place next to Jünger's *Das Wäldchen 125.*[4]

Nevertheless, Jünger has stamped his work with the *spirit* of the *front-line soldier,* desiring to keep him alive and to make this soldiership exemplary of a new human breed. But who [237] would deny that many others attempted and accomplished all of this much more loudly and pervasively?

The socialism of the "front-line soldiers," the "camaraderie" of the trench fighter, the "nationalism" of the true fighters: all of this was raised up as an "ideal" after the war. At the same time, forms of military life were transferred into the reformation of the political struggle and of communities. It was not just the breed of front-line soldiers that was determinative in this process, but also one that was essentially different—that of the volunteer corps fighter.[5]

While Ernst Jünger's thought is certainly based on the experiences of a front-line fighter, he leaves phenomena like socialism, nationalism, camaraderie, and community behind at once and with increasing certainty. For he realizes that these appearances either belong to the civil pre-war era, even if they are changed and fused together, like socialism and nationalism; or, as with camaraderie and community, that they are forms of human solidarity that remain valuable at all times, and can therefore never be *historical, shaping powers in themselves.*

Jünger sees the soldiership and even the humanity of World War I, and this war itself, as beyond—or rather this side of—socialism and nationalism; but this is because he, like no other, experiences that World War metaphysically, i.e., as an occurrence of beings as a whole. After the war, his thought did not return to the conventional regions of ideas about fate and humanity, in order to then [238] describe and explain the war from that angle. Instead, he

---

3. Friedrich Franz von Unruh, *Verlorener Posten: Schilderung aus der Loretto-Schlacht* (Hamburg, 1935).

4. [Ernst Jünger, *Das Wäldchen 125: Eine Chronik aus den Grabenkämpfen 1918* (Berlin, 1925). Translated by Basil Creighton as *Copse 125: A Chronicle of the Trench Warfare of 1918* (London: Chatto & Windus, 1930).—Tr.]

5. [The following is an insertion crossed out by Heidegger:] The prevalence of so-called "assault detachment speakers" [*Stoßtrupprednern*] for example, shows the extent of the transfer, but also the emptying, of military "forms of life." (Further, one can only understand the term if one avoids clear and distinct thinking—as with the term "junior driver" [*Nachwuchsfahrer*]; terms such as these are not only evidence of an unrestrained adulteration of language, but indications of the metaphysically grounded process of the destruction of the essence of language.)

attempts to confront the *different* essence of World War I, facing it in order to leave the *pre*-war era behind and determine anew—i.e. out of itself—what is present. That is the basic intention of his war books *In Stahlgewittern*,[6] 1920; *Das Wäldchen 125*, 1925; *Feuer und Blut*,[7] 1925. However, this intention only gradually found its secure form, which a comparison of the 1920 version of *In Stahlgewittern* with the final "revision" of 1933 demonstrates.

Throughout all of these efforts, Jünger realized that Nietzsche's teaching of the will to power already brought to mind and to word—i.e., grounded—*that* metaphysics on whose unrecognized foundation World War I and the post-war era became history.

This allusion to Nietzsche, however, means something essentially distinct from what the culture propaganda of Western democracy utters in the first and in this "World War": that the "war," brought about by the Germans, was an expression of Nietzsche's teaching of the "blond beast." Nietzsche realized, rather, that the Western democracies and their mode of preeminence in modernity stand at the decisive beginning of what we—beyond Nietzsche in a very broad but perhaps essential conception—must today call "communism." By this we mean neither a "party," nor a "world-view," but instead the ultimate metaphysical position of modernity. If one uses Nietzsche's name and selected phrases to attack German-ness, one [239] is not at all willing to think through his basic thoughts in this decisive direction; but even the Germans dare not and cannot pursue this. Only Ernst Jünger has grasped something essential here. It remains a separate question whether he has thereby already accessed the region of actual metaphysical decisions—i.e., whether he has initially even unfolded this region, and whether he can ever unfold it according to his way of thinking. In any case, Jünger's leap into Nietzsche's basic metaphysical position is more substantial than Spengler's[8] current superficial evaluation of Nietzsche's thinking.

One has naturally said too little if one points out that Jünger was substantially "influenced" by Nietzsche in his thinking, because: firstly, in such observations, Nietzsche remains solely a "name"; and secondly, only someone who brings a true inquiry *with* him, and toward an essential

6. Ernst Jünger, *In Stahlgewittern: Aus dem Tagebuch eines Stoßtruppführers v. Ernst Jünger, Kriegsfreiwilliger, dann Leutnant und Kompanieführer im Füs.-Regt. Prinz Albrecht v. Preußen* (Hannover, 1920). [Translated by Michael Hoffman as *Storm of Steel* (Harmondsworth: Penguin, 2004).—Tr.]

7. Ernst Jünger, *Feuer und Blut: Ein kleiner Ausschnitt aus einer großen Schlacht* (Magdeburg, 1925).
8. [Oswald Spengler, author of *The Decline of the West*.—Tr.]

thinker, can be influenced by the latter. To be "influenced" by great thinkers and poets is only the luck of those who have already left the region of the small. Jünger is neither a "Nietzschean" in the usual sense, nor has he simply appropriated certain ideas and demands, like D'Annunzio[9] and Mussolini— the latter of whom still manages to "harmonize" his supposedly Nietz- schean spirit quite well with his relations to the Vatican.[10] There is no trace of such questionable, perhaps even dubious, plundering of individual ideas of Nietzsche's in Jünger. Rather, being led by his own experiences and becoming clear-sighted through Nietzsche's thinking, he has experienced *that* which Nietzsche terms the lowest to which we descend: the *will to power* as the basic character of the real.

Jünger faces this reality and takes hold in a relation to it. He does not avoid the basic metaphysical position that Nietzsche's thought already oc- cupied. Nietzsche himself labeled this position with the name that was first shaped by the Russian poet Turgenev: nihilism.[11] But Nietzsche's nihilism is not the nihilism of "weakness," the mere letting-go [240] in the pessimistic "for nothing"—rather, it is "active nihilism."

> That something is a hundred times *more important* than the question of whether *we* feel well or not: fundamental instinct of all strong natures—and conse- quently also whether *others* feel well or not. In short, that we have a goal for which one does not hesitate to offer *human sacrifices*, to risk every danger, to take upon oneself whatever is bad and worst: the *great passion*.[12] (*The Will to Power* no. 26, 1887.[13] Cf. p. 11 below, at the top!)[14]

---

9. [Gabriele D'Annunzio (1863–1938), an Italian writer who prefigured many of the fascist ideals and cultural elements employed by Mussolini, most notably the notion of "superior" humans and the public display of nationalistic emotion.—Tr.]

10. [Heidegger probably has in mind the Lateran Treaty of 1929, a concordat signed between Italy and the Holy See, recognizing the full sovereignty of the latter in exchange for its neutrality in matters of foreign relations.—Tr.]

11. [This is presumably a reference to Turgenev's depiction of the "nihilist" Bazarov in *Fathers and Sons*, published in 1862. The word "nihilism" appears in German philosophical polemics at the end of the eighteenth century, but it is only with Turgenev's novel that it comes to characterize a type of "new man" in Europe.—Tr.]

12. "The great passion [. . .] makes him unhesitating [. . .] and uses up convictions [as a means . . .] The man of faith, the 'believer' of every kind, is necessarily a dependent person—one who cannot posit any end at all by themselves." In "Being able to see freely" (8, 294). [Heidegger's citation here is from Nietzsche's *The Antichrist*, § 54.—Tr.]

13. [The English version cited and slightly emended here is from Walter Kaufmann, *The Will to Power* (New York: Random House, 1967), 19.—Tr.]

14. [GA 90, 245–246.]

And what is the goal that this nihilism aims at, even though "nihilism means": "The aim is lacking" (*The Will to Power* no. 2, 1887)?[15] It is, in fact, the aim of aimlessness—the simple "yes"-saying to that which is and is recognized as being—to the will to power as the basic character of the real.

The "*analytic*" (*The Will to Power* no. 10, 1887)[16] is analogous to this affirmation. It dissects everything, not just to dissolve it, but rather to hit upon the lowest "to which we descend"; in distinction from "*historicism*," which disregards the real, explains and understands everything, does not acknowledge anything, and is therefore called the nihilism of weakness— "passive nihilism." And, with almost the same words that he uses to describe *active* nihilism, Nietzsche also determines the essence of the "heroic" attitude that says "yes" to that which is—to the "real," without concern for itself.

Active nihilism is thus utmost realism; more precisely, this "realism" is precisely authentic nihilism. What "realism" means here—what the real that he affirms looks like, whether or not he grasps the reality of this real, and thus [241] grasps himself—these are all questions from which we will not be able to retreat, but that all belong to the *one* question: what our history "is" at the moment.

Jünger himself describes his position—or rather the position of *that* humanity that he sees dawning—as "*heroic realism.*" His way of thinking corresponds to this: it is "analytic" through and through, in the sense of the constant, dissecting display of "reality." The fact that Jünger simultaneously and continually seeks out the dream world and invents dreamscapes does not contradict this. Just as metaphysics has mysticism as its necessary counterpart, so fantasy belongs to realism, especially of the nihilistic kind. These remarks are not intended to label Ernst Jünger and his writings with popular designations, but instead aim to indicate through which attitude World War I became the *decisive reality* for him.

This attitude, and its corresponding representation and achievement in Jünger's writings, offers a version of Nietzsche's basic metaphysical position that is closer and more comprehensible to our historical moment than Nietzsche's depictions of the historical situation in the seventies and eighties of the previous century. At the same time, it directly shows how independent Nietzsche's—and any thinker's—decisive thoughts are from the superficial images of his time, but from which he nevertheless cannot separate himself.

---

15. [Kaufmann, *The Will to Power*, 9.—Tr.]
16. [Ibid., 11.—Tr.]

If, however, Western metaphysics in general comes to completion in Nietzsche's metaphysics, and if metaphysics is the ground of Western history, then the ground of weak and of strong nihilism must be recognized in metaphysics itself.

In distinction from the realm of political and military struggles, one can only inquire, think, and decide *from extreme positions* in the all-surrounding and sheltering region of *spirit*.

In order to catch a glimpse, and perhaps one [242] day to gain a foothold in this region, we attempt an engagement with Ernst Jünger. Not as if we can expect a decision from him, or even the preparation of one. After all, heroic realism is in its essence not only the renunciation of the preparation and grounding of inceptive decisions, but must be recognized as a unique relation to devastation. By devastation, we do not mean the mere destruction of what is present, but instead the undermining of the possibility of any inceptive decision, on account of the taking-over of the real and, prior to this, of what is considered real. This does not prevent the fact that such an age can—from the horizon available to it alone—still have a sense of itself as a "transition" (*Blätter und Steine*,[17] 212–213).

The process of this metaphysically understood devastation does not rule out—but on the contrary *includes*—the maintenance and enjoyment of conventional culture and its most exquisite goods. Jünger himself is proof of this, in his peculiar way of moving among all the treasure houses of thinking, poetizing, and knowing. His acquaintance with the spirit and style of the French poets and "thinkers" stands at the forefront, as it does in Nietzsche—but without Nietzsche's substantial relation to the Greeks. This "education" is not just very unhistoriographical, but is especially *unhistorical* and is at times playful and almost coquettish.

The "active" part, the "action" of "heroic realism" is no longer a struggle, provided we understand it as the *execution*—i.e., the unfolding and grounding—of essential decisions.

Realistic heroism, heroism in the face of reality as such, is the definite "yes" to that which is and to the *way in which* the affirmer himself exists, and nothing more. This heroism despises noise; perhaps the only remainder of noise is the fact that it is [243] still called "heroism." Nietzsche already saw this clearly as well, as a note from 1888 attests (*The Will to Power*, no. 349): "However: Real heroism consists in *not* fighting under the banner of sacri-

---

17. Ernst Jünger, *Blätter und Steine*, 1934.

fice, devotion, selflessness, but in *not fighting at all*—'*This* is what *I* am; this is how *I* want it—*you* can go to hell!'"[18]

This conception of the "heroic spirit" is not an arbitrary one, and it also does not contain a so-called atemporal essence of the heroic, of hero-ness as such.

Nietzsche's and thus Jünger's determination of the "heroic spirit" is grounded in the metaphysics of modernity, according to which the human as subject—as that which is left to itself—must be grasped as a being that secures this position by mastering the world. The "heroism" arising from this, and from this alone, is unfathomably different from the Greek experience of the hero, who has his being in the middle position between the gods and humans, and whose condition thus lies in the reign of individual gods and the history of his own humanity. Hölderlin's experience of the hero and of the heroic is deeply related to this, yet substantially different. Thus it also stands—even if it falls within modernity according to historiographical time—*outside of this time* in an historical sense, in its own place (of the history of Beyng [*Seyn*]) that we have yet to recognize. "Heroic" and "heroic" are not the same—something that must be noted in an age that describes the death of a racecar driver, in the "mission" of a record-setting race, as heroic, and that offers heroism as a product. Nietzsche's notion of heroism, and Jünger's in its suit, must remain distinct over against this ordinary heroism, but *only in such a way* as essence over against non-essence. Jünger in particular, who thinks in terms of the material battle of World War I, never sees heroism as that blind brutality which, for instance, counts pain as something shameful and as mere weakness, that pretends not to know [244] fear, and that diminishes anxiety to the mere wretchedness of the coward. After all, on the first pages of his most powerful formulation of his war experience, Jünger writes (*Das Wäldchen 125*, p. 6): "Only I have lived among fighters long enough to know that there is no such thing as a human without fear. Without fear, even bravery would be senseless; fear is the dark shadow before which the risk appears more colorful and tempting." And he clearly does not want the description of his basic attitude as "heroic realism" to be misconstrued, since he remarks later on (*Blätter und Steine* 1934, p. 173):

> One cannot breed a "heroic world-view" artificially or proclaim it from the lecterns, for, to be sure, the hero gains this view by right of birth, but it sinks to

18. [The translation, with slight emendations, is from Kaufmann, *The Will to Power*, 191.—Tr.]

the level of common conceptions through the way in which the masses grasp it. [. . .] Likewise, a complete nation depends upon the existence of at least one complete human; and pure will, in the best of cases, creates a complete bureaucracy.

And at a different point (p. 218): "The one page on which Rabelais depicts Panurg soiling his pants out of fear has stronger energy than all books written about the heroic world-view." Jünger's essay "On Pain"[19] offers the best information for identifying his meaning of heroic realism, as well as for insight into his basic position (and its inner boundaries). According to that essay, "discipline" is the basic form in which humans sustain contact with pain. And the "commanding height" from which humans accomplish the objectification of pain and the sealing-off of life against it, decides the new rank of the future "race."[20]

"Tell me your relation to pain, and I wish to tell you [245] who you are! Pain, as measure, is immutable; conversely, the way in which humans face this measure is mutable."—"Our inquiry is as follows: What role does pain play in that new race that first distinguishes itself in its expressions of life, the one we called the *worker*?" (p. 155)

In his thoughts on pain, Jünger has not simply appropriated Nietzsche's basic views, but truly grasped them. For the many who cannot immediately see, in Jünger's way of seeing and mastering the real, how definitely he stands within the realm of Nietzsche's basic metaphysical position, Jünger gives hints that evince Nietzsche's spirit all the way down to the shape of his language. Near the end of the essay "On Pain," Jünger writes (pp. 210–211):

> Today [in 1934] we see the valleys and fields filled with military camps, deployments, and exercises. We see the states more threatening and armed than ever, poised toward power expansion in every minute respect, commanding ranks and arsenals whose purpose is clear. We also see the individual entering ever more clearly into that state in which he can be sacrificed without reservations. With this in view, the question arises whether we are witnessing the opening of the spectacle in which life appears as the *will to power,* and as *nothing* else.

At this point, it might help to bring to mind a passage of Nietzsche's *Will to Power* that can offer a preview of the realm in which Jünger's conception of "the worker" moves. The editors of *The Will to Power,* which in its *current ordering* of pieces has not retained Nietzsche's own order, have moved the

19. Ernst Jünger, "Über den Schmerz," in *Blätter und Steine,* 154–213.
20. Pain as touchstone and as means of determining a legitimate power: ibid., 13.

passage to the end of the whole work; however, it stems from 1885 and reads as follows (*The Will to Power*, no. 1067):[21]

> And do you also know what "the world" is to me? Should I show it to you in [246] my mirror? This world: a monster of force, without beginning, without end; a solid, iron magnitude of force that does not grow bigger or smaller, that does not expend itself, but only changes; immutable in its size as a whole, an economy without expenditures and losses, but also without growth or income; surrounded by "nothingness" as if by a boundary; nothing blurry, wasted, nothing infinitely expanded, but set as a definite force in a definite space, and not a space that would be "empty" anywhere, but more as force throughout, simultaneously one and many as a play of forces and force-waves, increasing here and at the same time thinning out there; a sea of forces storming and flooding together, eternally changing, eternally retreating, with tremendous years of recurrence, with an ebb and flood of its shapes, drifting from the simplest to the most complex, from the stillest, coldest, and most rigid out into the most glowing, most turbulent, most self-contradictory, and then again returning home to the simple from this abundance, from the play of contradictions back to the joy of harmony, still affirming itself in this uniformity of its courses and years, blessing itself as that which must return eternally, as a becoming that knows no satiety, no disgust, no weariness: this my *Dionysian* world of the eternally-self-creating, the eternally-self-destroying, this mystery-world of double lusts, this my "Beyond Good and Evil" without an aim, unless the joy of the circle is itself an aim; without a will, unless a ring feels good will toward itself—do you want a *name* for this world? A *solution* to all of its riddles? A light for you, too, you most-concealed, strongest, most intrepid, most midnightly?—*This world is the will to power*—and *nothing else*! And you yourselves are also this will to power—and nothing else!

But why not Nietzsche instead of Jünger, then, if we are attempting a reflection? After all, we do not want to acquaint ourselves with views and statements of Jünger the writer and [247] soldier, but find our way to what the real is and what is today becoming accessible as beings.

Jünger does not only see the real as will to power in phenomena that apply closely and especially to us. Rather, his vision moves within the *optics* of a reconnaissance scout who positions the real as if for an attack. Jünger's way of "describing" stems from that desire of Nietzsche's to guess what the ground of the foreground is, and this scouting-out is not an observation that is sharper by degrees, but something essentially different: a mastery of the

---

21. [This paragraph, with some emendations, can be found in Kaufmann, *The Will to Power*, 549–550.—Tr.]

real through exposure. Of course, all of this only becomes possible if, and to the extent that, the reality of the real is already decided as will to power, indeed even stands outside of the decision; for only thereby does the objectification, in allowing vision, obtain its own character of being the will to power. Jünger, in a grand fashion, often forces one into the real that is projected in this way, thus achieving an "introduction" to Nietzsche's basic metaphysical position, which means something different from a scholarly introduction to Nietzsche's philosophy.

One likes to dismiss Jünger with the excuse that his presentations stem from a "subjective view of essences" [*Wesensschau*]. If "subjective" is to mean that something is accomplished as if by a human and from out of his essential core, then every view of essences is "subjective"—and is more "objective" the more "subjective" it remains. If "subjective," on the other hand, means as much as "partial," "arbitrary," and "not objectively-empirically verifiable," then Jünger's view of the essence of the real, and Nietzsche's at its basis, and every philosophical view of essence, are the opposite of this. The "objectivity" of such a projection of the real does not, after all, consist in the correctness of the copying of what is supposedly present. Rather, it consists in the truth about beings as a whole—a truth that opens and shows itself in various depths of historical humanity. In every attempt to enter the realm of this truth insofar as it determines the current age, Ernst Jünger is a pointer with his own [248] "stature," and thus an essential human among his contemporaries.

But with this, we again touch upon the "biographical," whereas the matter at hand is the important thing. The matter, however, is not just the real that surrounds us, but the reality that determines the real. Indeed, it is important not only to know reality, but also the Being that has been sought and found in *reality*, here and for a long time in the history of Western humanity.

Perhaps the time has permanently passed that could have allowed one to know what really is, to at least gain a distance through this knowledge that could still serve as mastery of beings.

It is necessary to know the real without concealment. But if humans are at all to *be* among beings as a whole—to relate to them, that is, to build for beings a place of revealedness—it is more necessary to realize that concealment as well as disenchantment are already and ever unavoidable "occurrences" [*Ereignisse*].

It is necessary to know the real without concealment—and that is why we set out toward such knowledge. But it is more necessary to realize that all beings—and every relation to them—are nothing without the truth about *Beyng,* through which every being is first appropriated into what and how it is.

We can comb through all beings, but nowhere will we directly encounter Beyng. We can demolish and order anew all beings, but nowhere will we find a free place for the housing of Beyng! And how can we be surprised at such an abandonment by Beyng, if it has remained only an echo of a word to us—an echo that we thoughtlessly abuse in each spoken or unspoken "is"?

If Western history began from a knowledge of Beyng, indeed if this knowledge was the beginning itself, how should we prepare for another beginning, other [249] than through the knowledge that all beings are always *more than beings*?

We reach out for this knowledge when we attempt, on a single path, to see what is. In this process names, people, individual things, conditions, and incidents are unimportant; what counts is to face what is becoming, and what perhaps truly and solely "is" *as* this becoming.

The modesty out of which we attempt what is next guarantees us a hinting resonance [*Anklang*] of where, a long way off, the paths lead—but they are nevertheless already paths.

THIRTEEN

On Ernst Jünger (2)

═════◊◊◊═══════

1939–1940

The engagement with Western metaphysics as such and as a whole belongs essentially to the incipient reflective crossing into another beginning of the history of Beyng [*Seyn*]. The basic metaphysical position that Nietzsche founded stands closest to this engagement. This metaphysics, however, not only stands nearest to us *historiographically* [historisch], according to the calculation of time, but is much more immediate, since we historically [*geschichtlich*] act and "think" in its disclosed reality (of the real as will to power): even where one does not experience this real specifically in this way, even if one does not know Nietzsche's teaching, even if one rejects it. Nietzsche's metaphysics is just as little a "private system" (Dilthey) as Hegel's "system of science," and instead—in essential unity with the latter— prepares the completion and thus the end of Western metaphysics.

The engagement with Western metaphysics is not a discussion of teach-

───────────────

Bracketed numbers in this chapter refer to the pagination of GA 90; the chapter opens at page 253.—Tr.

ings, as "metaphysics" is here already conceived and experienced more essentially than the historical structure of the truth of beings as such and as a whole, a framework that will itself remain Western humanity's ground of history into the near future.

The engagement with metaphysics becomes a reflection on the truth of beings as a whole and must therefore be enacted from out of our belongingness to beings, which can only occur within the relation to the real that permeates us. However, this demands that we awaken within the basic position related by Nietzsche. And that requires an engagement with Nietzsche. Yet his metaphysics is presently and always thought as the end of that beginning in which the most ancient Greek thinkers (Anaximander, Heraclitus, Parmenides) questioned Being. We do not mean Nietzsche's historiographical relations to the distant antiquity of Western [254] thought. Rather, the historical proximity of that beginning is experienced in the metaphysics that is now complete.

But today's thinking, which remains only a calculative opining and "cipher"-play,[1] can no longer, or not yet, find its way into the accomplishment of an engagement with Nietzsche. The indiscriminate and ceaseless misinterpretation of Nietzsche is simply the consequence of this incapacity.

The arbitrary exploitation of his work for shifting purposes evokes the appearance, however, that this misinterpretation is Nietzsche's true historical "effect" in the present. This "effect" of Nietzsche's—and what one takes as this effect—nowhere encounters any boundaries or objections anymore: Otherwise Nietzsche could not simultaneously serve as a support for counter-Christian worldviews, as a defense of Christianity amid the contemporary contrivance of church teachings, as a revitalization of desolate freethinking, and as a goldmine for "psychological"-"biological" teachings. All of this ignores the fact that in Nietzsche's thinking, metaphysics reached the historical moment in which beings became disclosed as real in the sense of the will to power. One of course knows this "teaching" of Nietzsche's about the will to power, and provides crude and platitudinous "applications" in so-called "life"; but one takes over a "teaching" and recognizes therein a "position" of a person who, because he was sick and weak, simply attempted to preach health and violence as the highest values. "Race researchers" give themselves off as admirers of the teacher[2] of the will to

---

1. [Cf. Karl Jaspers, *Philosophie*, 3 vols. (Berlin, 1932). "Wesen der Chiffren" (Essence of Ciphers) is elaborated in volume 3, *Metaphysik*.]

2. [Heidegger first writes "philosopher," crosses this out and comments in the margin: "thus again ambivalent."]

power, while ignoring the fact that Nietzsche, precisely in the years of his work on *The Will to Power* in 1886–1887, wrote in his notebook: "Maxim: Not to deal with anyone who has a share in the fake race-swindle."—"The deceit and mire involved [255] in raising race questions in today's hodge-podge Europe!" (8, 356).

Nietzsche's supposedly "grand" effect is this stifling air of an enunciated, or concealed, or unnoticed "Nietzscheanism." This "effect" will still delay the knowledgeable appropriation of his basic experience for quite some time. And who would deny that some aspects of Nietzsche's way of expressing himself had to promote this "effect"? Nevertheless, one thing remains a dire necessity: experiencing the real in the truth of the historical moment. However, that does not entail understanding Nietzsche's basic metaphysical position as a teaching, but rather seeing the real in order to ponder it as it opens up out of, and for, this basic position. The more the layers disappear that were painted over what is essential in Nietzsche— layers that he himself contributed to and that were inevitable in his time— the clearer the actual horizon of his basic position will become.

Ernst Jünger's sole historical significance consists in freeing this real from the residual images of Romanticism, but also in raising it to visibility from the low and flat plane of positivism. This indication does not copy the real out for a tentative demonstration; instead the description inscribes us in the belongingness to this real. In order to see the will to power as the *reality* of the real, and thus bring the real into the open within this horizon, Nietzsche had to be *one who questions*.

Jünger, who presently moves in this open region, can remain a describer who subordinates himself to the answer of that questioner. However, that which could only be grounded through inquiry can itself only be overcome through a questioning if the necessity for this arises. Indeed, in order to even just experience reality over and "beyond" the real as described, we must question, be able to question, and desire to question. But due to the fear of concepts that haunts it, the age of "decided" thoughtlessness must detest all questioning of that kind as a [256] disturbance of its destruction-work. We must not be surprised, nor at all shocked; but we must also understand clearly that mere not-questioning here already means destruction, indeed even devastation.

And this is the point from which one must indicate the other side of Jünger's accomplishment. All description, particularly when it stems from Jünger's peering-power and agility, from his impressional capacity and taste, has the advantage of indulging freely in the diversity of appearances and its layers. An age of thoughtlessness must already accept the path through such descriptions of the real as the sole permissible thinking, as it remains near the real, particularly when there is plenty to be described. One will take such thinking, which in its descriptions always remains with the "substance" (i.e., the matter at hand) for "substantial" and, since that which is described makes the movements of the will to power visible, view this "substantial" thinking as "dynamic"—whereby one names the highest distinction that our age has to give. But this "substantial" and "dynamic" thinking is not at all the thought of a thinker, provided that we preserve this name's essential content and understand it as inquiring about the reality of the described real, questioning whether and how it is a true real, and which truth is being decided here.

Not as if we demand a "new thought" of Jünger. It would suffice if he were able to think an old, indeed the oldest thought; and if he thus resisted the ever-growing prejudice that description, as he practices it, is already thinking in an essential sense, whereas the thinking that does not describe remains a "mere" thinking that lives an illusory life, distant from "reality," in the so-called "system."

With these remarks, however, we touch upon a question that must intrude ever more urgently into our statements, for which reason an indication of this question may perhaps [257] promote our intention. The question at hand can be clarified most easily by looking to the ending of Jünger's essay "On Pain,"[3] already mentioned above. Jünger says here (pp. 212–213) that "new orders" of the new process, namely those of total mobilization as a planetary work-process, "have already pressed far ahead, but that the *values* corresponding to these orders have not yet become visible." The "new commanding signs" of the armament-process—i.e., in Nietzsche's language the "new values" and their tablets—must first be established. We glean two things from this:

1. The cross-section in which Jünger's description moves: total mobilization as a given work-process, in its prescribed orders; "the 'worker' the figure whose historical task consists in carrying out the process" (*Blätter und Steine*, p. 12); the "new values" that are to become visible. The title "worker" is the sober name for the figure of that human whom Nietzsche calls the "*Übermensch.*" For Jünger does not thereby mean— as the rabble and Nietzscheans-gone-wild believe—an exemplar of the human reaching beyond the "normal measure" of the citizen in his sexual desires and violent acts, overly developed in his muscles and

---

3. Ernst Jünger, "Über den Schmerz," in *Blätter und Steine*.

sexual tools, outfitted with a strong lower jaw and low forehead. Rather, he means that human who "historically" goes over and beyond the human so far—the "last" human—into another form. But Jünger does not state what he means by "value," holding instead to the current expression in the opinion of naming a matter of fact. But "value," to Nietzsche, means as much as "condition of the increase of life."

2. Jünger is of the opinion that the values that are to be decisive for the total mobilization will only later [258] become visible and established. Thus it is evident: the values are just the subsequent "expression" and almost the discharge of the process, but insofar as they provide the standard and goal, they only measure that on which they alone depend and to which they are supplementary. Jünger and others may oppose ever so loudly the "historical materialism" of "Marxism," according to which the ideas and ideologies only represent the supplemented "addition" to the economic production conditions—yet he fundamentally thinks along the same metaphysical path. Whether one says "life" or "body"—or race—instead of economic conditions, of which the so-called "ideas" are always just emanations, does not change the least thing about "materialism." Entirely apart from the question whether values and ideas are simply exudations of a brain-substance—not to mention the question whether the essence of the mind, and from this, the essence of the human, can be determined by the *modern* concepts of "idea" and "value"—the following question arises in light of Jünger's description of the current age: How is it ever guaranteed that the process of total mobilization can still accomplish, or even only *permit* something like the establishment of "new values"? How—if through this real in the sense of the will to power, precisely every area would be destroyed in which something "lasting" would be permitted to appear and establish itself out of its own ground?

In the horizon of these questions, the supposed "substance" and "dynamism" of Jünger's thinking disintegrates into the emptiness and nullity of the real, whose reality is lost and forgotten. And it must come to be shown—it can only be revealed, of course, to a questioning, and never to a mere description—that the "real" that Jünger experiences in the light of Nietzsche's metaphysics is no new reality, and not the indication of the crossing into a new age, but is just the utmost completion, boundless expansion, [259] and unleashing of what we must recognize as the reality of the "modernity" that has already endured three hundred years.

One often hears the observation that Jünger cannot be refuted. That is correct, not because Jünger is unassailable, but because he cannot at all embody the appropriate target of the only possible attack; for this target is Nietzsche's metaphysics alone, and that means: Western metaphysics as such and as a whole. An attack of such a kind, provided it understands itself, can never have a "refutation" as its aim, if this word should denote the correction of error[4] and discrepancy. A metaphysics will not care about such a rejection. This means: No essential thinker can be refuted, but his basic position must be overcome if the dire necessity arises.

But how? And especially how, when dealing with a final position in which the entire history up to this point is at hand in its simplest, essential form?

On the Struggle of the Describers and Questioners

In order to see (to think) the will to power as reality of the real, Nietzsche had to be *one who questions*.

In the region that Nietzsche opened up, Jünger is a *describer* who subordinates himself to the answer of that questioner. The age which to this hour still remains without clue or knowledge of Nietzsche prefers to take the descriptions and accept them as "truth." Such description of the real of such an reality is calming in its blindness and breaks from the necessity of questioning—which is suspected from the outset of being "foreign to the real," and is thus also already secured as being shocked or meaningless.

But for the longest time, it has no longer sufficed simply to oppose the latest projection [260] of beings with another—rather, one must experience the thrownness into the projected, and locate the abyss of the decisions concealed here.

That is "more real" than all reifications this side of "subjectivity" and "objectivity," and never graspable by any description or "intervention," no matter how well-practiced. No describer can grasp here unless he first becomes one grasped by Beyng—but this would be his annihilation. And this must first occur, so that the claim to explanation and predictability no longer becomes entangled in mere beings—but rather that questioning leads to a hope.

---

4. Error and *yet truth,* and this?

FOURTEEN

The Age of the World Picture

—⟞ᴥ⟝—

1938

In metaphysics, reflection on the essence of beings and a decision concerning the essence of truth is accomplished. Metaphysics grounds an age in that, through a particular interpretation of beings and through a particular comprehension of truth, it provides that age with the ground of its essential shape. This ground governs throughout all phenomena distinctive of the age. Conversely, in order for there to be an adequate reflection on these phenomena, their metaphysical ground must allow itself to be recognized in them. Reflection is the courage to place in question the truth of one's own presuppositions and the space of one's own goals (appendix 1).[1]

This chapter has previously been translated by Julian Young and Kenneth Haynes in *Off the Beaten Track* (New York: Cambridge University Press, 2002), 57–73. Small changes have been made for readability and to assure compatibility with the rest of this volume.

Bracketed numbers refer to the pagination of GA 5; the chapter opens at page 75. — Tr.

1. [Heidegger refers throughout this chapter to numbered appendices that were written at the same time as the essay, but were not delivered in public (cf. GA 5, 97ff.). They are not reproduced in this volume.]

One of the essential phenomena of modernity is its science. Machine technology is of equal importance. However, one may not misconstrue this as the mere application of modern mathematical science to practice. Machine technology is itself an autonomous transformation of practice such that this transformation first demands the employment of mathematical science. Machine technology still remains the most visible outgrowth of the essence of modern technology, one that is identical to the essence of modern metaphysics.

A third, equally essential phenomenon of modernity lies in the process of art moving into the purview of aesthetics. This means that the artwork becomes an object of experience and is consequently considered to be an expression of human life.

A fourth modern phenomenon announces itself in the fact that human action is understood and practiced as culture. Culture then becomes the realization of the highest values [76] through the care of humans' highest goods. It belongs to the essence of culture as such care that it, in turn, takes itself into care and then becomes the politics of culture.

A fifth phenomenon of modernity is the loss of the gods [*Entgötterung*]. This expression does not mean the mere elimination of the gods, crude atheism. The loss of the gods is a twofold process. On the one hand, the world picture is Christianized inasmuch as the ground of the world is posited as infinite and unconditioned, as the absolute. On the other hand, Christendom reinterprets its Christianity as a world-view (the Christian world-view) and thus makes itself modern and up to date. The loss of the gods is the condition of indecision about God and the gods. Christianity is chiefly responsible for bringing it about. But loss of the gods is far from excluding religiosity. Rather, it is on its account that the relation to the gods is transformed into religious experience. When this has occurred, the gods have fled. The resulting void is filled by the historical and psychological investigation of myth.

What conception of beings and what interpretation of truth lies at the basis of these phenomena?

We confine the question to the first of the phenomena mentioned above, natural science.

In what is the essence of modern science to be found?

What conception of beings and truth grounds this essence? If one can succeed in reaching the metaphysical ground that provides the foundation of science as a modern phenomenon, then it must be possible to recognize from out of that ground the essence of modernity in general.

When we use the word "science" these days, it means something essentially different from the *doctrina* and *scientia* of the Middle Ages; different, also, from the Greek ἐπιστήμη. Greek science was never exact precisely because, according to its essence, it neither could be nor needed to be. Hence, it makes no sense at [77] all to assert that contemporary science is more exact than the science of antiquity. Neither can one say that Galileo's doctrine of free-falling bodies is true while Aristotle's teaching that light bodies strive upwards is false. For the Greek understanding of the nature of body and place and of the relation between them rests on a different interpretation of beings. It therefore determines a correspondingly different way of seeing and questioning natural occurrences. No one would presume to say that Shakespeare's poetry is more advanced than that of Aeschylus. Yet it is even more impossible to say that the contemporary understanding of beings is more correct than that of the Greeks. If, then, we wish to grasp the essence of contemporary science, we must first free ourselves of the habit of comparing modern with older science—from the perspective of progress—merely in terms of degree.

The essence of what is today called science is research. What does the essence of research consist in?

It consists in the fact that knowing establishes itself as a procedure within some realm of beings in nature or history. Procedure here does not just mean methodology, how things are done. For every procedure requires, in advance, an open region within which it operates. But precisely the opening up of such a region constitutes the fundamental process of research. This is accomplished through the projection, within some region of (for example, natural) beings, of an outline [*Grundriss*] of natural processes. Such a projection maps out in advance the way in which the procedure of knowing is to bind itself to the region that is opened up. This commitment is the rigor of research. Through the projection of the outline and prescribing of rigor, procedure secures for itself, within the realm of being, its sphere of objects. A glance at mathematical physics—the earliest of modern sciences which is, at the same time, normative for the rest—will make clear what we mean. Insofar as modern [78] atomic physics still remains physics, what is essential—which is all that concerns us here—will be true of it as well.

Modern physics is called "mathematical" because it makes use, in a remarkable way, of quite a specific kind of mathematics. But it is only able to proceed mathematically because, in a deeper sense, it is already mathematical. For the Greeks, τὰ μαθήματα means that which, in their observation of beings and interaction with things, humans know in advance: the corporeality of bodies, the vegetable character of plants, the animality of animals, the humanness of human beings. Along with these, belonging to the already-known—i.e., the mathematical—are the numbers. When we discover three apples on a table, we recognize that there are three of them. But the number three, threeness, we know already. That is to say: Number is something mathematical. Only because numbers represent, so to speak, the most striking of the always-already-known, and therefore the best-known instances of the mathematical, is the mathematical directly reserved as a name for the numerical. The essence of the mathematical, however, is in no way defined in terms of the numerical. Physics is, in general, knowledge of nature. In particular, it is knowledge of material corporeality in its motion; for corporeality manifests itself immediately and universally—albeit in different ways—in all natural things. When, therefore, physics assumes an explicitly mathematical form, this means that through and for it, in an emphatic way, something is specified in advance as that which is already known. This specification concerns nothing less than what, for the sought-after knowledge of nature, is henceforth to count as nature: the closed system of spatio-temporally related units of mass. Pertaining to this outline, in accordance with its prior specification, are to be found, among others, the following definitions. Motion is change of place. No motion or direction [79] of motion takes precedence over any other. Every place is equal to every other. No point in time has precedence over any other. Every force is defined as—i.e., is nothing other than—its consequences as motion within the unity of time; and that means, again, change of place. Every natural event must be viewed in such a way that it fits into this outline of nature. Only within the perspective of this outline does a natural event become visible as such. The outline of nature is secured in place in that physical research, in each step of investigation, is obligated to it in advance. This obligation, the rigor of research, has, at a given time, its own character in keeping with the outline. The rigor of mathematical science is exactitude. Every event, if it enters at all into representation as a natural event, is determined in advance as a magnitude of spatio-temporal motion. Such determination is achieved by means of numbers and calculation. However, mathematical research into nature is not exact because it calculates precisely; rather, it must calculate precisely because the way it is bound to its domain of objects has the character of exactness. The human sciences, by contrast—indeed all the sciences that deal with living things—are necessarily inexact precisely in order to remain disciplined and rigorous. One can, indeed, also view living things as magnitudes of spatio-temporal motion, but what one apprehends is then no longer living. The inexactness of the historical human sciences is not a deficiency but rather the fulfillment of an essential requirement of this type of research. It is also true that the projecting and the securing of the domain of objects in the historical sciences is not only different, but far more difficult to achieve than the rigor of the exact sciences.

Science becomes research through the projection and its securing in the rigor of procedure [Vorgehens]. Projection and rigor, however, first develop into what they are in method [Verfahren]. Method constitutes the second [80] essential characteristic of research. If the projected region is to become objectified, then it must be encountered in the full multiplicity of its layers and interweavings. Procedure must therefore be free to view the changeableness in what it encounters. Only from within the perspective of the ever-otherness of change does the plenitude of the particular, of the facts, reveal itself. Yet the facts are to become objective. Procedure must therefore represent the changeable in its changing; it must bring it to a stop and yet allow the motion to remain a motion. The fixedness of the facts and the constancy of their change as such is the rule. The constancy of change in the necessity of its course is the law. Only from the perspective of rule and law do facts become clear as what they are. Research into the facts in the realm of nature is the setting up and confirmation of rule and law. The method by which a domain of objects is represented has the character of a clarification [Klärung] from out of the clear: of explanation [Erklärung]. Explanation always has two sides to it. It accounts for something unknown through something known, and at the same time confirms the known through that unknown. Explanation takes place in investigation. In the natural sciences this happens in the experiment, always according to the nature of the field of investigation and the kind of explanation aimed at. However, natural science does not first become research through experiment. Rather, conversely: Experiment is only possible where knowledge of nature has already transformed itself into research. It is only because contemporary physics is one that is essentially mathematical that it is capable of being experimental. Since neither the medieval doctrina nor the Greek ἐπιστήμη were science in the sense of research, there was for them no question of experiment. To be sure, Aristotle was the first to grasp the meaning of ἐμπειρία (experientia): the observation of the things themselves, their characteristics and alterations under changing [81] conditions, resulting in knowledge of the way in which they behave as a rule. But observation directed toward knowledge of this kind, the *experimentum*, is essentially different from that which belongs to science as research, the research-experiment. It remains essentially different even where ancient and medieval observation also works with number and measure, and even where it makes use of specific apparatus and instruments. For what is completely absent here is what is decisive about the experiment. This begins with the fundamental postulation of a law. To set up an experiment is to represent a condition according to which a specific nexus of motions can become capable of being followed in its necessary course, which is to say that it can be mastered in advance by calculation. The setting up of the law, however, is accomplished with reference to the outline of the sphere of objects. This provides the standard and constrains the anticipatory representation of the condition. Such representing with and within which the experiment begins is no arbitrary invention. This is why Newton says *hypotheses non fingo;*[2] the fundamental postulations are not arbitrarily thought up. They are, rather, developed out of the outline of nature and are sketched into it. Experiment is that method which, in its planning and execution, is supported and guided by what is postulated as a fundamental law, in order to bring forth the facts that either confirm the law or deny it such confirmation. The more exact the projection of the outline of nature, the more exact is the possibility of experiment. The frequently mentioned medieval scholastic, Roger Bacon, can therefore never be the forerunner of the contemporary experimental researcher but remains, rather, merely the successor of Aristotle. For in the meantime genuine possession of the truth has, through Christianity, been transferred to faith—to the truth preserved in the written word and in Church doctrine. The highest knowledge and teaching is theology, considered as interpretation of the divine word of revelation that is recorded in scripture [82] and proclaimed by the Church. Here, knowledge is not research but rather right understanding of the normative word and of the authorities who proclaim it. For this reason, discussion of the words and doctrinal opinions of the various authorities takes precedence in

---

2. [This phrase stems from Isaac Newton's response to challenges regarding his method: "I have not as yet been able to discover the reason for these properties of gravity from phenomena, and I *do not feign hypotheses.* For whatever is not deduced from the phenomena must be called a hypothesis; and hypotheses, whether metaphysical or physical, or based on occult qualities, or mechanical, have no place in experimental philosophy. In this philosophy particular propositions are inferred from the phenomena, and afterwards rendered general by induction" (*Philosophiae Naturalis Principia Mathematica, General Scholium,* 3d ed., trans. Bernard Cohen and Anne Whitman [Berkeley: University of California Press, 1999], 943: my stress).—Tr.]

the process of knowledge-acquisition in the Middle Ages. The *componere scripta et sermones*, the *argumentum ex verbo* is decisive and, at the same time, the reason why the Platonic and Aristotelian philosophy that had been adopted had to become Scholastic dialectic. If, then, Roger Bacon demands the *experimentum*—as he did—what he means is not the experiment of science and research. Rather he demands, in place of doctrinal opinions, observations of the things themselves—in other words, Aristotelian ἐμπειρία.

The modern research-experiment, however, is not merely an observation that is more precise in degree and scope. It is, rather, an essentially different process of verifying laws within the framework and in service of an exact projection of nature. In the historical human sciences, source-criticism corresponds to the experiment of physical research. Here this name covers the entire range of discovery, examination, verification, evaluation, preservation, and interpretation. To be sure, the historical explanation based on source-criticism does not subsume the facts under laws and rules. Yet it is also not reduced to a mere reporting of the facts. As in the natural sciences, method in the historical sciences aims at presenting what is constant and at making history an object. History can only be objectified when it is something past. That which is constant in the past, that on the basis of which historical explanation takes into account what is unique and diverse in history, is the having-always-already-been-there—that which can be compared. Through constant comparisons of everything with everything else, the intelligible is worked out [83] and, as the outline of history, verified and secured. The sphere of historical research extends only as far as the reach of historical explanation. The unique, the rare, the simple—in short, greatness in history—is never self-evident and thus remains inexplicable. Historical research does not deny greatness in history, but rather explains it as the exception. In such explanation, what is great is measured against the ordinary and average. There is no other kind of historical explanation, as long as explanation means subsuming under the intelligible, and as long as historical science remains research, i.e., explanation. Since history, as research, projects and objectifies the past as an explicable and surveyable nexus of effects, it demands source-criticism as the instrument of objectification. The standards of such criticism change to the degree that historical science approaches journalism.

As research, every science is based on the projection of a bounded domain of objects, and is thus necessarily an individual science. Each individual science, in developing its projection through its methodology, must focus on a particular field of investigation. However, this focus (specialization) is by no means merely the dire side effect of the increasing unsurveyability of research results. It is not a necessary evil, but rather the essential necessity of science as research. Specialization is not the consequence but instead the ground of the progress of all research. Research does not, through its methodology, become dispersed into random investigations so as to lose itself in them. For the character of modern science is determined by a third fundamental occurrence: constant activity [*Betrieb*] (appendix 2).

One will initially take this as the fact that a science today, whether natural or humanistic, only gains the proper recognition of being a science if it has become capable of being institutionalized. But research is not activity because its work is carried out [84] in institutions; rather, the institutions are necessary because science, as research, has the character of constant activity. The methodology through which individual object-domains are conquered does not simply amass results. Rather, it uses its results to direct itself toward a new procedure. The entirety of previous physics is contained in the machinery that enables physics to smash the atom. Similarly, in historical research the stock of sources only becomes usable when the sources themselves are secured through historical explanation. In these processes, the methodology of a science is encircled by its own results. More and more, methodology adapts itself to the possibilities of procedure that it itself opens up. This necessity of being based on its own results as the ways and means of a progressing methodology is the essence of the character of research as constant activity. This character, however, is the inner ground for the necessity of its institutional character.

It is in constant activity that the projection of the object-domain is, for the first time, built into beings. All of the arrangements that facilitate the planned amalgamation of methodologies, that promote the reciprocal checking and communication of results, and that regulate the exchange of labor, are measures that are by no means merely the external consequence of the fact that research work is expanding and diversifying. Rather, they are the distant and still by no means comprehended sign that modern science is entering the decisive phase of its history. Only now does science take possession of its own complete essence.

What occurs in the spread and entrenchment of the institutional character of the sciences? Nothing less than the establishment of the precedence of methodology over those beings (nature and history) that are objectified in research. On the basis of their character as constant activity, the sciences create for themselves the appropriate coherence [85] and unity. For this reason, historical or archaeological research that has become institutionally active is essentially closer to similarly organized research in physics than it is to a discipline of the humanities that has remained stuck within mere scholarship. The decisive unfolding of the character of modern science as constant activity produces, therefore, a human being of another stamp. The scholar disappears. He is replaced by the researcher engaged in research programs. These, and not the cultivation of scholarship, are what place his work at the cutting edge. The researcher no longer needs a library at home. He is, moreover, constantly on the move. He negotiates at conferences and educates himself at congresses. He commits himself to publishers' commissions. These now play a role in determining which books need to be written (appendix 3).

From his own compulsion, the researcher presses forward into the sphere of the technologist in the essential sense. Only in this way can he remain capable of being effective, and only then, in the eyes of his age, is he real. Alongside this, an increasingly thinner and emptier romanticism of scholarship and the university will still be able to survive for some time at certain places. Yet the effective unity, and thus the reality of the university, does not lie in the spiritual power that primordially unifies the sciences, a power emanating from the university because nourished and preserved by it. The reality of the university is that it is an establishment that still, on account of its administratively self-contained form, uniquely makes possible and visible both the fragmentation of the sciences into the specialties and the special unity of constant activity. As it is in constant activity that the essential forces of modern science become immediately and unambiguously effective, it is only self-directed research activities which, proceeding from themselves, can prefigure and establish an inner unity with other research activities.

[86] The real system of science consists in the planned coherence of procedure and stance with respect to the objectification of beings. The advantage demanded of this system is not the contrived and rigid unification of the contents of the object-domains. Rather, the advantage is the greatest possible free, though regulated, flexibility in changing and initiating research toward whatever the guiding tasks are. The more exclusively science focuses on the complete accomplishment and mastery of its work, and the more these activities are shifted—without delusion—into research institutes and professional schools for research, the more irresistibly do the sciences achieve the completion of their modern essence. The more unconditionally, however, science and research take seriously the modern shape of

their essence, the more unequivocally and immediately are they themselves able to stand ready to serve the common good; yet the more unreservedly, too, will they have to withdraw into the public anonymity of all commonly useful work.

Modern science simultaneously founds and differentiates itself in the projection of particular object-domains. These projections are developed by the respective methodologies that are secured by means of rigor. Each method establishes itself in constant activity. Projection and rigor, method and constant activity—each demanding the other—make up the essence of modern science, make it into research.

We are reflecting on the essence of modern science in order to discover its metaphysical ground. What conception of beings and what concept of truth ground the fact that science becomes research?

Knowledge, as research, calls beings to account regarding the way in which, and the extent to which, they can be placed at the disposal of representation. Research has beings at its disposal [87] when it can, through calculation, either predict their future course or retrace their past. In the prediction of nature and the tracing back of history, nature and history are set in place in the same way. They become objects of explanatory representation. Such representation counts on nature and takes account of history. Only what becomes an object in this way *is*—i.e., counts as existing. We first arrive at science as research when the Being of beings is sought in such objectness.

This objectification of beings is accomplished in a pre-senting [*Vorstellen*] that aims at bringing each being before it in such a way that the person who calculates can be sure—and that means certain—of the being. Science as research is first reached when, and only when, truth has transformed itself into the certainty of presentation. It is in the metaphysics of Descartes that, for the first time, the being is defined as the objectness [*Gegenständlichkeit*] of presentation, and truth as the certainty of presentation. The title of his main work reads *Meditationes de prima philosophia, Meditations on First Philosophy.* Πρώτη φιλοσοφία is the term coined by Aristotle for that which was later called "metaphysics." The whole of modern metaphysics, Nietzsche included, maintains itself within the interpretation of beings and of truth opened up by Descartes (appendix 4).

If, then, science as research is an essential phenomenon of modernity, it must follow that what constitutes the metaphysical ground of research determines the essence of modernity in general long in advance. The essence of modernity can be seen in humanity's freeing itself from the bonds of the Middle Ages, in freeing itself to itself. But this characterization, though correct, is merely the foreground. It leads to those errors that prevent one from grasping the essential ground of modernity and of assessing from there the breadth of that [88] essence. Certainly the modern age has, as a consequence of the liberation of humanity, introduced subjectivism and individualism. But it remains just as certain that no age before this one has produced a comparable objectivism, and that in no age before this has the non-individual, in the shape of the collective, come to have influence. What is essential here is the necessary interplay between subjectivism and objectivism. But precisely this reciprocal conditioning refers back to deeper processes.

What is decisive is not that humanity frees itself from previous bonds, but rather that the essence of humanity altogether transforms itself in that the human becomes a subject. Of course, this word "subject" must be understood as the translation of the Greek ὑποκείμενον. The word names that-which-lies-before, that which, as ground, gathers everything onto itself. This metaphysical meaning of the concept of the subject initially has no special relationship to the human, and none at all to the self.

When, however, the human becomes the primary and genuine *subjectum*, this means that it becomes that being upon which every being, in its way of Being and its truth, is founded. The human becomes the referential center of beings as such. But this is only possible when the understanding of beings as a whole shifts. Wherein does this change manifest itself? What is the essence of modernity, according to this transformation?

When we reflect on the modern age, we inquire about the modern world picture. We characterize this by contrasting it with the world picture of the Middle Ages and of antiquity. Yet why, in interpreting a historical age, do we inquire into its world picture? Does every historical epoch have its world picture—indeed, have it in such a way that it concerns itself about that picture? Or is it only a modern kind of representing that inquires into a world picture?

[89] What is this—a world picture? Obviously, a picture of the world. But what does world mean here? What does picture mean? World serves, here, as a name for beings in their entirety. The term is not confined to the cosmos, to nature. History, too, belongs to the world. But even nature and history—interpenetrating in their suffusion and exceeding of each other— do not exhaust the world. Under this term we also include the world-ground, no matter how its relation to the world is thought (appendix 5).

The word "picture" initially makes one think of a depiction of something. This would make the world picture, as it were, a painting of beings as a whole. But "world picture" means more than this. We mean by it the world itself: that totality of beings taken, as it is for us, as binding and providing standards. "Picture" does not mean mere imitation here, but rather that which sounds in the colloquial expression to be "in the picture" about something. This means: The matter itself stands in the way it stands to us, before us. To put oneself in the picture about something means: to place the being itself before one just as it is, and to keep it permanently before one as so placed. But a decisive determination in the essence of the picture is still missing. That we are "in the picture" about something does not just mean that the being is placed before us. It means, rather, that it stands before us in conjunction with the system of what belongs to and stands together with it. To be "in the picture" resonates with being well-informed, being equipped and prepared. Where the world becomes picture, beings as a whole are set in place as that for which the human is prepared; that which, therefore, he correspondingly intends to bring before him, have before him, and thereby, in a decisive sense, place before him (appendix 6). Understood in an essential way, world picture does not mean "picture of the world," but rather the world grasped as a picture. Beings as a whole are now taken in such a way that they solely and initially exist insofar as they are set in place by the human that presents and produces. Whenever we have a world picture, an essential decision [90] occurs concerning beings as a whole. The Being of beings is sought and found in the presentedness [*Vorgestelltheit*] of beings.

Yet wherever beings are *not* interpreted in this way, the world can also not come into the picture; there can be no world picture. That beings come to be through presentedness makes the age in which this occurs a new age distinct from those prior. The familiar phrases "world picture of modernity" and "modern world picture" say the same thing twice, and they presuppose something that could never have existed before—namely a medieval and ancient world picture. The world picture does not change from an earlier medieval to a modern one; rather, that the world becomes a picture at all is what distinguishes the essence of modernity. For the Middle Ages, by contrast, the being is the *ens creatum,* that which is created by the personal creator-God who is considered to be the highest cause. Here, to be a being means: to belong to a particular rank in the order of created things and, as thus created, to correspond to the cause of creation (*analogia entis*) (appendix 7). But here the being's Being never consists in its being brought before the human as the objective, in being placed in the realm of humans' cognizance and disposal such that, in this way alone, it exists.

The modern interpretation of beings is still further removed from that of the Greeks. One of the oldest expressions of Greek thought about the Being of beings reads: τὸ γὰρ αὐτὸ νοεῖν ἐστίν τε καὶ εἶναι. This statement of Parmenides means: the apprehension of beings belongs to Being, since it is from Being that it is demanded and determined. The being is that which rises up and opens itself; that which, as what is present, comes upon the human that is present—i.e., upon him who opens himself to what is present by apprehending it. The being does not first acquire Being by nature of the human looking upon it, in the sense of a presentation of subjective perception. Rather, the human is the one who is looked upon by beings—the one who is gathered by self-opening beings into presence [91] with them. To be looked at by beings, to be included and maintained and thus supported by their openness, to be driven about by their conflict and marked by their dividedness—that is the essence of humanity in the great age of Greece. That is why these humans, in order to fulfill their essence, must gather (λέγειν) and save (σώζειν), catch up and preserve, the self-opening in its openness—and they must remain exposed to all of its divisive confusion (ἀληθεύειν). The Greek human *exists* as the receiver of beings, which is the reason that, in the age of the Greeks, the world can never become a picture. On the other hand, however, is the fact that the beingness of beings is defined for Plato as εἶδος (look, view). This is the precondition for the world's having to become a picture—one that was sent far in advance, and that for a long time reigned mediately in concealment (appendix 8).

Modern presentation, whose signification is best expressed by the word *repraesentatio*, means something quite different from Greek apprehension. Presentation here means: to bring the present-at-hand before one as something standing over-and-against; to relate it to oneself, the presenter; and in this relation, to force it back to oneself as the decisive domain. Where this happens, the human puts himself in the picture concerning beings. Yet when he does this in this way, he places himself in the scene, i.e., into the open horizon of what is generally and publicly presented. Through this, the human situates himself as the scene in which beings must henceforth place themselves, present themselves, be a picture. The human becomes the representative of beings in the sense of the objective [*Gegenständigen*].

However, what is new in this occurrence is not at all that the position of the human in the midst of beings is simply other than it was for ancient or medieval humans. What is decisive is that the human specifically takes up this position as one constituted by himself, intentionally maintains it as that taken up by himself, and secures it as the basis [92] for a possible development of humanity. Now for the first time there exists such a thing as the position of the human. Humans make it depend on themselves how they are to stand toward beings as what is objective. This initiates that mode of being human that occupies the realm of human capacity as the domain of measuring and accomplishing the mastery of beings as a whole. The age that is determined by this event is not only new in retrospective comparison with what had preceded it. Rather, it explicitly sets itself up as the new. To be new belongs to a world that has become a picture.

If this clarifies the pictorial character of the world as the presentedness of beings, then in order fully to grasp the modern essence of presentedness we must scent out, in that worn-out word and concept "present," its original naming power: to place before and bring toward oneself. It is through this that the being comes to stand as an object and so first receives the seal of Being. The world becoming a picture is one and the same process as that whereby, in the midst of beings, the human becomes a subject (appendix 9).

Only because, and insofar as, the human has altogether and essentially become a subject is it necessary for him to confront, as a consequence, this explicit question: Is it as an "I" that is reduced to its random desires and abandoned to arbitrariness, or as the "we" of society; is it as individual or as community; is it as a personal being within the community or as a mere member of the body corporate; is it as a state, nation, or people, or as the general humanity of the modern human, that he wills and must be that subject which, *as* the essence of modernity, he *already is*? Only where the human is already essentially a subject does there exist the possibility of sliding into the nuisance of subjectivism in the sense of individualism. But only where the human also *remains* a subject does it make any sense to struggle explicitly [93] against individualism and for the community as the goal and arena of all achievement and utility.

The interweaving of these two processes—that the world becomes a picture and the human a subject—so decisive for the essence of modernity, illuminates the fundamental process of modern history, a process that at first sight seems almost nonsensical. For the more completely and comprehensively the world stands at humans' disposal as conquered, and the more objectively the object appears, the more subjectively (i.e., peremptorily) the *subjectum* rises up, and all the more inexorably do observations and teachings about the world transform themselves into a doctrine of the human—into an anthropology. It is no wonder that humanism first arises where the world becomes a picture. In the great age of the Greeks, however, it was as impossible for a humanism to gain currency as it was for there to be anything like a world picture. Thus humanism in the narrower, historical sense is nothing but moral-aesthetic anthropology. This label does not refer to some investigation of humanity by natural science. Neither does it mean the doctrine established within Christian theology concerning created, fallen, and redeemed humanity. It designates, rather, that philosophical interpretation of the human that explains and evaluates beings as a whole from the standpoint of, and in relation to, the human (appendix 10).

The ever more exclusive rooting of the interpretation of the world in anthropology, which has set in since the end of the eighteenth century, finds expression in the fact that humans' fundamental relation to beings as a whole is defined as a world-view. Since then this term has entered common usage. As soon as the world becomes a picture the position of the human is conceived as world-view. To be sure, it is easy to misunderstand the term "world-view"—to suppose it to have to do merely with a disengaged contemplation of the world. For this reason, one already rightly emphasized in the nineteenth century that "world-view" [94] also means, and even primarily means, "view of life." The fact that "world-view" has nonetheless asserted itself as the name for the position of the human in the midst of beings proves how decisively the world becomes a picture as soon as the human makes his life as subject the primary center of reference. This means: The being counts as existing only to the degree and extent that it is taken into, and referred back to, this life; i.e., insofar as it is lived out [er-lebt], and becomes life-experience [Er-lebnis]. Just as every humanism had to remain something unsuited to Greece, so a "medieval world-view" was an impossibility and a "Catholic world-view" an absurdity. Just as, the more unboundedly the modern human takes charge of the shaping of his essence, everything must necessarily and rightfully become experience for him—just as certainly, the Greeks at the Olympic festivals could never have had "experiences."

The fundamental event of modernity is the conquest of the world as picture. The word "picture" now means the formation of presenting production. Within this formation, the human fights for the position in which he can be that being that provides the measure for all beings, and draws up the guidelines. Because this position secures, organizes, and articulates itself as a world-view, the decisive unfolding of the modern relationship to beings becomes a confrontation of world-views. Not, indeed, just any set of world-views, but only those that have already taken hold of humans' most extreme fundamental stances with the utmost decisiveness. In this battle of world-views and according to its meaning, humanity sets in motion the unlimited process of calculating, planning, and breeding everything. Science as research is the indispensable form of this self-establishment in the world; it is one of the pathways along which, with a speed unrecognized by those who are involved, modernity races toward the fulfillment of its essence. With this battle of world-views, modernity first enters the decisive period of its history, and probably the one most capable of enduring (appendix 11).

[95] A sign of this event is the appearance everywhere, and in the most varied forms and disguises, of the gigantic. At the same time, the gigantic announces itself in the direction of the ever smaller. We have only to think of the numbers of atomic physics. The gigantic presses forward in a form that seems to make it disappear: in the eradication of great distances by the airplane, in the broadcast presentations of foreign and remote worlds in their everydayness produced at will by the flick of a switch. But one thinks too superficially if one takes the gigantic to be merely an endlessly extended emptiness of the purely quantitative. One thinks too briefly if one takes the gigantic, in the form of the continual never-having-been-here-before, to spring merely from a blind impulse to exaggerate and excel. One does not think at all if one takes oneself to have explained this appearance of the gigantic with the slogan "Americanism" (appendix 12).

The gigantic is, rather, that through which the quantitative acquires its own kind of quality, becoming thereby a remarkable form of the great. An historical age is not only great in a different way from others; it also has, in every case, its own concept of greatness. However, as soon as the gigantic—through planning, calculating, establishing, and securing—shifts from the quantitative into its own special quality, then the gigantic and the seemingly completely calculable become, through this shift, incalculable. This incalculability remains the invisible shadow cast over all things when the human has become the *subjectum* and the world has become a picture (appendix 13).

Through this shadow the modern world withdraws into a space beyond representation and so lends the incalculable its own determinateness and historical uniqueness. But this shadow points to something else, the knowledge of which is refused to us moderns (appendix 14). Yet the human will never even be able to experience [96] and think this refusal as long as he goes around merely negating the age. In itself, the flight into tradition, out of a combination of humility and presumption, achieves nothing but a closing of the eyes and blindness toward the historical moment.

Humans will know the incalculable—that is, safeguard it in its truth—only in creative questioning and forming from out of the power of genuine reflection. Reflection transposes the human of the future into that "in-between" in which he belongs to Being and yet, amidst beings, remains a stranger (appendix 15). Hölderlin knew about this. His poem, above which is written "To the Germans," closes:

> True, narrowly bounded is our lifetime,
> We see and count the number of our years
> But the years of the peoples,
> Have they been seen by mortal eye?
>
> Even if your soul soars in longing
> Beyond its own time, mourning
> You linger on the cold shore
> Among your own, and know them not.

> *Wohl ist enge begränzt unsere Lebenszeit,*
> *Unserer Jahre Zahl sehen und zählen wir,*
> *Doch die Jahre der Völker*
> *Sah ein sterbliches Auge sie?*
>
> *Wenn die Seele dir auch über die eigne Zeit*
> *Sich die sehnende schwingt, trauernd verweilest du*
> *Dann am kalten Gestade*
> *Bei den Deinen und kennst sie nie.*

FIFTEEN

On Nietzsche

———— ❦ ————

1944–1945

Nietzsche's thought, like all Western thought since *Plato,* is metaphysics. In what initially appears to be an arbitrary move, we here presume the concept of the essence of metaphysics and leave its origin obscure. Metaphysics is the truth of beings as such and as a whole. Truth brings that which beings are (*essentia,* beingness)—that they are and how they are within the whole—into the "unconcealed" of the ἰδέα, *per-ceptio,* of pre-sentation, of conscious-ness. But this (the unconcealed) itself changes according to the Being of beings. Truth—as such unconcealment and with its essence of unsheltering—determines itself from the beings that it itself permits, and in each case solidifies the shape of its essence according the Being that is thereby determined. Truth is therefore historical in its own Being. Truth always demands a humanity through which it can be ordained, grounded, shared, and thus preserved. Truth and its preservation belong together

---

Bracketed numbers in this chapter refer to the pagination of GA 50; the chapter opens at page 3.— Tr.

essentially, and in an historical way. In this way, a humanity always takes over the decision concerning the manner that is assigned to it of being amidst the truth of beings.[1] This manner of existing is essentially historical,[2] not because humanity progresses through the sequence of time, but because humanity remains transposed [4] into metaphysics, and the latter alone is capable of grounding an "epoch" insofar as it holds a humanity within a truth about beings as such and as a whole, and thereby "*seizes*" this humanity.

Beingness (what beings as such are) and the totality of beings (that and how beings are within the whole),[3] as well as the essential type of truth and the history of truth, and lastly the humanity that is transposed in order to preserve it, circumscribe the fivefold [*Fünffache*] in which the unified essence of metaphysics unfolds and takes hold again and again. Metaphysics as the truth of beings that belongs to Being[4] is never initially the view or judgment of a person, never a doctrinal system or "expression" of an age. It may also be these things, but always as a subsequent result and in the outwork. However, the manner in which someone who is called to safeguard truth in thought takes over the rare ordinance, grounding, communication, and preservation of truth in the advancing existential-ecstatic projection—and thus indicates and prepares a place for humanity within the history of truth—delimits what is called the *fundamental metaphysical position* of a thinker.[5]

If, therefore, the metaphysics that belongs to the history of Being itself is labeled with the name of a thinker (*Plato's* metaphysics, *Kant's* metaphysics), then this does not mean that in each case metaphysics is the achievement and property, or even the distinction, of these thinkers as figures of "cultural creation." The labeling now means that the thinkers are what they are insofar as the truth of Being has given itself over to them, demanding that Being—and within metaphysics that means the Being of beings—be spoken.

---

1. Only counts for *modern* metaphysics.

2. In what connection with the historicity of truth, whose essence is originally the essence of fate?

3. Determine this distinction itself historically as a metaphysical one, and retain its essential-historical modification.

4. To which Being, which essence?

5. This section, as well as the first, is only comprehensible from the standpoint of inceptive thought and is only presentable through Beyng-historical thought. More precisely: The essence of metaphysics is first speakable in the event [*Ereignis*] of its being overcome. (The Sounding), cf. *Contributions to Philosophy*.

[5] With the work *The Dawn* (1881), light comes upon Nietzsche's metaphysical path. In the same year, "6000 feet above sea level, and much higher above all things human!" (vol. 12, p. 425), he gained insight into the "eternal return of the same." For almost a decade after this, his path stands in the brightest light of this experience. Zarathustra uses the phrase. As the teacher of the "eternal return," he teaches the "*Übermensch*." It becomes clear and more certain that the fundamental character of beings is the "will to power," and that all interpretation of the world stems from it by being a type of valuation. European history unveils its basic trait of "nihilism" and leads to the necessity of "transvaluation of all previous values." This new valuation, based on the now decided and self-declared will to power, legislatively demands its own justification through a new "justice."

During this peak time of Nietzsche's, his thought wants to express the truth of beings as such and as a whole. One plan of execution succeeds another. One design after the other opens the structure of what the thinker wants to say. At one point the "eternal return" is the guiding term; at another "the will to power"; at another "the transvaluation of all values." Where one guiding term retreats, it reappears as a title for an epilogue to the whole, or as a subtitle. But everything rushes toward the "education of the higher human" (vol. 16, p. 414). They are the "*new true ones*" (vol. 14, p. 322) of a new truth.

One cannot misrepresent these plans and designs as the characteristics of something unaccomplished or unmastered. Their alternation does not attest to a first attempt and its insecurity. These sketches are not "programs" but rather the subsequent notation that preserves the silent but obvious paths that Nietzsche had to wander in the realm of the truth of beings as such.

[6] "The will to power," "nihilism," "the eternal return of the same," "the *Übermensch*," and "justice" are the five basic terms of Nietzsche's metaphysics. "The will to power" is the term for the Being of beings as such, the *essentia* of beings. "Nihilism" is the name for the history of the truth of these beings that are determined in this way. "Eternal return of the same" is the way that beings as a whole are, the *existentia* of beings. "The *Übermensch*" describes that humanity which is demanded by this totality. "Justice"[6] is the essence of the truth of beings as will to power.[7] Each of these basic terms

---

6. Justification—certainty of salvation, self-assurance—of the belongingness to beings as such; knowing oneself in it, about it, "truth" not as [. . .].

7. The essence of the truth of beings—according to the Being of beings—determined as the will

simultaneously names what the others say. The naming of each basic term is only exhausted if we think along what the others say with it.[8]

The present attempt can only be followed adequately through the basic experience of *Being and Time*. This experience consists in a perplexity that is constantly still growing, but that has perhaps reached clarity in a few places. It is the perplexity of the one occurrence: that, in the history of Western thinking, the Being of beings has indeed been thought, but that the truth of Being remains unthought; and that it is not only refused as a possible experience of thought but that, as metaphysics, [7] Western thinking veils the occurrence of this refusal, even if not knowingly.

The following interpretation of Nietzsche's metaphysics must therefore first attempt, from out of the aforementioned basic experience, to think Nietzsche's thought—which is no mere "philosophizing"—as metaphysics, i.e., through the fundamental traits of the history of metaphysics. The following attempt thus moves both toward a goal that is near, as well as toward the most distant one that thought can be burdened with.

Around 1881–1882, Nietzsche writes in his notebook: "The time is coming in which the fight for world domination will be fought—it will be fought in the name of *fundamental philosophical doctrines* [*Grundlehren*]" (vol. 12, no. 441, p. 207). At the time of writing, Nietzsche begins to know and speak about these "fundamental philosophical doctrines." It has not yet been considered that they develop in a peculiar sequence and manner. It therefore still remains unquestioned whether this sequence must have its basis in the essential unity of these "fundamental doctrines." The question of whether their manner of development sheds light on this essential unity demands its own reflection. The concealed unity of the "fundamental philosophical questions" determines the essential structure of Nietzsche's metaphysics. The completion of modernity unfolds its presumably long history on the foundation of this metaphysics and according to its meaning.

The immediate goal of the reflection attempted here is the recognition of the inner unity of those "fundamental philosophical doctrines." To this end, each of these "doctrines" must first be recognized and represented.

---

to power, is not a valuation as a securing of existence; or each is the same. Why then is it not stated, i.e., differentiated? Why is "justice" as such not grasped? Securing of existence as the Being of beings—because will to power is also Being, thus truth of the will to power as justice. Truth "of" Beyng. Truth of the Being of beings; truth of beings.

8. But Nietzsche himself could no longer think the inner essential joining of what these five terms refer to. Why not? The limit of the completion of metaphysics; here, the veiling of the essence of metaphysics at its most complete stage; even a "system" no longer helps here—Hegel.

Their unifying ground, however, receives its determination from the essence of metaphysics as such. Only if the age that is beginning can come to stand on this ground without reservation and without veiling, only then can it lead the "fight for world domination" from that highest *awareness* that corresponds to the Being that undergirds and reigns throughout this age.

The fight for world domination and the unfolding of the [8] metaphysics that undergirds it bring to completion an epoch of the earth and of historical humanity. For here, outermost possibilities of world domination come to realization, as well as attempts on the part of humans to decide purely from themselves about their essence.

With this completion of the epoch of Western metaphysics, however, a basic historical position is determined in the distance, one which, *after* the decision of that fight concerning world domination, can no longer open or sustain the realm of a fight. The basic position in which the epoch of Western metaphysics completes itself will then be drawn into a completely different confrontation [*Streit*], one with a different essence. The confrontation is no longer the battle over mastery of beings. Nowadays this mastery ubiquitously interprets itself and steers itself "metaphysically"—but already without metaphysical mastery of essences. The confrontation is the setting-apart [*Aus-einander-setzung*] of the power of beings and the truth of Beyng [*Seyn*]. The most distant goal of the reflection attempted here is to prepare this confrontation [*Auseinandersetzung*].

The immediate goal—the reflection on the inner unity of Nietzsche's metaphysics as the completion of Western metaphysics—is subordinated to the most distant one. To be sure, in terms of the temporal sequence of attestable facts and conditions, the most distant goal lies infinitely far away from the current age. But that only means that it belongs to the historical distance of another history.

This most distant goal is also "closer" than what is usually close and the closest—provided that the historical human belongs to Beyng and its truth; provided that Beyng never first needs to overcome the proximity of beings; provided that Beyng is the only goal of essential thought, though one that has not yet been put in place; provided that such thought is inceptive, and in the other beginning must precede even literature [*Dichtung*] in the sense of poetry [*Poesie*].

"Presentation" and "interpretation" are worked *into* [9] each other in the text that follows, so that it does not immediately become clear what is taken from Nietzsche's words and what is appended. Every interpretation, naturally, must not only be able to glean the matter from the text, but must also be able to add of itself from its own matter, without insisting on it. This contribution is what the layperson, measured by what he or she un-interpretively takes the content of the text to be, necessarily criticizes as imposition and arbitrariness. The "confrontation" with Nietzsche's metaphysics remains excluded.[9]

The Will to Power

[11] Anyone can experience in themselves what "will" means: willing is a striving for something. Everyone knows from daily experience what "power" is: the exertion of force [Gewalt]. What "will to power" means, then, is so clear that one prefers not to attach any special elaboration to the phrase. "Will to power" is obviously a striving for the possibility of exerting force, a striving for the possession of power. The "will to power" also expresses a "feeling of lack." The "will to" power is not yet itself the possession of power, i.e., not yet "power itself." This demand for something that is not yet counts as a sign of the "Romantic." Yet this will to power, as a drive toward grasping power, is at the same time also the pure greed of violence. Such interpretations of the "will to power," in which "Romanticism" and viciousness meet, deliver this basic phrase of Nietzsche's metaphysics to the common ear. Nietzsche thinks something different when he says "will to power."

Yet how are we to understand the "will to power" in Nietzsche's sense? Is not the "will" a mental capacity that psychological observation has long differentiated from "reason" and "feeling"? Nietzsche certainly also grasps the will to power "psychologically." But he does not delimit the essence of the will according to its usual [12] "psychology." Rather, conversely, he sets the essence and task of "psychology" according to the essence of the will to power. Nietzsche demands a psychology as "morphology and *theory of development of the will to power*" (*Beyond Good and Evil,* vol. 7, no. 23, p. 35).

What is the will to power? It is "the innermost essence of Being" (*The Will to Power,* vol. 16, no. 693, p. 156). That means: The will to power is the fundamental character of beings as such. The essence of the will to power can thus only be investigated and thought by looking to beings as such, i.e., metaphysically. The truth of this projection of beings onto Being, in the sense of the will to power, has a metaphysical character. This truth will not

9. On "confrontation," cf. the appended conclusion of the lecture-course from the summer semester of 1939, on Nietzsche's teaching of the will to power as knowledge [GA 47]. The level of confrontation is easier to exhibit, as an instructive lecture is also capable of this.

tolerate any grounding that relies on the manner and constitution of specific beings, since these indicated beings, after all, are only identifiable *as such*—i.e., as characterized by the will to power—if they have beforehand already been projected upon the fundamental character of the will to power as Being.

Does this projection remain solely within the whim of this thinker, then? So it appears. This appearance of arbitrariness also burdens the interpretation of what Nietzsche thinks when he speaks the phrase "will to power." But in the writings he himself published, Nietzsche hardly ever spoke of the "will to power"—an indication that he wanted to shelter for as long as possible this innermost aspect that he recognized of the truth about beings as such, and place it in the protection of a unique, simple saying [*Sagens*]. The will to power is mentioned, though without being distinguished as a basic term, in the second part of *Thus Spoke Zarathustra* (1883). The title of the section in which the first glimpse into the will to power is accomplished gives a hint toward the correct interpretation. In this section "On Self-Overcoming," Nietzsche says: "Where I found the living, there I found will to power; and even in the will of those who serve, I found the will to be a master." According to this, the will to power is the fundamental character [13] of "life." "Life," for Nietzsche, is just another word for Being. "'Being'—we have no other notion of this than as '*living*.'—How can something dead 'be'?" (*The Will to Power*, vol. 16, no. 582, p. 77). To will, however, is to want to be master. This will still exists in the will of him who serves, not insofar as he strives to free himself from the role of servant, but rather insofar as he is servant and attendant, and as such always still has something beneath him that he commands. But the servant also rules over the master insofar as he makes himself indispensable and thus forces the master closer to him and directs the master to him: being a servant is still a manner of the will to power. Willing would never be a will to be master if the will remained only a wishing and striving, instead of fundamentally and solely being a command.

But wherein lies the essence of the command? To command means to have the mastery of control *over* the possibilities, ways, manners, and means of active effect. What is ordered in the command is the accomplishment of this control. In the command, the one who commands obeys this control and thus obeys oneself. In this way, the one who commands is superior to oneself by still risking oneself. Are those who command thereby still obedient? (Being able to obey—being able to listen.) Commanding is self-overcoming and at times more difficult than obeying. Only the one that cannot obey oneself must be commanded. The command-character of the will sheds a first light upon the essence of the will to power.

Power, however, is not the "goal" that the will initially goes after, as something outside of itself. The will does not strive for power, but already and only reigns in the essential domain of power. However: the will is not simply power, and power is not simply will. Rather: the essence of power is *will to* power, and the essence of the will is will *to power*. Only from this knowledge of the essence can Nietzsche say "power" in place of "will" and "will" instead of "power." But this never amounts to the equation [14] of will and power. Yet Nietzsche also never combines the two as if they were separate things first put together into a formation. Rather, the phrase "will to power" is intended to name precisely the indivisible simplicity of a joined and singular essence: the essence of power.

Power only powers [*machtet*] by being master over each achieved level of power. Power is only power as long as it remains an increase in power and commands itself the "more" in power. The mere pausing within the increase of power, the standing still at a level of power, already initiates power-lessness. The overpowering of itself belongs to the essence of power. This stems from power itself insofar as it is command and, as command, em-powers itself to the overpowering of the power-level at hand. Thus power is constantly on its way "to" itself—yet not as a striving but as powering [*Machten*]—and not to another level of power, but to the empowering of its pure essence.

The counter-essence of the "will to power" is thus not the "ownership" of power that would be reached in contrast to the mere "striving for" power, but rather the "powerlessness to power" (*The Antichrist*, vol. 8, p. 233). But then "will to power" means nothing other than power to power. Certainly—except "power" and "power" do not here mean the same thing. Rather, "power to power" means: empowering to overpowering. Only the power to power understood in *this* way hits upon the complete essence of power. The essence of the will, as commanding, remains bound to this essence of power. However, insofar as commanding is an obeying of oneself, the will can be conceived, in correspondence to the essence of power, as a will to will. Here, too, "will" means different things: on the one hand, commanding, and on the other, control over the possibilities of acting.

But if power is now always power to power, and the will always will to will, are not will and power then the same thing? They are the same in the sense of the essential belonging-together [15] in the unity of *one* essence. They are not the same in the sense of the equivocal sameness of two otherwise separated beings. There is just as little such a thing as a "will" in itself as there is "power" in itself. "Will" and "power," each posited for themselves, stiffen into pieces that are artificially broken off of the essence of the "will to power." Only the will to will is a will—namely to power in the sense of the power to power. The will to power is the essence of power.

This essence of power, never merely a degree of power, naturally remains the "goal" of willing, in the essential meaning that the will can only itself be will in the essence of power. For this reason, the will necessarily "needs" this "goal." That is why a fear of emptiness reigns in the essence of the will. Emptiness entails the extinguishing of the will in not-willing. Thus it is said of the will: "it would rather still will *nothingness* than *not* will" (*On the Genealogy of Morals*, vol. 7, third essay, no. 1, p. 399). "Willing nothingness" here means willing diminution, negation, annihilation, destruction. In such willing, power still secures its possibility of commanding. Thus the negation of the world is only a hidden will to power.

All that lives is will to power. "Having and wanting to have more, in one word *growth*—that is life itself" (*The Will to Power*, vol. 15, no. 125, p. 233). Every mere maintenance of life is already the demise of life. Power is the command to more power. But in order that the will to power, as overpowering, be able to surpass a level, this level must not only be reached but also retained and secured. The power that is reached can only be surpassed out of such security of power. The heightening of power is thus at the same time also a maintenance of power. Power can thus only empower itself to overpower by commanding *both* increase and maintenance. This includes the fact that power itself, and only power, sets the conditions of increase and of maintenance.

[16] Of what kind are these conditions that the will to power itself sets and are thus conditioned by it? Nietzsche answers this with a note from the last year of his wakeful thinking (1888): "The aspect of 'value' is the point of view of *maintenance-conditions, increase-conditions,* with regard to complex formations of relative life spans within becoming" (*The Will to Power*, vol. 16, no. 715, p. 171).

The conditions that the will to power sets for the empowering of its own essence are points of view. Such points become what they are through the "punctuation" of a peculiar seeing. This punctuating vision turns its "regard to complex formations of relative life spans within becoming." The vision that sets such points of view takes a view toward "becoming." For Nietzsche, this faded term "becoming" retains the fulfilled content that revealed itself as the essence of the will to power. Will to power is the overpowering of power. "Becoming" does not mean the indeterminate flowing of a characterless change of any available circumstances. Yet "becoming" also does not mean "development to a goal." Becoming is the powering exceeding of each level of power. Becoming, in Nietzsche's language, means the movedness of the will to power that reigns from within itself as the fundamental character of beings.

For that reason, all being is "becoming." The wide view [*Ausblick*] toward "becoming" is the pre-view and vision into [*Vor- und Durchblick*] the powering of the will to power, with the single intention that the latter "be." This peering vision into the will to power, however, belongs to the latter itself. The will to power, as an empowering *to* overpowering, has the character of a pre-view and vision. Nietzsche says "perspectival." However, the "perspective" never remains a mere course of vision along which something is seen; rather, the peering vision sets its sights on "*maintenance-conditions, increase-conditions.*" As conditions, the "points of view" that are set in such "vision" [17] are of such a type that one must expect and reckon with them. They have the form of "numbers" and "measures"—and that means values. "Values" "are always *reducible* to that number- and measurement-scale of energy" (*The Will to Power*, vol. 16, no. 710, p. 169). Nietzsche always understands "energy" [*Kraft*] in the sense of power, i.e., as will to power.[10] Number, in its essence, is "perspectival form" (*The Will to Power*, vol. 16, no. 490, p. 17), and is thus bound to the "seeing" that belongs to the will to power, which according to its essence is a reckoning with values. "Value" possesses the character of the "point of view." Values are valid and "are" not "in themselves," in order occasionally to be sought out and brought into view, and thus subsequently also to become "points of view." Value is "essentially the point of view" of the powering-reckoning vision of the will to power (cf. *The Will to Power*, vol. 16, no. 715, p. 172).

Nietzsche speaks of the conditions of the will to power by calling them "*maintenance-conditions, increase-conditions.*" He intentionally does not say conditions of maintenance *and* increase, as if two different things were thereby brought together, where there really is only one. This one unified essence of the will to power regulates the complexity that inheres in it. Overpowering includes both that which is overcome as the level of power in each case, as well as that which overcomes. That which is to be overcome must pose a resistance and must therefore be something constant that holds and sustains itself. But that which overcomes must also have a firm place

---

10. Will to power as "force" [*Kraft*]; force, in a generalizing sense—life-force—"*energy*" [Energie].

234 · THE HEIDEGGER READER

and be stable, or else it could neither go beyond itself nor remain secure, without swaying, in the increase and its possibilities. Thus, conversely, all intentions toward maintenance are only for the sake of increase. Since the essence of the will to power has this complexity within itself, the conditions [18] of the will to power—i.e., the values—remain related to "complex formations." These forms of the will to power—e.g., science (knowledge), art, politics, and religion—Nietzsche also calls "forms of domination." He often not only designates the conditions for these forms of domination as values, but the forms themselves; for the latter create the paths and institutions and thus the conditions under which the world—which is essentially "chaos" and never an "organism"—orders itself as will to power. Thus, talk of "science" (knowledge, truth) and "art" being "values," initially perhaps strange, now becomes understandable. "How is the *value* objectively measured? Solely according to the amount of *increased* and *organized* power" (*The Will to Power*, vol. 16, no. 674, p. 137). Insofar as the will to power is the mutual interweaving of the maintenance and increase of power, each form of domination pervaded by the will to power remains steady as something that increases itself, but remains inconstant as something that maintains itself. Its inner constancy (duration) is thus essentially a relative one. This "relative duration" is appropriate to "life," to which "a flowing determination of power-boundaries [. . .] belongs," because it only is what it is "within becoming," i.e., within the will to power (*The Will to Power*, vol. 16, no. 492, p. 18). Since beings' character of becoming determines itself from the will to power, "all occurrence, all movement, all becoming [is] as an observation of relations of degree and energy" (*The Will to Power*, vol. 16, no. 552, p. 57). The "complex formations" of the will to power are of "relative life spans within becoming."

In this way, all beings are "perspectival" because they hold sway as will to power. It is "perspectivism" (i.e., the conception of beings as vision that sets points of view and reckons) "by virtue of which each center of energy— and not only the human—constructs the entire remaining world *from itself,* i.e., measures according to its energy, feels it, shapes it . . ." (*The Will to Power*, vol. 16, no. 636, p. 114). "If one wanted to get out of the world of perspectives, one would perish" (vol. 14, no. 15, p. 13).

[19] According to its innermost essence, the will to power is a perspectival reckoning with the conditions of its possibility, which it itself sets. The will to power is value-creating *in itself.* "The question of values is *more fundamental* than the question of certainty: the latter first obtains its se-

riousness under the condition of the value-question being answered" (*The Will to Power*, vol. 16, no. 588, p. 91).

"*Willing* in general amounts to wanting to become *stronger*, wanting to grow—and also wanting the *means to this*" (*The Will to Power*, vol. 16, no. 675, pp. 137–138). But the essential means are those "conditions" under which the will to power, in its essence, exists: the "values." "In all willing there is *valuing* . . ." (vol. 13, no. 395, p. 172). The will to power—and it alone—is the will that wants *values*. That is why it must finally expressly become and remain the source of all value-creation and that which dominates all estimation of values: the "principle of value-creation." As soon as the fundamental character of beings is recognized as such in the will to power, and the will to power thus dares to acknowledge itself, the thinking-through of beings as such in their truth—i.e., the truth of thinking the will to power—inescapably becomes a thinking according to values.

The metaphysics of the will to power—and only this—is rightly and necessarily a value-thinking. In reckoning with values and in valuing value-relations, the will to power reckons with itself. The self-consciousness of the will to power consists in value-thinking, whereas the name "consciousness" no longer means an indifferent "presenting," but is rather the powering and empowering calculation with itself. Value-thinking belongs essentially to the self-being of the will to power, to the manner in which it is a *subjectum* (something on its own that lies at the basis of all else). The will to power reveals itself as the subjectivity distinguished by value-thinking. As soon as beings as such are experienced in the sense of this subjectivity, i.e., as will to power, all [20] metaphysics—as the truth about beings as such—must be taken thoroughly for a value-thinking and value-creating. The metaphysics of the will to power interprets all previous basic metaphysical positions in light of the notion of value. All metaphysical engagement is a deciding about rankings of values.

Nihilism

[21] Plato, whose thought initiates metaphysics, conceives of beings as such, i.e., the Being of beings, as "idea." The ideas are the eternally one over against the many, the latter of which first appear in the ideas' light and in so appearing first *are*. As this one, the ideas are also the constant and true, in distinction to the changing and apparent. Conceived from the metaphysics of the will to power, the ideas must be thought as values, and the highest unities thought as the highest values. Plato himself illuminates the essence

of the "idea" by means of the *highest idea*, the idea of the good (ἀγαθόν). But "good," for the Greeks, means that which makes something suitable for something. The ideas, as Being, make beings suitable to being visible, thus to being present, and in Greek this means being beings. Since then— throughout all metaphysics—Being has the character of the "condition of possibility." Through the transcendental determination of Being as object-ness (objectivity), Kant gave this character of Being a "subjective" inter-pretation. Nietzsche, from the subjectivity of the will to power, grasped these "conditions of possibility" as "values."

However, Plato's Greek conception of the "good" does not contain the notion of value. Plato's "ideas" are not values, for the Being of beings is not yet projected as will to power. Against this, however, and from *his own* basic metaphysical position, Nietzsche may well read the Platonic interpretation of beings, of the ideas, and thus of the supersensual, as "values." All philoso-phy since Plato is metaphysics in the way he projected it: Beings as such are conceived on the whole [22] from the side of the supersensual, and this is simultaneously recognized as the truly existing—be it the supersensual "God" as creator and the redeemer-God of Christianity, be it the moral law, be it the authority of "reason," be it "progress," be it the "happiness of the majority." The sensual, immediately present-at-hand is everywhere mea-sured in terms of a "desirability," an "ideal." All metaphysics is Platonism. Christianity and the forms of its modern instantiations are "Platonism for the 'people'" (*Beyond Good and Evil*, vol. 7, preface, p. 5). Nietzsche thinks these desirabilities as the "highest values." Every metaphysics is a "system of valuations" or, as Nietzsche also says, "morality," "understood as the doc-trine of mastery-relations under which the phenomenon of 'life' is created" (*Beyond Good and Evil*, vol. 7, no. 19, p. 31).

The interpretation of all metaphysics from the side of the notion of value is a "moral" interpretation.[11] However, Nietzsche does not perform this interpretation of metaphysics and its history as a historical-scholarly observation of the past, but rather as a historical decision concerning what is to come. If the notion of value becomes the guiding thread for historical reflection on metaphysics as the ground of Western history, then this pri-marily means that the will to power is the sole principle of valuation. Where the will to power dares to declare itself as the fundamental character of beings, everything must be assessed in terms of whether it increases the will to power or decreases and inhibits it. As the fundamental character, the will

---

11. Value-thinking—consequence of the "moral"—ἀγαθόν.

to power conditions all beings in their Being. As this highest condition of beings as such, it is the authoritative value. Just as metaphysics, until now, has not particularly known the will to power as the principle of valuation, so in the metaphysics of the will to power, the latter becomes the "principle of a new valuation." [23] Since, from the vantage point of the metaphysics of the will to power, all metaphysics is grasped "morally" as a "valuation," the metaphysics of the will to power in Nietzsche's sense becomes a valuation— a "new" one in the sense of a "transvaluation of all previous values."

The completed essence of nihilism consists in *this* transvaluation. But does the name "nihilism" not already state that, according to this doctrine, everything is empty and nothing, and every will and every work is futile? According to Nietzsche's conception, however, "nihilism" is neither a "doctrine" and "opinion" nor does it at all mean what the name would have one think: the dissolution of everything into mere nothingness.

Nietzsche could not fit his understanding of nihilism—which stems from the metaphysics of the will to power and essentially belongs to it— into the closed framework that probably hovered before his metaphysical-historical vision, and yet whose pure form we do not know and will never be able to piece together from the fragments that have been preserved. Nevertheless, Nietzsche thought through what "nihilism" means in all aspects and levels and types that were essential for him within the domain of his thinking, and set these thoughts down in individual writings of varying extent and level of emphasis. One document reads: "What does nihilism mean?—*That the highest values devalue themselves.* The goal is lacking; the answer to the question 'Why?' is lacking" (*The Will to Power*, vol. 15, no. 2, p. 145). Nihilism is the process of devaluing the previously highest values. The fall of these values is the collapse of the previous truth about beings as such in the whole. The process of devaluing the previously highest values is thus not an historical happening among many others, [24] but rather the fundamental occurrence of Western history that is carried and led by metaphysics. Insofar as metaphysics has experienced its peculiar theological emphasis through Christianity, the devaluing of the previously highest values must also be expressed through the phrase "God is dead." "God" here means the supersensual in general, which makes itself valid as the actual and only goal, as the "true" eternal world "beyond" this "mundane" one. When the sacred-Christian faith wears out and loses its worldly domination, the rule of this God does not also disappear. On the contrary, its shape masks itself and its claim hardens in being unrecognizable. The authority of "conscience," the "mastery of reason," the "God" of historical "progress," the "social instinct," take the place of God's authority and of the Church. The fact that the previously highest values devalue themselves means that the ideals lose their power to shape history. But if the "death of God" and the fall of the highest values is nihilism, how can one claim that nihilism is nothing negative? What annihilates one more decisively into empty nothingness than death, indeed the death of God?

The devaluation of the previously highest values certainly belongs to nihilism as the fundamental occurrence of Western history, but it never exhausts its essence. The devaluation of the previously highest values initially leads to the world appearing valueless. The previous values are devalued, to be sure—but beings as a whole remain, and the dire need of setting up a truth about beings only increases. The indispensability of new values urges itself forward. The setting up of new values announces itself. A mediate condition is formed through which present world-history moves.[12] This mediate condition entails that at the same time [25] one hopes for the return of the previous world of values, indeed busies oneself with this—and yet one senses the presence of a new world of values, and acknowledges it even against one's will. This mediate condition—in which the historical peoples of the earth must decide their demise or new beginning—lasts as long as the appearance is maintained that the historical future can still be withdrawn through a mediating equalization between the old and the new values of the "catastrophe."

---

12. Hence the concept of *history*.

SIXTEEN

Logos and Language

―⟨ళ⟩―

1944

In the previous meetings we tried to bring to light the origin of "logic" from several angles. The motive for this was to at least roughly make clear [252] in what way logic is about λόγος. For we began these discussions of "logic" not for its own sake or for the sake of this subject, but for the sake of Λόγος, and so that we might achieve an adequate relation to it. With this, we still remain far from knowing about the essence and range of the origin of "logic." We should only note that, according to the origin of "logic" we have characterized, logic—as the science of the λόγος—grasps the λόγος itself according to particular perspectives and, within the firmly limited vicinity of these perspectives, solely investigates the forms and ways of the λόγος. The particular perspectives according to which logic thinks of the λόγος stem from the origin of "logic." The latter owes its essence and subsistence to that division of knowing and the knowable that became necessary in the

---

Bracketed numbers in this chapter refer to the pagination of GA 55; the chapter opens at page 251.—Tr.

realm of Platonic and Aristotelian thought. This division yields the three "sciences" of physics, ethics, and logic. Kant still claims that this division of philosophy is completely adequate to the nature of the matter. If we may now define *that* thinking out of which this whole division had to arise as "metaphysics"—more precisely as the decisive beginning of metaphysics, a conception that can neither be thoroughly presented nor specifically justified here—then logic, to put it succinctly, is nothing other than the metaphysical treatment and explanation of the λόγος. This claim does not say much at first. Indeed, it merely replaces something unexplained (the essence of logic) with something else that is also unexplained, namely with what we now call "metaphysical treatment." This determination of logic as the metaphysics of the λόγος, a determination that actually does not explain anything, thus appears to be a claim of desperation. But the desperation into which we fall here cannot be avoided, since metaphysics can largely only be illuminated through a clarification of the essence of "logic." At the same time, however, the opposite is true: "Logic" can only be clarified from the essence of metaphysics. [253] We thus move in a circle. As soon as thought enters such a circular path, it is often, though not always, a sign that thought can linger in the vicinity of the essential, or at least approach its edges.

We shall stick to the statement that at first remains a mere assertion: Logic is the metaphysics of the λόγος. We will take this statement as a somewhat abruptly, almost forcefully erected pathmarker that should merely direct our reflections toward the fact that logic treats the λόγος in a particular way—namely "metaphysically." What this is supposed to mean, however, must at least admit of being approximately indicated, without us getting lost in an extensive discussion "about" metaphysics. This is, in fact, possible; but only with some reservations and in such a way that much remains unclarified.

For "logic," the λόγος is stating [*Aussagen*]—λέγειν τι κατά τινος— stating something about something. In order for something to be able to be stated about something, that which is being talked about there must already be addressed, namely as that which it is. As a statement, the λόγος is thus already in itself—and that means more originarily—the addressing of something with respect to what that addressed thing is. Something appears as what it is, provided that the "is" and "to be" are somehow experienced as appearing. The sight [*Anblick*] that the thing offers, the look [*Aussehen*] and vision [*Ansehen*] in which it stands, are that as which the thing appears and shows itself. What appears there, for instance that house there, shows itself in vision and stands in the look of "house" and the "house-like"—and so *is a* house. What appears here shows itself, for instance, in the look of a book and in the book-like—and so *is a* book. The look in which something appears as that which it is thus contains the what-being [*Was-sein*] of the thing in question—in short, the Being of the being [*Sein des Seienden*]. Plato was the first to think the Being of beings from the side of, and as, the look of [254] what appears. In Greek, "look" is εἶδος—ἰδέα—"idea." The look in which it becomes visible what a house even is—not this or that sensibly perceivable house—the look of the house-like is something non-sensory, the supersensory. To think the being from the side of the idea, from the super-sensory, is the distinguishing mark of that thinking that bears the name "metaphysics."

If we make the statement "That house is tall," then this is already based on addressing what encounters us as what it is—namely house, the εἶδος. Now λόγος, in Greek, does not only mean addressing, λέγειν, but at the same time and more frequently, even predominantly, what is addressed in such an addressing. Τὸ λεγόμενον—that which is addressed—is nothing other than the look: εἶδος—ἰδέα. In a certain respect, then, εἶδος and λόγος mean the same thing. In other words, the λόγος conceived of as addressing and stating is grasped with regard to the ἰδέα; the λόγος taken as a state-ment is that conception of the λόγος that moves in the vicinity of thought that thinks beings from ideas, i.e., metaphysically. The λόγος that logic thinks is thought metaphysically. Logic is the metaphysics of the λόγος.

So far it has only been shown from the outside that logic, along with the other two subjects of "philosophy" (physics, ethics), arose within the hori-zon of Platonic thought. Now we recognize what this heritage from Plato's thought means for logic and the λόγος. The condition for the λόγος being able to be grasped in steps as the addressing of something in its what-being is the determination, accomplished by Plato, of what-being and of Being as εἶδος and ἰδέα. This determination is accomplished in such a way that beings themselves are projected onto Being by way of beings, and that the Being of beings is thought as the most general of all beings. To think the Being of beings in this way is the distinguishing mark of all metaphysics. As long as metaphysics, in whatever form, dominates Western thought in its foundations—and that [255] has occurred until this very moment—the λόγος and all inquiry about it will be mastered, but also limited, by "logic."

A circumstance that we have by far not thought through adequately, but to which we are still subject today as if it were the most self-evident thing in the world, reveals how—in the beginning of metaphysics, and thus decisively for all subsequent influential metaphysics—the λόγος is decidedly delimited, in the way we described, as addressing and stating. This circumstance consists in the fact that the fundamental traits of the Being of the thing—those determinations of the thing in which it shows itself according to its most general look—are called "categories." The Greek word κατηγορία means "statement." Indeed this word, according to its root and composition, much more properly means "statement" than does the word λόγος. Κατ-αγορεύειν means: to publicly—in the market or in court—adjudge someone to be guilty and the cause of something, so that this adjudging, as a stating, announces an accusation or the findings of a case. Κατηγορία is the statement in the sense of the highlighting, announcing, communicative stating.

Κατηγορία is the statement in the distinguished sense. Λόγος, too, means statement. However, λόγος and κατηγορία do not mean exactly the same thing. On the contrary, Plato and Aristotle both realize—the former implicitly, the latter more explicitly—that κατηγορία holds sway in every λόγος taken in the sense of a common statement. In any statement about any possible or impossible thing, there reigns a further, distinguished statement. How so?

In order to see this, we now merely need to accomplish more decidedly the step we took earlier with regard to the general characterization of the "idea." When we say "This tree here is healthy," then in saying "this tree here" it is already stated, though not voiced: "this that is present [256] from itself." When we say "is healthy," it is already said in this, though not voiced: "is constituted in such and such a way." "To be constituted" and "to be present from oneself"—both of these are already, indeed necessarily, stated along with the λόγος about this tree here. For if this were not stated, or in this case silently thought alongside, then we could neither say "this tree here" nor "is healthy." The same "being present from itself" and "being constituted" are stated in the statement "That house there is tall," and this goes for all similar statements. All common stating rests and resonates in this distinguished stating in which, e.g., the present-from-itself, the constitutedness, the relatedness and such are stated about the being. These stated things are the fundamental traits of Being—that from which all beings have their origin: γένος. Plato calls these fundamental traits of the Being of beings γένη or εἴδη—the highest ideas. Why should this saying that simultaneously supports all common stating, this distinguished stating in which a fundamental trait of Being comes to appearance—as Aristotle says, ἐμφαίνεται—not also receive the name of authentic stating, of κατηγορία?

Thus the word κατηγορία becomes the name for the Being that is stated in every λόγος about any being. "Being"—fundamental trait of a being—is called "statement," what is stated. Something thoroughly strange comes to light here. Category and *logos* stand in an essential relation that the Greek thinkers did not at all themselves illuminate, let alone justify. Plato and Aristotle simply move on the paths of this relation between λόγος and category. One day, when an insight into the essence of the λόγος has become an urgent need for us, we will have to ask why this was possible, indeed even necessary.

If we now only preliminarily think about the relation of category and λόγος, we will learn to understand what is otherwise not at all graspable, namely that the highest determinations of [257] beings bear the name "categories," i.e., statements in the sense we have discussed. The name and substance of "category" were later transformed (e.g., externalized) such that "category" merely designates an external "schema" and "label" under which something falls. Since Plato and Aristotle—i.e., since the beginning of metaphysics as the fundamental trait of Western thought—it has remained the concern of this thought about beings as a whole to set up and configure the most general determinations of Being, the categories, into a "doctrine of categories." Yet in the history of metaphysics, the relation between category and *logos*—in the sense of statement and judgment—rarely still becomes visible.

It is no coincidence that in Kant's thought—in which metaphysics experiences the final decisive change—this relation between category and statement rises to the surface. Kant apparently and, according to many interpreters' and critics' opinions, arbitrarily selects "the logical function of reason in judgments" (i.e., the λόγος as statement) as the "guiding thread for the discovery of all concepts of pure reason"[1] (i.e., the categories). But the fact that the λόγος becomes the guiding thread for setting up the categories reveals the occurrence at work since the beginning of metaphysics, and which can be stated as follows: Logic is the guiding thread, indeed the proper horizon of metaphysical thought. For Kant, this role of logic stood entirely unquestioned, for which reason he also never particularly thought about the relation between λόγος and κατηγορία, or even about the origin and ground of this relation. But logic can only form the guiding thread and the horizon of metaphysical thought because logic is nothing other than the metaphysics of the λόγος—this taken as the state-

---

1. Immanuel Kant, *Critique of Pure Reason*, B 91–92.

ment in the proper sense, i.e., as κατηγορία, and that means as ἰδέα and εἶδος. If metaphysics counts [258] as the highest form of deep thought—which is unavoidable in light of tradition—and if "logic" is precisely the metaphysics of the λόγος, then the essence of the λόγος must be thought most deeply in "logic." From this standpoint pre-Platonic thought becomes pre-metaphysical thought, something that is still incomplete and on its way to metaphysics. What the pre-Platonic thinkers said about the λόγος can only be thought from out of subsequent metaphysics. That is, in fact, how it happened and still happens. Indeed it is even thanks to metaphysics and its thinking about the λόγος, that statements about the λόγος by pre-Platonic thinkers—especially those of Heraclitus—have remained preserved.

The path that our considerations have attempted to follow, in order to think the essence of the Λόγος, requires a different procedure. We do not take "logic" as a God-given and conclusively decided doctrine of the λόγος—one that is at most modifiable. We inquire through logic into the Λόγος and ask more precisely how it became possible that the λόγος, as statement, could achieve the role of a guiding thread for the discovery of the fundamental traits of beings within metaphysics. We think about whether and how one used to think within metaphysics prior to the creation of "logic," and whether and how one used to think about the Λόγος prior to metaphysics. If we seek to understand what a pre-Platonic thinker, namely Heraclitus, thought about the Λόγος, then we set aside the metaphysical conception of the λόγος. Yet this elimination of the horizon of metaphysics is at first only something negative. In addition to this, we also need another horizon within which what Heraclitus says about the λόγος can become visible and [259] graspable and speakable. But nothing can be directly reported about this horizon that guides us here. Within it, of course, we come upon a mystery. The mystery consists of the fact that from early on for the Greeks, λόγος means "saying" and "speaking," but that this is not the original meaning of λόγος—indeed that around the time that the metaphysical concept of λόγος had already been solidified, something simultaneously remained of the original meaning in the concept of λόγος.

The point now is not to solve this mystery of the multiple meanings of the λόγος, but rather to first acknowledge this mystery and let ourselves be guided by it.

We will listen to several sayings by Heraclitus that deal with the λόγος, in a particularly selected order. The first is fragment 50. It reads:

οὐκ ἐμοῦ, ἀλλὰ τοῦ λόγου ἀκούσαντας ὁμολογεῖν σοφόν ἐστιν ἓν πάντα εἶναι.

(In the preliminary yet already clarifying translation, we will leave the decisive word Λόγος untranslated. Although we render the other word, ὁμολογεῖν—which also sounds like Λόγος—as "saying" [*sagen*], this translation is not intended to decide anything concerning the essence of the Λόγος.) The translation reads:

> If you have not only heard me, but have instead (obeying the Λόγος) listened to the Λόγος, then knowledge is (that which consists of) saying the same with the Λόγος, saying: All is one.

There is talk in this fragment of a hearing. If it is supposed to be a real hearing, it should direct itself not toward the voiced sounds of the thinker, but toward the Λόγος. Thus, when referred to hearing, the Λόγος is indisputable, something hearable—so a kind of saying or word. The correct knowledge [260]—σοφόν—springs from, and is, the correct listening to the Λόγος. Since this knowledge, after all, is grounded in a relation to the Λόγος, it consists in ὁμολογεῖν; we "literally" translate this as saying the same that the Λόγος says. One would have difficulty disputing that Λόγος and ὁμολογεῖν are thought here from within the vicinity of saying and hearing. Yet what do saying and hearing mean? Hearing is a matter for the ears. Whoever has ears to hear shall hear. But what are the "ears"? The ears that are anatomically and physiologically present do not make or create hearing, not even if we conceive of it as a perception of sounds and reverberations and noises. Perception is neither anatomically discoverable, nor physiologically provable, nor biologically graspable. If this ability to perceive did not exist, what then would the ear and the entire hearing apparatus be? Hearing, as the sensation of sounds, always occurs on the basis of that hearing that is a listening to something in the sense of hearkening [*Horchens*]. Our hearkening, however, itself already hearkens in each case and in some way to what is to be heard, ready for it or not ready, [and is] somehow an obedience [*Gehorsam*]. The ear, which is necessary for correct hearing, is the obedience. That which is able to be heard—the hearkeningly perceivable—need not be anything sound-like or noise-like. It is not so easy to say what the obedience consists in. We only glean from Heraclitus's fragment that knowledge springs from the hearkening listening to the Λόγος which, in contrast to the human speech of the thinker, is no sounding-out; and that this knowledge consists in ὁμολογεῖν—saying the same that another, in this case, what the Λόγος says. Saying the same here does not mean to parrot, but rather to repeat in such a way that the same is said in a different way, such that the repetition pursues and "follows," i.e., abides by what is said and is obedient to it. This is what the obedience in ὁμολογεῖν might consist in: obedient repetition. Yet what does this repetition, that is supposed to be proper knowledge, say?

[261] The Λόγος obviously does not say anything arbitrary and individuated. It says something about "all" and it says that this is one. It is not possible to speak about more than the all. And it is also not possible to say anything more simple about it than that it is one. The Λόγος says both this broad and this simple thing at the same time.

How easily this statement is spoken: All is one! The fleeting superficiality of approximate opinion can meet in this statement with the hesitant carefulness of questioning thought. The hurried explanation of the world through a formula that is correct at all times and places can help itself to the claim "All is one." But a thinker's first steps that decide all the fate of thought can also lie concealed in this saying. How should *we* now be allowed—*we* the unprepared and those who have become even more helpless through much historical information—to directly approach this ἕν πάντα εἶναι, "all is one," precisely in order to wrest from it a meaning that is graspable to *us* or, in case it does not offer this, to substitute one for it?

ἕν—"one"—what does this mean? According to number, it means "one" —so one rather than two or three. Or does ἕν mean not the singular, the one—but rather "the one" that we think when we say "one and the same"? But even here it is not entirely clear what the one means, if it is to mean something in addition to the added word "the same." ἕν πάντα εἶναι—"All is one and the same"—does this perhaps mean all is of one kind? Spoken of everything, does "one and the same" mean the erasing of all differences? "All," πάντα, would then correspond to the [262] undifferentiated. That, however, is the indifference of the emptiness of the non-existent nothingness. Or does ἕν neither mean the one of the singular nor the one of selfsameness, but rather the one in the sense of the one that is called such because it joins and unifies? But how, and in what respect, is this one then to be thought? Is the unifying, the πάντα that unites everything, a volume still separate from the "all"? In that case the πάντα, the all, would in turn not be the all. The one unifying thing would thus stand over against everything and would reign over it. The ἕν would be the one and the πάντα the other, and there would be two and not ἕν—one.

Or is the ἕν, the one, something like the unique that excludes everything else, but excluding it in such a way that it barely still includes the other, the everything (πάντα)? Then there would not merely be a unification of the manifold, not only a cohesion of the plural, but a unification that originarily retains everything in its "one."

How opaque the easily pronounceable ἕν is, and how lacking in footholds for flexible thought. Perhaps we cannot even separate the meanings of the ἕν—the one of singularity, the one of selfsameness, the one of the unifying unity, the one of uniqueness—or exclude them from each other by means of either/or distinctions. Perhaps all the cited meanings of the ἕν are thought along in the ἕν that Heraclitus thinks. But then our question only becomes more pointed: In what unity and one are the aforementioned meanings of the ἕν themselves united? It is easy to see that all questions concerning the possible meaning of the ἕν will recur if we attempt to think the πάντα in a similarly clearly joined and valid way. [263] Does πάντα just mean the "all" in the sense of a sum of the possible many, a sum that is somehow completed? Is the "all" just the accumulation of various and most different things? Is the "all" the totality of variously scattered and divisible parts? Wherein does the totality of the whole lie?

What are we to make use of in order to determine the "totality" that we have appealed to so much of late, if the unity and the essence of the one remains undetermined? It is easy to say that the whole determines the parts and their divisibility in the division, and is thus not first the result of an accumulation of pieces. It is also somewhat clear that the way in which the number of pieces first establishes a sum is different from the way that the whole already and solely predetermines the ability to join its partitions and parts. In its generality and indeterminacy, this distinction of sum and totality, which has long been known to thought, hardly helps us to think the πάντα—the all—and its relation to the ἕν.

From what just been discussed concerning the ἕν and the πάντα, we see that these words presumably name something essential but that, to the degree that they mean something essential, they also remain ambiguous and empty and are occasionally only spoken as mere shells of words. Thought tries, again and again, to achieve clarity and a solid ground concerning the ἕν and the πάντα with the help of the statement ἕν πάντα εἶναι. But again and again, these attempts fly apart and combine into new mixtures. It suffices here to name the term "pantheism" in order to call to mind the manifold efforts of experience and thought that strove to clarify the ἕν πάντα εἶναι and thus clarify the world as a whole. One cannot deny what is strangely vague and futile about all of these endeavors. But it is also about time to ask about the reason for this undeniable state of affairs. The [264] reason is that thought forgets—and until now has forgotten—to initially even seek out the measuring space [*Maßraum*] from which the dangerously harmless words ἕν and πάντα receive what is nameable and determinable in them.

ἕν and πάντα are named in what is perceivable out of the λόγος itself, and this is: ἕν πάντα εἶναι, that all *is* one. In Being and as Being the one unites all that is. The all is the being that has the fundamental trait of its Being in the ἕν. How are we ever to arrive at an adequate conception of the ἕν and the πάντα, as long as we do not think clearly that in which they weave and come to presence [*weben und wesen*]? The πάντα as beings as a whole, and the ἕν as the fundamental trait of beings, weave and come to presence in Being. But we must certainly first ask how Being, the εἶναι, is thought in the ἕν πάντα εἶναι—or even how it must be thought according to Heraclitus's way of thinking. As long as we do not set about thinking the εἶναι (Being) according to Heraclitus's way and that of early Greek thought—indeed if we do not even sense the direction of the path or the region of this thought—every effort to think and to thoughtfully experience the ἕν and the πάντα will remain thoroughly futile.

Let us now pay attention to the entirety of the saying that speaks of listening to the λόγος:

οὐκ ἐμοῦ, ἀλλὰ τοῦ λόγου ἀκούσαντας ὁμολογεῖν σοφόν ἐστιν ἕν πάντα εἶναι.

We see that the saying closes with the word εἶναι. Yet the εἶναι (Being) that is last in the order of words remains, in the totality of the saying, the first of all words—the first according to the rank and worth and breadth of the speaking. But Heraclitus's saying does not speak of Being; it deals instead with the λόγος and ὁμολογεῖν. This, the obedient speaking in which knowledge proper consists, says that same as the λόγος. The λόγος says that ἕν πάντα εἶναι—always provided that the λόγος is a speaking and only such. The ἕν πάντα εἶναι is heard in and from the hearkening [265] listening to the λόγος. The ἕν πάντα εἶναι comes from the λόγος. It is what is perceivable in listening to the λόγος and is thus what is taken from the λόγος. But how should the ἕν πάντα εἶναι stem from the λόγος if it does not belong to the latter? How should the ἕν πάντα εἶναι belong to the λόγος if the λόγος itself does not preserve the ἕν πάντα εἶναι in itself? How should the λόγος preserve it, however, if the λόγος does not conform to the ἕν πάντα εἶναι, nor is at least equal to it? But what can the λόγος itself still be, "beyond" and "in addition to" the ἕν πάντα εἶναι? The πάντα, as the totality of beings, holds sway in Being. Similarly and especially, the ἕν holds sway in Being as the fundamental trait of beings. Thus the λόγος, which is perceivable in the ἕν πάντα εἶναι, cannot hold sway as anything other than Being itself. But according to the interpretation so far, the λόγος is at least that which speaks—the word and the literal meaning. The ἕν and the πάντα and the εἶναι, on the other hand, are nothing λόγος-like in this sense—i.e., nothing word-like. At most, rather, they are that which is spoken in the λόγος. However, as long as we think back and forth in this manner, we still inadvertently insist on that determination of the λόγος that "logic" has fixed in place by thinking the λόγος as statement and thus as "speaking," thereby claiming to know what "speaking" is. Nevertheless we find this determination of the λόγος insightful, since λέγειν and λόγος do, in fact, mean "talking" and "saying" for the early Greeks. But against all this, Heraclitus's saying again indisputably yields the fact that the ἕν πάντα εἶναι somehow originates from the λόγος itself. The λόγος itself must therefore allow the εεν, the πάντα, and the εἶναι—each in itself and all in their relation—to hold sway. The λόγος itself must hold sway in the way of their essencing [*Wesens*], and thus hold sway in the essence [*Wesen*] of the one, of the all, of Being.

Is it not finally time to ponder, for once, that what reveals itself in the λόγος and perhaps as this λόγος itself—the ἕν πάντα εἶναι—that just this and only [266] this gives us the right hint for grasping the essence of the Λόγος, purely according to what it allows us to perceive about it? Is it not time to set aside all habitual perspectives and views of the later and thoroughly metaphysical interpretations of the λόγος?

What, then, does the perceivable ἕν πάντα εἶναι tell us, if the Λόγος itself dissolves in it, and makes itself perceivable by showing itself? If we ponder this and retain it, what does the ἕν πάντα εἶναι tell us about the Λόγος itself? If we now try to glimpse the essence of the λόγος from out of the ἕν πάντα εἶναι, we naturally remember that the ἕν πάντα (εἶναι) has remained thoroughly ambiguous. But we especially avoided demonstrating the undetermined ambiguity of the third word, εἶναι. In all their ungraspability the ἕν and the πάντα, their relation, and even the grounds for their relation nevertheless remain something graspable, which we here call the uniting and conjoining of the all, i.e., of that which is—the totality of beings. The uniting and conjoining in relation to beings as a whole—and that also means in relation to beings as such—must also be the fundamental trait of the Λόγος if the ἕν πάντα εἶναι, as the perceivable, becomes perceivable out of, and as, the Λόγος.

What do λόγος and λέγειν now actually mean if, as we claimed, the word originally has nothing to do with saying and stating, with talk and speech? Λέγειν, the Latin *legere*, is the same word as our German *"lesen"*—but not the *"lesen"* [to read] that we apply to writing and thus to the written word and thus in turn to talk and speech. For now and henceforth, we will here take *"lesen"* [to gather] in a further and at the same time more originary sense: "to glean [267] the field," "to harvest the grapes in the vineyard," "to gather wood in the forest." Λέγειν, *lesen*, λόγος, the gathering [*die Lese*]. But just as the Greek word λόγος means λέγειν and λεγόμενον, so the German word *"die Lese"* means, on the one hand, the process of gathering—e.g., the wine harvest in process—but on the other hand also what is gathered in the sense of the yield of the harvest, as when we speak of a *Spätlese* as a type of wine.

(If only, after all considerations and consequences, we were to succeed in our attempt to think the essence of the λόγος purely according to the meaning of λέγειν we have just shown, i.e., to unfold the region of thought that it indicates!)

Not much is accomplished, however, and even less is gained by the mere display of the obviously verifiable root-meaning of λέγειν = *lesen*, in the sense of gleaning. It is important, rather, to illuminate the intended meaning of gathering according to its fundamental traits; but also to attempt to elucidate the λέγειν and the λόγος, along the guiding thread of this meaning, from out of the Greek realm of experience and thought. We therefore ask two things:

1. What lies in gathering?
2. How does the gathering, λέγειν, properly understood, give us an indication by which to think the λόγος, insofar as the latter reveals itself as the ἕν πάντα εἶναι?

To 1: What does *gathering* mean? To gather is to take up and pick up from the ground, to bring together and place together, λέγειν, collecting [*Sammeln*]. What is picked up and placed together in gathering, however, is not simply brought together in the sense of an accumulation that just ends at some point. Gathering first has its completion in that picking up that preserves what is taken up and brought in. Gathering is simultaneously picking up [*Aufheben*] in the sense of taking something up from the ground, and in the sense of preservation [*Aufbewahrens*]. With the latter, gathering first reaches its completion. Properly speaking, however, gathering does not end with the preservation that picks up and brings in. Rather, [268] true gathering already begins in the preserving picking-up insofar as gathering, in advance, already intends such a preservation that brings in, and remains constantly attuned by it. Gathering contains the predominant fundamental trait of preservation. At the same time, however, there is another trait to be grasped in gathering: Gathering is not an arbitrary grasping, a snatching-up that rushes from one thing to the next; the preserving bringing-in is always an attentive taking-in. But this only becomes possible on the basis of a reaching-out that reigns in advance, and that gets its breadth and narrowness from what it has to preserve and care for. If we are to thoughtfully even approximate gathering in its full sense, we must think all of these traits and relations as one.

Instead of "*lesen*" in the sense discussed, we can also say "collecting" [*sammeln*]. This word is even less equivocal in relation to what is meant with "*lesen*," since we usually immediately relate "*lesen*" to "writing." On the other hand, talk of "collecting" easily tempts us to simply take "gathering" superficially as some mere scraping-together. The gathering, however, is the collection that brings in and reaches out, whose collecting is already held together by what is determined to be preserving and preserved. For that reason, every real collecting must have already taken itself together—i.e., be collected [*gesammelt*] and gathered [*versammelt*] with itself in its own determination. In gathering, this originarily collected gatheredness [*Versammlung*] reigns over what is to be preserved. The gatheredness taken in this way is the originary collectedness and "collection" that already holds sway in every collecting that picks up.

Of course, we only still know this wonderful word "gatheredness" [*Versammlung*] in a very narrow and common meaning. Now, on the contrary, we think it in the clarified sense of the gathering, while paying special attention not to simply add the collecting as an additional bringing-together. [269] Rather, collecting means the originary collectedness of what is to be preserved, from which all collecting originates and in which it is held, i.e., gathered [*ver-sammelt*], collected out of originary collection and sheltered in it. If we think this "gatheredness" that reigns throughout all collecting and gathering, then we give this word a unique worth and determinacy. Gatheredness is the originary retention in a collectedness, a retention that first determines all reaching-out and bringing-in, but also first permits all dispersion and scattering. Just as all real "concentration" is only possible out of a concentrating center that already holds sway, so all common collecting is carried by, and joined to, a gatheredness that reigns throughout the totality of reaching-out, picking-up, bringing-in and taking-in, and taking-up, and thus properly "collects." To be sure, it is not easy for us immediately to think "collecting" in this originary, origin-giving and full sense, since we are accustomed to merely seeing collecting as a pushing-together and rounding-up that, in a certain sense, always only occurs after the fact.

To 2: If we try to think the gathering and the harvest, the collecting and the gatheredness in the sense we have discussed, then perhaps we will reach a point where we can intimate the originary essence of the Λόγος—i.e., think its essence as one with what the early Greek thinkers named with it when they used the name Λόγος: φύσις—ἀλήθεια. We glean from Heraclitus's fragment that the λόγος reveals itself as the ἕν πάντα εἶναι—as the all-uniting one. There is hardly a need for any special indication that the Λόγος, as originary gathering and gatheredness, cannot at all reveal itself as anything other than the unifying [270] one. Yet with all this, we only stand at the beginning of our attempt to think the Λόγος. Only one thing has already been gained, namely that the usual meaning of λέγειν and λόγος—in the sense of stating, saying, talk and word and literal meaning—does not bring the originary essence of the Λόγος to appearance. But we also already see that the usual meaning of λόγος as talk and statement is not suitable to making the demonstrated essence of the λόγος—as gathering and gatheredness—accessible and understandable. On the contrary, that a path could very well offer itself that would allow one to understand the usual meaning of "lesen"—as taking up and grasping writing and the written word, and the word and speech in general—from out of the λέγειν as originally thought, as collecting.

SEVENTEEN

Bremen Lectures
Insight into That Which Is

———————————— ❧ ————————————

1949

The Indication

All distances in time and space are decreasing. People used to be underway for weeks or months to get somewhere, and can now get there overnight by airplane. What people used to only come to know after years, if at all, they today immediately find out every hour on the radio. The sprouting and flourishing of plants, which remained hidden throughout the seasons, is now openly displayed on film within a minute. Film shows the distant sites of ancient cultures as if they just now stood in the middle of today's traffic. Furthermore, film also attests to its object in that it simultaneously presents the recording instrument and the person at work operating it. Television epitomizes all removal of distance, and will soon pervade and dominate the gears and bustle of all interaction.

Bracketed numbers in this chapter refer to the pagination of GA 79; the chapter opens at page 3. — Tr.

Humans cross the longest stretches in the shortest time. They put great distances behind themselves, and thus put everything at a short distance from themselves.

However, the hasty elimination of all distances does not bring about nearness; for nearness does not consist in a small measure of distance. Something that stands closest to us in terms of distance—through images in film, through sound on the radio—can remain remote from us. Something that is ungraspably far away from us can be close. Short distance is not already nearness. Great distance is not yet remoteness.

What is nearness if, despite the decrease of the longest stretch to the shortest distance, it is still lacking? What is nearness, if it is even prevented by the restless elimination of distances? What is nearness if, along with its privation, remoteness remains lacking as well?

[4] What is happening if, when we eliminate great distances, everything stands equally near and remote? What is this uniformity, within which everything is neither near nor remote—without distance, as it were?

Everything is swept into the distance-less uniformity. How? Is the convergence into the distance-less not more uncanny than everything blowing apart? The human stares at what could be coming with the explosion of the atomic bomb. The human does not see what *has* long already arrived, and indeed *has* happened, of which the atomic bomb and its explosion are only final eruptions—to speak nothing of the one hydrogen bomb whose detonation could suffice, in the furthest of possibilities, to extinguish all life on earth. What is this helpless fear still waiting for, if the dreadful *has* already happened?

The displacingly dreadful is what removes everything that is from its prior essence. What is that which is dreadful? It shows itself and conceals itself in the way that everything comes to presence, namely in the way that, despite all overcoming of distances, the nearness of what is remains lacking.

The Thing

[5] How does it stand with nearness? How can we experience its essence? It appears that nearness cannot be found immediately at hand. We might be more successful by pursuing that which is near. What is near is what we tend to call things. Yet what is a thing? How long have humans already looked at things and asked about them? In what various ways have they used things, and indeed also used them up? How invasively have humans explained things—i.e., traced them back to their origins—on the basis of these inten-

tions? Humans have for a long time proceeded this way with regard to things, and still do, without ever considering the thing *as thing*.

Until now, humans have considered the thing as thing just as little as they have considered nearness. The pitcher is a thing. What is the pitcher? We say: a container, that which contains something else. The containing parts of the pitcher are the bottom and sides. This containing is itself graspable at the handle. As a container, the pitcher is something that stands in itself. Standing-in-itself [*Insichstehen*] characterizes the pitcher as something independent [*selbstständiges*]. As the self-standing of something independent, the pitcher differs from an object [*Gegenstand*]. Something independent can become an object if we place it in front of ourselves, be it in direct perception or in the presentation of memory. The thingness of the thing, however, neither consists in it becoming an object of a presentation, nor can the thingness of a thing at all be determined by the objectness [*Gegenständlichkeit*] of the object—even if we do not merely account for the position of the object through our presentation, but leave it to the object as its own matter.

The pitcher remains a container whether we perceive it or not. As [6] a container, the pitcher stands in itself. Yet what does it mean that the containing stands in itself? Does the standing-in-itself of the container already determine the pitcher as a thing? Certainly the pitcher only stands as a container insofar as it was brought into place. This, of course, occurred, and it happens through a placing [*Stellen*]—namely production [*Herstellen*]. The potter makes the earthen pitcher out of earth selected and prepared specifically for it. The pitcher consists of this earth. It can stand on the earth through that in which it consists, be it immediately or be it mediately through table and bench. What persists through such production is what stands in itself. If we take the pitcher as a produced container, then we seemingly grasp it as a thing and not as a mere object.

Or do we even now still take the pitcher as an object? Certainly. Granted, it no longer only counts as an object of mere presentation, but it is an object that a producing places before us and over against us. The standing-in-itself seemed to characterize the pitcher as a thing. In truth, however, we think of the standing-in-itself from the side of production. The standing-in-itself is what the production aims at. The standing-in-itself is thus still, and despite everything, thought from the perspective of objectness, even if the position of the product is no longer based in mere presentation. But no path leads from the objectness of the object or from independence to the thingness of the thing.

What is thing-like about the thing? What is the thing in itself? We will only reach the thing in itself if our thought has first reached the thing as thing.

The pitcher is a thing as a container. To be sure, this container requires production—but having been produced by the potter does not in any way make out what is appropriate to the pitcher insofar as it is a pitcher. The pitcher is not a container because it was produced; rather, the pitcher had to be produced because it is this container.

[7] Production certainly lets the pitcher enter what is its own. But this ownness of the pitcher's essence is never fabricated by production. Separated from fabrication, the pitcher has gathered itself in order to contain. In the process of production, however, the pitcher must first show its look to the producer. But this self-showing, the look (εἶδος, ἰδέα), merely characterizes the pitcher in the respect in which the container stands over against production, as that which is to be produced.

The view toward the look, the ἰδέα, can never bring to experience—let alone adequately think—what the container that looks this way is, or what and how the pitcher is as this pitcher-like thing. That is why Plato, who imagines the presence of what is present to stem from its look, thought the essence of the thing just as little as did Aristotle and all subsequent thinkers. Moreover, and quite decisively for what followed, Plato experienced all present things as objects of a producer—instead of object [Gegenstand], we say more precisely: standing-forth [Herstand]. In the full essence of standing-forth, there reigns a dual standing: on the one hand, the standing-forth in the sense of stemming from . . . be it a self-presentation or a being-produced; on the other hand, the standing-forth in the sense of standing into the unconcealment of the already-present.

Yet all presentation of what is present, either in the sense of standing-forth or of being object-like, never reaches the thing as thing. The thingness of the pitcher consists in it being a container. We notice the containing of the container when we fill the pitcher. The bottom and sides of the pitcher evidently take over the task of containing. But easy there! When we fill the pitcher with wine, do we pour it into the sides and the bottom? At most, we pour it between the sides and onto the bottom. The sides and the bottom are the impenetrable aspects of the container. However, the impenetrable is not yet the containing. When we fill the pitcher, the liquid flows into the empty pitcher. The emptiness is the containing of the container. The [8] emptiness—this nothingness that belongs to the pitcher—is what the pitcher, as a containing container, is.

Yet the pitcher does consist of sides and a bottom. It stands by virtue of that of which it consists. What would a pitcher be that did not stand? At the very least, a failed pitcher; so still a pitcher—namely one that could contain—but one that would spill everything by constantly falling over. Yet only a container can spill [what it contains].

The sides and bottom, of which the pitcher consists and by virtue of which it stands, are not the actually containing aspects. If the latter, however, consists in the pitcher's emptiness, then the potter who shapes the sides and bottom at the wheel does not actually produce the pitcher. He merely shapes the clay. No—he shapes the emptiness. He forms the clay into its shape for this emptiness, in it, and through it. The potter initially and always grasps the ungraspable of the emptiness and places it into the shape of the container as the containing. The emptiness of the pitcher determines every movement of production. The thingness of the container in no way rests in the material that it is made of, but in the emptiness that contains.

Yet is the pitcher really empty?

Physics assures us that the pitcher is filled with air and with everything that makes up the mixture of air. We let ourselves be deceived by pseudo-poetic considerations when we spoke of the pitcher's emptiness.

But as soon as we condescend to investigating the real pitcher scientifically, with regard to its reality, another state of affairs reveals itself. When we pour the wine into the pitcher, the air that already fills it is simply expelled and replaced with a fluid. To fill the pitcher means, scientifically speaking, to exchange one content with another.

These accounts by physics are correct. Through them, science presents something real, according to which it can orient itself objectively. But—is this real thing the pitcher? No. Science [9] only ever meets with what its mode of presentation has already permitted as its possible object.

One says that the knowledge of science is absolute. Certainly. Yet wherein does its absoluteness lie? In our case, the compulsion is to surrender the wine-filled pitcher and replace it with an empty space filled with a liquid. Science turns the pitcher-thing into something invalid, insofar as it does not permit things to be decisive.

In its realm—that of objects—the absolute knowledge of science had already destroyed things as things long before the atomic bomb exploded. That explosion is only the crudest of all crude confirmations of the destruction of things that occurred a long time ago—a confirmation of the fact that the thing as thing remains unimportant. The destruction is so monstrous because it involves a double delusion. On the one hand there is the opinion that science, above all other experiences, meets the real in its reality. On the other hand there is the appearance that, unharmed by the scientific exploration of reality, things could still be things—which presumes that they were already present things at all. But if things had always already shown themselves as things, then the thinghood of the thing would have become obvious. It would have made a claim upon thought. In truth, however, the thing as thing remains barred, invalid, and in that sense destroyed. This occurred and occurs in such an essential manner that not only are things no longer permitted as things, but they were never able to appear as things at all.

What is the basis for the thing's non-appearance as a thing? Did humans simply neglect to present the thing as thing? Humans can only neglect something that was already assigned to them. They can only present, equally and in equal fashion, that which has previously cleared itself of its own accord and shown itself in the light thus brought about.

[10] But what is the thing as a thing, then, such that its essence has never been able to appear?

Did the thing never come near enough, such that humans did not learn to pay enough attention to the thing as thing? What is nearness? We already asked this. We asked it in order to experience the pitcher in its nearness.

Wherein does the pitcher-ness of the pitcher lie? We suddenly lost it from sight, in the moment that it appeared that science could tell us about the reality of the real pitcher.

We presented the effective part of the container—its containing, the emptiness—as a hollow space filled with air. That is emptiness thought physically and actually; but it is not the emptiness of the pitcher. We did not allow the emptiness of the pitcher to be its own emptiness. We thus did not heed what is containing about the container. We did not think about how containing itself holds sway. Thus we also failed to grasp what the pitcher contains. For the scientific presentation, the wine became a mere liquid—a general possible aggregate state of substances. We ceased thinking about what the pitcher contains and how it contains.

How does the emptiness of the pitcher contain? It contains by taking what is poured in. It contains by holding onto what is taken in. Emptiness contains in a twofold fashion: by taking in and by holding onto. The word "contain" is therefore ambiguous. Yet the taking of what is poured in and its retention belong together. Their unity, however, is determined by the pouring-out—for which purpose the pitcher, as a pitcher, is determined.

The emptiness' dual containing thus rests in the pouring-out. As this, containing is properly what it is. The pouring-out of the pitcher is a pouring [*Schenken*]. The containing of the container holds sway in the pouring. The containing needs the emptiness as what contains. The essence of the containing emptiness is gathered into the pouring. But pouring is richer than mere pouring-out. The pouring, in which the pitcher is what it is, gathers the twofold containing into itself, namely [11] in pouring out. We call the gathering of mountains [*Berge*] a mountain range [*Gebirge*]. We call the gathering of the twofold containing into the pouring-out, which together first amounts to the complete essence of pouring, the gift [*Geschenk*].[1] The pitcher-ness of the pitcher holds sway in the gift of the pouring. Even the empty pitcher retains its essence from the gift, despite its not being able to pour anything out. But this inability belongs to the pitcher and only to the pitcher. A scythe or a hammer are not capable of an inability to pour out.

The gift of the pouring-out can be a drink. There is water, there is wine to drink.

The spring lingers in the water of the gift. The stone and all the dark slumber of earth, which receives rain and dew from the sky, lingers in the spring. The marriage of sky and earth lingers in the water from the spring. It lingers in the wine that the fruit of vine offers, and that has mutually entrusted the nourishment of the earth and the sun of the sky to each other. Sky and earth linger in both the gift of water and the gift of wine. But the gift of pouring is the pitcher-ness of the pitcher. Sky and earth linger in the essence of the pitcher.

The gift of the pouring is the drink for the mortals. It quenches their thirst. It refreshes their leisure. It enlivens their sociability. But the gift of the pitcher has occasionally also been poured in consecration. If the pouring is in consecration, it does not quench [12] a thirst. It calms and elevates the celebration of the feast. Now, the gift of the pouring is neither poured in a tavern, nor is it a drink for the mortals. The libation is the drink offered to the immortals. The gift of the pouring as a drink is the authentic gift. In pouring the consecrated drink, the pouring pitcher holds sway as the pouring gift. The word "libation" properly names the consecrated drink: offering and sacrifice. "Libation" [*Guß*] and "to pour" [*gießen*] are in Greek: χέειν, in Indo-Germanic: *ghu*. Both mean sacrifice. Pouring is where it is essentially accomplished, adequately thought, and actually stated: to offer, to sacrifice, and thus to give. It is only for this reason that pouring, as soon as its essence

---

1. [*Schenken* can mean both "to give" and "to pour" in German. — Tr.]

is stunted, becomes a mere pouring in and out, until it finally decays in the common pouring-out. Pouring is not mere pouring in and out.

The mortals linger in their own way in the gift of the pouring that is a drink. The immortals, who receive the gift of the pouring back as a gift of donation, linger in their way in the gift of the pouring that is a drink. The mortals and the immortals linger differently in the gift of the pouring. Earth and sky linger in the gift of the pouring. Earth and sky, immortals and mortals, linger at the same time in the gift of the pouring. These four belong together from their own unity. Prior to all that is present, they belong enfolded together in a fourfold [Geviert].

The unity of the four lingers in the gift of the pouring.

The gift of the pouring is a gift insofar as it houses earth and sky, the immortals and mortals. But dwelling is now no longer the mere persistence of something present at hand. Dwelling appropriates. It brings the four into the clearing of what is its own. They are entrusted to each other from out of its simplicity. Unified in this togetherness, they are unconcealed. The gift of the pouring houses the simplicity of the fourfold of the four. Yet in the gift the pitcher, as a pitcher, holds sway. The gift gathers what belongs to pouring: the twofold containing, that which contains, [13] the emptiness and the pouring-out as offering. What is gathered in the gift gathers itself by appropriatingly housing the fourfold. This diverse, simple gathering is what holds sway in the pitcher. Our language uses an old word to name what gathering is: thing.[2] The essence of the pitcher is the pure, giving gathering of the simple fourfold into a period of time. The pitcher holds sway as a thing [Ding]. The pitcher is a pitcher as a thing. But how does the thing hold sway? The thing things. Thinging gathers. It gathers, appropriating the fourfold and its time into something that lingers: into this or that thing.

To the essence of the pitcher experienced and thought in this way, we give the name "thing." We think this name from the subject-matter of the thing, from the thinging as the gathering-appropriating dwelling of the fourfold. At the same time, however, we recall the Old High German word thing. This etymological indication easily tempts us to misunderstand the way that we now think the essence of the thing. It could appear as if the intended essence of the thing were twisted, as it were, out of the incidentally grasped meaning of the Old High German word thing. The suspicion arises that the experience of the essence of the thing that we just attempted rests

---

2. [Heidegger here uses the Old High German word thing, as elaborated below. We will distinguish this from the English "thing" (Ding) by means of italics.—Tr.]

upon the arbitrariness of an etymological game. The opinion gains ground and is already commonly accepted that, rather than pondering the matter at hand, we simply use the dictionary.

But the opposite of such fears is the case. For in fact, the Old High German word *thing* means gathering, namely gathering into discussion an affair or point of dispute that is talked about. Accordingly, the Old High German words *thing* and *dinc* become words for "affair" or "concern": they name that which concerns humans in some respect, what is thus talked about. The Romans call that which is talked about *res;* ῥέειν, ῥῆμα is Greek for talking or negotiating about something. *Res publica* does not mean the state, but what openly concerns all the people and is thus publicly discussed.

[14] *Res* can only enter the combinations *res adversae, res secundae* because it means that which one concerns oneself with; the former is that which concerns humans in a contrary way, the latter what accompanies them favorably. Yet dictionaries translate *res adversae* as bad luck, *res secundae* as luck; they say nothing about what these words speak as thought. Thus it is not the case here or elsewhere that our thinking thrives on etymology, but rather that etymology, along with the dictionaries, does not think enough.

The Roman word *res* names that which concerns humans—the affair, the point of dispute, the case. The Romans also use the word *causa* for this; it actually in no way initially means "cause." *Causa* means the case, and thus also that which is the case, that something proceeds and becomes due. *Causa* can only obtain the meaning of cause—in the sense of the causality of an effect—because, almost synonymous with *res,* it means case. The Old High German words *thing* and *dinc,* with their meaning of gathering an affair into discussion, are suitable unlike any other to adequately translate the Roman word *res:* that which concerns someone. From the Roman word that corresponds to the word *res,* from the word *causa*—in the sense of case and affair—we get the Romantic *la cosa* and the French *la chose.* We say: *das Ding.* In English, "thing" still bears the fulfilled naming power of the Roman word *res:* "He knows his things"—he understands his matters, what concerns him. "He knows how to handle things"—he knows how one must deal with things, i.e., with things that are of concern from case to case. "That's a great thing"—it is a great (distinguished, immense, grand) thing, i.e., something that comes from itself and concerns humans.[3]

[15] Yet what is decisive is not at all the history of meaning we have

---

3. [These three phrases are in English in the original.—Tr.]

briefly mentioned here of the words *res, Ding, causa, cosa* and *chose,* and "thing." What is decisive is something entirely different and that has not yet been considered. The Roman word *res* names that which concerns humans in some way. What concerns them is the reality of the *res.* The *realitas* of the *res* is experienced by the Romans as the concern [*Angang*].[4] But the Romans never thought in its essence what was thus experienced. Rather, the Roman *realitas* of the *res* is taken over from late Greek philosophy, and is presented in the sense of the Greek ὄν. ῍Ον—*ens* in Latin—means what comes to presence in the sense of standing forth [*Herstandes*]. The *res* becomes the *ens:* that which comes to presence, in the sense of what stands forth and is presented. The peculiar *realitas* of the *res* as originally experienced by the Romans—the concern—remains covered over as the essence of what comes to presence. Conversely, in subsequent times and especially in the Middle Ages, the word *res* serves to designate every *ens qua ens*—i.e., every thing that somehow comes to presence, even if it only stands forth and holds sway in presentation, like the *ens rationis.* The same thing that happens to the word *res* occurs with the word *dinc* that corresponds to it. For *dinc* means that which somehow is. Accordingly, Meister Eckhardt uses the word *dinc* for both God and for the soul. For him, God is the "highest and most supreme *dinc.*"[5] The soul is a "great *dinc.*"[6] This master of thought by no means intends to say that God and the soul are the same kinds of thing as a rock, a material object. *Dinc* is here a careful and moderate name for something that is at all. Thus, according to a phrase of Dionysius the Areopagite,[7] Meister Eckhardt says: "love is of such a nature that it transforms humans into the things that he loves."[8]

[16] Since the word "thing," in the usage of Western metaphysics, names that which is at all and is somehow something, the meaning of the word "thing" accordingly changes in correspondence to the interpretation of that which is—i.e., of beings. Kant speaks of things in the same way as Meister Eckhardt, and means by this something that is. But for Kant, that which is becomes an object of presentation which occurs in the self-

---

4. [It is difficult to render this word in English, since it refers not to the act of being concerned, but to the object of concern. Further, in German it carries the sense that the object of concern "affects," "goes to" those concerned.—Tr.]

5. Meister Eckhardt, Sermon 51. *Deutsche Mystiker des vierzehnten Jahrhunderts,* ed. Franz Pfeiffer, vol. 2: *Meister Eckhardt* (Leipzig: 1857), p. 169.

6. Ibid., Sermon 42, p. 141.

7. [Heidegger presumably means Augustine.]

8. Cf. *Meister Eckhart,* Sermon 63, p. 199, and Sermon 20, p. 86.

consciousness of the human self. The thing-in-itself means, for Kant, the object in itself. The character of the "in itself" means, for Kant, that the object is an object for itself, without reference to human presentation, i.e., without the "over against" [Gegen] through which it first arises for this presentation. "Thing-in-itself," in a strict Kantian fashion, means an object that is no object [Gegenstand], because it is to stand without any possible "over against" toward the human presentation that faces it.

In our dire situation, however, neither the long-expended general meaning of the word "thing" as used in philosophy nor the Old High German meaning of the word thing help us in the least to experience and adequately think the essence of what we have now spoken of as the essence of the pitcher. It is rather the case that "gathering," an aspect of the word thing from old usage, makes a claim upon that previously-thought essence of the pitcher.

The pitcher is a thing—but neither in the sense of the res of the Romans, nor in the sense of the ens as presented in the Middle Ages, nor even in the sense of the object presented in modernity. The pitcher is not a thing as an object, be it as one of production or of mere presentation. The pitcher is a thing insofar as it things. The coming to presence of what is present first occurs and determines itself from out of the thinging of the thing.

Today, all that is present is equally near and equally remote. Distance-less-ness reigns. Yet all shortening and elimination of distances [17] does not bring about nearness. What is nearness? We pondered the pitcher in its nearness in order to find the essence of nearness. We sought the essence of nearness and found the essence of the pitcher as a thing. But in this discovery, we also notice the essence of nearness. The thing things. In thinging, it houses earth and sky, the immortals and the mortals. In housing, the thing brings the four near to each other. This bringing near is the nearing [das Nähern]. Nearing is the essence of nearness. Nearness nears what is remote, and it does so as what is remote. Nearness preserves remoteness. Preserving remoteness, nearness holds sway in its nearing. Nearing in such a way, nearness conceals itself and in its way remains what is closest.

The thing is not "in" nearness, as if the latter were a container. Nearness reigns in nearing as the thinging of the thing.

As thinging, the thing houses the united four—earth and sky, the immortals and the mortals—in the simplicity of their fourfold that unites from itself.

The earth is that which builds and carries, which bears fruit in nearing, and which tends waters and stones, plants and animals.

The sky is the course of the sun, the path of the moon, the shining of the stars, the seasons of the year, light and twilight of the day, darkness and brightness of the night, favor and desolateness of the weather, passage of clouds and the blue depth of the ether.

If we say sky, then we already think—if we are thinking—the other three along in the unity of the four.

The immortals are the hinting messengers of divinity. Out of their concealed reign, the god appears in its essence, which withdraws from any comparison with what is present.

If we name the immortals, then we think—if we are thinking—the other three along in the unity of the four.

The mortals are the humans. They are called mortals because they can die. To die means to be capable of death as death. Only the human dies. The animal perishes. It has [18] death, as death, neither in front of it nor behind it. Death is the shrine of the nothing, namely of that which from any perspective is never a mere being, but which nevertheless holds sway as Being itself. Death, as the shrine of the nothing, harbors in itself that which holds sway as the essence of Being. As the shrine of the nothing, death is the harboring of Being. We now call the mortals such not because their earthly life ends, but because they are capable of death as death. The mortals are who they are as mortals, holding sway in the harboring of Being. They are the relation that holds sway to Being as Being.

Metaphysics, on the other hand, presents the human as *animal,* as a living being. Even if *ratio* pervades *animalitas,* human being remains determined by life and experience [*Leben und Erleben*]. The mortals must first arise from the rational beings.

If we say "the mortals," then we think—if we are thinking—the other three along in the unity of the four.

United from themselves, earth and sky, the divine and the mortals belong to the simplicity of the united fourfold. Each of the four mirrors, in its own way, the essence of the others. Each is thereby reflected, in its own way, back into its ownness within the simplicity of the four. This mirroring is no representation of an image. Clearing each of the four, the mirroring appropriates their own essence together into the simple appropriation. Mirroring in this appropriative-clearing fashion, each of the four passes itself to each of the others. The appropriative mirroring frees each of the four into its ownness, but binds these free things together in the simplicity of their essence.

The mirroring that binds into freedom is the game that each of the four credits to the other out of the folding hold of the appropriation. None of the four hardens itself toward its own separate peculiarity. Rather, within their appropriation, each of the four is disappropriated to its ownness. This disappropriating appropriation is the mirror-game of the fourfold. The simplicity of the fourfold is dared from within this appropriation.

[19] The appropriative mirror-game of the simplicity of earth and sky, divine and mortal, we call the world. World holds sway by worlding. This means that the worlding of world is neither explainable nor fathomable through other things. This impossibility lies not in the fact that our human thinking is incapable of such explaining and fathoming. Rather, the inexplicable and unfathomable about the worlding of the world lies in the fact that such things as causes and reasons remain unsuited to it. As soon as human knowledge demands an explanation, it does not exceed the essence of world but rather falls beneath it. The human desire to explain does not even reach into what is simple in the simplicity of worlding. The united four are already suffocated in their essence if one simply presents them as individual real things that are to be confusedly reasoned and separately explained.

The unity of the fourfold is the fouring [Vierung]. Yet the fouring in no way embraces the four and only subsequently comes to them as this embracing. Neither does the fouring exhaust itself by virtue of the four simply standing by one another as just being present at hand.

The fouring holds sway as the appropriative mirror-game of those that are simply credited to one another. The fouring holds sway as the worlding of world. The mirror-game of world is the round [Reigen] of the appropriation [Ereignens]. For this reason, the round does also not reach around the four like a tire. The round is the ring that rings by playing as the mirroring. Appropriating, it clears the four into the gleam of their simplicity. Gleaming, the ring everywhere and openly appropriates the four into the mystery of their essence. The gathered essence of the mirror-game of the world that rings in this way is the ringing [Gering]. In the ringing of the mirroring-playing ring, the four cling to their united and yet own essence. Pliant in this way, they obediently and worldingly ordain the world.

In our old German language "pliant, malleable, flexible," "obedient," and "light" are ring and gering. The [20] mirror-game of the worlding world, as the ringing of the ring, wrests the united four into their own obedience, the ring of their essence. The thinging of the thing then occurs through the mirror-game of the ringing of the ring.

The thing houses the fourfold. The thing things the world. Each thing houses the fourfold into something that respectively lingers of the simplicity of the world.

If we let the thing come to presence in its thinging from the worlding world, we think of the thing as the thing. Thoughtful in this way, we let ourselves be concerned with the worlding essence of the thing. Thinking in this way, we are affected by the thing as the thing. We are, in the strict sense of the word, the thinged, conditioned ones [Be-Dingten]. We have left behind the presumption of everything unconditioned.

If we think the thing as thing, we protect the essence of the thing in the area from which it comes to presence. Thinging is the nearing of the world. Nearing is the essence of nearness. Insofar as we protect the thing as the thing, we inhabit nearness. The nearing of nearness is the actual and only dimension of the mirror-game of the world.

The absence of nearness, despite all elimination of distance, has brought the distance-less to rule. In the absence of nearness, the thing remains negated as a thing, in the sense mentioned. But when and how are things as things? We ask this in the midst of the domination of the distance-less.

When and how do things arrive as things? They do not arrive through human machinations. But they also do not arrive without the watchfulness of mortals. The first step toward such watchfulness is the step back from merely presentational—i.e., explanatory—thought into commemorative thought [andenkende Denken].

The step back from one thinking into another is, naturally, not a mere change of mindset. It can never be such because all mindsets, along with their modes of change, remain tied to the domain of presentational thought. The step back, however, completely leaves [21] the domain of merely taking a stance. The step back resides in a correspondence that, in being addressed in and by the essence of the world, answers it from within. A mere change of mindset cannot do anything to help the arrival of the thing as thing, just as what now stands as an object in the distance-less cannot simply be changed into a thing. Things also never arrive as things by virtue of us evading objects and remembering old objects that may have once been underway to becoming things, or even coming to presence as things.

Whatever becomes a thing occurs from the ringing of the mirror-game of the world. Only when world worlds as world—presumably suddenly— the ring gleams from which the ringing of earth and sky, divine and mortals wrests itself into the ring of its simplicity.

According to this ringing, the thinging itself is flexible and each respectively lingering thing is pliant, inconspicuously obedient to its essence. The thing is pliant: the pitcher and the bench, the bridge and the plow. But, in their own way, the tree and the pond, the stream and the mountain are also things. Respectively lingering and thinging in their way, heron and deer, horse and bull are things. Respectively lingering and thinging according to their way, mirror and buckle, book and picture, crown and cross are things.

Yet things are also pliant and malleable in numbers, measured by the immense amount of objects that count as the same everywhere, and measured by the enormity of the massive that belongs to the human, a living being.

The first to inhabit the world as world are humans, as the mortals. Only what rings forth from the world can at some point become a thing.

The *Ge-Stell*

[24] At the beginning of our path, it became evident that no mastery of distances achieves nearness anywhere. But with nearness, remoteness is also canceled. Everything is leveled down into the distance-less. Now we see more clearly: nearness comes to presence insofar as the thing things. The thing things the world. Thinging is nearing that holds the world in nearness as the world. The essence of nearness lies in nearing.

Nearness is not the shortness of distance, remoteness is not its length. Finally, remoteness is not the nullification of nearness. Remoteness first "remotes," and remains preserved as remoteness, in the nearing of nearness. That is why, where the thing does not thing and thus nearness does not near, remoteness also remains remote. Nearness and remoteness both remain lacking. The distance-less dominates.

"Gap" is what we know as the stretch between two points. Yet if we step out of the house into the shade under the tree, then the gap between the house and the tree does not consist in the measured stretch between the two. The gap consists much more in how the house and tree and shade, in their relation to each other, collectively concern us. Such concern attunes the gap (distance) between what is present within coming-to-presence. Such concern attunes the gap between us and everything that is present or absent. That which, among itself, possesses this distance to us, concerns us precisely in this distancing, be it that something lies remote from us or that it comes near. Even that which, as we say, is none of our business, concerns us very much in its own way. For the trivial concerns us in the way that we constantly pass it by and let it lie.

All that is present or absent has the character of a concern [*Anganges*]. Distance lies in concern. Concern lies in nearness. Too easily we think that distance, from our point of view, lies in something standing [25] over against us. Accordingly, distance first appears to be reached in this standing-over, and to be secured in what stands in this way. But what stands over [*Gegenständige*] is only the final interval and the last remainder of the distant. When what is present becomes that which stands over against presentation, the domination of the distance-less, if still inconspicuous, has already set in. In what is objective [*Gegenständlichen*], we have before us that which concerns us. In this way it stands apart from us, and we from it. Yet this objective presentation, which apparently first allows us to encounter what is present, is essentially already an attack upon what concerns us. In the appearance of pure presence that the standing-over-against—the objective—offers us, there lies hidden the greed of presentational calculation. The states in which we face ourselves, within which we pursue and dissect ourselves, are also things that stand over against us. Psychology and the mastery of psychological explanation contain the onset of the leveling of the psychical-intellectual to what is always accessible to everyone, to what is basically already distance-less. The domination of what stands over against us will not secure the distance. In this distance already lurks the onrush of the distance-less. If the distance rests in concern, then where the distance-less reigns, nothing is any longer specifically our concern. Everything slides into the basic trait of being equally valid, even if some things still lie close to us, here and there, like lost embedded crystals. The concern of the equally valid is a tearing-away into the uniformity, which goes, stands, and falls neither near nor far. The uniform distance-less concerns humans so decisively that they are everywhere equally concerned with it. The uniformity of this concern with the distance-less consists in the fact that humans, concerned with it in this way, continually fall prey to it in the same, empty fashion. Yet what comes to presence without distance is neither lacking in concern nor in position. Rather, the distance-less has its own standing. Its constancy circulates in the eerie concern of what is equally valid everywhere. The human stands toward this by falling prey to it. The distance-less is [26] never without a standing. It stands insofar as everything that is present is an inventory or standing reserve [*Bestand*]. Where the inventory comes to power the object, as a character of what is present, decays.

The inventory endures. It endures as long as it is geared toward a demand [*Bestellen*]. Being turned toward demand, it is put to use. Use places everything in advance in such a way that what is placed pursues whatever succeeds. Placed in this way, everything is "as a succession of . . ." But the succession is demanded as a success from the outset. Success is that type of succession that remains geared toward the result of further sequences. The inventory endures through a peculiar placing. We call it "besetting" [Be-Stellen].

What does "placing" [stellen] mean? We know the word from the phrases: to present something [vor-stellen], to produce something [her-stellen]. Yet we must still doubt whether our thinking is adequate to the simple and underestimated reach of these phrases.

What does "placing" mean? Let us begin by thinking it from the side of production. The joiner produces a table, but also a coffin. What is produced is not equatable with what is merely fabricated. What is placed forth stands in the region of that which concerns us. It is placed forth into a nearness. The joiner in the mountain village does not fabricate a box for a corpse. The coffin is placed in advance at the preferred location of the farm where the dead farmer still remains. There, the coffin is still called Totenbaum.[9] In it, the death of the deceased thrives. This thriving determines house and farm, those that live there, their family, and their neighborhood.

In a motorized burial industry of the city, everything is different. Here, no Totenbaum is produced.

In order to tow felled trees from the forest onto the woodpath, the farmer gets his draft bull. He does not place the bull in order for it to stand somewhere. He produces the draft beam [Gestell] in such a way that it turns into a use.

Men and women must report [stellen] to a labor service. They are ordered [bestellt]. They are affected by a placement [Stellen] that challenges them—i.e., that demands something of them. One blocks [stellt] the other, stops them. He [27] bars [stellt] them, demands information, and calls them to account. He challenges them. We will engage this meaning of the word stellen in order to glean what occurs in that ordering [Bestellen] through which the inventory stands and thus is a standing reserve.

Placing [Stellen] now means: challenging, demanding, forcing to surrender. This placing occurs as the Gestellung.[10] In the Gestellung-order, it applies to humans. But within all that is present, the human is not the only thing present that is affected by the Gestellung.

---

9. [Literally "tree for the dead," also frequently called "tree-coffin," this is the name for a coffin made out of a hollowed-out tree trunk.—Tr.]

10. [I have chosen not to translate the terms Ge-Stell and Gestellung in this chapter, as there is no single English word that could convey the many connotations that Heidegger has in mind, and since he explicitly develops these aspects throughout this section. Since Gestellung denotes the process of the Ge-Stell's forceful "framing," the former concept will become more clear as Heidegger elucidates the latter in subsequent pages.—Tr.]

A stretch of land is forced to supply [*gestellt . . . auf*] coal and ores that appear as outcrops. The presence of ores is presumably already presented within the horizon of such a forcing [*Stellens*], and is only imaginable from within it. The outcropped rock that as such is already sized up for surrender [*Sichstellen*] is challenged [*herausgefordert*] and thus transported out [*herausgefördert*]. The earth is drawn into such a supplying [*Stellen*] and seized by it. It is beset [*be-stellt*], affected by *Gestellung*. That is how we understand the word *bestellen* now and in what follows.

Through such besetting, the land becomes a coal dispensary, the ground a warehouse for ores. This besetting is already of another kind than that formerly used by the farmer to occupy his field. The farmer's doing does not challenge the soil of the field; rather, it gives the seed over to the powers of growth; it shelters the seed in its thriving. In the meantime, however, farming has switched over to the same besetting that makes the air surrender nitrogen, makes the ground surrender coal and ores, makes the ores supply uranium, makes the uranium supply atomic energy, makes the latter supply destruction on command. Farming is now a motorized nutrition-industry, in essence the same as the fabrication of corpses in gas chambers and destruction camps, the same as the blockade and starving-out of countries, the same as the fabrication of hydrogen bombs.

[28] Yet toward what, for instance, is the coal geared that the coal dispensary is made to surrender? It is not placed forth as the pitcher on the table. Just as the ground is made to supply the coal, the latter is challenged for heat; this is already made to supply steam, whose pressure drives the machinery that keeps a factory in production; a factory that is made to supply machines that make tools with which, in turn, machines are brought to and kept in working order.

One forcing [*Stellen*] challenges the other, besets it with *Gestellung*. This does not occur through the mere sequence of forcing actions. The *Gestellung* occurs, according to its essence, secretly and in advance. Only in this way does the *Gestellung* enable a useable planning and the measures of the individual plans of the forcing. But what does the sequencing of this besetting aim at?

The hydroelectric plant is placed into the flow of water. The latter is made to supply pressure which makes the turbines turn, which drives the machine whose gears supply electricity, which allows the long-distance power station and its grid to transport electricity. The electric plant in the Rhine—the dam complex, the turbines, the dynamos, the switching center, the grid—all of this only exists insofar as it immediately stands in place for supply, not in order to come to presence, but rather in order to be forced to supply something else.

Only what is beset in this way, standing immediately in place for supply, endures as standing reserve and remains constant [*beständig*] in the sense of an inventory [*Bestand*]. The constancy consists in the pervasive assailability [*Bestellbarkeit*] within such *Gestellung*.

Again we ask: What does the chain of such besetting ultimately aim at? It aims at nothing—for the besetting [29] does not produce anything that could have a presence for itself outside of the forcing. What is beset is always already and only ever forced to supply and bring something else to success as its result. The chain of besetting does not aim at anything; instead, it just enters its cycle. Only in this does the assailable [*Bestellbare*] have its persistence [*Bestand*]. The flow of the Rhine, for example, only exists as the assailed object of the besetting. The hydroelectric plant is not built into the flow of the Rhine, but rather the flow is built into the power plant and only is what it is by virtue of the plant's essence. In order to assess the monstrosity that reigns here, let us pay attention for a moment to the contrast expressed in these two titles: "the Rhine," built into the power plant—"the Rhine," spoken in Hölderlin's hymn of the same name.

The standing reserve persists [*Der Bestand besteht*]. It endures in besetting. What, in itself, is the besetting? The forcing has the character of challenging [*Herausfordern*]. Accordingly, it becomes a hauling-out [*Herausfördern*]. This happens with coal, with ores, with oil, with streams and seas, with the air. One says that the earth is being exploited with regard to the material harbored within it, but that the exploitation is the action and business of the human.

According to this, the besetting would merely be a machination of the human, accomplished in the mode of exploitation. Yet the besetting of the inventory initially and only appears in this character so long as we present it within the horizon of everyday meaning. This appearance, that the besetting is in essence only a human machination with the character of exploitation, is even inevitable. Nevertheless, it remains a mere illusion.

The besetting forces. It challenges. Yet if we reflect, not on possible effects but on its essence: The besetting does not pursue bounty and gain, but rather always something that is assailable. "Always" here means: in [30] advance, because essential. The besetting is only drawn from one assailable thing to another because it has in advance torn everything present into complete assailability and forced it there, whether what is present had already respectively been placed in a certain way or not. This all-encompassing violence of the besetting merely draws the separate acts of besetting along behind it. This violence of besetting allows one to surmise that what is here called "besetting" is no mere *human* doing, even if the human belongs to its accomplishment.

The question remains to what extent the human is already entailed in the essence of the besetting. However, what does "the human" mean here? "The human" does not exist anywhere. Yet provided that humans challenge the force of the water flow for its pressure, and force the latter to supply electricity—they are only capable of this insofar as they are already ordered into this besetting [*in dieses Bestellen bestellt sind*]. Humans, in their relation to what is present, are already challenged to present what is present as the assailable object of besetting [*das Bestellbare des Bestellens*], in advance and thus everywhere, and therefore constantly. Insofar as human presentation has already forced what is present, as what is assailable, into the calculation of besetting, the human—whether knowingly or not—in its essence remains placed [*bestellt*] into besetting [*Bestellen*] for the forcing [*Bestellen*] of what is assailable [*Bestellbaren*].

Humans themselves now stand in such a *Gestellung*. The human offered himself to the accomplishment of such *Gestellung*. Now he stands ready to take over and accomplish this besetting. Thus, the human is the employee [*Angestellte*] of the besetting. That is why humans, alone and *en masse*, are being set aside [*abgestellt*]. The human is now the one assailed by and for the besetting.

The besetting is no human creation—for the human effect that operates along in each besetting must [31] first be capable of being forced, through the besetting, into a certain doing and letting.

The besetting does not only seize the materials and forces of nature with *Gestellung*. It at the same time seizes the fate of the human. The essence of the human is forced to help accomplish the besetting in a human way. The besetting affects nature and history, everything that is, and in all ways that what is present exists. What is present is, as such, forced into assailability and thus forced in advance into what is constant, whose standing holds sway from within the besetting. What is constant in this way, and constantly present, is the inventory.

That is why the besetting can never be explained through some individual inventory, just as little as it can be presented in the sum of all discoverable inventories, as something general hovering above them. The besetting cannot be clarified at all—i.e., it cannot be reduced to that clarity that we inadvertently pass off for what is immediately and commonly known, and generally take to be unquestionable. Whatever we tend to clarify with this clarity is thereby just given over to the unreflective and thoughtless. We must not desire to clarify the besetting in which the inventory holds sway. We must rather first attempt to experience its essence that still remains unthought.

For this, it is necessary that we note how the besetting besets in advance everything that is: nature and history, the human and the divine—for if today's ill-advised theology helps itself to the results of modern atomic physics in order to secure its proofs of God, then God is thereby forced into the region of the assailable.

The besetting affects everything present with [32] respect to its presence, and affects it with *Gestellung*. The besetting is only geared toward one thing, *versus unum*—namely: to secure, as an inventory, *the one whole* of what is present. In itself, the besetting is universal. It gathers within it all possible kinds of securing [*Stellens*] and all modes of their connection. The besetting has already gathered itself, in itself, toward the thorough securing of the assailability of *all* that is present.

We call the gathering of mountains [*Berge*] that from itself is already gathered in a unified way—and never after the fact—a mountain range [*Gebirge*]. We call the collection of the ways we can and do feel [*zumute*] our feeling [*Gemüt*].

We now call the collection of securing, gathered from itself, in which everything assailable holds sway in its inventory, the *Ge-Stell*.

This word now no longer indicates an individual object such as a book-case or a draw-well. *Ge-Stell* also does not signify something constant that is part of the assailed inventory. *Ge-Stell* names the universal besetting—gathered from itself—of the complete assailability of present things as a whole. The circularity of besetting occurs in and as the *Ge-Stell*.

In the *Ge-Stell*, the presence of all that is present becomes an inventory. The *Ge-Stell* constantly draws what is assailable into the cycle of besetting, holds it firmly there, and deposits it, as constant, into the inventory. This depositing does not take what is constant out of the cycle of securing. It merely deposits away into an assailability that will follow, i.e., back into the besetting.

The *Ge-Stell* forces [*stellt*]. It pulls everything together into assailability. It pulls [*rafft*] everything present into assailability and is thus the gathering of this pulling. The *Ge-Stell* is a pulling [*Geraff*]. But this [33] pulling never merely accumulates the inventory. Rather, it constantly pulls what is beset away into the cycle of assailability. Within the pulling, one thing forces another. One drives the other forward, but forward into the "away" of besetting.

The *Ge-Stell*'s forcing, gathered into itself, is the collection of work [*Treibens*] that circles in itself. The *Ge-Stell* is mechanism [*Getriebe*]. The pulling pulls, and it does so away into the mechanism of operation [*Getriebe des Betriebes*].

The *Ge-Stell* holds sway as the pulling of the mechanism that demands [*bestellt*] the constant assailability of the complete inventory.

What we thus think as *the Ge-Stell,* is *the essence of technology.*

We say "of technology" and mean modern technology. One often designates it as machine technology. This designation hits upon something correct, but it does not yet contain truth—it does not point into the essence of modern technology, because the mode of presentation that gives rise to the designation of modern technology as machine technology can never point into the essence of technology. One thinks that modern technology, in contrast to all previous kinds, is determined by the machine. Yet what if the opposite were the case? Modern technology is not what it is because of the machine, but rather the machine only is what it is and how it is out of the essence of technology. One therefore says nothing about the essence of modern technology if one presents it as machine technology.

In advance, the *Ge-Stell* as such secures all inventory such that it can only persist through the machine. How? The *Ge-Stell* is the gathering of the pulling of the mechanism of the reservation of what is assailable, the latter of which is solely geared to immediately standing in place for supply. The *Ge-Stell* is the gathering of the circling besetting of what is assailable. In itself, the *Ge-Stell* is the pulling, working circulation of the ordering of what is assailable into besetting [*Bestellens des Bestellbaren in das Bestellen*]. The *Ge-Stell* forces everything into this equality of the assailable, such that it constantly secures itself again in [34] the same shape, into the sameness of assailability.

The *Ge-Stell,* as this circulation of besetting, in itself erects the essence of the machine. The latter includes rotation without it necessarily having the shape of a wheel; for the wheel is determined by rotation, not the other way around.

Rotation is the turning that runs back into itself, and that turns something assailable (fuel) into the besetting of the assailable (propelling force). The rotation of the machine is forced—i.e., challenged and made constant —in the circulation that lies in the mechanism, the essential character of the *Ge-Stell.*

Long before the first steam engine was invented and put to work in

England, toward the end of the eighteenth century, the *Ge-Stell*—the essence of technology—was in gear in a concealed fashion. This means: The essence of technology already reigned beforehand, in such a way that it first cleared the realm within which something like the invention of engines could even begin its pursuit and make its experiments.

Thus, no matter how technically we describe the most modern machine and explain its construction with precision, we will always only grasp the machine technologically. We never think the machine from the *essence* of technology. But the essence of technology is not itself something technological. Every construction of every machine already moves within the essential sphere of technology. Yet, as technological construction, it can never design the *essence* of the machine. That is just as impossible as the attempt to calculate the essence of mathematics through mathematical means, or delimiting the essence of history through historical research.

[35] It must suffice, on our path, to indicate the essential location of the machine. The machine is not something that comes to presence in its own special way. It is not just a more convoluted form of tool or equipment—just a collection of wheels that powers itself, in contrast to the farmer's spinning wheel or the bucket-wheel from the rice paddies of China. In general, the machine does not merely stand in for equipment and tools; just as little as it is an object. The machine only stands insofar as it goes. It goes insofar as it runs. It runs in the mechanism of operation. The mechanism works as the machination of the besetting of the assailable. When the machine stands still, its standing-still is a condition of the mechanism: its cessation or its interruption. Machines are within a machinery. But the latter is not a heap of machines. The machinery runs on the pulling of the mechanism, as which the *Ge-Stell* besets the inventory.

Even if it does not become immediately and presently obvious, the *Ge-Stell* has already in advance removed all those places [*Stellen*] where the spinning wheel and the water mill used to stand. Through its machinery, the *Ge-Stell* occupies [*bestellt*] in advance a different kind and order of places [*Stellen*]. In these, something can only come to stand if it immediately and uniformly, as something assailable, stands in place for supply.

That is also why the way in which the machine produces something is essentially different from the labor of hands, provided that there even is still something like production with the *Ge-Stell*.

Tractors and trucks are brought out, spit out one by one in a line. Where does this stand, that which is brought forth is such a way? Into what standing is it placed?

The automobile is brought out in such a way that it immediately stands in place for supply, i.e., is instantly and constantly deliverable. It is not produced so as to stand there and remain there like the pitcher. The automobile is rather placed in such a way that it goes off as something assailable that can be [36] challenged, namely for transportation, which serves the advancement of interaction.

That which the machine puts out piece by piece, it places in the inventory of the assailable. What is put out is a piece of the inventory [*Bestand-Stück*]. This term is now taken in a new and strict sense.

The piece is something different than the part [*Teil*]. The part joins, with other parts, into the whole. It takes part in the whole, belongs to it. The piece on the other hand is separate and, as what it is, is sectioned off against other pieces. It never joins into a whole with these. The piece of the inventory also never joins into the inventory with other pieces. Rather, the inventory is what is pieced-apart into the assailable. This piecing-apart does not break the pieces, but instead precisely brings about their persistence. Each of them is drawn and locked into a cycle of assailability. The sectioning off of pieces against each other corresponds to each piece being locked into an operation of besetting.

If one wanted to place the pieces of an automobile inventory away somewhere piece by piece, then these pieces would be torn out of the cycle of their assailability. The result would be a kind of car cemetery. The parking garage is different, in which each vehicle is ready on hand in its assailability and as the secured piece of an assailed inventory.

The inventory-pieces are the same piece by piece. Their character as pieces demands this uniformity. As the same, the pieces stand against each other in the utmost separation; in this way, they increase and secure their character as pieces. The uniformity of the pieces allows one piece to be exchanged for the other without further ado—i.e., on the spot: the piece is thus on hand. One inventory-piece is replaceable [37] through the other. As a piece, the piece is already geared toward replaceability. Inventory-piece means: what is sectioned off as a piece is—exchangeably—locked into a besetting.

Even what we call a machine part is, strictly speaking, never a part. To be sure, it is fitted into the mechanism, but as an exchangeable part. Conversely, my hand is not a piece of me. I myself am completely in each respective gesture of the hand.

We tend to imagine something lifeless under the name "piece," even if one speaks of a "piece" of cattle. The inventory-pieces, however, are each stretched into a besetting, forced by it. In their own way humans also belong to what is forced in such a way, be it as those who operate the machine or as those who construct and build the machine within the besetting of the machinery. The human is, in the age of technology's domination, essentially forced into the essence of technology, into the *Ge-Stell*, and beset by it. In their own way, humans are inventory-pieces, in the strict sense of the words "inventory" and "piece."

The human is exchangeable within the besetting of inventory. Being an inventory-piece remains the prerequisite for the human being able to become a functionary of besetting. Nevertheless, the human belongs into the *Ge-Stell* in a completely different way than the machine. This way can become inhuman. The *in*human, however, is always still in*human*. The human will never become a machine. Of course, the inhuman that remains human is more terrible than the human that is merely a machine, because the former is more vicious and more fateful.

But the humans of this age are forced into the *Ge-Stell* even if they do not stand immediately in front of machines and in the operation of a machinery. The forester, for example, who measures the [38] felled timber in the forest and appears to follow the paths in the same way as his grandfather, is today put to use by the timber industry. Whether he knows it or not, he is in his own way an inventory-piece of the cellulose-inventory and its assailability for paper, which is delivered to newspapers and magazines, which then through the public stand to be consumed.

Broadcast and film belong to the inventory of that besetting through which the public as such is forced, challenged, and thus first established. The machineries of broadcast and film are inventory-pieces of that inventory which brings everything into the public and thus assails the public for everything and anything without differentiation. It is not only the machineries that are the inventory-pieces of this inventory of the public's installation and direction, but also in their own way the employees of these operations, all the way to the council on broadcasting. The latter is secured by the inventory called broadcasting—i.e., is challenged to beset this operation. As an inventory-piece of this inventory, it remains locked within it. Let us imagine the improbable case that the broadcasting council were to recommend eliminating broadcasting. The council would be deposed overnight because it only is what it is as the secured piece of an inventory within the *Ge-Stell* of the public's besetting.

Sealed off into the piece-character of the inventory-piece, every radio listener who turns their dial is sectioned off as a piece of the inventory in which they remain locked, even if they believe that the switching on and off of the device is within their freedom. Yet they are only still free in the sense that each time, they must free themselves from a compulsion of the pressing public, which unavoidably persists either way.

At this point, humans are not just secondarily inventory-pieces of broadcasting. Already in their essence, they are forced toward this character of being inventory-pieces. Let us picture another, even more unlikely scenario, namely that suddenly, everywhere on earth, all radios were to [39] disappear —who could imagine the helplessness, boredom, and emptiness that would seize humanity with one blow, disturbing its everyday life through and through?

Let it be clear that this is not a judgment upon radio listeners, and also not upon broadcasting itself. The point is merely to indicate that, in the inventory called broadcasting, there reigns a besetting and forcing that has interfered with the essence of the human. Because this is the case, and because the human never decides about his essence solely from and through himself, the besetting of the inventory—the Ge-Stell, the essence of technology—cannot be anything solely human. One therefore ultimately loses one's way if one tries to derive technology from human intelligence, or even from artistic intelligence. The artistic presumes the ars, the ars presumes τέχνη, and this presumes the essence of what is τέχνη-like.

The inventory of the Ge-Stell consists of the inventory-pieces and the ways of their besetting. The inventory-pieces are the persistent part of the inventory. We must therefore think their persistence from the essence of the inventory—i.e., out of the Ge-Stell.

One commonly presents the persistent as what perseveres. This is the constantly present. But what is present can concern humans in different ways of presence. These various ways determine the epochs of the Western history of Beyng [Seyn]. What is present can hold sway as that which comes forth from itself, out from concealment, forth into unconcealment. We call what is present in this way, in its coming-to-presence, what stands forth [Herstand].

What is present can announce itself as the created thing of the creator, who himself is constantly and everywhere present in everything. What is present can offer itself as that which is placed forth for, and over against, human presentation. What is present is thus the objective for the presentation: As percipere, presentation is the cogitare of the ego cogito [40] of conscientia—of consciousness, of the subject's self-awareness. The object is the object for the subject.

But what is present can also exist as the persistent in the sense of the inventory-pieces of that inventory which, as the constantly assailable, is forced into that placing as which the *Ge-Stell* reigns.

The *Ge-Stell* is the essence of technology. Its placing is universal. It turns toward the unity of the whole of all that is present. The *Ge-Stell* then determines the way that each present thing now comes to presence. All that exists is—openly or still concealed, in the more various ways and their variations—an inventory-piece of the inventory in the besetting of the *Ge-Stell*. The persistent persists, through the same that is beset, in the assailable replaceability.

The *Ge-Stell* is the essence of technology. The *Ge-Stell* besets. It besets what is present with *Gestellung*.[11] It orders what is present into an inventory. What is persistent in the inventory are the inventory-pieces. Their persistence consists in the assailable replaceability through what is constantly the same, that which is immediately in place for supply. Yet here a doubt announces itself. If the essence of technology consists in the *Ge-Stell*, but technology aims at forcing the forces and materials of nature—i.e., to challenge them as that which, when hauled out, advances everything that leads to success—then the essence of technology precisely shows that it is not universal. The forces and materials of nature set such a decisive limit to technology that the latter remains dependent on nature as the source and support of the technological inventory. We thus cannot claim that all that is present comes to presence in the form of the persistent—the persistent that comes to stand in the besetting of the *Ge-Stell*. The *Ge-Stell* does not affect all that is present. Technology is only one real thing among others. Technology remains far from deciding the reality of all that is real.

How does it stand with the essence of technology? Is it universal or [41] not? What is the relation between technology and nature?

Yet what is nature, which supposedly comes to presence outside the realm of the technological inventory, and as that to which besetting must always return? How does nature come to presence insofar as technology, dependent on nature, takes the power of its power plants and its materials from it? What are the forces of nature that are secured in technology? Natural science gives the answer. The fundamental discipline in the science of the physical is physics. To be sure, the latter does not tell us anything about the essence of force; but physics provides an opportunity for thought to pursue how natural science presents what it calls force. Physically, the

---

11. [Recall that *Gestellung* denotes the process of the *Ge-Stell*'s forceful "framing."—Tr.]

force of nature is only accessible in its effect—for only in its effect does force demonstrate its calculability. In calculation, force becomes object-like. Natural science depends solely on this object of calculation. Nature is presented as that reality which is secured in measurement and number, and that objectively comes to presence in its effect. This effect, in turn, only counts as present insofar as it has an effect itself and proves to be effective. That which is present in nature is the real. The real is the effective. The coming-to-presence of nature consists in effectiveness. In it, nature can immediately bring something into place, i.e., make it occur.

Force is that which brings one thing to effect something else out of it in a surveyable fashion. The forces of nature are presented by physics in the sense of a forcing through which the Ge-Stell secures what is present. Nature stands over against technology only in such a way that it persists as a system of ordering successes out of the effective that is secured. Kant was the first to decisively think this essence of nature, albeit without recourse to the Ge-Stell. The effectiveness of the real—of nature—is nothing other than the capacity to order [Bestellfähigkeit] success. This means: Nature does not stand over against technology as something undetermined, [42] present in itself. It does not stand over against technology as an object at all, one that is occasionally exploited. In the age of technology, nature belongs in advance to the inventory of the assailable within the Ge-Stell.

One will rejoin that this might apply to the forces of nature, which technology taps and draws out, as it were. The materials of nature, on the other hand, have existed outside the technological inventory for a long time, long before technology began. Chemistry determines what the materials themselves are in their objective reality.

Yet how does science take the material of nature? It presents it as matter. What is the fundamental physical trait of matter? It is inertia. What does physics mean by inertia? Presented physically, inertia is the persistence in the state of motion. Rest is also such a state, which counts physico-calculatively as a limit case of motion. Inertia is resistance against change of motion. Resistance is counter-movement, namely against acceleration. Material, as matter, is presented within the horizon of motion and with respect to what is effective, i.e., from the side of force. This force must be expended (i.e., secured) in order to change the respective state of motion—in order to occupy another state.

For physics, nature is the inventory of energy and matter. They are the inventory-pieces of nature. Matter is determined with respect to inertia and from the side of energy. Energy, however, is what is effective, what is capable of ordering [*Bestellfähige*] the secured besetting of a success. Force itself is the assailable that is capable of being ordered, capable of being geared toward capacities of preservation, transformation, and storage—all characteristics that are geared toward a constantly available assailability of energy.

Not only the forces of nature but the materials of nature as well are presented [43] physically-chemically as a besetting and assailable [*bestellend-bestellbarer*] inventory. They are "pre-sented" [*vor-gestellt*] in an essential ambiguity of this word, namely: forced in advance into the aspect of calculation.

Nature, which appears to stand over against technology, is already employed by the essence of technology in the inventory of the *Ge-Stell* as a basic inventory. The essence of modern technology begins to reign historically with the onset of modern science three and a half centuries ago. What does this mean? It does not mean that modern technology was initially just natural science and only later came to exist as its application. Rather, it means that the essence of modern technology, the *Ge-Stell,* began with the fundamentally essential act of besetting, insofar as it first secured nature in advance as the fundamental inventory. Modern technology is not applied natural science; instead, modern natural science is the application of the essence of technology through which the latter turns to its fundamental inventory in order to secure it into usability.

Something is only present for natural science if, and insofar as, it can be pre-calculated. The pre-calculability of natural processes, decisive for all natural-scientific presentation, is the presentational assailability of nature as the inventory of a success. Whether this calculability ends up being univocal and certain, or only remains probable and thus merely statistically graspable, does not change the least thing about the essence of nature—as inventory—as solely permitted by the essence of technology. Atomic physics, to be sure, is experimentally-calculatively different than classical physics. Thought from its essence, however, it remains the same physics.

In the age of technology, nature is no limit to technology. Nature is much more the basic inventory-piece of the technical inventory—and nothing else.

[44] Nature is not even something that stands over against [*Gegenstand*] anymore. As the basic piece of the inventory, it is something constant in the *Ge-Stell,* something whose standing and constancy are solely determined by the besetting. Everything present, even nature, comes to presence in the manner of that which is constant in the inventory that the *Ge-Stell* besets.

The *Ge-Stell* is universal in its placing. It concerns all that is present—not just in its sum or sequence, but insofar as everything present as such, in its persistence, is forced by the besetting. It therefore does not matter whether we immediately notice and take note of this character of presence every time, or whether we overlook it for a long time and, as is largely the case, continue to present the reality of the real in an habitual fashion which, considered strictly, is completely muddled.

In the age of technology, all that is present comes to presence in the manner of the constancy of the inventory-pieces. The human also comes to presence in this way even if it may appear—for some stretches of time and in some areas—that his essence and presence are not affected by the forcing of the *Ge-Stell*.

What is constant in the inventory-pieces is characterized by uniformity. In the *Ge-Stell*, everything is geared toward constant replaceability of the same by the same. Only in this way does the *Ge-Stell* remain completely pulled together in what is constant in its mechanism. The *Ge-Stell* in advance pulls everything assailable into the same of unlimited assailability of the complete inventory. The same that is constantly replaceable counts as the same in all that is constant. What is equally valid in all that is constant secures for the latter its constancy through the replaceability that is assailable on the spot. The inventory consists of the *Ge-Stell*'s besetting. Everything stands as equally valid in the inventory. The inventory besets what is without distance.

Everything real moves together into the uniform distance-less. [45] Nearness and remoteness of what is present remain eschewed. Our reflection began with this indication. The airplane and all traffic devices that continually increase their speed shorten the distances. Everyone today knows this. Everyone assures us that the world is getting smaller. Everyone knows that technology is doing this.

We possess this insight without needing to agree to such intricate detours as we have just gone, detours in which we thought about the thing in its thinging, the *Ge-Stell* and its forcing, the inventory and its pieces.

Why do we nevertheless follow this path of thought in order to gain insight into that which is? Because we do not want to merely assert again, through a number of perceptions that could be multiplied at will, what everyone in the technological age already knows. What is decisive is not that distances are decreasing through the help of technology, but rather that nearness remains eschewed. Yet we do not merely take note of this. We think about the essence of nearness in order to experience the way in which it is lacking, in order to think about what occurs in this absence. We do not pursue the effects of technology in order to display their results. We think into the essence of technology in order to experience how the absence of nearness goes together with the unfolding of technology's essence. Technology's machines can only diminish distances—and refrain from bringing nearness—because the essence of technology refuses nearness and remoteness in advance. But we do not think about the essence of technology in order to erect a philosophy of technology or even just design it. Technology holds sway as *Ge-Stell*. Yet what reigns within the *Ge-Stell*? Whence and how does the essence of the *Ge-Stell* occur?

EIGHTEEN

The Principle of Identity

27 June 1957

According to a familiar formulation, the principle of identity is A = A. The principle counts as the highest law of thinking. We shall try to think about this principle for a while, for through it, we would like to find out what identity is.

When thought, engaged by something, pursues this matter, it can occur that thought changes in the process. In what follows, therefore, it is advisable to pay attention to the path and less to the content. The progress of the lecture already prevents us from properly dwelling with the content.

What does the formula A = A, with which one customarily represents the principle of identity, state? The formula expresses the equality of A and A. An equation requires at least two elements. One A equals another. Is this

---

This chapter was previously translated by Joan Stambaugh in *Identity and Difference* (New York: Harper & Row, 1969). Several emendations have been made, both to correct missing sentences, and to take seriously Heidegger's claim that *Er-eignis* cannot be translated.

Bracketed numbers refer to the pagination of GA 11; the chapter opens at page 33. — Tr.

what the principle of identity is supposed to mean? Obviously not. What is identical, *idem* in Latin, is τὸ αὐτό in Greek. Translated into our German language, τὸ αὐτό means "the same" [*das Selbe*]. If someone continuously says the same thing, for example: "the plant is a plant," he speaks in a tautology. For something to be the same, one thing is always enough. One does not need two, as one does with equality.

The formula A = A speaks of equality. It does not speak of A as the same. The common formulation of the principle of identity thus conceals precisely what the principle is trying to say: A is A, that is, every A is itself the same.

While we elaborate what is identical in this way, we are reminded of an old phrase through which Plato makes the identical distinct—a phrase that points back to a still older one. In the dialogue *Sophist,* at 254d, Plato speaks of στάσις and κίνησις, rest and motion. At this point, Plato has the stranger say: οὐκοῦν αὐτῶν ἕκαστον τοῖν μὲν δυοῖν ἕτερόν ἐστιν, αὐτὸ δ'ἑαυτῷ ταὐτόν.

"Each one of them is different from the (other) two, but itself [34] the same for itself." Plato does not just say: ἕκαστον αὐτὸ ταὐτόν, "each itself the same," but says ἕκαστον ἑαυτῷ ταὐτόν, "each itself the same for itself."

The dative ἑαυτῷ means: each thing itself is returned to itself, each itself is the same, namely for itself and with itself. Our German language, like the Greek, offers the advantage of illustrating the identical by means of the same word, but in the jointure [*Fuge*] of its various forms.

Accordingly, the more fitting formulation of the principle of identity "A is A" does not only state that every A is itself the same, but rather that every A is itself the same with itself. Sameness contains the relation of "with"— that is, a mediation, a connection, a synthesis: the unification into a unity. This is why, throughout the history of Western thought, identity has appeared in the form of unity. But this unity is by no means the stale emptiness of that which, in itself without relation, persists in monotony. Yet Western thought has required more than two thousand years to arrive at the point where the relation of the same with itself—which prevails in identity and that resounded early on—emerges as this mediation in a decisive and decided way, and until an abode can even be found for this radiant emergence of mediation within identity. For it is only the philosophy of speculative idealism, prepared by Leibniz and Kant, which through Fichte, Schelling, and Hegel founds an abode for the essence of identity—an essence that is synthetic in itself. This abode cannot be demonstrated here. One thing must be kept in mind: Since the age of speculative idealism, it has remained forbidden for thought to represent the unity of identity as mere sameness, and to ignore the mediation [35] that prevails in the unity. Wherever this occurs, identity is only represented abstractly.

Even in the improved formula "A is A," only abstract identity appears. Does it get that far? Does the principle of identity say anything about identity? No, at least not directly. Rather, the principle already presupposes what identity means and where it belongs.

How do we find anything out about this presupposition? The principle of identity supplies it, if we listen carefully to its fundamental tone and reflect on it, instead of thoughtlessly mouthing the formula "A is A." Actually, the principle states: A *is* A. What do we hear? With this "is," the principle says how every being is, namely: It itself is the same with itself. The principle of identity speaks of the Being of beings. As a law of thought, the principle is valid only insofar as it is a principle of Being that reads: To every being as such there belongs identity, the unity with itself.

Heard from its fundamental tone [*Grundton*], what the principle of identity states is exactly what the whole of Western European thought thinks—and that is: The unity of identity forms a basic characteristic in the Being of beings. Wherever and however we are related to beings of every kind, we find identity making its claim on us. If this claim were not made, beings could never appear in their Being. Accordingly, no science would exist. For if the identity of its object were not guaranteed ahead of time in each case, science could not be what it is. [36] Through this guarantee, research assures itself of the possibility of its work. Still, the guiding notion of the identity of the object is never of any palpable use to the sciences. Thus, what is successful and fruitful about scientific knowledge is everywhere based on something useless. The claim of the identity of the object *speaks*—whether the sciences hear it or not, whether they throw to the winds what they have heard or let themselves be strongly affected by it.

The claim of identity speaks from the Being of beings. In the place, however, where the Being of beings comes to its earliest and particular expression in Western thought, namely in Parmenides, there τὸ αὐτό—the identical—speaks in a way that is almost too powerful. One of Parmenides' fragments reads: τὸ γὰρ αὐτὸ νοεῖν ἐστίν τε καὶ εἶναι. "For the same is perceiving (thinking) as well as Being."[1]

Different things, thinking and Being, are here thought of as the same. What does this tell us? Something completely different in comparison to

---

1. [Since Heidegger glosses this phrase in his own peculiar way, I have given a direct translation of his German rendering here.—Tr.]

what we otherwise know as the teaching of metaphysics that identity belongs to Being. Parmenides says: Being belongs to an identity. What does identity mean here? What does the word τὸ αὐτό, "the same," say in Parmenides' fragment? Parmenides does not give us an answer to this question. He places us before an enigma that we may not evade. We must acknowledge the fact that in early ages of thought, long before thinking arrives at a principle of identity, identity itself speaks out in a pronouncement that decrees: Thinking and Being belong together in the same and by virtue of this same.

We have now unintentionally already interpreted τὸ αὐτό, "the same." We interpret sameness to mean belonging together. It would be obvious to represent this belonging-together in the sense of identity as it was thought and generally understood later on. What could [37] prevent us from doing so? Nothing less than the principle itself that we read in Parmenides. For it says something else, namely: Being belongs—together with thinking—in the same. Being is determined from an identity as a characteristic of that identity. The identity that is thought later in metaphysics, however, is presented as a trait of Being. Thus we cannot attempt to determine the identity that Parmenides speaks of in terms this metaphysically represented identity.

The sameness of thinking and Being that speaks in Parmenides' fragment arrives across a greater distance than the identity determined by metaphysics as a characteristic of Being.

The guiding word in Parmenides' fragment—τὸ αὐτό, "the same"—remains obscure. We shall leave it obscure. But we shall at the same time take a hint from the sentence that begins with this word.

Meanwhile, we have already established the sameness of thinking and Being as the belonging-together of both. That was premature, perhaps necessarily so. We must reverse the rashness. And we can do so, since we do not consider the aforementioned belonging-together as the ultimate, or even the only authoritative, interpretation of the sameness of thinking and Being.

If we think of the belonging-*together* in a habitual way, then the meaning of belonging, as the emphasis already indicates, is determined by the "together"—i.e., by its unity. In this case, "belonging" means as much as: assigned and placed in the order of a together, established in the unity of a manifold, combined into the unity of a system, mediated through the unifying center of a standardizing synthesis. Philosophy represents this belonging-together [38] as *nexus* and *connexio,* the necessary connection of the one with the other.

However, belonging-together can also be thought of as *belonging-*

288 · THE HEIDEGGER READER

together. This means: The "together" is now determined by the belonging. Yet we must still ask here what "belong" means, and how its peculiar "together" is first determined from it. The answer to these questions is closer than we imagine, but it is not obvious. It suffices if, through this indication, we pay attention to the possibility of no longer representing "belonging" from the unity of the "together," but rather experience this "together" from the side of "belonging." But does the indication of this possibility not exhaust itself in an empty play of words that makes something up and lacks any grounding in verifiable states of affairs?

So it appears, until we look closer and let the matter speak.

The notion of a belonging-together in the sense of a *belonging*-together arises in respect to a matter that has already been mentioned. Due to its simplicity, it is naturally difficult to keep in view. Yet it immediately comes closer to us if we note the following: In the interpretation of belonging-together as *belonging*-together, according to Parmenides' hint, we already had in mind thinking as well as Being, and thus what belongs to each other in the same.

If we take thinking to be the distinctive characteristic of the human, then we reflect on a *belonging*-together that pertains to the human and to Being. Immediately we find ourselves beset by the questions: What does Being mean? Who or what is the human? Everyone can see that, without a sufficient answer to these questions, we lack the ground on which to determine anything reliable about the *belonging*-together of human and Being.

Yet as long as we inquire in this way, we are confined within the attempt to represent the "together" of human and Being as a [39] coordination, and to establish and explain this coordination either in terms of the human or in terms of Being. In this, the traditional concepts of human and Being constitute the basis for the coordination of the two.

How would it be if, instead of only tenaciously representing a coordination of the two in order to produce their unity, we were for once to note whether and how a belonging-together is at stake in this "together"? There is even the possibility of already catching sight, even if only from a distance, of the belonging-together of human and Being in the traditional determinations of its essence. How so?

The human is obviously a being. As such, it belongs to the totality of Being just as do the stone, the tree, and the eagle. To "belong" here still means to be in the order of Being. But what is distinctive about the human is that as the thinking being, open to Being, it is placed before Being, remains related to Being and thus corresponds to Being. The human *is* actually this relation of correspondence [*Entsprechung*], and is only this. "Only"—this is not a limitation, but an excess. A belonging to Being reigns within the human, a belonging that listens to Being because it is *appropriated* [übereignet] to it. And Being? Let us think Being according to its original meaning, as presence. Being is present to the human neither incidentally nor only occasionally. Being is present and abides only as it concerns the human through its claim. [40] For it is initially the human, open for Being, that lets the latter arrive as presence. Such coming-to-presence [*An-wesen*] needs the open of a clearing, and through this need remains *appropriated* to human being. This does not at all mean that Being is initially and solely posited by humans. On the contrary, the following becomes clear:

Humans and Being are appropriated to one another. They belong to each other. From this belonging-together that has not been thought about more closely, humans and Being have first received those determinations of essence by which they are grasped metaphysically in philosophy.

As long as we only represent everything in categories and mediations, be it with or without dialectics, we stubbornly misunderstand this prevailing *belonging*-together of human and Being. We only ever find connections that are established either in terms of Being or in terms of the human, and that represent the belonging-together of the human and Being as an intertwining.

We do not, as yet, enter into the *belonging*-together. But how [41] can such an entry come about? By turning away from the attitude of representational thinking. This move is a jump [*Satz*] in the sense of a leap [*Sprunges*]. It leaps off, away from the common notion of the human as the rational animal, who in modernity has become the subject for his objects. Simultaneously, the leap also leaps away from Being. But Being, from the early ages of Western thought, has been interpreted as the ground in which every being as such is grounded.

Where does the leap go that leaps from the ground? Does it leap into an abyss? Yes, as long as we only represent the leap within the horizon of metaphysical thinking. No, insofar as we leap and let ourselves go. Where to? To where we are already accepted: into the belonging to Being. Being itself, however, belongs to us; for only with us can it prevail [*wesen*] as Being, that is, come to presence [*an-wesen*].

Thus, in order to experience the *belonging*-together of human and Being, a leap is necessary. This leap is the abruptness of the unbridged entry into that belonging which alone can grant a toward-each-other of human and Being, and thus the constellation of the two. The leap is the abrupt entry into the realm in which human and Being have already reached [*erreicht*] each other in their essence, since both are mutually appropriated [42] to each other in a handing-over [*Zureichung*]. The entry into the realm of this appropriation first attunes and determines [*stimmt und be-stimmt*] the experience of thinking.

What a strange leap, which presumably yields us the insight that we do not yet sufficiently linger in the place where we actually already are. Where are we? In what constellation of Being and human?

Today we no longer need complicated indications, as we did years ago, to catch sight of the constellation by virtue of which humans and Being concern each other. Or so at least it seems. One would like to think that it is enough to utter the phrase "atomic age" in order to evoke the experience of how Being becomes present to us in today's technological world. But may we simply equate the technological world with Being? Obviously not, even if we imagine this world as the totality in which atomic energy, the calculating plans of humans, and automation are conjoined. Why does such an indication concerning the world of technology—no matter how extensively it depicts the latter—never let us catch sight of the constellation of Being and the human? Because every analysis of the situation falls short in its thinking, insofar as the aforementioned totality of the world of technology is interpreted in advance in terms of humans—as being of their making. Technology, conceived in the broadest sense and in its manifold manifestations, is the plan that humans [43] project—a plan that finally compels the human to decide whether he will become servant to his plan or remain its master.

Through this conception of the totality of the technological world, everything is reduced to the human, and one at best comes to the point of demanding an ethics of this world. Caught up in this conception, one compounds one's own opinion that technology has only to do with humans. One fails to hear the claim of Being that speaks in the *essence* of technology.

Let us finally cease conceiving technology as something purely technological, i.e., in terms of the human and his machines. Let us pay attention to the claim that in our age is placed not only upon the human, but upon all beings, nature and history, with regard to their Being.

Which claim do we mean? Our entire human existence is challenged everywhere—now playfully, now urgently, now rushed, now pushed—to devote itself to the planning and calculating of everything. What speaks in this challenge? Does it merely stem from a self-induced mood [*Laune*] of the human? Or are we here already concerned with beings themselves, in such a way that they make a claim upon us with respect to their aptness to be planned and calculated? Then Being itself would be challenged to let beings appear in the horizon of calculability? Indeed. And not only this. To the same degree that [44] Being is challenged the human, too, is challenged —that is, forced to secure all beings that are his concern as the substance for his planning and calculating, and to carry this manipulation on past all bounds.

The name for the gathering of this challenge that places [zu-stellt] human and Being face to face in such a way that they mutually challenge [stellen] each other is the Ge-stell.² One has taken objection to this phrasing. But we also say "posit" [setzen] instead of "place" [stellen], and see nothing wrong with using the term "positive law" [Ge-setz]. Then why not also use Ge-Stell, if the matter at hand demands it?

That in which and from which humans and Being are of concern to each other in the technological world claims us in the manner of the Ge-Stell. In the mutual surrender [Sichstellen] of human and Being, we hear the claim that determines the constellation of our age. The Ge-Stell concerns us everywhere directly. The Ge-Stell, if we may still speak in this manner, is more in existence [seiender] than all atomic energies and the whole world of machinery—more in existence than the driving power of organization, communications, and automation. Since we no longer encounter what is called the Ge-Stell within the horizon of representation that lets us think [45] the Being of beings as presence—the Ge-Stell no longer concerns us as something that is present—it seems strange at first. It remains strange especially because it is not something ultimate, but rather first gives us that which actually prevails throughout the constellation of Being and human.

The belonging-together of human and Being in the manner of mutual challenge drives home to us with startling force that, and how, the human is delivered over [vereignet] to the ownership of Being and Being is appropriated [zugeeignet] to the essence of the human. There reigns within the Ge-Stell a peculiar ownership and appropriation [Vereignen und Zueignen]. It is necessary to simply experience this owning [Eignen] in which the human and Being are delivered over to each other [ge-eignet], that is, to enter into what we call the appropriative event [Ereignis]. The word Ereignis is taken from natural language. Er-eignen originally meant er-äugen, i.e., to catch

---

2. [As in the previous chapter, since Heidegger goes to some lengths to circumscribe this term, it has been left untranslated here.—Tr.]

sight of, to call something to oneself through looking, to appropriate [*an-eignen*]. The word *Ereignis,* thought in terms of the matter just indicated, should now serve as a guiding word in the service of thinking. As such a guiding word, it can no more be translated than the Greek λόγος or the Chinese *Tao.* The word *Ereignis* here no longer means what we would otherwise call a happening, an occurrence. The word is now used as a *singulare tantum* [a noun that has no plural form]. What it indicates happens only in the singular—no, not even in any number, but uniquely. What we experience in the *Ge-Stell* as the constellation [46] of Being and the human through the modern world of technology is a *prelude* [*Vorspiel*] to what is called the *Er-eignis.* Yet this latter does not necessarily persist in its prelude. For in the *Er-eignis,* the possibility exists that it might twist the mere reign of the *Ge-Stell* into a more originary appropriation. Such a warping of the *Ge-Stell,* out of the *Er-eignis* and back into it, would effect the appropriative recovery of the technological world—a recovery that could never be made by humans alone—from its dominance back to servitude in the realm through which the human reaches more truly into the *Er-eignis.*

Where has the path led us? To the entry of our thinking into that simplicity that we call, in the strict sense, the *Er-eignis.* It appears that we now risk directing our thought all too carelessly toward something that is remote and general, while in fact what the word *Er-eignis* wishes to indicate really speaks to us directly from the very nearness of the proximity in which we already linger. For what could be closer to us than what brings us nearer to where we belong, to where we are those who belong [*Gehörende*]: the *Er-eignis?*

The *Er-eignis* is that realm, resonating in itself, through which human and Being reach each other in their essence, achieve their essence by losing those determinations with which metaphysics had endowed them.

To think the appropriating event as *Er-eignis* means to help build this self-resonating realm. Thought receives the tools for this [47] self-suspended structure from language. For language is the most delicate, but also[3] the most susceptible, all-embracing resonance in the suspended structure of the appropriation. We dwell in the appropriation inasmuch as our essence is given over to language.

We have now reached a point on our path where the crude but inevitable question besets us: What does appropriation have to do with identity?

---

3. [Joan Stambaugh notes that in conversation with her, Heidegger emended the original *aber auch* to *und daher.* We have retained the original, published phrasing here.—Tr.]

Answer: nothing. Identity, on the other hand, has a lot, if not everything, to do with appropriation. How so? We answer this by retracing our path in a few steps.

The appropriation delivers the human and Being over to their essential togetherness. In the *Ge-Stell* we glimpse an initial, oppressing flash of the appropriation that constitutes the essence of the modern technological world. In the *Ge-Stell* we glimpse a *belonging*-together of human and Being, in which the letting-belong [*Gehörenlassen*] first determines the manner of the "together" and its unity. We let Parmenides' fragment, "For the same is thinking as well as Being," introduce us to the question of a belonging-together in which belonging has precedence over "together." The question of the [48] meaning of this same is the question of the essence of identity. The doctrine of metaphysics represents identity as a fundamental characteristic of Being. Now it becomes clear that Being belongs with thinking to an identity whose essence stems from that letting-belong-together that we call the *Ereignis*. The essence of identity is a property of the *Er-eignis*.

If the attempt to direct our thinking to the place of the essential origin of identity is tenable, then what would become of the title of our lecture? The meaning of the title "The Principle of Identity" would have changed.

At first, the principle appears in the form of a fundamental principle that presupposes identity as a trait of Being, i.e., of the ground of beings. This principle [*Satz*] in the sense of a statement has meanwhile become a jump [*Satz*] in the manner of a leap that leaps off from Being as the ground of beings, and so jumps into the abyss. Yet this abyss is neither empty nothingness nor a murky confusion, but rather the *Er-eignis*. There resounds in the *Er-eignis* the essence of what speaks as language, which at one time was called the house of Being. "Principle/jump of identity" now means: a leap that the essence of identity demands because it needs that leap if the *belonging*-together of human and Being is to attain the essential light of the *Ereignis*.

On its way from thinking the principle as a statement about identity to the jump as a leap into the essential origin of identity, thought has undergone a transformation. Thus, looking toward the present, beyond the situation of the human, thought sees the constellation [49] of Being and the human in terms of that which joins the two—in terms of the *Er-eignis*.

Assuming we could look forward to the possibility that the *Ge-Stell*—the mutual challenging of human and Being into the calculation of the calculable—were to address itself to us as the *Ereignis* that first surrenders humans and Being to what is authentically theirs, then a path would be open for humans to experience beings—the totality of the modern technological world, nature and history, and above all Being—in a more originary way.

As long as reflection on the world of the atomic age, however earnestly and responsibly, strives only for the peaceful use of atomic energy and will also not be content with any other goal, thinking stops short halfway. Such incompleteness only secures the technological world all the more in its metaphysical predominance.

Yet where is it decided that nature as such should for all times remain the nature of modern physics, and that history must only present itself as the object of historiography? Of course, we cannot reject today's technological world as devil's work, nor may we destroy it—assuming it does not destroy itself.

However, we may still less cling to the view that the technological world is such that it could absolutely prevent a leap out of it. For this view is obsessed by what is current, and regards it as the only thing that is real. This view is indeed fantastical. The same is not true, however, of a thinking-ahead that looks toward what approaches us as the call of the essence of identity between human and Being.

Thought needed more than two thousand years to really grasp such a simple relation as that of the mediation within [50] identity itself. May we then think that the thoughtful entry into the essential origin of identity could be achieved in one day? Precisely because this entry requires a leap, it needs its time: the time of thinking that is of another sort than that of calculation, which today pulls at our thoughts from all sides. Today, the thinking machine calculates thousands of relations in one second. Despite their technical use, they lack an essence.

Whatever and however we attempt to think, we are thinking within the space of tradition. It reigns whenever it frees us from a thinking-after [Nachdenken] into a thinking-ahead [Vordenken] that is no longer a planning.

Only when we thoughtfully face what has already been thought will we be made of use for what remains to be thought.

NINETEEN

The Language of Johann Peter Hebel

———— ❧ ————

1955

Hebel's *Alemannic Poems* were written in Karlsruhe in the course of a few years between 1800 and 1803. They are born of the longing for home. One often takes note of this, but ponders it too little. Let us assume, for a moment, that Hebel's dream had come true, and that he had been allowed to be head pastor in a margrave village: he would have had even more abundant opportunities to write about the countryside and people and customs of home. Indeed—to write, if only the point had been to depict the countryside and "its folk" folklorically, as it were. But something else was demanded of the professor who ended up in Karlsruhe: to poetize home— to raise its essence into luminosity through the word. True and high poetry only ever accomplishes one thing: it makes the inconspicuous shine. But that which pervades and determines everything ordinary and superficial

---

Bracketed numbers in this chapter refer to the pagination of GA 13; the chapter opens at page 123.—Tr.

remains inconspicuous. The homely itself only begins to shine and enters our view if we step back from it, if we are far enough away. The essence [124] of home only reaches its luminosity abroad. Everything the great poets sing and say is seen from homesickness and is called into the word through this pain.

But—thus many will have already replied—how are these *Alemannic Poems* supposedly great, worldwide poetry, if alone in their language they already remain restricted to a specific landscape and its folklore?—So the world of Hebel's poems is indeed a limited world, because they are "only" Alemannic poems?

One often also takes dialect to be a maltreatment and disfiguration of elevated and standard language. But in truth it is the opposite: dialect is the mysterious source of every mature language. Everything that the spirit of language harbors in itself flows toward us out of this source. Thus, a valuable asset is still preserved unharmed for Swiss country and valley communities: they not only speak in their dialect, but think and act in it as well.

What does the spirit of a language harbor? It retains in itself the inconspicuous yet crucial relationships to God, to the world, to people and their works, and to things. The spirit of language harbors in itself that all-pervading height from which everything has its origin, so that it counts and is of use. This height and validity comes to life in language, and dies out with it as soon as a language has to make do without the influx from the source, the source that is dialect. The poet Hebel knew this well. He therefore writes in a letter that the *Alemannic Poems* may in fact remain "within the character and horizon of the folk," but are at the same time "noble poetry."

Hebel collected the most beautiful stories and reflections that he had contributed to the calendar[1] up to 1811 in the *Schatzkästlein des Rheinischen Hausfreundes* [*Treasure Chest of the Rhenish Family Friend*], which appeared in 1811 through the Cotta publishing house that also published [125] works of Goethe and Schiller. If nowadays you encounter the name *Schatzkästlein* on the radio or anywhere else, you should think of Hebel.

------

1. [The calendar in question is the *Volkskalender,* a kind of almanac containing recipes, holidays, and household tips as well as short, didactic, entertaining stories.—Tr.]

Until today, however, only few have fully appreciated the treasures hidden in Hebel's *Chest*. The standard German in which Hebel's stories and reflections speak is the simplest, brightest, simultaneously most delightful and most contemplative that has ever been written. The language of the *Treasure Chest* remains lofty schooling for anyone preparing to speak and write authoritatively in this language.

Wherein does the secret of Hebel's language lie? Not in an affected stylistic will, and also not in the aim of writing as folklorically as possible. The secret of the *Treasure Chest*'s language lies in the fact that Hebel could capture the language of the Alemannic dialect in standard language, and let the latter sound as a pure echo of the former. And that, at the same time, gives us a clue to the secret of the *Alemannic Poems*.

Hebel did not have poetic insights and moods from somewhere that he then, in distinction from other poets, expressed in Alemannic dialect. Rather, Hebel held himself listeningly toward the influx of the language-spirit of this dialect, in such a way that this language continually sprang together into single poems, in the way that crystals are formed.

And since these poems are rooted in the local, they reach into the distance and surmount all limits seemingly given by dialect.

TWENTY

Letter to Father William J. Richardson

—◦◦◦—

1962

Dear Father Richardson,

It is with some hesitation that I attempt to answer the two main questions you posed in your letter of 1 March 1962. The first question deals with the initial impetus that determined my path of thinking. The other question seeks information about the much-discussed reversal [*Kehre*].

I hesitate with the answers because by necessity they will remain mere indications. The lesson of long experience leads me to surmise that such indications will not be taken as an instruction to set about on one's own path and think independently about the indicated matter. One will take the indications as an opinion I have expressed, and propagate them as such. Every attempt to bring what has been thought closer to prevailing modes of

---

This letter was originally translated by its recipient, Fr. Richardson, and published in his *Heidegger: Through Phenomenology to Thought* (The Hague: Martinus Nijhoff, 1974), ix–xxiii. I have altered the translation slightly for stylistic purposes, and for consistency within the present volume.

Bracketed numbers refer to the pagination of GA 11; the chapter opens at page 145.—Tr.

presentation must assimilate what is to be thought to those presentations and thereby inevitably deform the matter.

This prefatory remark is not the lament of a man misunderstood, but rather the observation of an almost insurmountable difficulty in making oneself understood.

The first question of your letter reads: "How are we properly to understand your first experience of the Being-question in Brentano?"

"In Brentano." You have in mind the fact that the first philosophical text through which I worked my way, again and again from 1907 on, was Franz Brentano's dissertation *On the Manifold Sense of Being in Aristotle* (1862). On the title page of his work, Brentano quotes Aristotle's phrase: τὸ ὂν λέγεται πολλαχῶς. I translate: "A being becomes manifest (with regard to its Being) in many ways." Latent in this phrase is the *question* that determined the path of my thought:

What is the simple, unified determination of Being that pervades all of the various meanings? This question [146] raises the following ones: What does Being even mean? To what extent (why and how) does the Being of beings unfold in the four modes which Aristotle constantly affirms, but whose common origin he leaves undetermined? It suffices to run through the names assigned to them in the language of the philosophical tradition to be struck by the fact that they seem, at first, irreconcilable: Being as property, Being as possibility and actuality, Being as truth, Being as schema of the categories. What sense of Being is expressed in these four headings? How can they be brought into a comprehensible accord?

We cannot grasp this accord until we have first inquired and clarified whence Being as such (not merely beings as beings) receives its determination.

Meanwhile a decade went by and I needed many detours and false paths through the history of Western philosophy for the questions above to even reach an initial clarity. Three insights were crucial for this clarity, though, to be sure, they were not yet sufficient for venturing a discussion of the question of Being as a question concerning the meaning of Being.

Dialogues with Husserl provided the immediate experience of the phenomenological method that prepared the concept of phenomenology explained in the introduction to *Being and Time* (§7). In this preparation, a decisive role was played by the reference back to fundamental words of Greek thought, λόγος (to make manifest) and φαίνεσθαι (to show oneself), which I interpreted accordingly.

A renewed study of the Aristotelian treatises (especially book 9 of the

Metaphysics and book 6 of the *Nicomachean Ethics*) resulted in the insight into ἀληθεύειν as a process of revealing, and in the characterization of truth as unconcealment, to which all self-manifestation of beings pertains. One thinks too superficially, or does not think at all, if one contents oneself with the observation that Heidegger conceives truth as unconcealment. As if, with ἀ-λήθεια, what is properly worthy of thought did not first come to an approximate appearance. The [147] situation is not improved by proposing the translation "unforgottenness" in place of "unconcealment," since "forgottenness" must be thought in Greek fashion as withdrawal into concealment. Correspondingly, the counter-phenomenon to forgetting, remembering, must receive a Greek interpretation: as a striving for, an attaining to, the unconcealed. Plato's ἀνάμνησις of the Ideas implies: the catching-sight-once-again, the revealing, of beings—i.e., of beings in their look.

Along with the insight into ἀλήθεια as unconcealment came recognition of the fundamental trait of οὐσία, the Being of beings: presence. But a literal translation—i.e., a translation drawn out of the matter itself—is not expressed until the heart of the matter, in this case presence as such, is brought before thought. The disquieting, ever watchful question concerning Being as presence (present) developed into the question concerning Being in terms of its temporal character. Through this process it became clear that the traditional concept of time was in no way adequate for even correctly posing the question concerning the temporal character of presence, let alone for answering it. Time became questionable in the same way as Being. The ecstatic-horizonal temporality delineated in *Being and Time* is not by any means already the most proper element of time that is sought as a correlate of the question of Being.

With this preliminary clarification of ἀλήθεια and οὐσία, the meaning and scope of the principle of phenomenology, "to the things themselves," became clear. Working my way into phenomenology through actual practice rather than merely through texts, the question concerning Being that was aroused by Brentano's work nevertheless always remained in view. The doubt thus arose whether the "thing itself" was to be characterized as intentional consciousness or even as the transcendental ego. If phenomenology, as the process of letting things show themselves, was to characterize the decisive method of philosophy, and if the guiding question of philosophy has perdured since ancient times in the most diverse forms as the question about the Being of beings, [148] then Being had to remain the first and last thing itself of thought.

Meanwhile, phenomenology in Husserl's sense was developed into a distinctive philosophical position according to a pattern set by Descartes, Kant, and Fichte. The historicity of thought remained completely foreign to such a position (see the insufficiently noted work of Husserl: "Philosophy as a Rigorous Science," which appeared 1910–1911 in the journal *Logos*, 289ff.).

The question of Being developed in *Being and Time* set itself apart from this philosophical position, on the basis of what I consider to this day to be a more faithful adherence to the principle of phenomenology.

What can thus be sketched in a few strokes—in retrospect that continually verges on *retractatio*[1]—was in its historical reality a tangled process that was opaque even to me. This process inevitably remained captive to contemporary modes of presentation and language, and was accompanied by insufficient explanations of its own intentions.

Now if by the title of your book, *From Phenomenology to Thought* [*Seinsdenken*], you understand "Phenomenology" in the sense just described as a philosophical position of Husserl, then the title is to the point, insofar as the Being-question as posed by me is something completely different from that position. The title is fully justified, if the term "Thought" is shorn of that ambiguity according to which it covers both metaphysical thought (the thinking of the Being of beings) as well as the Being-question, i.e., the thinking of Being as such (the revealedness [*Offenbarkeit*] of Being).

If, however, we understand "Phenomenology" as allowing the most proper concern of thought to show itself, then the title should read "*Through* Phenomenology to the Thinking of Being."[2] This genitive [*of* Being] says, then, that Being as such (Beyng) [*Seyn*] [149] shows itself simultaneously as that which is to be thought and as that which needs a thinking that corresponds to it.

With this indication, I am already touching upon your second question. It reads: "Granted *that* a 'reversal' [*Kehre*] has occurred in your thinking, *how* has it occurred? In other words, how is one to think this occurring itself?"

Your question admits of an answer only if we first make clear what "reversal" means—more precisely, if one is ready to think through what has already been said concerning this, instead of constantly circulating unwarranted assertions. The first time in my published writings that I spoke of the

---

1. [In his translation, Fr. Richardson underscores the connotation of *retractatio* as "retouching" rather than "recantation," and notes the allusion to St. Augustine that this word implies—namely to the *Retractationes*, a text which Heidegger knew.—Tr.]

2. [Fr. Richardson states that this suggestion urged him to change the title of his book at the last minute before it went to press.—Tr.]

"reversal" was in the *Letter on Humanism*. One therefore concludes that, since 1947, Heidegger's thought has undergone an "inversion" [*Umkehr*] or even, since 1945, a "conversion" [*Bekehrung*]. One does not make allowance for the fact that many years are needed before the thinking-through of so decisive a matter can find its way into the clear. The passage cited below may serve to show that the matter thought in the term "reversal" was already at work in my thought a decade prior to 1947. The thinking of the reversal *is* a change in my thought. But this change is not a consequence of altering the standpoint, much less of abandoning the fundamental issue, of *Being and Time*. The thinking of the reversal results from the fact that I stayed with the matter that was to be thought in *Being and Time*, i.e., that I inquired into that perspective which already in *Being and Time* (p. 39) was designated as "Time and Being."

The reversal is above all not an operation of interrogative thought; it is inherent in the very matter designated by the headings "Being and Time," "Time and Being." That is why the aforementioned passage from the *Letter on Humanism* reads: "Here the whole is reversed." "The whole": this means the matter of "Being and Time," "Time and Being." The reversal is in play within the matter itself. It is neither invented by me, nor related [150] solely to my thought. Up to now I know of no attempt to reflect on this matter and analyze it critically. Instead of the groundless, endless chatter about the "reversal," it would be more advisable and fruitful for people to first engage with the matter mentioned. Refusal to do so obliges one to demonstrate that the Being-question developed in *Being and Time* is unjustified, superfluous, and impossible. Any criticism of *Being and Time* that begins in this fashion, however, must obviously first be set straight.

Whoever is ready to see the simple fact that, in *Being and Time*, the starting point of subjectivity is deconstructed [*abgebaut*], that every anthropological inquiry is kept at a distance, and moreover that the sole decisive experience is that of Da-sein with a constant look ahead to the Being-question, will agree that the "Being" which *Being and Time* inquires into cannot remain something that the human subject posits. Rather, Being is something that matters to Da-sein as the presence determined by its time-character. Accordingly thought is also already called upon, in the initial steps of the Being-question of *Being and Time*, to undergo a change whose movement corresponds with the reversal. Yet the inquiry of *Being and Time* is not in any way given up thereby. Thus, the prefatory note to the seventh unrevised edition of *Being and Time* (1957) contains the remark: The "way still remains even today a necessary one, if the question about Being is to stir our Dasein." But the thinking of the reversal supplements [*er-gänzt*] the inquiry of *Being and Time* in a decisive way. Only someone who sees the whole [*das Ganze*] can supplement [it]. This supplementation also first brings about the adequate determination of Da-sein, i.e., of the essence of the human as thought in terms of the truth of Being as such (cf. *Being and Time* §66). Thus the first draft of the lecture-course for the winter semester 1937–1938, which tries [151] to analyze the necessity of the question of truth in the perspective of the question of Being, reads in part:

> Over and over again we must insist: In the question of truth as posed here, what is at stake is not only an alteration in the traditional conception of truth, nor a comportment of its current presentation; what is at stake is a transformation in human Being itself. This transformation is not demanded by new psychological or biological insights. Here, humans are not the objects of any anthropology. Humans come into question here in the deepest and broadest, in the genuinely fundamental perspective: humans in their relation to Being—in the reversal: Beyng and its truth in relation to humans.

The "occurrence" of the reversal that you inquire about "is" Beyng as such. It can only be thought *out of* the reversal. There is no special kind of occurrence proper to the reversal. Rather, the reversal between Being and time, between time and Being, is determined by the way Being is granted, time is granted [*wie Es Sein, wie Es Zeit gibt*]. I tried to say a word about this "is granted" [*Es gibt*] in the lecture "Time and Being" which you heard yourself here [in Freiburg], on 30 January 1962.

If instead of "Time" we substitute the clearing of the self-concealing of presence, then Being is determined by the scope of time. Yet this only results insofar as the clearing of self-concealment makes use of a thinking that corresponds to it.

Presence (Being) belongs in the clearing of self-concealment (time). The clearing of self-concealment (time) brings about presence (Being).

[152] The fact that this belonging and bringing-forth rests in appropriation [*Er-eignen*] and is called event [*Ereignis*] is an accomplishment neither of my questioning nor of the proclamation of my thought (cf. *Identity and Difference*, 30ff.). The fact that what we thoughtlessly enough call "truth" the Greeks called Α-Λήθεια, in poetic as well as *non*-philosophical and philosophical language, is not their invention and caprice. It is the richest endowment of their language, in which that which comes to presence as such attained both unconcealment and concealment. Whoever has no sense with which to see the granting of such a gift to humans, the sending of someone

destined in that way, will never understand what is said about the destiny of Being [*Seinsgeschick*]—just as little as the naturally blind person can ever experience what light and color are.

Your distinction between Heidegger I and Heidegger II is justified only on the condition that this is kept constantly in mind: Only by way of what Heidegger I has thought, does one gain access to what is to be thought by Heidegger II. But Heidegger I only becomes possible if it is contained in Heidegger II.

Meanwhile, all that is expressed in formulas is open to misunderstanding. According to the intrinsically manifold matter of Being and time, all words that give utterance to it (like reversal, forgottenness, sending) are always ambiguous. Only a manifold thought gains access to the expression of the heart of such a matter.

To be sure, this manifold thought does not require a new language, but rather a transformed relationship to the essence of the old one.

My wish for your work, for which you alone bear the responsibility, is that it may help set in motion the manifold thinking of the simple business of thought, which, by reason of its very simplicity, abounds in hidden plenitude.

Freiburg im Breisgau, early April 1962.

Martin Heidegger

TWENTY-ONE

Art and Space

—⌇⌇⌇—

1969

"If one thinks a lot, one finds much wisdom inscribed into language. It is not likely that one inscribes all of it oneself; rather, there is actually a lot of wisdom in it, just as in proverbs."

—GEORG CHRISTOPH LICHTENBERG

Δοκεῖ δὲ μέγα τι εἶναι καὶ χαλετὸν ληφθῆναι ὁ τόπος.
  "It appears, however, to be something overwhelming and hard to grasp, the *topos*."—that is, place-space.

—ARISTOTLE, *PHYSICS* BOOK 4

These remarks on art, space, and their interplay remain questions, even when uttered in the form of assertions. They restrict themselves to visual art [*bildende Kunst*] and, within this, to sculpture. Sculptural formations are bodies. Their matter, consisting of different materials, is formed in various ways. The forming occurs in a demarcation as enclosing and excluding. With this, space comes into play. The sculpted formation occupies space

---

Previously translated by Charles H. Seibert in *Man & World* 3 (1973): 3–8. I have made minor emendations to this chapter. Heidegger originally etched this essay onto lithographic stone, which is why it is frequently printed as a series of unconnected paragraphs. This format has been altered for the present volume.

Bracketed numbers refer to the pagination of GA 13; epigraphs appear on page 203 and the chapter opens on page 204.—Tr.

and casts it as a closed, breached, and empty volume. Familiar states of affairs, and yet puzzling.

The sculptural body embodies something. Does it embody space? Is sculpture a seizing occupation of space, a domination of space? Does sculpture thus correspond to the technical-scientific conquest of space?

As art, of course, sculpture is a confrontation with artistic space. Art and scientific technology view space and work upon it with different aims and in different ways.

But space—does it remain the same? Is it not that space that was first determined by Galileo and Newton? Space—that homogeneous separation that is not distinct in any of its possible places, that is equivalent in all directions, but not sensibly perceptible?

The space which, in the mean time, increasingly and ever more obstinately challenges the modern human to its ultimate controllability?

Does not modern visual art also pursue this challenge, insofar as it understands itself as dealing [205] with space? Does it not thereby find its contemporary character validated?

Yet can space, construed physically-technologically—and however it may be determined in the future—count as the only true space? Compared with this one, are all spaces that are construed differently—the artistic space, the space of everyday action and commerce—just subjectively conditioned prefigurations and derivations of the one objective, cosmic space?

But how, if the objectivity of the objective world-space inevitably remains the correlate of the subjectivity of a consciousness that was foreign to the epochs that preceded European modernity?

Even if we acknowledge the various ways of experiencing space in past epochs, do we thereby gain insight into the peculiarity of space? The question of what space as space is, is not yet asked with this, let alone answered. It remains undecided in what way space *is*, and whether an existence can even be attributed to it.

Space—does it belong to the primal phenomena at the discovery of which, according to Goethe, humans are overcome by a kind of awe, even to the point of fear? For it appears that behind space, there is nothing more to which it could be traced back. In front of it, there is no evasion to something else. What is proper to space must show itself from space itself. Can its peculiarity still be uttered?

The urgency of such inquiry demands the following confession:

[206] As long as we do not experience the peculiarity of space, the dis-

course about artistic space remains obscure as well. For the time being, the way in which space pervades the artwork is suspended in indeterminateness.

The space within which the sculpted formation can be encountered as an available object; the space that the volume of the figure encloses; the space that subsists as emptiness between volumes—are not these three spaces, in the unity of their interplay, always merely derivatives of the one physical-technological space, even if calculative measurements are not permitted to interfere with artistic formation?

If it is granted that art is the bringing-into-work of truth, and truth means unconcealment of Being, then must not true space—that space which uncovers its ownmost peculiarity—become decisive in the work of visual art?

Yet how can we find what is peculiar to space? There is an emergency bridge, one that is narrow and swaying. We attempt to listen to language. Whereof does it speak, in the word "space" [Raum]? Clearing-away [Räumen] speaks in it. This means: to clear out [roden], to make the wilderness open. Clearing-away brings forth what is free, the open for humans' settling and dwelling.

Clearing-away, thought on its own, is the freeing of places through which the fates of dwelling humans turn toward the safety of a home, toward the calamity of homelessness, or even toward indifference concerning both.

Clearing-away is freeing of the places at which a god appears, the places from which the gods have fled, places at which the appearance of the divine hesitates for a long time. Clearing-away brings forth each place that prepares a dwelling. [207] Profane spaces are always the privation of sacred spaces, often ones which lie far back.

Clearing-away is freeing of places.

In clearing-away, a happening at once speaks and conceals itself. This character of clearing-away is all too easily overlooked. And even if it is seen, it still remains difficult to determine, especially so long as the physical-technological space counts as the space to which all designation of what is spatial should adhere from the outset.

How does clearing-away happen? Is it not making-space [Einräumen], and this again in the twofold way of granting and arranging [Einrichtens]?

On the one hand, making-space admits something. It lets what is open hold sway, which among other things grants the appearance of present things to which human dwelling sees itself consigned.

On the other hand, making-space prepares for things the possibility of belonging to their respective whither and, out of this, to each other.

The granting of places happens in this twofold making-space. The character of this happening is such a granting. Yet what is place, if its peculiarity should be determined by the guideline of freeing making-space?

Place, in each case, opens a region in which it gathers things into their belongingness in the region.

Gathering plays in a place, in the sense of the freeing sheltering of things in their region.

And the region [*Gegend*]? The older form of the word is "that-which-regions" [*Gegnet*]. It names the free expanse. Through it, the open is urged to let each thing unfold into its resting in itself. But this means at the same time: preserving, [208] the gathering of things in their belonging-together.

The question arises: Are places initially and merely the result and consequence of making-space? Or does making-space acquire its peculiarity from the reign of gathering places? If this were the case, we would have to seek the peculiarity of clearing-away in the grounding of locality, and ponder locality as the combined play of places.

We would have to take heed both that, and how, this play receives the consignment to the belongingness of things out of the free expanse of the region.

We would have to learn to recognize that things themselves are places and do not merely belong in a place.

In this case, we would be obliged for a long time to accept a strange state of affairs: Place is not located in a pre-given space after the manner of physical-technological space. The latter first unfolds itself through the reigning of a region's places.

The interplay of art and space would have to be pondered from out of the experience of place and region.

Art as sculpture: no occupation of space. Sculpture would not be a confrontation with space.

Sculpture would be the embodiment of places which, opening and preserving a region, hold something free gathered around them, granting a stay to each thing, and a dwelling to humans in the midst of things.

[209] If this is the case, what becomes of the volume of the sculpted formation, each embodying a place? Presumably, it will no longer demar-cate spaces from one another, in which surfaces surround an interior over against an exterior. That which is named by the word "volume"—a meaning

that is only as old as modern technological science—would have to lose its name.

The place-seeking and place-forming characteristics of sculptured embodiment would initially remain nameless.

And what would become of the emptiness of space? Often enough, it simply appears to be a deficiency. Emptiness then counts as the filling-out that cavities and gaps lack.

Presumably, however, emptiness is precisely related to the peculiarity of place, and thus is not a lack but rather a bringing-forth.

Once again, language can give us a hint. The word "collecting" [*lesen*] speaks in the verb "to empty" [*leeren*], in the original sense of the gathering that holds sway in a place.

To empty the glass means: to gather it, as that which can contain something, into its having been freed.

To empty the collected fruit into a basket means: to prepare this place for it.

Emptiness is not nothing. It is also not a deficiency. In sculptural embodiment, emptiness plays in the manner of the seeking-projecting instituting of places.

The preceding remarks certainly do not reach so far that they show with sufficient clarity the peculiarity of sculpture as a kind of visual art. Sculpture: an embodying bringing-into-work of places, and with them an opening of regions of possible dwelling for humans, of possible tarrying of things that surround and concern humans.

[210] Sculpture: the embodiment of the truth of Being in its work of instituting places.

Even a cautious insight into the peculiarity of this art arouses the suspicion that truth, as the unconcealedness of Being, is not necessarily dependent on embodiment.

Goethe says: "It is not always necessary that what is true should embody itself; it suffices for it to float about intelligibly and evoke harmony as it drifts through the air like a serious but friendly sound of a bell."

TWENTY-TWO

Cézanne

From the series Gedachtes *for René Char*

L'Herne *1971*

Last version 1974

————✧————

Transformed, afflictingly experienced
duality of the "present" (ἐόν),*
sheltered in the image of the mountain,
treasure of authority,
ordaining simplicity.
  Collectedly beckoning:
  the thoughtfully released,
  the earnest stillness of the shape
  of the old gardener Vallier,
  who cares for what is inconspicuous
  on the *chemin des Lauves.*

Path granting the view
to what is across from it,

---

* Cf. *Was heißt Denken?* 1954, p. 144; *Unterwegs zur Sprache,* 1959, p. 269.

to the same that is always newly sought:
presence of the "mountain
of holy victory."

The likeness: gardener and mountain—
barely noticeable signs
of the transformative path
of duality into simplicity,
directing into the same the shaping and thinking
that anticipate the origin.

What Cézanne calls *la réalisation* is
the appearance of the present in the clearing
of coming-to-presence—such that the duality of both
is bound up in the simplicity of the pure
shining of its images.
For thought, this is the question of
twisting free of the ontological difference between
Being and beings. But the twisting free only becomes
possible if the ontological difference is first experienced
and pondered as such, which in turn can only occur
on the basis of the "question of Being" posed
in *Being and Time.* Its unfolding demands the experience
of the sending of Being. The insight into this first prepares
the venture into the region of paths, a journey that finds its way into
the simple saying, in the mode of naming what is withheld,
a naming to which thinking remains deferred.

SUPPLEMENT 1.

Der Spiegel *Interview with Martin Heidegger*

———————————— ‿∾∾‿ ————————————

On 23 September 1966, Heidegger received Rudolf Augstein, Georg Wolf, and the photographer Digne Meller-Marcovic for this *Spiegel* interview which, in keeping with his terms, was not published until after his death in 1976.

Der Spiegel: Professor Heidegger, we have noted time and again that your philosophical work is somewhat adumbrated by events of your life that did not last very long, but which have never been cleared up, either because you were too proud or because you did not consider it necessary to speak about them.

Martin Heidegger: You mean '33?

S: Yes, before and after. We would like to put this in a larger context and from that perspective arrive at several questions that seem important, e.g.: What possibilities exist of affecting reality, even political reality, from the point of philosophy? Does this possibility even still exist? If so, what does it consist in?

H: Those are indeed important questions; I wonder whether I can answer

———————————————

In preparing this translation, I have consulted the previous translation by Maria P. Alter and John D. Caputo, "Only a God Can Save Us: *Der Spiegel's* Interview with Martin Heidegger," *Philosophy Today* 20, no. 4 (1976): 267–284, as well as the translation by William J. Richardson, "Only a God Can Save Us: The *Spiegel* Interview with Martin Heidegger," in *Heidegger: The Man and the Thinker*, ed. Thomas Sheehan (Chicago: Precedent Publishing Co., 1981), 45–67. However, since the basis for this supplement was the complete version from the *Gesamtausgabe* rather than the edited version ultimately published in *Der Spiegel*, I have been able to fill in gaps in previous translations. Unless otherwise noted, all footnotes are either the editor's or Dr. Hermann Heidegger's, Martin Heidegger's executor.

Bracketed numbers in the interview refer to the pagination of GA 16; the interview opens at page 652.—Tr.

them all. But first of all I must state that, before my rectorship, I was in no way politically active. I was on leave in the winter semester of 1932–1933 and spent most of the time up at my cabin.

S: Then how did it happen that you became rector of the University of Freiburg?

H: In December 1932, my neighbor von Möllendorff, Professor of Anatomy, was elected rector. The term of office for the new rector at the University of Freiburg begins on 15 April. During the winter semester of 1932–1933, he and I often spoke of the situation—not just the political one, but especially that of the universities, and of the partially hopeless situation of the students. My judgment was this: As far as I can judge things, there only remains the one possibility, to attempt to head off the coming development by means of the constructive powers that are actually still alive.

[653] S: So you saw a connection between the situation of the German university and the overall political situation in Germany?

H: Naturally, I followed the political events between January and March 1933, and occasionally spoke about them with younger colleagues. But my work was dedicated to a comprehensive interpretation of pre-Socratic thought. I returned to Freiburg at the beginning of the summer semester. In the meantime, Professor von Möllendorff had begun his office as rector. Barely two weeks later, the Badish Minister of Culture at the time, Wacker, relieved him of his office. Presumably, the desired occasion for the minister's decision was the rector's prohibition against posting the so-called Jew Notice [Judenplakat] in the university.

S: Professor von Möllendorff was a social democrat. What did he do after his removal?

H: On the same day he was fired, von Möllendorff came to me and said: "Heidegger, now you must take over the rectorship." I said that I lacked any experience in administrative activity. The vice-rector at the time, Professor Sauer (Theology), likewise urged me to run in the rectoral election, since otherwise there might be the danger that a party functionary would be elected rector. Younger colleagues, with whom I had been discussing the shaping of the university for many years, besieged me to take over the rectorship. I hesitated for a long time. Finally, I declared myself willing to take over the office in the interest of the university, but only if I could be certain of a unanimous agreement of the board. My doubts about my suitability for the rectorship persisted such that, on the morning of the election day, I went to the rector's office and explained to von Möllendorff (who, though no longer rector, was present there) and to Professor Sauer that I could not take [654] over the position. Both colleagues then responded that the election was prepared in such a way that I could no longer withdraw my candidacy.

S: Then you decidedly declared yourself ready. How did your relationship to the National Socialists take shape?

H: On the second day after I had assumed office, the "student leader" appeared in my office with two companions, and demanded again the posting of the "Jew Notice." I declined. The three students left, remarking that the prohibition would be reported to the National Student Leadership. After a few days a telephone call came from the Office of Higher Education [*SA Hochschulamt*], in the highest SA echelons, from the SA Leader Dr. Baumann.[1] He demanded the posting of the notice, which had already been posted in other universities. In the case of my further refusal, I would face removal, if not the closing of the university. I refused, and tried to win the support of the Badish Minister of Culture for my prohibition. He explained that he could not do anything against the SA. Nevertheless, I did not retract my prohibition.

S: That was not known until now.

H: The fundamental motive that even determined me to take over the rectorship is already indicated in my inaugural address at Freiburg in the year 1929, *What is Metaphysics?* (p. 8): "The fields of the sciences lie far apart. Their methods of treating their objects are fundamentally different. Today, this fragmented multiplicity of disciplines is only held together by the technical organization of universities and faculties, and kept together in one meaning through the practical orientation of the academic departments. However, the rootedness of the sciences in their essential ground has died off." What I attempted to do during my term of office with regard to this state of the university (a state that has, by today, extremely deteriorated) is presented in my rectoral address.[2]

[655] S: We will attempt to find out whether, and how, this statement from 1929 aligns with what you said in your in your inaugural address as rector in 1933. We will tear a sentence out of its context: "The much-praised 'academic freedom' is being banished from the German university because this freedom was false, as it was only negating." We find it plausible that this sentence at least partially expresses notions that you have not distanced yourself from.

H: Yes, I still stand behind it. For this "academic freedom" was fundamentally a merely negative one. It was *freedom from* the exertion of entering into what scientific study demands in terms of thinking and reflective awareness. But the sentence that you have picked out should not be read in isolation. Rather, it should be read in context, for then it becomes evident what I meant by "negative freedom."

S: Agreed; that is understandable. But we nevertheless seem to perceive a new tone in your rectoral address when you speak, four months after Hitler was named Chancellor of the Reich, of the "glory and greatness of this new beginning."

H: Yes, and I was convinced of that.

---

1. [SA stands for *Sturmabteilung*, or Storm Troop.—Tr.]
2. [See chapter 7 of the present volume.—Tr.]

S: Could you elaborate a little more?

H: Gladly. At the time I saw no alternative. In the general confusion of opinions and the political trends of thirty-two parties, it was necessary to find a national, and above all social, point of view, along the lines attempted by Friedrich Naumann. To give just one example, I could cite an essay by Eduard Spranger, which goes far beyond my rectoral address.[3]

S: When did you start to concern yourself with political situations? After all, the thirty-two parties had been there a long time. And there were millions of unemployed people before 1930 as well.

[**656**] **H:** During this time, I was still completely taken up with the questions that are developed in *Being and Time* (1927) and the writings and lectures of the years following it. These are basic questions of thinking that also, in an indirect way, address the national and social questions. As a teacher at the university, the question that I had most directly in view was that of the meaning of the sciences, and the determination of the university's task. This effort is expressed in the title of my rectoral address: "The Self-Assertion of the German University." No one had dared use such a title in a rectoral address at the time. But who, among those who polemicize against this speech, has read it thoroughly, thought it through, and understood it in terms of the situation back then?

S: "Self-assertion of the university," does that not come across as slightly inappropriate in such a turbulent world?

H: Why would it? The "self-assertion of the university" goes against the so-called "political science" that was demanded at the time in the party and by the National Socialist Students. This term had a completely different meaning then: It did not mean, as it does today, the science of politics; rather, it meant that science as such, its meaning and value, is determined according to the practical use for the people. The rectoral address expresses precisely the counter-position to *this* politicizing of science.

S: Do we understand you correctly? By drawing the university along into something that you perceived to be a new beginning, you wanted to brace the university against overpowering currents that would no longer have left the university's peculiarity to itself?

H: Certainly. But the self-assertion was to simultaneously set itself the task of retrieving, through reflection on the tradition of Western European thought, a new meaning over against the merely technical organization of the university.

S: Professor, are we to understand that you [657] thought it possible at the time that the university might regain its health in alliance with the National Socialists?

---

3. [This essay appeared in the journal *Die Erziehung*, ed. A. Fischer, W. Flitner, T. Litt, H. Nohl, and E. Spranger, 1933, pp. 401ff.]

H: That does not express it correctly. Not together with the National Socialists. Rather, the university was to renew itself through its own reflection, and thus gain a solid position over against the danger of politicization of the sciences—in the sense already described.

S: And that is why you proclaimed these three pillars in your rectoral address: labor service, military service, knowledge service. Did you mean to say by this that the knowledge service was to be elevated to the same status as the others, a position that the National Socialists had not granted it?

H: There is no talk of "pillars." If you read it carefully, you see that the knowledge service stands third in the enumeration, but is placed first in terms of meaning. One should realize that labor and the military, like all human action, are grounded in knowledge and are illuminated by it.

S: But we must—and we are almost done with this miserable quoting—still mention one more sentence, which we could not imagine you still subscribe to today. You said in the fall of 1933: "Doctrines and ideas shall not be the rules of your being. The Führer himself and he alone *is* the present and future German reality and its rule."

H: These sentences are not in the rectoral address, but rather only appear in the local *Freiburg Student Newspaper,* at the beginning of the 1933–1934 winter semester. When I took over the rectorship, I knew that I would not make it through without compromises. Today, I would no longer write these cited sentences. Even by 1934 I no longer said such things. But I would still today, and today more decidedly than ever, repeat the speech about the "Self-Assertion of the German University," naturally without reference to National Socialism. Society has entered in place of the "people" [*Volk*]. Nevertheless, the speech would be just as much a waste of breath today as it was then.

[**658**] **S:** May we ask another related question? It has become clear in the conversation so far that your position in the year 1933 fluctuated between two poles. First, you had to say many things *ad usum Delphini;*[4] that was one pole. The other pole was more positive, and you express that as follows: "I had the feeling that there is something new here, there is a new beginning here"—as you put it.

H: That is right.

S: Between these two poles there was—that is completely understandable given the situation . . .

H: Certainly. But I must emphasize that the expression "*ad usum Delphini*" does not say enough. I believed at the time that, in engagement [*Auseinandersetzung*] with National Socialism, a new path could open itself up—one that was the only remaining possibility of a renewal.

S: You are aware that several accusations are raised against you in connec-

---

4. ["For the use of the Dauphin," i.e., for public consumption.—Tr.]

tion with this, concerning your collaboration with the NSDAP[5] and its groups, accusations which are still considered unrefuted in the public eye. Thus you have been accused of participating in book burnings organized by the student body or the Hitler Youth.

H: I prohibited the planned book burning that was to take place in front of the university hall.

S: Then you were also accused of having books by Jewish authors removed from the university library or from the Philosophical Seminar.

H: As Director of the Seminar, I only had control over its library. I did not comply with the repeated demands to remove the books of Jewish authors. Former participants of my seminars can bear witness today not only that no books by Jewish authors were removed, but that these authors, especially Husserl, were cited and discussed just as they were prior to 1933.

[659] S: We would like to take note of that. But how do you explain the origin of such rumors? Is it maliciousness?

H: According to my knowledge of the sources, I am inclined to believe that. But the motives for the defamation lie deeper. My taking over the rectorship is probably only an occasion, but not the determining reason. The polemics will probably flare up again and again, whenever an occasion presents itself.

S: You had Jewish students even after 1933. Your relationship to some of these students, probably not all of them, is supposed to have been quite warm, even after 1933.

H: My attitude after 1933 remained unchanged. One of my oldest and most gifted students, Helene Weiß, who later emigrated to Scotland, was awarded her doctorate in Basel—for this was no longer possible at Freiburg—with a very important dissertation, "Causality and Chance in the Philosophy of Aristotle," printed at Basel in 1942. At the conclusion of the foreword, the author writes: "The attempt at a phenomenological interpretation, which we here submit in its preliminary stage, was made possible by M. Heidegger's unpublished interpretations of Greek philosophy." Here you see the copy that the author sent me in April 1948, with her own dedication. I visited Dr. Weiß several times in Basel prior to her death.

S: You and Jaspers were friends for a long time. After 1933, this friendship began to be strained. The story goes that this strain was connected to the fact that Jaspers's wife is Jewish. Would you like to comment on that?

H: What you bring forward here is a lie. I had been friends with Jaspers since 1919. I visited him and his wife in Heidelberg during the summer semester of 1933, when I was there giving a lecture. Karl Jaspers sent me all of his publications between 1934 and 1938, "with warm regards." I'll present the writings to you here.

---

5. [This stands for *Nationalsozialistische Deutsche Arbeiterpartei*, literally the National Socialist German Worker's Party, usually simply referred to as National Socialists. — Tr.]

[**660**] **S:** It says here: "A warm greeting." Now, certainly the greeting would not have been "warm" if there had been a strain at an earlier time.[6] Another, similar question: You were a student of Edmund Husserl, your Jewish predecessor in the Chair of Philosophy at Freiburg University. He recommended you to the faculty to be his successor as professor. Your relationship with him must have included some gratitude.

H: You have the dedication to *Being and Time,* after all.

S: Of course.

H: In 1929, I edited the volume dedicated to his seventieth birthday, and at the celebration at his house I delivered the speech that was printed in the academic newsletters that May.

S: Now, later this relationship became strained. Can you, and would you like to, tell us what brought this about?

H: The differences with regard to philosophical matters became more sharp. In the early thirties, Husserl publicly settled accounts with Max Scheler and me, the distinctness of which left nothing in doubt. I was never able to find out what moved Husserl to set himself off against my thought in such a public way.

S: On what occasion was this?

H: Husserl spoke at the University of Berlin, in front of an audience of 1600 people. In one of the big Berlin newspapers, Heinrich Mühsam reported a "kind of *Sportpalast*-mood."[7]

S: The controversy itself is not of interest in our context. What is interesting is that the controversy had nothing to do with the year 1933.

H: Not in the least.

S: That was our observation as well. Is it not true, then, that you later [661] left out the dedication to Husserl in *Being and Time*?

H: That is true. I explained this matter in my book *On the Way to Language,* 1959, p. 269. The text reads: "To counter widely circulated, untrue allegations, let it be explicitly noted here that the dedication to *Being and Time* mentioned on p. 92 of the *Dialogue* remained in *Being and Time* until its fourth edition of 1935. In 1941, when the publisher felt that the printing of the fifth edition was endangered, even at risk of being banned, I finally agreed, at the suggestion and wish of Niemeyer,[8] to omit the dedication from this edition, under my condition that the remark on page 38 be retained, a note which actually gives the reason for the dedication and that reads: "If the following investigation has taken any steps forward in the disclosure of the 'things themselves,' then the author must first of

---

6. [The book that Heidegger presents is *Reason and Existence.* Heidegger also presents Jaspers's book *Descartes and Philosophy,* which bears a dedication to Heidegger from 1937.]

7. [The *Sportpalast* was a large sports venue in Berlin, where many political meetings of the National Socialists also took place.—Tr.]

8. [Hermann Niemeyer, Heidegger's publisher at the time.]

all thank *E. Husserl*, who, through his own incisive personal guidance and by freely turning over his unpublished investigations, familiarized the author with the most diverse areas of phenomenological research during his student years at Freiburg."

S: Then we hardly need to ask whether it is true that, as rector of the University of Freiburg, you forbade Professor Emeritus Husserl from entering or using the university library or the library of the Philosophical Seminar.

H: That is a slander.

S: And there is also no letter that contains this prohibition? How did this rumor arise?

[662] H: I do not know, I cannot find an explanation for it. I can demonstrate the impossibility of this whole matter by means of something that is not known. When I was rector I was able, through a meeting I had with the minister, to retain Professor Thannhauser, the Director of the medical clinic at the time, and von Hevesy, Professor of Physical Chemistry and later Nobel Prize winner. Both men were Jews whom the Ministry had ordered to be removed. It is absurd that I would retain these two men and at the same time act against Emeritus Husserl, my own teacher, in the way that is rumored. I also prevented students and lecturers from holding a demonstration against Professor Thannhauser in front of his clinic. In the obituary that the Thannhauser family published in the local newspaper, it reads: "Until 1934, he was the honored Director of the University Medical Clinic in Freiburg. [Died] Brookline, Massachusetts, 18 December 1962." The *Freiburg University Pages* report about Professor von Hevesy in issue 11 from February 1966: "Von Hevesy was Director of the Physical-Chemical Institute of the University of Freiburg from 1926 to 1934." After I had relinquished my rectorship, both directors were removed from their posts. At the time there were lecturers stuck without students, who thought: "The time has come to move up." Whenever these people met with me about this, I turned them down.

S: You did not attend Husserl's funeral in 1938. Why not?

H: I would only like to say the following about that: The accusation that I broke off my relations with Husserl is unfounded. In May 1933, my wife wrote a letter to Mrs. Husserl in both our names, expressing our "unchanged gratitude," and sending the letter along with a bouquet of flowers. Mrs. Husserl responded with a brief and formal thank-you, stating that the relations between our families were broken off. It is a human failure of mine not to have expressed my gratitude once [663] again at Husserl's sickbed and death. I later asked Mrs. Husserl's forgiveness for this in a letter.

S: Husserl died in 1938. By February of 1934, you had already resigned from the rectorship. How did it come to that?

H: I will have to expand a little in order to answer that. I had the intention of overcoming the technical organization of the university, that is, of renewing the faculties from the inside out according to the tasks of their disciplines. With this in mind, I proposed for the winter semester of 1933–1934 to nominate younger and especially outstanding colleagues as deans of the individual faculties, and this without regard to their position in the party. Thus the deans were appointed as follows: in the Law School, Professor Erik Wolf; in Philosophy, Professor Schadewaldt; in Natural Sciences, Professor Soergel; in Medicine, Professor von Möllendorff, who had been removed as rector in the spring. But by Christmas of 1933 it was clear that I could not carry through my imagined renewal of the university, because of the resistance both within the faculty and from the party. The faculty, for example, resented that I included students in the responsible administration of the university, much as is the case today. One day I was called to Karlsruhe, where the minister demanded through his assistant, and in the presence of the regional Student Leader, that I replace the deans of the Law School and Medical School with other colleagues that would be acceptable to the party. I refused this demand and declared that I would resign my rectorship if the minister persists in his request. That is what happened. That was in February 1934. I stepped down after ten months in office, whereas rectors at that time remained in office two or more years. While the foreign and domestic press commented in diverse ways about the appointment of the new director, they were silent about my resignation.

[**664**] **S:** Did you negotiate with Rust[9] at the time?

H: At what time?

S: One still hears of a trip that Rust made here to Freiburg in 1933.

H: There were two different episodes. I gave a brief formal greeting to the minister on the occasion of a memorial service for Schlageter in his home at Schönau im Wiesental. The minister made no special notice of me, and I did not make any effort to engage in conversation at the time. Schlageter was a student from Freiburg and a member of a Catholic association. The conversation with Rust took place in November 1933, on the occasion of a rectors' conference in Berlin. I presented to him my views on the sciences and the possible shaping of the faculties. He took note of everything so attentively that I gained hope that my presentation would have an effect. But nothing happened. I do not understand why I get reproached for this conversation with the Reichsminister of Education, while at the same time all foreign governments hastened to recognize Hitler and to show him the customary international courtesies.

S: How did your relation to the NSDAP develop after you resigned the rectorship?

H: After the resignation I focused on my teaching tasks. In the summer semester of 1934, I lectured on "Logic." During the following semester of 1934–1935, I gave the first Hölderlin-lecture. The Nietzsche-lectures began in 1936.

---

9. [Bernhard Rust was Reichsminister for Science, Pedagogy, and Education from 1934 to 1945.—Tr.]

Anyone with ears to hear heard in these lectures a confrontation [*Auseinander-setzung*] with National Socialism.

S: How did the transfer of office take place? You did not take part in the ceremony?

H: Yes, I declined to take part in the ceremonial transfer of the rectorship.

S: Was your successor an active party member?

[665] H: He was a member of the law faculty. The party newspaper *Der Alemanne* announced his appointment as rector with the banner headline: "The First National Socialist Rector of the University."[10]

S: Did you have difficulties with the party afterwards, or how did that work out?

H: I was constantly under surveillance.

S: Do you have an example of this?

H: Yes, the case with Dr. Hancke.

S: How did you find out?

H: Because he came to me himself. He had already received his doctorate and was a participant in my advanced seminar in the winter semester of 1936–1937 and the summer semester of 1937. He had been sent here to keep me under surveillance.

S: What brought him to suddenly come to you?

H: Because of my Nietzsche-seminar in the summer semester of 1937 and the way in which work was done there, he confessed to me that he could not continue with his assigned task of surveillance. He wanted to bring this situation to my attention in view of my future activity as a teacher.

S: Otherwise you had no difficulties with the party?

H: I only knew that my writings were not allowed to be discussed, for example the essay "Plato's Doctrine of Truth." The Hölderlin lecture that I delivered at the Germanic Institute in Rome in the spring of 1936 was attacked in an insidious way in the Hitler Youth magazine *Wille und Macht.* Those who are interested should read the polemics against me beginning in the summer of 1934 in E. Krieck's magazine, *Volk im Werden.* I was not a German delegate at the International Congress of Philosophy in Prague in 1934, nor was I even invited to participate. I was to remain excluded in the same fashion from the International Descartes-Congress in Paris in 1937. This seemed so strange in Paris that [666] the leadership of the congress there—Professor Bréhier at the Sorbonne—inquired on his own why I did not belong to the German delegation. I responded that the leaders of the congress should direct this inquiry to the Reich's Ministry of Education. After some time, a request came from Berlin that I belatedly join the delegation. I refused to do so. My lectures "What is Metaphysics?" and "On the Essence of Truth" were sold under the counter without title covers. After

---

10. [This citation has not been found to date.]

1934, the rectoral address was immediately withdrawn from circulation at the instigation of the party. One was only allowed to discuss it in the National Socialist lecturer's camps [*NS-Dozentenlagern*], as an object of partisan polemics.

S: As the war, then, in 1939 . . .

H: In the final year of the war, 500 of the most important scholars and artists of every kind were exempted from war duty.[11] I was not among the exempted. On the contrary, in the summer of 1944 I was ordered to work on the fortifications over at the Rhine by Kaiserstuhl.

S: Karl Barth worked on the fortifications on the other, Swiss side.

H: It is interesting how this took place. The rector called the entire faculty into lecture hall 5. He gave a brief speech to the effect that what he was going to say was in coordination with the county and regional Nazi leaders. He would divide the whole faculty into three groups. First, those who could be dispensed with entirely; second, those who could only be partially dispensed with; third, those who were indispensable. The first to be named in the category of the completely dispensable were Heidegger, then G. Ritter.[12] In the [667] winter semester of 1944–1945, after completing the fortification work at the Rhine, I gave a lecture with the title "Poetry and Thought." In a certain sense, this was a continuation of my Nietzsche lectures, that is, of my engagement with National Socialism. After the second session, I was drafted into the *Volkssturm*, the oldest member of the faculty to be called up.

S: I believe that the events leading up to your actual—or should we say rightful—retirement [*Emeritierung*], are well-known, such that we do not need to discuss them.

H: Those events are not well-known in the least. It is not a pretty matter.

S: Except if you would like to say something to this issue.

H: No.

S: Perhaps we may summarize: In 1933, you were—as an unpolitical person in the strict sense, not in the wider sense—caught up in the politics of this supposed new beginning . . .

H: . . . by way of the university . . .

S: . . . caught up by way of the university in this supposed new beginning. After about half a year, you gave up the function you had assumed in this regard. But in a lecture you gave in 1935, which was published in 1953 as *Introduction to Metaphysics*, you stated: "What is being peddled about nowadays"—that is, in

---

11. [This insertion on *Der Spiegel's* part is a revised statement by Dr. Heinrich-Wiegand Petzet that Heidegger accepted in the final draft, as it concerned the matter at hand.]

12. [Professor Gerhard Ritter, then full Professor of Modern History at the University of Freiburg, was imprisoned on 1 November 1944, in connection with the assassination attempt on Hitler on 20 July of the same year. He was finally released by Allied troops on 25 April 1945. He was named Professor Emeritus in 1956, and died in 1967. (From *Carl Goerdeler und die deutsche Widerstandsbewegung.*)]

1935—"as a philosophy of National Socialism, but which really has nothing to do with the inner truth and greatness of this movement (namely, the encounter between global technology and the modern human), pulls its catch from the murky waters of 'values' and 'totalities.'" Did you only insert the parenthetical remark in 1953, when it was printed—in order perhaps to clarify for your reader of 1953 how you viewed the "inner truth and greatness of this movement," i.e., of National Socialism—or was this explanatory remark already present in the 1935 version?

[668] **H:** It was written in my manuscript and corresponded exactly to my conception of technology at the time, though not yet with the later interpretation of the essence of technology as *Ge-Stell*. The reason that I did not read this passage aloud was that I was convinced of my audience's correct understanding. The idiots, spies, and snoopers understood it differently—but they wanted to.

S: Certainly you would also include the communist movement in this category?

H: Yes, definitely, as determined by global technology.

S: Would you not also classify the sum total of American pursuits in this way?

H: I would say that, too. Meanwhile, it should have become more evident in the last thirty years that the global movement of modern technology is a force whose scope in determining history can hardly be overestimated. It is a decisive question for me today how any political system can be assigned to the current technological age—and if so, which system? I do not have an answer to this question. I am not convinced that it is democracy.

S: Now "democracy" is merely a catch-all word under which quite different ideas can be brought together. The question is whether a transformation of this political structure is still possible. After 1945, you commented on the political aspirations of the West, speaking also about democracy, about the Christian world-view expressed in a political fashion, and about constitutional statehood— and you called all three of these aspirations "half-truths."

H: First of all, I would ask you to tell me where I spoke of democracy and the other things you mentioned. I would characterize them as half-truths because I do not see in them an actual engagement with the technological world, [669] since behind them, on my view, there still stands the presupposition that humans have control over the essence of technology. In my opinion, this is not possible. The essence of technology is not something that humans can master by themselves.

S: Which of the directions just mentioned would be the most timely, in your opinion?

H: That I do not see. But I see a decisive question here. First, one would have to clarify what you mean by "timely," what "time" means here. Moreover, one would have to inquire whether timeliness is the standard for the "inner truth" of human action, or whether the decisive action is not "poetizing and thinking," despite all heretical misuse of this phrase.

S: It is conspicuous that humans never master their own tools; think of "The Sorcerer's Apprentice." Is it not somewhat pessimistic to say that we will not be able to manage this certainly much greater tool of modern technology?

H: Pessimism, no. Pessimism and optimism are positions that do not go far enough in the domain of the reflection currently being attempted. Above all, modern technology is not a "tool," and no longer has anything to do with tools.

S: Why should we be so thoroughly overpowered by technology?

H: I do not say overpowered. I say that we do not yet have a path that corresponds to the essence of technology.

S: One could counter completely naïvely: What is to be overcome here? Everything is functioning. More and more power plants are being built. People are hard at work producing. People in the highly technologized parts of the world are well provided for. We live in prosperity. What is actually missing here?

H: Everything is functioning. That is precisely what is strange [*unheimlich*], that it is functioning and that the functioning always [670] drives to further functioning, and that technology increasingly tears humans away from the earth and uproots them. I do not know if you were alarmed, but I was just recently alarmed when I saw the pictures of the earth taken from the moon. We do not need an atomic bomb at all; the uprooting of humans has already taken place. We only have purely technological relationships anymore. This is no longer earth, on which humans live today. As you know, I recently had a long conversation in Provence with René Char, the poet and resistance fighter. They are building rocket bases in Provence, and the countryside is being devastated in an incredible way. This poet—who could certainly not be suspected of sentimentality or of glorifying the idyllic—told me that the uprooting of the human that is taking place there will be the end, unless poetry and thought reach a position of power without violence.

S: Well, we have to say that—although we prefer to be here, and will probably not have to leave in our lifetimes—who knows if humans are determined to be on this earth? It would be unthinkable for humans not to have any determination at all. But it could, after all, be seen as one possibility for humans that they reach out from this earth toward other planets. This will not occur for a long time, of course. But where is it written that they have their place here?

H: As far as my own orientation goes, in any case: I know that, according to our human experience and history, everything essential and great has arisen solely out of the fact that humans had a home and were rooted in a tradition. Contemporary literature, for example, is largely destructive.

S: The word "destructive" is bothersome in this case, especially since the word "nihilistic" has received a comprehensive context of meaning through you and your philosophy. [671] It is jarring to hear the word "destructive" applied to literature, which you could—or might be compelled to—see as part of this nihilism.

H: I would like to say that the literature I had in mind is not nihilistic in the sense that I have given to that word. (Cf. *Nietzsche II*, 335ff.)

S: Obviously, you see a world movement—and you have expressed as much —that either is bringing about the absolute technological state, or has done so already?

H: Yes! But the technological state corresponds precisely in the least degree to the world and society determined by the essence of technology. The technological state would be the most submissive and blind bailiff over against the power of technology.

S: Fine. Then the question arises, of course: Can the individual still even influence this web of inevitabilities? Or can philosophy influence it, or can both together influence it, with philosophy guiding the individual or several individuals to a specific action?

H: With these questions, you return to the beginning of our conversation. If I may answer briefly and perhaps somewhat gravely, but after long reflection: Philosophy will not be able to effect any immediate transformation of the present condition of the world. This is not only true of philosophy, but of all human reflection and striving. Only a god can still save us. I see the only possibility of salvation in the process of preparing a readiness, through thinking and poetizing, for the appearance of the god or for the absence of the god in the decline. We will not "croak," to put it bluntly, but rather, if we go under, we will do so face-to-face with an absent god.

S: Is there a connection between your thinking and the emergence of this god? Is there, on your view, a causal relation here? Do you think that we can think god into presence?

[672] **H:** We cannot think him into presence; at most, we can prepare the readiness of awaiting.

S: But can we help?

H: The preparation of the readiness would be the first help. The world cannot be what and how it is through humans, but also not without humans. This is connected, in my opinion, with the fact that "Being"—what I have named with this longstanding, traditional, multifaceted, and now worn-out word— needs humans, that Being cannot be Being without needing humans for its revelation, preservation, and formation. I see the essence of technology in what I call the *Ge-Stell.* The name, which is at first easily misunderstood, when thought correctly points back into that innermost history of metaphysics that still determines our Dasein. The *Ge-Stell* holding-sway means: Humans are beset [*gestellt*], claimed, and challenged by a power that manifests itself in the essence of technology. It is precisely in humans' experience of being forcibly beset [*Gestelltseins*] by something that is not they and that they do not control, that the possibility exists of realizing that Being needs humans. Precisely the possibility of experience, of being needed, and of being prepared for these new possibilities is concealed in the ownmost core of modern technology. To assist with this realization is all that one can expect from thought, and philosophy is over.

S: In earlier times, nevertheless (and not only in earlier times), philosophy was thought to accomplish a great deal indirectly—directly only seldom—but it was able indirectly to do much, to help new currents break through. Even if one thinks merely of great names among the Germans, such as Kant, Hegel through Nietzsche, not to mention Marx, it is evident that philosophy had a tremendous effect in roundabout ways. Do you now think that this effect of philosophy is over? And when you say [673] that philosophy is dead, that it no longer exists, does this include the notion that this effect of philosophy, if it was once there, is no longer present, at least not today?

H: I said just now: A mediated effect is possible through another kind of thinking, but not a direct one, such that thought could, so to speak, causally change the state of the world.

S: Pardon us, we do not wish to philosophize—we are not up to that—but after all we have here the seam between politics and philosophy, so please forgive us for drawing you into such a conversation. You just said that philosophy and the individual could do nothing but . . .

H: . . . prepare for the readiness of holding oneself open for the arrival, or absence, of the god. Even the experience of this absence is not nothing, but instead a liberation of humans from what I called "fallenness amidst beings" in *Being and Time*. Reflecting on what *exists* today is part of the preparation for the aforementioned readiness.

S: But indeed the well-known impetus would still have to come from outside, from a god or whomever. Thus thinking could today no longer effect anything autonomously and from its own resources? This used to be the case according to earlier contemporaries' opinions, and even, I believe, according to ours.

H: But not immediately.

S: We already named Kant, Hegel, and Marx as men who caused a great stir. But even Leibniz gave many an impetus as well—for the development of modern physics and therefore for the origin of the modern world in general. We believe you said earlier that you no longer expect such an effect.

H: Not in the sense of philosophy, not any more. The sciences have today taken over the role that philosophy played up until now. To adequately clarify the "effect" [674] of thinking, we would have to discuss in more detail what "effect" and "effecting" can mean. For this, we would need a fundamental distinction between occasion, stimulus, challenge, assistance, hindrance, and cooperation.

But we only gain the appropriate dimension for these distinctions when we have adequately analyzed the Principle of Sufficient Reason [*Satz vom Grund*]. Philosophy dissolves into individual sciences: psychology, logic, and political science.

S: And who now takes the place of philosophy?

H: Cybernetics.

S: Or the pious one who keeps himself open?

H: But that is no longer philosophy.

S: What is it, then?

H: I call it the "other thinking."

S: You call it the "other thinking." Would you like to formulate that a little more clearly?

H: Were you thinking of the sentence at the ending of my lecture "The Question Concerning Technology": "For questioning is the piety of thought"?

S: We found a sentence in your Nietzsche-lectures which is enlightening. You state there: "It is because the highest possible bond prevails in philosophical thought that all great thinkers think the same. This sameness, however, is so essential and rich that one individual can never exhaust it, so each only binds himself to the other all the more strictly." But it appears that, in your opinion, precisely this philosophical edifice has come to a certain end.

H: It has come to an end, but it has not become null and void for us; rather, it has become newly present through dialogue. My entire work in lectures and exercises in the past thirty years was mainly just an interpretation of Western philosophy. The return to the historical foundations of thought, the thinking-through of the questions that have remained unasked since the time of Greek philosophy, that is no severance from the tradition. But I am saying: the traditional metaphysical [675] mode of thinking that ended with Nietzsche no longer offers any possibility of thoughtfully experiencing the basic traits of the technological age, an age that is just beginning.

S: Approximately two years ago, in a conversation with a Buddhist monk, you spoke of "a completely new way of thinking," and stated that "only a few people are capable of" this new way of thought. Did you mean by this that only very few people can have the insights that on your view are possible and necessary?

H: To "have" them in a very primordial sense, so that they can say them, in a certain sense.

S: Yes, but you did not make clear in your conversation with the Buddhist monk just how this realization is to take place.

H: I cannot make this clear. I do not know how this thinking "has an effect." It may also be that the path of thinking today leads to silence, in order to protect thought from being sold at a loss in the course of a year. It may also be that it takes three hundred years to "have an effect."

S: We understand that very well. But since we do not live three hundred years in the future, but rather right here and now, silence is denied us. We politicians, half-politicians, citizens, journalists, etc.—we constantly have to make decisions of one kind or another. We have to adapt to the system we live in, must try to change it, must look for the narrow door of reform, and the still narrower one of revolution. We expect help from the philosopher, even if just indirect help, help in a roundabout way. And now we hear: I cannot help you.

H: And I cannot.

S: That must surely discourage the non-philosopher.

H: I cannot, because the questions are so difficult [676] that it would be contrary to the meaning of the task of thought to step up publicly, as it were, to preach and to impose moral judgment. Perhaps one might risk the following: To the mystery of the global dominance of the unthought essence of technology, there corresponds the tentativeness and inconspicuousness of thought, which attempts to thoughtfully pursue this unthought essence.

S: You do not count yourself among those who could show a way, if they were only heard?

H: No! I know of no paths to the immediate transformation of the present state of the world, assuming that such a transformation is even humanly possible. But it seems to me that attempted thought could already awaken, clarify, and strengthen the aforementioned readiness.

S: A clear answer. But can, and may, a thinker say: Just wait, something will occur to us within three hundred years?

H: It is not a matter of simply waiting until something occurs to humans after three hundred years go by, but of thinking ahead, without prophetic proclamations, into the time which is to come; of thinking from the fundamental traits of the present age, which have scarcely been thought through. Thinking is not inactivity but is in itself the action that stands in dialogue with the fate of the world. It seems to me that the distinction, stemming from metaphysics, between theory and practice—as well as the notion of a transmission between the two—blocks the way to an insight into what I understand by thinking. Perhaps I may refer here to my lectures which appeared in 1954 with the title *What is Called Thinking?* Maybe it is also a sign of our times that of all my publications, this one is read the least.

S: Naturally, it has always been a misunderstanding of philosophy to think that the philosopher could have some kind of direct effect with his philosophy. Let us return to our beginning. Would it not be conceivable to regard National [677] Socialism on the one hand as the realization of that "global encounter," on the other as the last, worst, strongest and simultaneously most impotent protest against this encounter of "globally determined technology" with the modern human? It appears that you embody a disparity in your person, such that many byproducts of your activity can really only be explained by the fact that, with different parts of your being that do not pertain to the philosophical core, you attach yourself to many things; things that you, as a philosopher, know not to have any substance: concepts such as "home," "rootedness," and the like. How do global technology and home fit together?

H: I would not say that. It seems to me that you are taking technology too absolutely. I do not see humans' situation in the world of global technology as a fate that cannot be unraveled or escaped. Instead, I see the task of thought precisely in thinking along at its limits, so that humans can even first achieve an adequate relationship to the essence of technology. To be sure, National Socialism moved in this direction. But those people were much too inexperienced in their thinking to attain a really explicit relationship to what occurs today and has been going on for three centuries.

S: Do the Americans today perhaps have this explicit relationship?

H: They do not have it either, and are still entangled in a thinking which, as pragmatism, indeed abets technical operation and manipulation, but at the same time blocks the path to a reflection on what properly belongs to modern technology. Meanwhile, here and there in the U.S.A., some attempts to dissociate from pragmatic-positivistic thought are stirring. And who of us can say whether or not one day, in Russia and China, the ancient traditions of a "thought" will awaken that will assist in enabling for humans a free relationship to the technical world?

[678] S: But if no one has it, and the philosopher cannot give it to them . . .

H: It is not for me to decide how far I will get with my attempt to think, and in what way it will be taken up and fruitfully transformed in the future. In a lecture I gave in 1957 on the anniversary of the University of Freiburg, called "The Principle of Identity,"[13] I ventured to demonstrate, in a few steps, how a thoughtful experience of what is most proper to modern technology opens the possibility for humans of the technical age to come into relationship with a claim—a claim that humans are not only capable of hearing, but to which they themselves belong. My thought stands in an unavoidable relationship to the poetry of Hölderlin. Yet I do not take Hölderlin to be just any poet whose work the literary historians take as a subject next to many others. For me, Hölderlin is the poet who points to the future, who awaits the god—and who can thus not simply remain an object of Hölderlin research in literary-historical presentations.

S: Speaking of Hölderlin—we are sorry to have to read once more—you state in your Nietzsche lectures that the "widely known opposition between the Dionysian and the Apollonian, between the sacred passion and the sober presentation, is a hidden stylistic law of the historical destiny of the Germans, and that we must be prepared and ready one day to be formed by it. This opposition is not a formula by which we can merely describe 'culture.' With this opposition, Hölderlin and Nietzsche have placed a question mark before the Germans' task of finding their essence historically. Will we understand these signs? One thing is

---

13. [Chapter 18 of the present volume.—Tr.]

certain: History will take revenge upon us if we do not understand." We do not know in what year you wrote that. We guess it was in 1935.

[**679**] **H:** The quotation probably belongs to the Nietzsche lecture "The Will to Power as Art," 1936–1937. It may have been spoken in the following years.

S: So, would you like to clarify it a little? After all, it leads us from generalities to a concrete determination of the Germans.

H: I could rephrase what was read in the quotation in the following way: It is my conviction that any reversal of the modern technological world can only occur from out of the same location in which it originated. It cannot take place through the adoption of Zen Buddhism or other Eastern experiences of the world. In order to achieve a shift in thinking [*Umdenken*], one needs the European tradition as well as a new appropriation of it. Thinking will only be transformed through thought that has the same origin and determination.

S: At precisely this location where the technological world arose, it must, you think, also . . .

H: . . . be sublated [*aufgehoben*] in the Hegelian sense. Not set aside, instead sublated—but not by humans alone.

S: You particularly assign the Germans a special task in this?

H: Yes, in the sense of the dialogue with Hölderlin.

S: Do you believe that the Germans have a particular qualification for this reversal?

H: I have in mind the special inner relationship of the German language with that of the Greeks and with their thought. The French continually confirm this for me nowadays. When they begin to think, they speak German, assuring that they could not get by with their own language.

S: Do you take this as the explanation for why you have had such a strong effect on the Romance countries, especially the French?

H: Since they see that they can no longer get by in today's world with all their rationality, when it [680] comes down to understanding the world in the origin of its essence. One can translate thinking no more than one can poetry. One can circumscribe it at best. As soon as one takes to translating literally, everything is transformed.

S: A discomforting thought.

H: We would do well to take this discomfort seriously and on a large scale, and to finally consider the momentous transformation that Greek thought underwent through its translation into Roman Latin. This is an event that still today prevents us from adequately reflecting on the fundamental words of Greek thought.

S: Professor, we would actually always begin with the optimistic assumption that anything can be communicated and even translated. For if this optimism about the communicability of thought-contents across linguistic boundaries were to cease, we would be threatened by provincialism.

H: Would you characterize Greek thought in its distinction from the mode of presentation in the Roman Empire as "provincial"? Business correspondence can be translated into all languages. The sciences, which today include the natural sciences with mathematical physics as the fundamental science, are translatable into all world languages. More accurately: They are not translated, but instead the same mathematical language is spoken. Here we touch upon an area that is broad and difficult to survey.

S: Perhaps the following is also part of the topic. It is no exaggeration to state that we are experiencing, at the moment, a crisis of the democratic-parliamentary system. We have had it for a long time. It exists especially in Germany, but not only in Germany. It also exists in the classical democratic countries, England and America. In France it is not even a crisis anymore. Now the question: Could not thinkers provide indications, even just as a byproduct, [681] either that this system must be replaced by a new one, and what the new one should look like, or that reform must be possible and how this would take place? Otherwise we are left with the situation that the person not trained in philosophy—and that tends to be the person in charge of things even though he does not determine them, and who is controlled by things—might come to faulty conclusions, perhaps even make disastrous mistakes. So should not the philosopher be prepared to ponder how humans can establish their community in this world, a world that they themselves have made technological but that has now perhaps overpowered them? Does one not rightly expect from the philosopher that he indicate what he sees as the possibility of life? And does he not neglect a part of his task and vocation—even if just a small part—if he does not contribute something to this issue?

H: As far as I can see, an individual is not capable of grasping the world as a whole in thought, to the point that he could give practical directions—especially in light of the task of first finding once again a basis for thought itself. So long as thought takes itself seriously with regard to the great tradition, it is overwhelmed if one demands that it also give instructions. By what authority could this take place? There are no authoritative assertions in the realm of thinking. The only measure for thought derives from the matter which is to be thought. This matter, however, is what is questionable before all else. In order to clarify this state of affairs, one would need to discuss the relationship between philosophy and the sciences, whose technical-practical successes make thinking, in the philosophical sense, appear today more and more superfluous. The difficult situation into which thought is placed with regard to its own task thus corresponds to an alienation of thought that is fed by the powerful position of the sciences, and when confronted with the [682] daily demand for answers to practical questions pertaining to world-views, thought must necessarily fail.

S: Professor, there are no authoritative assertions in the realm of thinking. Thus it cannot be of any surprise that even modern art finds it difficult to make authoritative assertions. Nevertheless, you call the latter "destructive." Modern art frequently considers itself experimental art. Its works are attempts . . .

H: I do not mind being taught.

S: . . . attempts from within the isolated situation of the human and the artist. And out of a hundred attempts, now and again something hits the mark.

H: That is precisely the great question. Where does art stand? What place does it occupy?

S: Fine, but with this, after all, you are demanding something of art that you no longer demand of thinking.

H: I demand nothing of art. I am only saying that there is a question concerning the place that art occupies.

S: If art does not know its place, is it therefore destructive?

H: All right, cross that comment out. But I would like to note that I do not see how modern art shows the way, especially since we are left in the dark as to how modern art perceives, or at least seeks, what is most proper to art.

S: The artist, too, lacks a sense of being bound to what tradition has passed down. He can find it beautiful, and can say: Yes, one could have painted like that six hundred years ago or three hundred years ago, or even thirty years ago. But he, after all, can no longer do it. Even if he wanted to, he could not. Otherwise the greatest artist would be the ingenious forger, Hans van Meergeren, who could paint "better" than the others. But that simply does not work anymore. So the artist, writer, and poet are in a similar situation to that of the thinker. How often must we say: Close your eyes?

H: If one takes the "culture industry" as a framework for [683] relating art and poetry and philosophy, then the comparison is justified. However, if not only the notion of an industry becomes questionable, but also that which we call "culture," then the reflection on this questionability itself belongs to the realm of those tasks which are assigned to thinking, whose distressing situation can barely be thought through. But the greatest emergency of thinking consists in the fact that today, as far as I can see, no thinker speaks who would be "great" enough to bring thinking before its subject matter in an immediate and formed fashion, and to thereby set it on its way. For us contemporaries, the greatness of what is to be thought is too great. We can perhaps work at building the narrow and short planks of a crossing.

S: Professor Heidegger, we thank you for this interview.

SUPPLEMENT 2.

Chronology of Heidegger's Life

———————————⟡⟡⟡———————————

1889   Martin Heidegger is born on 26 September in Meßkirch. His parents are Friedrich Heidegger, master cooper and sexton, and Johanna Heidegger, née Kempf.

1892   On 12 November, sister Marie Heidegger is born (died 8 March 1956).

1894   On 6 February, brother Fritz Heidegger is born (died 26 June 1980).

1903   Heidegger enters the Gymnasium in Constance. He lives in the St. Conrad dormitory of the seminary there.

1906   Transfer to the Bertold-Gymnasium in Freiburg and to the arch-episcopal seminary there.

1907   Conrad Gröber, prefect of the seminary in Constance, gives Heidegger Franz Brentano's book *On the Manifold Meaning of Being According to Aristotle.*

1909   After his *Abitur,* Heidegger enters the Jesuit novitiate in Tisis near Feldkirch (Vorarlberg), on 30 September. He is released on 13 October on account of heart trouble.

1909   Enrollment at the Albert-Ludwig-University of Freiburg. Heidegger studies theology and philosophy. First publications in Catholic journals.

1911   Heidegger breaks off his theological studies. He studies history, natural sciences, and especially philosophy. Heidegger's most important teacher is Heinrich Rickert. Intensive reading of Husserl's *Logical Investigations.*

This chronology was researched by Martin Heidegger's son and executor, the historian Dr. Hermann Heidegger. It was produced in collaboration with the editor of this volume, Günter Figal. — Tr.

1913   Graduates on 26 July, with a thesis on "The Teaching of Judgment in Psychologism." Thesis advisor: Arthur Schneider.

1914   At the outbreak of the war, Heidegger voluntarily registers for the military. He is selected on 10 October, but released again on 15 October for health reasons.

1915   On 26 July, Heidegger qualifies for teaching (*Habilitation*) with the dissertation "Duns Scotus' Teachings on Categories and Meaning." Advisor and director: Heinrich Rickert. On 27 July, Heidegger gives an examination lecture on "The Concept of Time in the Historical Sciences (*Geschichtswissenschaft*)."

       On 18 August Heidegger is drafted into the services. After basic training in Müllheim (Baden), he works as a private in the militia at the censure office in Freiburg after 1 November.

1916   Heidegger becomes engaged to Elfride Petri, a student of economics that he met in the winter semester of 1915–1916. The engagement is kept secret from March until August, when it becomes official.

       Husserl comes to Freiburg as successor to Rickert.

1917   Closer acquaintance with Husserl, who becomes a promoter of Heidegger.

       On 20 March, marriage to Elfride Petri.

1918   Heidegger is called to the front-line weather service and, after training in Berlin, is ordered to the army weather station at Verdun.

       Acquaintance with Elisabeth Blochmann.

1919   After 1 January, Heidegger is Husserl's research assistant.

       On 21 January, birth of son Jörg.

       Heidegger holds his first lecture course after the war: "The Idea of Philosophy and the Problem of the World-view" (War emergency semester). It is the earliest course retained word for word, and demonstrates clear lines of independent philosophical thought.

1920   On 20 August, birth of son Hermann.

       Beginning of friendship with Karl Jaspers.

1922   Heidegger is a promising candidate for professorial positions in Marburg (as successor to Nicolai Hartmann) and Göttingen (as successor to Hermann Nohl). To make up for not having published since his dissertation, Heidegger writes the sketch of a planned book on Aristotle. This text, "Phenomenological Interpretations of Aristotle," is a concentrated summary of his lectures and, as such, the nucleus of *Being and Time*.

       On 8 August, the Heidegger family moves into the Todtnauberg cabin that was planned and designed by Elfride Heidegger, and which thereafter serves as Heidegger's refuge and preferred workspace.

1923   Hans-Georg Gadamer studies in Freiburg. Heidegger takes him up into his closer circle of students.

1923   As an *ad personam* full professor, Heidegger is called to an associate professorship at the University of Marburg (Lahn). He begins his teaching activity in the winter semester of 1923–1924 with the lecture-course "Introduction to Phenomenological Research," in which he openly criticizes Husserl's philosophy. Beginning of friendship with Rudolf Bultmann. Among Heidegger's students at Marburg are Karl Löwith, Hans-Georg Gadamer, Gerhard Krüger, Hans Jonas, and Herbert Marcuse.

1924   Heidegger meets Hannah Arendt at the end of the year. A secret amorous relationship quickly develops.

1925   Heidegger is recommended by the faculty for the position of first chair of philosophy at Marburg, to replace Nicolai Hartmann. To qualify for the position, Heidegger prepares a publication based on materials from his lectures.

1926   Separation from Hannah Arendt. On Heidegger's suggestion, she goes to Heidelberg and studies under Jaspers there.

1927   On 1 October, Heidegger succeeds Nicolai Hartmann as chair of philosophy at Marburg. The first part of *Being and Time* appears in the "Yearbook for Phenomenology and Phenomenological Research," which is edited by Husserl. The lecture course of the summer semester, "Basic Problems of Phenomenology," is an approach to a continuation of *Being and Time*, the second part of which is never completed.

1928   On 1 October, Heidegger is called to the University of Freiburg as successor to Husserl. His first lecture-course in the winter semester of 1928–1929 is an "Introduction to Philosophy." The Heidegger family moves into a house designed by Elfride Heidegger, Rötebuckweg 47, in Freiburg-Zähringen.

    Heidegger holds talks at the Herder-Institute of Riga.

1929   On 24 July, Heidegger delivers his inaugural address, "What is Metaphysics?"

    From 17 March to 6 April, Heidegger takes part in the Second Higher Education Courses at Davos. He gives three talks under the title "Kant's *Critique of Pure Reason* and the Task of Grounding Metaphysics." Heidegger and Ernst Cassirer voice their different understandings of philosophy in discussions about Kant.

    Heidegger publishes the book *Kant and the Problem of Metaphysics*.

    Speech at Husserl's seventieth birthday, on 9 April.

    In the lecture-course for the winter semester of 1929–1930, "The Fundamental Concepts of Metaphysics: World-Finitude-Solitude," Heidegger develops a new philosophical orientation that goes beyond *Being and Time*.

1930   Heidegger is offered a position at the University of Berlin, which he turns down.

He holds the talk "On the Essence of Truth," which is determinative of the new paths of his thinking.

1931   In the lecture-course for the winter semester of 1931–1932, "On the Essence of Truth," Heidegger continues work on the problematic of truth in his engagement with Plato.

1933   On 21 April, Heidegger is elected almost unanimously to the position of rector of the University of Freiburg (with three abstentions and one vote against). On 3 May, backdated to 1 May, he joins the National Socialist Party (NSDAP).

The official assumption of office is on 27 May. Heidegger gives a speech with the title "The Self-Assertion of the German University," in which on the one hand he advocates a revolutionary beginning with politico-educational dimensions, and on the other turns against the political exploitation of philosophy and the sciences. Heidegger does not mention the *Führer* or *Reichskanzler* Adolf Hitler; the words "National Socialism" or "national-socialist" do not occur in the speech. In a letter, Karl Jaspers congratulates Heidegger on this speech.

In September, Heidegger receives his second invitation to the University of Berlin, this time connected to a "political task," as well as an invitation to the University of Munich. Heidegger organizes a "summer camp" in Todtnauberg that aims to educate lecturers and teaching assistants about the "National-Socialist upheaval of higher education." He decides to stay in Freiburg and turns down both offers.

On 1 October, Heidegger appoints his colleague Wilhelm von Möllendorff, whom the National Socialists had forced to "voluntarily" resign his post as rector because of his social-democratic leanings, as dean of the faculty of medicine.

1934   At the end of February, Heidegger is ordered by the Ministry of Education in Karlsruhe to fire Wilhelm von Möllendorff as dean of the faculty of medicine and Erik Wolf as dean of the law faculty. Heidegger refuses, and resigns his rectorship. He is urged to keep his resignation secret until a successor can be nominated. Despite this, Heidegger publicly announces his resignation in April. A successor is only named afterwards. Heidegger does not take part in the transition ceremony.

1934   Heidegger holds his first lecture course on Hölderlin in the winter semester of 1934–1935, "Hölderlin's Hymns 'Germania' and 'The Rhine.'"

1935   Heidegger holds the lecture course "Introduction to Metaphysics," which is important for his thinking in the later thirties. On 13 November, he gives the talk "The Origin of the Artwork" at the Freiburg Art Association.

1936   Speaking tour to Rome. On 2 April Heidegger speaks on "Hölderlin and the Essence of Poetry," and on 8 April he speaks on "Europe and German

Philosophy." He meets with his student Karl Löwith, who had emigrated to Italy.

The exchange of letters with Karl Jaspers is broken off. Heidegger continues to send his publications to Jaspers.

Heidegger speaks again on the origin of the artwork, this time in three talks at the Freies Deutsches Hochstift in Frankfurt am Main (17 and 24 November, 4 December).

In the winter semester of 1936–1937, he holds the first of four total lecture courses on Nietzsche: "Nietzsche: The Will to Power as Art." The occupation with Nietzsche serves as impetus for an engagement with his own time. The Gestapo watches over Heidegger's lectures.

1937   Heidegger turns down traveling to Paris as a member of the official German delegation to the International Philosophy Congress.

1938   Heidegger completes the manuscript of *Contributions to Philosophy*

1939   Completion of the manuscript of *Mindfulness* (*Besinnung*). Together with *Contributions to Philosophy*, this text is Heidegger's attempt to unfold the thoughts developed in the thirties.

Heidegger publishes the treatise "On the Essence and Concept of Φύσις: Aristotle's *Physics* B, 1," which is central to his thinking, in Italy.

1944   Heidegger is conscripted into the *Volkssturm* and deployed to the Alsace region. After a heavy bombing attack on Freiburg, he brings his manuscripts to Meßkirch. The philosophy faculty of the University of Freiburg is relocated to the Wildenstein castle near Beuron.

Heidegger publishes *Elucidations of Hölderlin's Poetry*.

1945   After the war ends, Freiburg falls under French military administration. Heidegger is called before the *Bereinigungsausschuß* (purification committee), a university commission formed by the military. Karl Jaspers submits an extremely critical letter about Heidegger.

Correspondence with Jean-Paul Sartre.

1946   On 28 December, Heidegger is banned from teaching. He suffers a physical and emotional breakdown and is treated by Victor Freiherr von Gebsattel, a student of the psychoanalyst Ludwig Binswanger.

Heidegger gets to know the French philosopher Jean Beaufret. He writes the "Letter on Humanism" to him.

1948   On 16 September, Ernst Jünger, whose essay "The Worker" (1932) had had a lasting effect on Heidegger, makes his first visit to Todtnauberg, arranged by Vittorio Klostermann.

1949   In the "Club of Bremen" on 1 December, Heidegger gives the talks "Insight Into That Which Is," which are dedicated to an interpretation of modernity.

The teaching ban is lifted in September.

The correspondence with Karl Jaspers resumes.

1950 The Bremen lectures are repeated at the Bühlerhöhe near Baden-Baden on 26 and 27 March. On 6 June, Heidegger speaks on "The Thing" at the Bavarian Academy of Fine Arts in Munich.

Hannah Arendt, who had emigrated to the United States, returns to Germany and visits Heidegger for the first time.

Heidegger publishes *Holzwege,* a collection of works written between 1936 and 1946.

1951 Heidegger retires properly on 26 September. At the same time, he resumes his teaching with the lecture-course "What is Called Thinking?"

On 5 August, Heidegger speaks on "Building—Dwelling—Thinking" at the "Darmstädter Gespräch II."

1953 On 18 November, Heidegger gives the talk "The Question Concerning Technology" at the Bavarian Academy of Fine Arts in Munich.

Beginning of friendship with Erhart Kästner.

1954 Heidegger publishes *Lectures and Essays.*

1955 At the Conradin Kreutzer memorial celebration in Meßkirch on 30 October, Heidegger speaks on "Releasement" (*Gelassenheit*). Heidegger gets to know the poet René Char through Jean Beaufret.

1957 At the five-hundredth anniversary celebration of the University of Freiburg, Heidegger gives the talk "The Principle of Identity."

Reception into the Heidelberg Academy of Sciences.

Reception into the Berlin Academy of Arts.

1959 Beginning of seminars with doctors and psychotherapists in the clinic at Zollikon, near Zurich, which is directed by Medard Boss.

Heidegger is named honorary citizen of Meßkirch.

On the Way to Language appears.

1960 Heidegger receives the Hebel-Award.

1961 In two volumes under the title *Nietzsche,* Heidegger publishes a reworked and supplemented version of his Nietzsche lectures from the thirties.

1962 The first trip to Greece. Heidegger captures the experience in his journal "Sojourns."

1966 The first seminar in Thor (Provence), René Char's hometown.

Heidegger receives Rudolf Augstein, Georg Wolf, and the photographer Digne Meller-Marcovic for a *Spiegel* interview which, in keeping with his terms, is not published until after his death.

1967 Heidegger publishes *Pathmarks,* a collection of works from 1919 to 1961.

In Freiburg, Heidegger meets Paul Celan, who is there for a reading. They go together to Todtnauberg, and Celan captures this visit in his poem "Todtnauberg."

1969 Reception into the Bavarian Academy of Fine Arts.

Heidegger's last publication, the book *On the Matter of Thinking,* appears.

1971   In the fall, Heidegger moves into the retirement home planned by Elfride Heidegger (owner: Hermann Heidegger). It is at Fillibachstrasse 25, behind the old Heidegger residence on Rötebuckweg.

1975   The first volume of the Heidegger *Gesamtausgabe* appears.

1976   Heidegger dies on 26 May, and is buried on 28 May in Meßkirch. The Freiburg theologian Bernhard Welte, who is also from Meßkirch, speaks at the service. At the open grave, Hermann Heidegger reads poems by Hölderlin that his father had selected.

1985   Founding of the Martin Heidegger Society.

2002   Opening of the Heidegger Museum in Meßkirch.

SUPPLEMENT 3.

Sources for the Present Volume

———————————— ~∞~ ————————————

Unless otherwise noted, the texts in this volume stem from and contain page references to the Martin Heidegger *Gesamtausgabe* (GA), which is published by Vittorio Klostermann, Frankfurt am Main. The complete plan of the *Gesamtausgabe* is presented in this volume as supplement 4: "The Heidegger *Gesamtausgabe* and English Translations." The reader is directed to that supplement for bibliographic details. Below is a concise and unified reference source for locating selections in this volume in the original.

1. "The Environmental Experience" is from GA 56/57, 2d ed. (1999), 70–75.

2. "Indication of the Hermeneutical Situation" is from GA 62, 346–375.

3. "The Problem of *Being and Time*" is from GA 26, 3d ed. (2007), 171–177.

4. "Transcendence" is from GA 26, 3d ed. (2007), 238–252.

5. "Description of the Situation: Fundamental Attunement" is from GA 29/30, 3d ed. (2004), 89–123.

6. "The Projection of Being in Science and Art" is from GA 34, 2d ed. (1997), 60–64.

7. "Rectorship Address: The Self-Assertion of the German University" is from GA 16, 107–117.

8. "Hölderlin and the Essence of Poetry" is from GA 4, 3d ed. (forthcoming), 33–48.

9. "On the Origin of the Work of Art: First Version" is from *Heidegger Studies* 5 (1989), 5–22. The following remark by the editor, Dr. Hermann Heidegger, precedes the text in *Heidegger Studies* 5:

"The Origin of the Work of Art" (1935–1936) appeared in *Holzwege* (GA 5), in the autumn of 1949 (© 1950).

Martin Heidegger's thoughts on the mystery of art did not presume to solve it, but rather to see it. The version submitted at that time included the three lectures given at the *Freien Deutschen Hochstift* of Frankfurt am Main in 1936. They constituted the third development of this theme.

The second development was the first version in lecture form. This lecture was delivered to the *Kunstwissenschaftliche Gesellschaft* of Freiburg im Breisgau on 13 November 1935.

In 1987, this second draft was published in France as a bilingual, pirated printing, on the basis of a photocopy of the typed copy of the handwritten manuscript. It did not adhere to Martin Heidegger's written emendations of the typed text.

Presented here is the undelivered, heretofore unpublished and thus unknown first draft of "On the Origin of the Work of Art." Martin Heidegger had kept it, along with the other lectures on the same topic, in a drawer.

—Hermann Heidegger

10. "As When on a Holiday . . ." is from GA 4, 2d ed. (1996), 49–77.

11. "*Ereignis*" is from GA 65, 3d ed. (2000), 4–6, 10–20.

12. "On Ernst Jünger (1)" is from GA 90, 235–249.

13. "On Ernst Jünger (2)" is from GA 90, 253–260.

14. "The Age of the World Picture" is from GA 5, 2d ed. (2003), 75–96.

15. "On Nietzsche" is from GA 50, 3–25.

16. "*Logos* and Language" is from GA 55, 3d ed. (1994), 252–270.

17. "Bremen Lectures: Insight Into That Which Is" is from GA 79, 2d ed. (2005), 3–21, 24–45.

18. "The Principle of Identity" is from GA 11, 33–50.

19. "The Language of Johann Peter Hebel" is from GA 13, 2d ed. (2002), 123–125.

20. "Letter to Father William J. Richardson" is from GA 11, 145–152.

21. "Art and Space" is from GA 13, 2d ed. (2002), 203–210.

22. "Cézanne" is from the 1991 yearbook of the Martin Heidegger Society (unpaginated).

Supplement 1. "*Der Spiegel* Interview with Martin Heidegger" is from GA 16, 652–683.

The Heidegger Gesamtausgabe *and English Translations*

———— ✑✑✑ ————

This list is intended as a definitive overview of Martin Heidegger's collected works: the Heidegger *Gesamtausgabe* (GA), which is published by Vittorio Klostermann, Frankfurt am Main. In addition, it provides details on published or planned English translations. However, since the publication of Heidegger's works is an ongoing process—in German, as well as in translation—some of the information here remains incomplete or subject to change.

Division I: Published Writings, 1910–1976

GA 1 *Frühe Schriften (1912–16)*
Editor: Friedrich-Wilhelm v. Herrmann
1978, 454 pages.

GA 2 *Sein und Zeit (1927)*
Editor: Friedrich-Wilhelm v. Herrmann
1977, 586 pages.
Translated by John Macquarrie and Edward Robinson as *Being and Time*. Harper & Row, 1962. Translated by Joan Stambaugh as *Being and Time*. State University of New York Press, 1996.

GA 3 *Kant und das Problem der Metaphysik (1929)*
Editor: Friedrich-Wilhelm v. Herrmann
First edition 1991, 318 pages. Second edition in preparation.
Translated by Richard Taft as *Kant and the Problem of Metaphysics*. Indiana University Press, 1990. Fifth, enlarged edition 1997.

GA 4 *Erläuterungen zu Hölderlins Dichtung (1936–68)*
Editor: Friedrich-Wilhelm v. Herrmann
First edition 1981. Second edition 1996, 208 pages. Third edition in preparation.
Translated by Keith Hoeller as *Elucidations of Hölderlin's Poetry*. Humanity Books, 2000.

GA 5 *Holzwege (1935–46)*
Editor: Friedrich-Wilhelm v. Herrmann
First edition 1977. Second edition 2003, 382 pages.
Translated by Julian Young and Kenneth Haynes as *Off the Beaten Track*. Cambridge University Press, 2002.

GA 6.1 *Nietzsche I. (1936–39)*
Editor: Brigitte Schillbach
1996, 596 pages.

GA 6.2 *Nietzsche II. (1939–46)*
Editor: Brigitte Schillbach
1997, 454 pages.

GA 7 *Vorträge und Aufsätze (1936–53)*
Editor: Friedrich-Wilhelm v. Herrmann
2000, 298 pages.

GA 8 *Was heißt Denken?*
Editor: Paola-Ludovika Coriando
2002, 268 pages.
Translated by J. Glenn Gray as *What Is Called Thinking?* Harper & Row, 1968.

GA 9 *Wegmarken (1919–61)*
Editor: Friedrich-Wilhelm v. Herrmann
First edition 1976, 490 pages. Second, revised edition 1996. Third edition 2004, 488 pages.
Translated by various translators as *Pathmarks*. Cambridge University Press, 1998.

GA 10 *Der Satz vom Grund (1955–56)*
Editor: Petra Jaeger
1997, 192 pages.
Translated Reginald Lilly as *The Principle of Reason*. Indiana University Press, 1991.

GA 11 *Identität und Differenz*
(1) Was ist das—die Philosophie? (1955)
(2) Der Satz der Identität (1957)
(3) Die onto-theo-logische Verfassung der Metaphysik (1956–57)

(4) Die Kehre (1949)
(5) Grundsätze des Denkens (1957)
(6) Brief an Pater William J. Richardson (1962)
(7) Brief an Takehiko Kojima (1963)
Editor: Friedrich-Wilhelm v. Herrmann
2006, 168 pages.
Part of this volume has been translated by Joan Stambaugh as *Identity and Difference*. Harper & Row, 1969.

GA 12 *Unterwegs zur Sprache (1950–59)*
Editor: Friedrich-Wilhelm v. Herrmann
1985, 262 pages.
Translated by Peter D. Hertz as *On the Way to Language*. Harper & Row, 1971.

GA 13 *Aus der Erfahrung des Denkens (1910–76)*
    Abraham a Sankta Clara (1910); Frühe Gedichte (1910–1916); Schöpferische Landschaft: Warum bleiben wir in der Provinz? (1933); Wege zur Aussprache (1937); Winke (1941); Chorlied aus der Antigone des Sophokles (1943); Zur Erörterung der Gelassenheit. Aus einem Feldweggespräch über das Denken (1944–45); Aus der Erfahrung des Denkens (1947); Der Feldweg (1949); Holzwege ("Dem Künftigen Menschen . . .") (1949); Zu einem Vers von Mörike. Ein Briefwechsel mit Martin Heidegger von Emil Staiger (1951); Was heißt Lesen? (1954); Vom Geheimnis des Glockenturmes (1954); Für das Langenharder Hebelbuch (1954); Über die Sixtina (1955); Die Sprache Johann Peter Hebels (1955); Begegnungen mit Ortega y Gasset (1955); Was ist die Zeit? (1956); Hebel—der Hausfreund (1957); Aufzeichnungen aus der Werkstatt (1959); Sprache und Heimat (1960); Über Igor Strawinsky (1962); Für René Char (1963); Adalbert Stifters "Eisgeschichte" (1964); Wink in das Gewesen (1966); Die Kunst und der Raum (1969); Zeichen (1969); Das Wohnen des Menschen (1970); Gedachtes (1970); Rimbaud vivant (1972); Sprache (1972); Der Fehl heiliger Namen (1974); Fridolin Wiplingers letzter Besuch (1974); Erhart Kästner zum Gedächtnis (1975); Grußwort für Bernhard Welte (1976)
Editor: Hermann Heidegger
First edition 1983. Second, revised edition 2002, 254 pages.

GA 14 *Zur Sache des Denkens (1962–64)*
Editor: Friedrich-Wilhelm v. Herrmann
Translated by Joan Stambaugh as *On Time and Being*. Harper & Row, 1972.

GA 15 *Seminare (1951–73)*
Editor: Curd Ochwadt
First edition 1986. Second, revised edition 2005, 448 pages.
Part of this volume has been translated by Andrew Mitchell and François Raffoul as *Four Seminars*. Indiana University Press, 2003. Another part is translated by Charles H. Seibert as *Heraclitus Seminar*. Northwestern University Press, 1993.

GA 16 *Reden und andere Zeugnisse eines Lebensweges (1910–1976)*
Editor: Hermann Heidegger
2000, 842 pages.

Division II: Lectures, 1919–1944
(WS = winter semester, SS = summer semester)

Marburg Lectures (1923–1928)

GA 17 *Einführung in die phänomenologische Forschung (WS 1923–24)*
Editor: Friedrich-Wilhelm v. Herrmann
First edition 1994. Second edition 2006, 332 pages.
Translated by Daniel Dahlstrom as *Introduction to Phenomenological Research*.
Indiana University Press, 2005.

GA 18 *Grundbegriffe der aristotelischen Philosophie (SS 1924)*
Editor: Mark Michalksi
2002, 418 pages.
Translated by Robert D. Metcalf and Mark Basil Tanzer as *Basic Concepts of Aristotelian Philosophy*. Indiana University Press, 2009.

GA 19 *Platon: Sophistes (WS 1924–25)*
Editor: Ingeborg Schüßler
1992, 668 pages.
Translated by Richard Rojcewicz and André Schuwer as *Plato's Sophist*. Indiana University Press, 1997.

GA 20 *Prolegomena zur Geschichte des Zeitbegriffs (SS 1925)*
Editor: Petra Jaeger
First edition 1979. Second, revised edition 1988. Third, revised edition 1994, 448 pages.
Translated by Theodore Kisiel as *History of the Concept of Time, Prolegomena*. Indiana University Press, 1985.

GA 21 *Logik: Die frage nach der Wahrheit. (WS 1925–26)*
Editor: Walter Biemel
First edition 1976. Second, revised edition 1995, 418 pages.
Translation in preparation by Thomas Sheehan as *Logic: The Question of Truth*.

GA 22 *Grundbegriffe der antiken Philosophie (SS 1926)*
Editor: Franz-Karl Blust
First edition 1993. Second edition 2004, 344 pages.
Translated by Richard Rojcewicz as *Basic Concepts of Ancient Philosophy*. Indiana University Press, 2007.

GA 23 *Geschichte der Philosophie von Thomas v. Aquin bis Kant (WS 1926–27)*
Editor: Helmuth Vetter
2006, 256 pages.

GA 24 *Die Grundprobleme der Phänomenologie (SS 1927)*
Editor: Friedrich-Wilhelm v. Herrmann
First edition 1975. Second edition 1989. Third edition 1997, 474 pages.
Translated by Albert Hofstadter as *The Basic Problems of Phenomenology*. Indiana
University Press, 1982.

GA 25 *Phänomenologische Interpretation von Kants Kritik der reinen Vernunft (WS
1927–28)*
Editor: Ingtraud Görland
First edition 1977. Second edition 1987. Third edition 1995, 436 pages.
Translated by Parvis Emad and Kenneth Maly as *Phenomenological Interpretation
of Kant's Critique of Pure Reason*. Indiana University Press, 1997.

GA 26 *Metaphysische Anfangsgründe der Logik im Ausgang von Leibniz (SS 1928)*
Editor: Klaus Held
First edition 1978. Second, revised edition 1990. Third, revised edition 2007, 292
pages.
Translated by Michael Heim as *The Metaphysical Foundations of Logic*. Indiana
University Press, 1984.

Freiburg Lectures (1928–1944)

GA 27 *Einleitung in die Philosophie (WS 1928–29)*
Editors: Otto Saame and Ina Saame-Speidel
First Edition 1996. Second, revised edition 2001, 404 pages.
Translation in preparation by Eric Sean Nelson and Virginia Lyle Jennings as
Introduction to Philosophy.

GA 28 *Der Deutsche Idealismus (Fichte, Hegel, Schelling) und die philosophische
Problemlage der Gegenwart (SS 1929)*
Editor: Claudius Strube
1997, 368 pages.
Translation in preparation by Peter Warnek as *German Idealism*.

GA 29/30 *Die Grundbegriffe der Metaphysik: Welt, Endlichkeit, Einsamkeit (WS
1929–30)*
Editor: Friedrich-Wilhelm v. Herrmann
First edition 1983. Second edition 1992. Third edition 2004, 544 pages.
Translated by William McNeill and Nicholas Walker as *The Fundamental Con-
cepts of Metaphysics*. Indiana University Press, 1995.

GA 31 *Vom Wesen der menschlichen Freiheit. Einleitung in die Philosophie* (SS 1930)
Editor: Hartmut Tietjen
First edition 1982. Second, revised edition 1994, 308 pages.
Translated by Ted Sadler as *The Essence of Human Freedom*. Continuum Books, 2002.

GA 32 *Hegels Phänomenologie des Geistes* (WS 1930–31)
Editor: Ingtraud Görland
First edition 1980. Second edition 1988. Third edition 1997, 224 pages.
Translated by Parvis Emad and Kenneth Maly as *Hegel's Phenomenology of Spirit*. Indiana University Press, 1988.

GA 33 *Aristoteles: Metaphysik IX* (SS 1931)
Editor: Heinrich Hüni
First edition 1981. Second, revised edition 1990. Third, revised edition 2006, 224 pages.
Translated by Walter Brogan and Peter Warnek as *Aristotle's Metaphysics Θ 1–3: On the Essence and Actuality of Force*. Indiana University Press, 1995.

GA 34 *Vom Wesen der Wahrheit. Zu Platons Höhlengleichnis und Theätet* (WS 1931–32)
Editor: Hermann Mörchen
First edition 1988. Second, revised edition 1997, 338 pages.
Translated by Ted Sadler as *The Essence of Truth: On Plato's Parable of the Cave and the Theaetetus*. Continuum, 2005.

GA 35 *Der Anfang der abendländischen Philosophie (Anaximander und Parmenides)* (SS 1932)
Editor: Heinrich Hüni

GA 36/37 *Sein und Wahrheit*
(1) *Die Grundfrage der Philosophie* (SS 1933)
(2) *Vom Wesen der Wahrheit* (WS 1933–34)
Editor: Hartmut Tietjen
2001, 306 pages.
Translation in preparation by Richard Polt and Gregory Fried as *Being and Truth*.

GA 38 *Logik als die Frage nach dem Wesen der Sprache* (SS 1934)
Based on the lecture notes by Wilhelm Hallwachs
Editor: Günter Seubold
1998, 176 pages.

GA 39 *Hölderlins Hymnen "Germanien" und "Der Rhein"* (WS 1934–35)
Editor: Susanne Ziegler
First edition 1980. Second, revised edition 1989. Third, unrevised edition 1999, 296 pages.

Translation in preparation by William McNeill as *Hölderlin's Hymns "Germanien" and "Der Rhein."*

GA 40 *Einführung in die Metaphysik (SS 1935)*
Editor: Petra Jaeger
1983, 234 pages.
Translated by Gregory Fried and Richard Polt as *An Introduction to Metaphysics.* Yale University Press, 2000.

GA 41 *Die Frage nach dem Ding. Zu Kants Lehre von den transzendentalen Grundsätzen (WS 1935–36)*
Editor: Petra Jaeger
1984, 254 pages.
Translated by W. B. Barton and Vera Deutsch as *What Is A Thing?* Henry Regnery Company, 1967.

GA 42 *Schelling: Vom Wesen der menschlichen Freiheit (1809) (SS 1936)*
Editor: Ingrid Schüßler
1988, 290 pages.
Translated by Joan Stambaugh as *Schelling's Treatise on the Essence of Human Freedom.* Ohio University Press, 1984.

GA 43 *Nietzsche: Der Wille zur Macht als Kunst (WS 1936–37)*
Editor: Bernd Heimbüchel
1985, 298 pages.
Translated by David F. Krell as *Nietzsche I: The Will to Power as Art.* Harper & Row, 1979.

GA 44 *Nietzsches Metaphysische Grundstellung im abendländischen Denken: Die ewige Wiederkehr des Gleichen (SS 1937)*
Editor: Marion Heinz
1986, 254 pages.
Translated by David F. Krell as *Nietzsche II: The Eternal Recurrence of the Same.* Harper & Row, 1984.

GA 45 *Grundfragen der Philosophie. Ausgewählte "Probleme" der "Logik" (WS 1937–38)*
Editor: Friedrich-Wilhelm v. Herrmann
First edition 1984. Second edition 1992, 234 pages.
Translated by Richard Rojcewicz and André Schuwer as *Basic Questions of Philosophy: Selected "Problems" of "Logic."* Indiana University Press, 1994.

GA 46 *Zur Auslegung von Nietzsches II. Unzeitgemäßer Betrachtung "Vom Nutzen und Nachteil der Historie für das Leben" (WS 1938–39)*
Editor: Hans-Joachim Friedrich
2003, 382 pages.

GA 47 *Nietzsches Lehre vom Willen zur Macht als Erkenntnis (SS 1939)*
Editor: Eberhard Hanser
1989, 330 pages.
Translated by Joan Stambaugh as *Nietzsche III: The Will to Power as Knowledge.*
Harper & Row, 1987.

GA 48 *Nietzsche: Der europäische Nihilismus (SS 1940)*
Editor: Petra Jaeger
1986, 340 pages.

GA 49 *Die Metaphysik des deutschen Idealismus. Zur erneuten auslegung von Schelling: Philosophische Untersuchungen über das Wesen der menschlichen Freiheit und die damit zusammenhängenden Gegenstände (1809) (1941)*
Editor: Günter Seubold
First edition 1991. Second, revised edition 2006, 210 pages.

GA 50 *Nietzsches Metaphysik (announced for WS 1941–42, but not delivered). Einleitung in die Philosopie—Denken und Dichten (WS 1944–45)*
Editor: Petra Jaeger
First edition 1990. Second, revised edition 2007, 162 pages.
Translation in preparation by Phillip Braunstein as *Introduction to Philosophy: Thinking and Poetizing.*

GA 51 *Grundbegriffe (SS 1941)*
Editor: Petra Jaeger
First edition 1981. Second, revised edition 1991, 128 pages.
Translated by Gary Aylesworth as *Basic Concepts*. Indiana University Press, 1994.

GA 52 *Hölderlins Hymne "Andenken" (SS 1941–42)*
Editor: Curd Ochwadt
First edition 1982. Second edition 1992, 204 pages.
Translation in preparation by William McNeill as *Hölderlin's Hymn "Andenken."*

GA 53 *Hölderlins Hymne "Der Ister" (SS 1942)*
Editor: Walter Biemel
First edition 1984. Second edition 1993, 210 pages.
Translated by William McNeill and Julia Davis as *Hölderlin's Hymn "The Ister."*
Indiana University Press, 1997.

GA 54 *Parmenides (WS 1942–43)*
Editor: Manfred S. Frings
First edition 1982. Second edition 1992, 252 pages.
Translated by André Schuwer and Richard Rojcewicz as *Parmenides*. Indiana University Press, 1993.

GA 55 *Heraklit.*
(1) Der Anfang des abendländischen Denkens (SS 1943)
(2) Logik. Heraklits Lehre vom Logos (SS 1944)
Editor: Manfred S. Frings
First edition 1979. Second, revised edition 1987. Third edition 1994, 406 pages.

Early Freiburg Lectures (1919–1923)

GA 56/57 *Zur Bestimmung der Philosophie*
(1) Die Idee der Philosophie und das Weltanschauungsproblem (emergency semester 1919)
(2) Phänomenologie und transzendentale Wertphilosophie (SS 1919)
(3) Anhang: Über das Wesen der Universität und des akademischen Studiums (SS 1919).
Editor: Bernd Heimbüchel
First edition 1987. Second, revised and expanded edition 1999, 226 pages.
Translated by Ted Sadler as *Towards the Definition of Philosophy*. Continuum Books, 2000.

GA 58 *Grundprobleme der Phänomenologie (WS 1919–20)*
Editor: Hans-Helmuth Gander
1992, 274 pages.

GA 59 *Phänomenologie der Anschauung und des Ausdrucks. Theorie der philosophischen Begriffsbildung (SS 1920)*
Editor: Claudius Strube
1993, 202 pages.
Translation in preparation by Ted Sadler and Jan Lyne as *Phenomenology of Intuition and Expression.*

GA 60 *Phänomenologie des religiösen Lebens*
(1) Einleitung in die Phänomenologie der Religion (WS 1920–21)
Editors: Matthias Jung and Thomas Regehly
(2) Augustinus und der Neuplatonismus (SS 1921)
(3) Die philosophischen Grundlagen der mittelalterlichen Mystik (plans for an undelivered lecture 1918–19)
Editor: Claudius Strube
1995, 352 pages.
Translated by Jennifer Gosetti and Matthias Fritsch as *The Phenomenology of Religious Life*. Indiana University Press, 2004.

GA 61 *Phänomenologische Interpretationen zu Aristoteles: Einführung in die phänomenologische Forschung (WS 1921–22)*
Editor: Walter Bröcker and Käte Bröcker-Oltmanns
First edition 1985. Second, revised edition 1994, 204 pages.

Translated by Richard Rocjewicz as *Phenomenological Interpretations of Aristotle*. Indiana University Press, 2001.

GA 62 *Phänomenologische Interpretationen ausgewählter Abhandlungen des Aristoteles zur Ontologie und Logik (SS 1922). Anhang: Phänomenologische Interpretationen zu Aristoteles (Anzeige der hermeneutischen Situation) (developed for the philosophical faculty of Marburg and Göttingen 1922)*
Editor: Günther Neumann
2005, 452 pages.

GA 63 *Ontologie: Hermeneutik der Faktizität (SS 1923)*
Editor: Käte Bröcker-Oltmanns
First edition 1988. Second edition 1995, 116 pages.
Translated John van Buren as *Ontology: The Hermeneutics of Facticity*. Indiana University Press, 1999.

Division III: Unpublished Treatises

Lectures — Thoughts

GA 64 *Der Begriff der Zeit (1924)*
I. Die Fragestellung Diltheys und Yorcks Grundtendenz
II. Die ursprünglichen Seinscharaktere des Daseins
III. Dasein und Zeitlichkeit
IV. Zeitlichkeit und Geschichtlichkeit
Anhang: Der Begriff der Zeit (lecture for the Marburg theology faculty July 1924)
Editor: Friedrich-Wilhelm v. Herrmann
2004, 134 pages.

GA 65 *Beiträge zur Philosophie (Vom Ereignis) (1936–38)*
Editor: Friedrich-Wilhelm v. Herrmann
First edition 1989. Second, revised edition 1994. Third edition 2003, 522 pages.
Translated Parvis Emad and Kenneth Maly as *Contributions to Philosophy: (From Enowning)*. Indiana University Press, 1999.

GA 66 *Besinnung (1938–39)*
Editor: Friedrich-Wilhelm v. Herrmann
1997, 438 pages.
Translated by Parvis Emad and Kenneth Maly as *Mindfulness*. Continuum Books, 2006.

GA 67 *Metaphysik und Nihilismus*
(1) Die Überwindung der Metaphysik (1938–39)
(2) Das Wesen des Nihilismus (1946–48)
Editor: Hans-Joachim Friedrich
1999, 274 pages.

THE HEIDEGGER *GESAMTAUSGABE* AND ENGLISH TRANSLATIONS · 353

GA 68 *Hegel*
(1) *Die Negativität (1938–39)*
(2) *Erläuterung der "Einleitung" zu Hegels "Phänomenologie des Geistes" (1942)*
Editor: Ingrid Schüßler
1993, 154 pages.

GA 69 *Die Geschichte des Seyns*
(1) *Die Geschichte des Seyns (1938–40)*
(2) *Κοινόν. Aus der Geschichte des Seyns (1939)*
Editor: Peter Trawny
1998, 230 pages.
Translation in preparation by Jeffrey Powell and William McNeill as *History of Being*.

GA 70 *Über den Anfang (1941)*
Editor: Paola-Ludovika Coriando
2005, 200 pages.

GA 71 *Das Ereignis (1941–42)*
Editor: Friedrich-Wilhelm v. Herrmann

GA 72 *Die Stege des Anfangs (1944)*
Editor: Friedrich-Wilhelm v. Herrmann

GA 73 *Zum Ereignis-Denken*
Editor: Hans-Joachim Friedrich

GA 74 *Zum Wesen der Sprache*
Editor: Thomas Regehly

GA 75 *Zu Hölderlin—Griechenlandreisen*
Editor: Curd Ochwadt
2000, 408 pages.

GA 76 *Zur Metaphysik—Neuzeitlichen Wissenschaft—Technik*
Editor: Claudius Strube

GA 77 *Feldweg-Gespräche (1944–1945)*
(1) *Άγχιβασίν. Ein Gespräch selbdritt auf einem Feldweg zwischen einem Forscher, einem Gelehrten und einem Weisen*
(2) *Der Lehrer trifft den Türmer an der Tür zum Turmaufgang*
(3) *Abendgespräch in einem Kriegsgefangenenlager in Rußland zwischen einem Jüngeren und einem Älteren*
Editor: Ingrid Schüßler
1995, 250 pages.
Translation in preparation by Bret Davis as *Country Path Conversations.*

GA 78 *Der Spruch des Anaximander (1946)*
Editor: Ingrid Schüßler

GA 79 *Bremer und Freiburger Vorträge*
(1) Einblick in das was ist. Bremer Vorträge 1949: Das Ding—Das Ge-stell—Die Gefahr—Die Kehre
(2) Grundsätze des Denkens. Freiburger Vorträge 1957
Editor: Petra Jaeger
First edition 1994. Second, revised edition 2005, 182 pages.

GA 80 *Vorträge (1915–1967)*
Includes: *Frage und Urteil (lecture in the Rickert seminar 10 July 1915); Wahrsein und Dasein. Aristoteles, Ethica Nicomachea Z (lecture at the Kant-Society in Cologne, winter semester 1923–24); Kasseler Vorträge (1925); Begriff und Entwicklung der Phänomenologischen Forschung (lecture at the Marburger kulturwissenschaftlichen Kränzchen 4 December 1926); Phänomenologie und Theologie. I. Teil: Die nichtphilosophischen als positive Wissenschaften und die Philosophie als transzendentale Wissenschaft (lecture for the Protestant theology faculty at Tübingen 8 July 1927); Die heutige Problemlage der Philosophie (lecture at the Kant-Society in Karlsruhe 4 December 1929, and at the scientific association in Amsterdam 21 March 1930); Philosophische Anthropologie und Metaphysik des Daseins (lecture at the Kant-Society in Frankfurt 24 January 1929); Hegel und das Problem der Metaphysik (lecture at the scientific association of Amsterdam 22 March 1930); Augustinus: Quid est tempus? Confessiones XI (lecture in Beuron 26 October 1930); τὸ ψεῦδος (lecture at the Freiburger Kränzchen 22 July 1932); Der Satz vom Widerspruch (lecture in Zurich 18 January 1936); Von der Grundbestimmung des Wissens (lecture at the Freiburger Kränzchen 9 June 1939); Der Spruch des Parmenides (lecture at the Freiburger Kränzchen June 1940); Zur Geschichte des Existenzbegriffs (lecture at the Freiburger Kränzchen 7 June 1941); Über die Be-stimmung der Künste im gegenwärtigen Weltalter (lecture at the Schweizer Haus in Baden-Baden 7–8 May 1959); Max Kommerell (lecture at the memorial celebration of Max Kommerell 27 February 1962); Überlieferte Sprache und technische Sprache (lecture for teachers at Comburg 18 July 1962); Bemerkungen zu Kunst—Plastik—Raum (lecture at St. Gallen 3 October 1964); Die Herkunft der Kunst und die Bestimmung des Denkens (lecture at the academy of arts and sciences in Athens 4 April 1967); Die Bestimmung der Sache des Denkens (lecture at W. Bröcker's 65th birthday in Kiel 19 July 1967)*
Editor: Bernd Heimbüchel

GA 81 *Gedachtes*
I. Frühe unveröffentlichte Gedichte
Among others: Ich mied der Gottesnähe heldenschafte Kraft; Fernes Land; Hast die Sonne du verloren
II. Aus der Erfahrung des Denkens
Includes: *Auf dem Heimweg; Der Ring des Seyns; Wende; Dann sind wir bedacht; Amo: volo ut sis; Sonata sonans; Ankunft; Winke; An-fang und Beginn im Ereignis*

"der" Freyheit; Aus der Werkstatt; Hütte am Abend; Pindari Isthmia V, 1–16;
Ἡράκλειτος ὁ σκοτεινός. *Dem Freunde zu Weihnachten 1946; Furchen*
III. Gedachtes für das Vermächtnis eines Denkens
Includes: *Lerchensporn; Wage den Schritt; . . . durchrasend die Irrnis; Seynsfuge;*
Tod; Nichtendes Nichts; Gegnet noch Gegend; Die Nähe des letzten Gottes; Der
Schritt Zurück; Vermächtnis der Seynsfrage
Editor: Paola-Ludovika Coriando
2007, 360 pages.

Division IV: Indications and Notes

GA 82 *Zu eigenen Veröffentlichungen*

GA 83 *Seminare: Platon—Aristoteles—Augustinus*
Editor: Mark Michalski

GA 84 *Seminare: Leibniz—Kant*
Editor: Günther Neumann

GA 85 *Seminar: Vom Wesen der Sprache*
Die Metaphysik der Sprache und die Wesung des Wortes. Zu Herders Abhandlung
"Über den Ursprung der Sprache."
Editor: Ingrid Schüßler
1999, 220 pages.
Translated by Wanda Torres Gregory and Yvonne Unna as *On the Essence of*
Language: The Metaphysics of Language and the Essencing of the Word: Concerning
Herder's Treatise on the Origin of Language. State University of New York Press,
2004.

GA 86 *Seminare: Hegel—Schelling*
Editor: Peter Trawny

GA 87 *Nietzsche: Seminare 1937 und 1944*
(1) Nietzsches metaphysische Grundstellung (Sein und Schein)
(2) Skizzen zu Grundbegriffe des Denkens
Editor: Peter von Ruckteschell
2004, 324 pages.

GA 88 *Seminare*
(1) Die metaphysischen Grundstellungen des abendländischen Denkens
(2) Einübung in des philosophische Denken
Außerdem: Die neuzeitliche Wissenschaft; Die Bedrohung der Wissenschaft (gesehen
aus dem anderen Anfang, nicht neuzeitlich) (WS 1937)
Editor: Alfred Denker

GA 89 *Zollikoner Seminare*
Editor: Medard Boss
Third, expanded edition 2006, 382 pages.
Translated by Franz K. Mayr and Richard R. Askay as *Zollikon Seminars*. Northwestern University Press, 2001.

GA 90 *Zu Ernst Jünger*
Editor: Peter Trawny
2004, 472 pages.

GA 91 *Ergänzungen und Denksplitter*

GA 92 *Ausgewählte Briefe I*
Editor: Alfred Denker

GA 93 *Ausgewählte Briefe II*
Editor: Alfred Denker

GA 94 *Überlegungen II–VI*

GA 95 *Überlegungen VII–XI*

GA 96 *Überlegungen XII–XV*

GA 97 *Anmerkungen II–V*

GA 98 *Anmerkungen VI–IX*

GA 99 *Vier Hefte I—Der Feldweg*
Vier Hefte II—Durch Ereignis zu Ding und Welt

GA 100 *Vigiliae I, II*

GA 101 *Winke I, II*

GA 102 *Vorläufiges I–IV*

———————————————— ⤚๑๑⤛ ————————————————

Günter Figal
is Professor of Philosophy at the
University of Freiburg in Breisgau, Germany.
He is the author of several books on Gadamer,
Heidegger, hermeneutics, and social and
political philosophy.

Jerome Veith
is completing his doctorate in philosophy
at Boston College, specializing in
Gadamer's hermeneutics of history.

CPSIA information can be obtained
at www.ICGtesting.com
Printed in the USA
JSHW032135280721
17348JS00004B/355